The
SHORT BIBLE

An American Translation

. . .

Edited by

EDGAR J. GOODSPEED

AND

J. M. POWIS SMITH

THE UNIVERSITY OF CHICAGO PRESS
CHICA~~GO~~

D1248964

Date Due

THE UNIVERSITY OF CHICAGO PRESS
CHICAGO, ILLINOIS

· ·

THE BAKER & TAYLOR COMPANY
NEW YORK

THE CAMBRIDGE UNIVERSITY PRESS
LONDON

THE MARUZEN-KABUSHIKI-KAISHA
TOKYO, OSAKA, KYOTO, FUKUOKA, SENDAI

THE COMMERCIAL PRESS, LIMITED
SHANGHAI

Date Due

PREFACE

. . .

A cultivated woman once remarked that she had always supposed the Bible was to look up references in. It is too true that many people actually know no other use for it. Its size, variety, and obscurity bewilder them. They need a bridge to carry them over these gulfs to the understanding and appreciation of it.

This is why so many shortened Bibles have made their appearance of late years. They are not meant as substitutes for the Bible but as introductions to it. They seek to present those parts of it which everyone ought to be acquainted with, from a literary, historical, or religious point of view.

It is at once plain that such a book must be based upon an intelligible modern translation that has taken advantage of the great advances made in recent years in the understanding of both Old and New Testaments. After consultation with many experienced teachers of the English Bible it has become clear that, to be most useful, it should present the various books in the chronological order of their composition, so that earlier religious ideas come first and more developed ones later. So arranged, the book becomes an introduction to the development of Hebrew and Christian religious thought, and the great messages of the prophets and evangelists stand out in their full originality. And, finally, each book should be preceded by a brief account of its origin and purpose; a statement of when and why it was written, for historical study has shown how essential such introductions are to any real understanding of the books.

With the generous assistance of Mr. Bean, the manager, and Mr. Laing, the editor, of the University of Chicago Press, this *Short Bible* was undertaken. It is based upon the translation especially designed for American readers, recently edited by Professor J. M. P. Smith and myself. The books selected for inclusion have been arranged in the probable order of their production, and each is prefaced with a brief account of its origin and purpose, and of its chief interest for history, literature, or religion.

The selections from Genesis, Exodus, Leviticus, Numbers, Deuteronomy, Joshua, Judges, and Ruth are in the translation of Professor Theophile J. Meek. Those from the books of Samuel, Kings, Ezra, Nehemiah, and Esther are in that of Professor Leroy Waterman. Those from Proverbs, Isaiah, Jeremiah, Ezekiel, and Daniel are in that of Professor Alex. R. Gordon, and those from Job, Psalms, Ecclesiastes, and the Minor Prophets are in that of Professor Smith. The New Testament selections and the one from the Apocrypha are in my translation. On account of limitations of space, no selections have been included from Chronicles, the Song of Songs, Lamentations, Obadiah, Malachi, II Peter, II John, III John, or Jude.

The lamented death of my lifelong friend and colleague, Dr. Smith, left his introductions to the books of the Old Testament fully drafted but unrevised. Subsequent changes in the plan of the book made it necessary to recast their form, and this task fell to me. I have moreover been without his counsel in the matter of the order in which the books are arranged. In both these matters I have sought to adhere to the historical positions reached by him, in so far as they could be ascertained.

The accuracy of the verse-numbering in this volume is due to the kindness and care of Miss Mary D. Alexander, of the University of Chicago Press, and my brother, Charles T. B. Goodspeed, has greatly obliged me by carefully reading all the proofs.

The preparation of this volume has greatly increased my own enthusiasm for the interest and value of the Bible for modern life. I sincerely hope the book may convey the same impression to all its readers.

EDGAR J. GOODSPEED

PARADISE ISLAND
July 20, 1933

AIDS TO FURTHER STUDY

THE OLD TESTAMENT

MOORE, G. F. *The Literature of the Old Testament.*

BOX, G. H. *A Short Introduction to the Literature of the Old Testament.*

GRAY, G. B. *A Critical Introduction to the Old Testament.*

FOWLER, H. T. *A History of the Literature of Ancient Israel from the Earliest Times to 135 B.C.*

BEWER, J. A. *The Literature of the Old Testament in Its Historical Development.*

CORNILL, G. H. *A Short Introduction to the Canonical Books of the Old Testament.*

DRIVER, S. R. *An Introduction to the Literature of the Old Testament.*

CREELMAN, H. *Introduction to the Old Testament, Chronologically Arranged.*

THE NEW TESTAMENT

GOODSPEED, E. J. *The Story of the New Testament.*

FOWLER, H. T. *The History and Literature of the New Testament.*

PEAKE, A. S. *A Critical Introduction to the New Testament.*

BACON, B. W. *An Introduction to the New Testament.*

SCOTT, E. F. *The Literature of the New Testament.*

McNEILE, A. H. *An Introduction to the Study of the New Testament.*

JUELICHER, A. *An Introduction to the New Testament.*

MOFFATT, J. *An Introduction to the Literature of the New Testament.*

AIDS TO FURTHER STUDY

THE OLD TESTAMENT

THE NEW TESTAMENT

TABLE OF CONTENTS

THE OLD TESTAMENT

TRANSLATED BY J. M. POWIS SMITH, THEOPHILE
J. MEEK, ALEX. R. GORDON,
LEROY WATERMAN

THE OLD TESTAMENT

THE BOOK OF AMOS
· · ·

The literature of Western Asia was for the most part anonymous. It arose as a social product, with no individual authors associated with it. The principal exception to this rule is found in the Jewish literary prophets —those great individuals who beginning with the eighth century before Christ not only uttered but wrote their religious messages. These early prophets were also poets and cast their oracles in poetic form.

It is the voice of a peasant, a shepherd and a laboring man, that first makes itself heard. He does not speak as a prophet, for the prophets of his time were in bad repute. They were notoriously mercenary and self-seeking, and he declares that he has nothing to do with them. Yet God has taken him from following his flock, and said to him, "Go, prophesy to my people Israel."

His name was Amos, and he lived in Tekoa, a village a few miles south of Jerusalem. His visits to the chief markets of the land to sell his produce have shown him the wrongs of the poor and the cruelty of the rich, and he bursts out in fierce denunciation of such things. God will punish the nations around them for their awful wickedness, and just as surely he will not spare Israel for the injustice and oppression that go on in it. The Day of the Lord is to be a day of doom.

The Jewish nation had already broken into two kingdoms, the Northern and the Southern. Amos says these things in Bethel, a famous sanctuary of the Northern

[3]

Kingdom, but Amaziah the priest drives him away, telling him that his denunciation of Israel will be more welcome in the Southern Kingdom of Judah, and better paid for there. Amos denounces social injustice and declares that God will punish the nation for such ruthless selfishness. Exile and destruction will be the penalty.

Amos preached probably between 765 and 750 B.C. With him begins what has been called the ethical monotheism of the prophets. God is righteous, and his judgment of all the nations is impartially just. There is little hope in any of his prophecies. His book, however, like many others in the Old Testament, was afterward supplemented with prophecies of subsequent restoration.

. . .

THE TITLE AND PURPOSE OF THE BOOK 1:1–2

The words of Amos, who was among the shepherds of   1
Tekoa, which he prophesied regarding Israel, in the days
of Uzziah, king of Judah, and in the days of Jeroboam,
the son of Joash, king of Israel, two years before the
earthquake; saying,
> "The LORD roars from Zion,   2
> And from Jerusalem he utters his voice;
> And the pastures of the shepherds mourn,
> And the top of Carmel withers."

DOOM UPON THE SURROUNDING NATIONS, 1:3–2:3

Thus says the LORD,   1
> "For three transgressions of Damascus,
> And for four, I will not turn it back;
> Because they have threshed Gilead
> With threshing-tools of iron.
> So I will send a fire upon the house of Hazael,   4
> And it shall devour the palaces of Ben-hadad.
> And I will break the bar of Damascus,   5
> And cut off the inhabitants from the valley of Aven,

[4]

And the holder of the scepter from Beth Eden;
And the people of Syria shall go captive to Kir,"
Says the Lord.

6 Thus says the Lord,
  "For three transgressions of Gaza,
    And for four, I will not turn it back;
    Because they carried into exile a whole people,
    To hand them over to Edom.
7 So I will send a fire upon the wall of Gaza,
    And it shall devour her palaces.
8 And I will cut off the inhabitants from Ashdod,
    And the holder of the scepter from Askelon,
    And I will turn my hand against Ekron,
    And the remnant of the Philistines shall perish,"
      Says the Lord God.

9 Thus says the Lord,
  "For the three transgressions of Tyre,
    And for four, I will not turn it back;
    Because they handed over a whole people as captives
      to Edom,
    And did not remember the agreement between
      brothers.
10 So I will send a fire upon the wall of Tyre,
    And it shall devour her palaces."

11 Thus says the Lord,
  "For three transgressions of Edom,
    And for four, I will not turn it back;
    Because he pursued his brother with the sword,
    And did violence to his feelings,
    And kept his anger perpetually,
    And cherished his wrath forever.
12 So I will send a fire upon Teman,
    And it shall devour the palaces of Bozrah."
13 Thus says the Lord,
  "For three transgressions of the Ammonites,
    And for four, I will not turn it back;

[5]

Because they ripped up the pregnant women of
   Gilead,
That they might enlarge their boundary.
So I will kindle a fire upon the wall of Rabbah,   14
And it shall devour her palaces;
With shouting in the day of battle,
With a storm in the day of tempest.
And their king shall go into exile,
He and his princes also,''
                Says the LORD.

Thus says the LORD,   2
  ''For three transgressions of Moab,
  And for four, I will not turn it back;
  Because he burned the bones
  Of the king of Edom to lime.
  So I will send a fire against Moab,   2
  And it shall devour the palaces of Kerioth.
  And Moab shall die with uproar,
  With shouting and the sound of the trumpet.
  And I will cut off the chieftain from the midst of her,   3
  And slay all her princes with him,''
                Says the LORD.

THE SIN AND DOOM OF ISRAEL, 2:6-16

Thus says the LORD,   2
  ''For three transgressions of Israel,
  And for four, I will not turn it back;
  Because they have sold the innocent for silver,
  And the needy for the sake of a pair of sandals.
  And they trample upon the heads of the poor,   7
  And they turn the humble from the way.
  A man and his father go to the harlots,
  So that they profane my holy name.
  Garments taken in pledge they spread out   8
  Besides every altar;
  And the wine of those who have been fined they
    drink
  In the houses of their gods.

[6]

9 "Yet it was I who destroyed the Amorite from before
  them,
  Whose height was like that of the cedars,
  And he was strong as the oaks;
  But I destroyed his fruit above,
  And his roots below.

10 And it was I who brought you up from the land of
  Egypt,
  And led you through the wilderness for forty years,
  That you might seize the land of the Amorites.

11 And I raised up some of your sons as prophets,
  And some of your young men as Nazirites.
  Is this not so, indeed, O Israelites?"
    An oracle of the Lord.

12 "But you made the Nazirites drink wine;
  And you laid command upon the prophets, saying,
  'You shall not prophesy.'

13 "I am going to make a groaning under you,
  As a wagon groans that is loaded with sheaves.

14 Flight shall perish from the swift;
  And the strong shall not exert his strength;
  And the warrior shall not save himself.

15 And he who handles the bow shall not stand firm,
  Nor shall the swift of foot save himself;
  And he who rides upon horseback shall not save
  himself.

16 And the stoutest of heart among the warriors
  Shall flee away naked in that day."
    An oracle of the Lord.

PRIEST AGAINST PROPHET, 7:10–17

7 Then Amaziah, the priest of Bethel, sent to Jeroboam,
king of Israel, saying,

 "Amos has conspired against you in the midst of the
11 house of Israel. The land is unable to endure all his
words. For thus says Amos,

 'By the sword shall Jeroboam die,

And Israel shall surely be carried into exile away
from its soil.' "

Then Amaziah said to Amos,   12
"O seer, take your flight to the land of Judah,
And there eat bread, and there prophesy;
And never again come to Bethel to prophesy,   13
For this is the king's sanctuary, and the royal
palace."

Then Amos replied to Amaziah, saying,   14
"I am no prophet, nor am I a member of a prophetic
order;
But I am a shepherd and a dresser of sycamores.
And the LORD took me from behind the flock,   15
And the LORD said to me,
'Go, prophesy to my people Israel.'
And now hear the word of the LORD.   16
You are saying, 'You shall not prophesy against
Israel
Nor drop a word against the house of Isaac.'
Therefore, thus says the LORD,   17
'Your wife shall practice harlotry in the city,
Your sons and your daughters shall fall by the
sword,
Your land shall be parcelled out by measure,
And you yourself shall die upon unclean soil,
And Israel shall surely be carried into exile away
from its soil.' "

THE BOOK OF HOSEA

. . .

The Jewish prophets often embodied their messages in symbolic acts which engaged the public attention more effectively than any mere words could have done. The supreme example of this is the marriage of Hosea. He was a man of the Northern Kingdom, the religion of which was contaminated with nature worship and idolatry. The woman Hosea has married proves unfaithful to him. She later leaves Hosea and lives with another man, apparently becoming a slave. Hosea is greatly distressed and humiliated by this, but he still loves her and seeks to bring her back.

In all this domestic tragedy Hosea sees a symbol of Israel's unfaithfulness to God, who nevertheless still loves his people and would restore them, if they would repent. Hosea is the prophet of the love of God as Amos was the prophet of his impartial justice. His whole message is an attempt to awaken Israel to a sense of its guilt and to arouse it to repentance. He clearly foresees its destruction for its sins.

Hosea prophesied between 745 and 735 B.C. His reading of the future proved only too true, for within twenty years the Northern Kingdom fell before Assyria (721 B.C.).

. . .

THE SUPERSCRIPTION, 1:1

1 The word of the LORD that came to Hosea, the son of Beeri, in the days of Uzziah, Jotham, Ahaz and Hezekiah,

kings of Judah, and in the days of Jeroboam, son of Joash,
king of Israel.

THE MARRIAGE OF HOSEA, 1:2–9

In the beginning, when the LORD spoke through 1
Hosea, then the LORD said to Hosea,
> "Go, and take to yourself a harlotrous wife, and
> harlotrous children;
> For the land has committed great harlotry, turning·
> from following the LORD."

So he went and took Gomer, the daughter of Diblaim, 3
and she became pregnant and bore him a son. And the 4
LORD said to him,
> "Call him Jezreel; for but a little while,
> And I will demand the blood of Jezreel from the
> house of Jehu;
> And I will bring to an end the dominion of the house
> of Israel.

> And it shall come to pass in that day, 5
> That I will break the bow of Israel, in the valley of
> Jezreel."

When she became pregnant again and bore a daughter, 6
he said to him,
> "Call her 'She-who-is-unpitied'; for I will not again
> Have pity upon the house of Israel, that I should
> ever forgive them.

> But upon the house of Judah I will have pity; 7
> And I will deliver them through the LORD, their
> God;
> And I will not deliver them by bow,
> Nor by sword, nor by war,
> Nor by horses and horsemen."

Then she weaned "She-who-is-unpitied," and became 8
pregnant, and bore a son. And he said, 9
> "Call him, 'Not-my-people';
> For you are not my people,
> And I am not your God."

HOSEA'S OWN ACCOUNT OF HIS MARRIAGE AND ITS MEANING, 3:1-5

3 "The LORD said to me again,
'Go, love a woman that is beloved of a paramour, and is an adulteress; even as the LORD loves the Israelites, though they turn to other gods and are lovers of raisin-cakes.'

2 "So I bought her for myself for fifteen pieces of silver
3 and a homer and a half of barley. Then I said to her,
'Many days you must dwell as mine;
You must not play the harlot, nor have a husband;
nor will I myself come near you.'

4 "For the Israelites shall abide many days with no king, no prince, no sacrifice, no pillar, no ephod, and no
5 teraphim. Afterward, the Israelites shall return and seek the LORD, their God, and David their king; and they shall hasten eagerly toward the LORD, and his goodness in the days to come."

ISRAEL MUST GO INTO EXILE, 9:1-9

9 Do not rejoice, O Israel!
Do not exult, like the peoples!
For you have apostatized from your God.
You have loved a harlot's hire
Upon all threshing-floors for grain.

2 But threshing-floor and wine-vat shall not know them,
And wine shall fail them.

3 They shall not remain in the land of the LORD,
But Ephraim shall return to Egypt,
And in Assyria they shall eat unclean food.

4 They shall not pour out libations of wine to the LORD;
Nor shall they prepare their sacrifices for him.
Their food shall be like mourners' food,
In that all who eat of it will defile themselves;
For their food is for themselves only,
It may not come into the house of the LORD.

What will you do on the festival day;   5
And on the day of the feast of the LORD?
For lo, they shall go to Assyria;   6
Egypt shall gather them,
Memphis shall bury them.
Their desirable places nettles shall possess;
Thorns shall be in their tents.
The days of punishment will come;   7
The days of requital will come;
Israel shall know.

The prophet is distracted,
The man of the spirit is crazed,
Because of your great guilt.
Great is the opposition to the watchman of Ephraim,   8
   the people of my God.
The prophet—the fowler's snare is upon all his
   ways;
Opposition is in the house of his God.
They have dug a deep pit for him   9
As in the days of Gibeah.
He will remember their guilt,
He will punish their sins.

ISRAEL'S FAITHLESSNESS AND ITS PUNISHMENT, 11:12—12:14

"Ephraim surrounds me with lies,   11
And the house of Israel with deceit;
But Judah still seeks after God,
And is loyal to the holy one.
Ephraim feeds upon wind,   12
And pursues the East wind all the time;
They multiply lies and falsehood;
They make a treaty with Assyria,
And carry oil to Egypt.

"The LORD has a quarrel with Judah;   2
And he will punish Jacob according to his ways;
According to his deeds will he requite him.
In the womb he seized his brother's heel;   3
And in his full vigour he strove with God.

[12]

4　　Then he fought against an angel and prevailed;
　　　He wept and entreated him for mercy.
　　　At Bethel he found him,
　　　And there he talked with him.
12　　Then Jacob fled to the field of Aram,
　　　And Israel worked for a wife,
　　　And for a wife he watched sheep.

5　　"And the LORD, the God of hosts,
　　　The LORD, is his name.
6　　But do you return to your God,
　　　Practice kindness and justice,
　　　And wait for your God constantly.

7　　"A Canaanite, in whose hands are false balances,
　　　He loves to oppress.
8　　But Ephraim says, 'Indeed, I am rich;
　　　I have found power for myself.'
　　　All his gain will not suffice
　　　For the guilt which he has incurred.
9　　I am the LORD, your God,
　　　From the land of Egypt;
　　　I will again make you dwell in tents,
　　　As in the days of old.

10　　"I spoke to the prophets
　　　And I gave many visions.
　　　And through the prophets I gave parables.
11　　Gilead, indeed, is wickedness; yea, they are false-
　　　　hood;
　　　In Gilgal they sacrifice to demons;
　　　Their altars, also, are like heaps,
　　　Upon the furrows of the field.
13　　And by a prophet the LORD brought Israel up from
　　　　Egypt,
　　　And by a prophet he was kept.
14　　Ephraim has provoked him bitterly;
　　　So he will hurl his blood upon him;
　　　And his disgrace his Lord will requite to him."

THE BOOK OF MICAH

· · ·

The evils attacked by Amos and Hosea were bitterly assailed within a few years of Hosea's time by a Judean prophet named Micah. He lived in Moresheth Gath, a small town in the western part of Judah, near the Philistine border. The idolatry of Israel and the oppression of the poor by the ruling classes of Judah roused him to denounce both peoples, especially for the sins so rife in their respective capitals, Samaria and Jerusalem.

Micah was a peasant and spoke for the oppressed peasantry of his land. His message, like that of Amos, is a plea for social justice. He preached about the time of the fall of the Northern Kingdom before Assyria, 721 B.C., and predicted the destruction of Samaria which occurred a few years later. But he foretold the destruction of Jerusalem too; and he was the first prophet to do this.

The book of Micah as we know it includes portions from later hands, but in the first three chapters at any rate is the work of Micah himself, and they are still like the prophet, full of power, " to declare to Jacob his crimes and to Israel his sins."

· · ·

THE SUPERSCRIPTION, 1:1

The word of the LORD which came to Micah, the 1 Morashtite, in the days of Jotham, Ahaz, and Hezekiah, kings of Judah, which he prophesied against Samaria and Jerusalem.

[14]

THE DOWNFALL OF ISRAEL, 1:2–9

1   Hear, O peoples, all of you!
Give heed, O earth, and everything in it!
And let the Lord GOD be a witness against you,
The Lord from his holy temple.

3   For, lo, the LORD is coming forth from his place;
And he will descend and tread upon the heights of
      the earth;
4   And the mountains shall melt under him,
And the valleys be cloven asunder,
Like wax before the fire,
Like waters poured down a precipice.

5   For the transgression of Jacob is all this,
And for the sin of the house of Judah.
What is Jacob's transgression?
Is it not Samaria?
And what is Judah's sin?
Is it not Jerusalem?

6   So I will turn Samaria into a ruin of the field,
Into a planted vineyard.
And I will pour down her stones into the valley,
And lay bare her foundations.

7   All her carved images shall be smashed to pieces;
And all her images shall be burned with fire;
And all her idols I will lay waste.
For from the harlot's hire they were gathered,
And unto the harlot's hire they shall return.

8   For this let me lament and wail;
Let me go barefoot and stripped.
Let me make lamentation like the jackals,
And mourning like the ostriches.

9   For her stroke is incurable;
For it has come even to Judah;
It reaches the gate of my people,
Even to Jerusalem.

THE DOWNFALL OF PROPHETS, PRIESTS AND PRINCES, 3:1–12

And I said,   3
"Hear now, you heads of Jacob,
And rulers of the house of Israel,
Is it not your place to know justice,
You who hate the good, and love wickedness,   2
Snatching their skin from upon them,
And their flesh from upon their bones?"

They eat the flesh of my people,   3
And strip them of their flesh,
And lay bare their bones and break them,
Like meat in the pot and flesh within the cauldron.

Then shall they cry unto the LORD,   4
And he will not answer them,
But will hide his face from them, at that time,
Inasmuch as they have done wicked deeds.

Thus has the LORD said,   5
Regarding the prophets who lead my people astray,
Who preach prosperity when their mouth is filled;
But if one does not put something in their mouths,
They declare war against him!

"Therefore, it shall be night for you, without vision,   6
And darkness for you, without divination.
For the sun shall set upon the prophets,
And the day shall become dark over them.

"The seers shall be abashed,   7
And the diviners shall blush;
And they shall all cover the upper lip,
Because there is no answer from God."

But I am full of power,   8
The spirit of the LORD, justice, and strength,
To declare to Jacob his crimes,
And to Israel his sins.

Hear this, now, you heads of the house of Jacob,   9
And rulers of the house of Israel,

Who abhor justice,
And distort everything that is right;
10   Who build Zion with blood,
And Jerusalem with guilt.

11   Her chiefs pronounce judgment for a bribe,
And her priests declare oracles for hire,
And her prophets divine for cash.
Yet they lean upon the LORD, saying,
"Is not the LORD in the midst of us?
No misfortune can befall us."

12   Therefore, because of you,
Zion shall be plowed like a field,
And Jerusalem shall become a ruin,
And the temple hill a high place in a forest.

THE BOOK OF ISAIAH
. . .

The later years of the eighth century before Christ were trying times for the Jews of Jerusalem. The Northern Kingdom combined with Syria to attack Judah in 735–734 B.C.; the Northern Kingdom fell before the Assyrians in 721 B.C.; Sargon of Assyria defeated Hanno of Gaza at Raphia in 715 B.C., and captured Ashdod in 711 B.C.; and Sennacherib invaded Judah itself in 701 B.C. The whole generation was full of anxiety and difficulty for the little people of Judah.

In this troubled period there lived in Jerusalem a fearless, brilliant, and high-minded prophet named Isaiah, who came of an aristocratic family and was therefore in close touch with court and king. In the vicissitudes of his generation, his voice was repeatedly raised in warning and direction. Called to the prophetic office about 740 B.C. (6:1–13), he realized the awful holiness of God and the punishment demanded by his people's sins. In the war with Syria and the Northern Kingdom, 7:1–25, he calls upon Ahaz, king of Judah, to stand firm, and put his faith in God, for in two or three years the two hostile kingdoms will be ruined and desolate, and even Judah itself will be invaded and laid waste by the Assyrians. Again and again the prophet denounces the sinfulness, luxury, and extravagance of his own people, and predicts its destruction. As for himself and his disciples, they will wait upon God. In one of the latest of his prophecies, 10:5 ff., probably about 701 B.C., he fore-sees the destruction of Assyria itself.

The work of Isaiah himself is preserved in the bulk of chapters 1–39. Later prophets added prophecies of joy-ous return from exile and golden ages of restoration to his work, until his book became a veritable anthology of prophecy. Chapters 40–66 are generally recognized as belonging to later times, chapters 40–55 expressing the hopes of return from exile that were aroused in the breast of an exiled prophet between 549 and 538 B.C. by the successes of Cyrus the Persian; they are among the finest utterances in all the literature of religion. The rest of the book, chapters 56–66, comes from various peri-ods a century or more later.

Isaiah's prophetic career seems to have lasted from 740 to 701 B.C. Tradition says that he met a martyr's death, being sawn asunder in the time of Manasseh, who came to the throne a few years later.

. . .

SUPERSCRIPTION, 1:1

1 The vision of Isaiah, the son of Amoz, which he saw concerning Judah and Jerusalem, in the days of Uzziah, Jotham, Ahaz, and Hezekiah, kings of Judah.

FAITHLESS CHILDREN, 1:2–3

1 Hear, O heavens, and give ear, O earth,
　For the LORD has spoken:
"Sons have I reared and brought up,
　And they have rebelled against me!
3 The ox knows its owner,
　And the ass its master's crib;
But Israel does not know,
　My people shows no understanding."

[19]

THE DESOLATION OF JUDAH, 1:4-9

Ah! sinful nation, guilt-laden people;   1
Brood of evil-doers, children who deal corruptly;
Who have forsaken the Lord, and spurned the Holy
    One of Israel,
And gone back in estrangement from him!
Where will you still be smitten, that you revolt   5
    again and again?
The whole head is ailing, and the whole heart sick;
From the sole of the foot to the head there is no   6
    health in it—
Nought but blows and bruises and bleeding wounds,
That have not been pressed nor bound up nor
    softened with oil.
Your land is a desolation, your cities are burned   7
    with fire;
Your soil—in your presence aliens devour it:
It is a desolation like the overthrow of Sodom.
And the daughter of Zion is left like a booth in a   8
    vineyard,
Like a hut in a cucumber-field, like a watchman's
    tower.
Unless the Lord of hosts had left us a handful of   9
    survivors,
We should have become like Sodom, we should have
    resembled Gomorrah.

TRUE AND FALSE WORSHIP, 1:10-17

Hear the word of the Lord,   1
    You rulers of Sodom;
Give ear to the instruction of our God,
    You people of Gomorrah!
"Of what use is the multitude of your sacrifices to   11
    me,"
    Says the Lord;
"I am sated with burnt-offerings of rams
    And the fat of fed beasts;
In the blood of bullocks and lambs and he-goats
    I take no delight.

12   When you come to see my face,
      Who demands this of you—
            The trampling of my courts?
13   Bring no more worthless offering!
      Foul smoke it is to me.
      New moon and sabbath, the holding of assemblies—
      Fasting and festival I cannot endure.
14   Your new moons and your appointed seasons I hate;
      They are a burden upon me, which I am weary of
            bearing.
15   So, when you spread out your hands,
            I will hide my eyes from you;
      Though you make many a prayer,
            I will not listen.
      Your hands are full of bloodshed—
16   Wash yourselves clean;
      Put away the evil of your doings
            From before my eyes;
17   Cease to do evil, learn to do good;
      Seek justice, restrain the oppressor;
      Uphold the rights of the fatherless, defend the cause
            of the widow!"

THE WAGES OF SIN, 1:18-20

18   "Come now, and let us reason together,"
            Says the LORD:
      "If your sins be like scarlet,
      Can they become white as snow?
      If they be red like crimson,
      Can they become as wool?
19   If you prove willing and obedient,
      You shall eat the good of the land;
20   But if you refuse and rebel,
      You shall taste the sword;
      For the mouth of the Lord has spoken.

THE MOUNTAIN OF THE LORD'S HOUSE, 2:1-4

2   The word that Isaiah, the son of Amoz, received con-
      cerning Judah and Jerusalem.

Now in the end of the days   2
The mountain of the LORD's house will be
Established on the top of the mountains,
    And lifted above the hills.
And all the nations will stream to it,
Many peoples will go and say: 3
"Come! let us go up to the mountain of the LORD,
To the house of the God of Jacob;
That he may instruct us in his ways,
And that we may walk in his paths;
For out of Zion goes forth instruction,
The word of the LORD out of Jerusalem."
Then will he judge between the nations,   4
And will arbitrate for many peoples;
And they will beat their swords into plowshares,
    And their spears into pruning-hooks:
Nation will not lift up sword against nation,
And they will learn no more the art of war.

A JUDGMENT SCENE, 3:13–15

The LORD comes forward to plead,   3
He stands up to arraign his people;
The LORD will bring an indictment   14
Against the elders and princes of his people:
"It is you that have ravaged the vineyard—
The plunder of the poor is in your houses.
What mean you by crushing my people,   15
And grinding the face of the poor?"
Is the oracle of the Lord, the GOD of hosts.

THE SONG OF THE VINEYARD, 5:1–7

Let me sing for my Loved One   5
    My love song of his vineyard.

My Loved One had a vineyard
    On a fertile hill;
He trenched it, and cleared it of stones,
    And planted it with choice vines;   2
He built a watchtower in the midst of it,

And hewed out a winevat;
And he looked for it to yield grapes,
But it yielded wild grapes.

3 Now, O citizens of Jerusalem, and men of Judah,
Judge, I pray, between me and my vineyard!
4 What more could have been done for my vineyard
Than that which I have done for it?
Why, then, when I looked for it to yield grapes,
Did it yield wild grapes?

5 So now, I pray, let me tell you
What I will do to my vineyard:
I will remove its hedge, and it shall be ravaged;
I will break down its wall, and it shall be trampled
under foot;
6 I will make it a waste, unpruned and unhoed,
That shall spring up with briers and thorns;
And the clouds will I command
That they rain no rain upon it.

7 For the vineyard of the LORD of hosts is the house of
Israel,
And the men of Judah are his cherished plantation;
And he looked for justice, but lo! bloodshed,
For righteousness, but lo! a cry.

THE VISION OF THE LORD, 6:1-13

6   In the year that King Uzziah died, I saw the Lord
sitting upon a throne, high and uplifted, the skirts of his
2 robe filling the temple. Over him stood seraphs, each
having six wings, with two of which he covered his
face, with two he covered his loins, and with two he hov-
3 ered in flight. And they called one to another, and said,
"Holy, holy, holy, is the LORD of hosts;
The whole earth is full of his glory."
4   And the foundations of the thresholds shook at the
sound of those who called, and the house filled with
smoke.

[23]

Then said I,   5
  "Ah me! I am lost—
    For I am a man of unclean lips,
    And I dwell among a people of unclean lips—
    For my eyes have seen the King,
      The LORD of hosts."
Then flew one of the seraphs to me, with a red-hot   6
stone in his hand, which he had taken with tongs from
the altar; and he touched my mouth with it, and said,   7
  "See! this has touched your lips;
    And your guilt is removed, and your sin forgiven."
And I heard the voice of the Lord, saying,   8
  "Whom shall I send,
    And who will go for us?"
And I said,
  "Here am I! send me."
Then said he,   9
  "Go and say to this people:
    'Keep on hearing, but understand not;
    And keep on seeing, but know not!'
    Make the mind of this people gross,   10
    Dull their ears, and besmear their eyes;
    Lest they see with their eyes, and hear with their
      ears,
    And have a mind to understand, and turn, and be
      healed."
And I said,   11
  "Lord, how long?"
And he said,
  "Till cities lie waste, without inhabitant,
    And houses without man;
    And the soil be left a desolation,
    And the LORD have removed man far away,   12
    And many be the forsaken places in the midst of the
      land.
    Even if a tenth remain in it,   13
    This must pass through the fire again,
    Like a terebinth, or an oak,
    Whose stump remains when it is felled."

THE SIGN OF "GOD IS WITH US," 7:10–17

7   Once more the LORD spoke to Ahaz, saying,

11   "Ask a sign of the LORD your God; make it deep as Sheol, or high as the heavens!"

12   And Ahaz said,
"I will not put the LORD to the test by asking such a thing."

13   And he said,
"Hear now, O House of David! Is it too slight a thing for you to weary men, that you must weary my God also?

14 Therefore the Lord himself will give you a sign: Behold! a young woman is with child, and is about to bear a son;

15 and she will call him 'God is with us.' Curds and honey will be his food when he knows how to refuse the bad

16 and choose the good. For before the child knows how to refuse the bad and choose the good, the land before whose

17 two kings you stand in dread will be forsaken. The LORD will bring upon you, and upon your people, and upon your father's house, such days as have not come since the day that Ephraim parted from Judah, even the king of Assyria."

THE TEACHING AND THE TESTIMONY, 8:16–18

8   I will bind up my testimony, and seal my teaching

17 in the heart of my disciples. And I will wait for the LORD, who is hiding his face from the house of Israel: I

18 will set my hope on him, while I and the children whom the LORD has given me remain as signs and symbols in Israel from the LORD of hosts, who dwells on Mount Zion.

THE PRINCE OF PEACE, 9:1–7

9   But there will be no more gloom to her that was in anguish. As in days gone by he brought contempt upon the land of Zebulon and the land of Naphtali, so in the time to come will he bring glory upon the land along the Sea Road, beyond Jordan—the Circle of the Nations.

[25]

The people that walked in darkness   2
Have seen a great light;
Those who dwelt in a land of deep darkness—
On them has light shone.
Thou hast multiplied the nation, thou hast in-   3
    creased its joy:
They rejoice before thee as with the joy in harvest,
As men exult when they divide the spoil.
For the yoke that was their burden,   4
And the bars upon their shoulder,
The rod of their master,
Thou hast broken in pieces as on the day of Midian.
For every boot worn by booted warrior in the fray,   5
And war cloak stained with blood,
Will be for burning—food for the fire.
For a child is born to us, a son is given to us;   6
And the government will be upon his shoulder;
And his name will be
"Wonderful counsellor, Godlike hero,
Father forever, Prince of peace."
Of the increase of his government, and of peace,   7
There will be no end,
Upon the throne of David, and over his kingdom,
To establish it, and to uphold it,
In justice and in righteousness,
From henceforth, even forever.
The zeal of the Lord of hosts will do this.

THE DOWNFALL OF ASSYRIA, 10:5-15

Oh! Assyria, rod of my anger,   **10**
        And staff of my fury!
Against a godless nation I send him,   6
And against the people of my wrath I charge him,
To spoil them, and to prey on them,
And to trample them down like mire of the streets.
But not so does he think,   7
And not so does he plan;
For destruction is in his mind,
And to cut off nations not a few.

8   For he says,
           "Are not my captains all of them kings?
9   Is not Calno like Carchemish?
           Is not Hamath like Arpad?
           Is not Samaria like Damascus?
10   Inasmuch as my hand has reached to the kingdoms
              of the idols,
           Whose carved images were more than those of
              Jerusalem and Samaria,
11   Shall I not do to Jerusalem and its images,
           As I have done to Samaria and its idols?"

12   But when the Lord has finished all his work on Mount
    Zion and Jerusalem, he will punish the arrogant boasting
13 of the king of Assyria, and his vainglorious pride. For
    he says,
           "By the strength of my hand have I done it,
           And by my wisdom, for I have understanding;
           I have removed the boundaries of peoples,
                 And have plundered their treasures;
           I have brought down to the dust
                 Cities and their inhabitants.
14   My hand has seized like a nest
                 The wealth of the peoples;
           And as one gathers eggs that are left,
                 And the earth have I gathered;
           And there was none that moved a wing,
                 Or opened the mouth, or chirped."

15   Shall an axe boast over the man that hews with it,
           Or a saw lord itself over the man that plies it?
           As though a rod were to sway the man that wields
              it,
           Or a staff were to wield what is not wood!

THE AGE OF GOLD, 11:1-9

11   A shoot will spring from the stem of Jesse,
           And a sprout from his roots will bear fruit.
2   And the spirit of the LORD will rest upon him—
           The spirit of wisdom and understanding,

The spirit of counsel and might,
The spirit of knowledge and the fear of the Lord—
And his delight will be in the fear of the Lord.   3
He will not judge by that which his eyes shall see,
Nor decide by that which his ears shall hear;
But with justice will he judge the needy,   4
And with fairness decide for the poor of the land;
He will smite the ruthless with the rod of his mouth,
And with the breath of his lips he will slay the
     wicked.

Righteousness will be the girdle round his loins,   5
And faithfulness the girdle round his waist.
Then the wolf will lodge with the lamb,   6
And the leopard will lie down with the kid;
And the calf and the young lion will graze together,
And a little child will lead them.
The cow and the bear will be friends,   7
Their young ones will lie down together;
And the lion will eat straw like the ox.
The suckling child will play on the hole of the asp,   8
And the weaned child will put his hand on the
     viper's den.
They will do no harm nor destruction   9
     On all my holy mountain;
For the land will have become full of the knowledge
     of the Lord,
          As the waters cover the sea.

THE INVASION OF SENNACHERIB, 36:1–10; 37:21–38

Now in the fourteenth year of King Hezekiah's reign, 36
Sennacherib, king of Assyria, went up against all the
fortified cities of Judah, and took them. And the king of   2
Assyria sent his Commander from Lachish to Jerusalem,
against King Hezekiah, with a strong army. And he took
up his position near the conduit from the upper pool, on
the highway to the fuller's field. Then Eliakim, the son   3
of Hilkiah, who was steward of the palace, and Shebna,
the secretary, and Joah, the son of Asaph, the recorder,
went out to meet him. And the Commander said to them,   4

"Say now to Hezekiah, 'Thus says the great king, the king of Assyria: "What sort of confidence is this which
5 you cherish? Do you suppose that a mere word of the lips can pass for warlike counsel and strength? Now in whom
6 do you trust, that you have rebelled against me? You trust, forsooth, in the support of this broken reed, Egypt, on which if a man lean, it will run into his hand, and pierce it—for such is Pharaoh, king of Egypt, to all who
7 trust in him! Or if you say to me, 'We trust in the Lord our God'; is not he the one whose sanctuaries and altars Hezekiah has removed, saying to the people of Judah and
8 Jerusalem, 'Before this altar shall you worship'? And now, pray, make a wager with my lord, the king of Assyria: I will supply you with two thousand horses, if
9 you are able to supply them with riders! How then will you repel the attack of one of the least of my lord's officers? Yet you trust in Egypt for chariots and horse-
10 men! Or is it without the sanction of the Lord that I have come up against this land to destroy it? The Lord himself said to me, 'Go up against this land and destroy it!' " ' "

37   Then Isaiah, the son of Amoz, sent to Hezekiah, saying,

"Thus says the Lord, the God of Israel: 'Because you have prayed to me concerning Sennacherib, king of
22 Assyria, this is the word which the Lord has spoken against him:

"The virgin daughter of Zion
    Scorns you and mocks you;
The daughter of Jerusalem
    Shakes her head at you.
23 Whom have you insulted and blasphemed?
And against whom have you raised your voice,
And lifted your eyes on high?
    The Holy One of Israel!
24 By the mouth of your servants you have insulted
    the Lord,
And have said, 'With the multitude of my chariots
I have scaled the height of the mountains,

[29]

The recesses of Lebanon;
I have cut down its tallest cedars,
Its choicest cypresses;
I have pierced to its farthest retreat,
Its densest thicket;
I have dug and drunk   25
Foreign waters;
With the sole of my foot have I dried up
All the streams of Egypt!'
Have you not heard how I planned this   26
Long ago,
How I prepared it in days gone by,
And now have brought it about—
That you should be able to lay fortified cities
Into ruinous heaps,
While their inhabitants, shorn of their strength,   27
Are dismayed and confounded,
Are become like grass in the field,
Like tender green grass,
Like grass on the housetops,
Blasted before it is grown up.
I know your rising and sitting,   28
Your going and coming, and your raging against me.
Because you have raged against me   29
And your rioting has come up to my ears,
I will put my hook in your nose,
And my bridle in your lips,
And will turn you back by the way
By which you came.''

" 'And this is the sign to you: This year you shall eat 30
what grows of itself, and next year what springs from it;
but in the third year you shall sow and reap, plant vineyards and eat the fruit of them. And the remnant that 31
survives of the house of Judah shall once more strike root
downward and bear fruit upward; for a remnant shall 32
escape from Jerusalem, and a body of survivors from
Mount Zion. The zeal of the Lord of hosts shall do
this.' "

33   "Therefore thus says the Lord concerning the king of
            Assyria:
        'He shall not come to this city,
        Nor shoot an arrow there;
        He shall not bring a shield before it,
        Nor cast up a mound against it.
34   By the way that he came,
        By the same shall he return;
        And to this city shall he not come,'
        Is the oracle of the Lord.
35   'For I will shield and save this city,
        For my own sake, and for my servant David's
            sake.' "

36   Then the angel of the Lord went forth, and slew in
        the camp of the Assyrians one hundred and eighty-five
        thousand; and when men rose early in the morning, lo!
        they were all dead bodies.

37   So Sennacherib, king of Assyria, broke up his camp,
38   and returned home, and dwelt at Nineveh. And one day,
        as he was worshipping in the temple of Nisroch his god,
        Adrammelech and Sarezer, his sons, smote him with the
        sword, and made good their escape to the land of Ararat.
        And Esarhaddon, his son, reigned in his place.

THE FIRST RETURN FROM EXILE

VOICES FROM THE HEAVENS, 40:1–11

40   "Comfort, O comfort my people,"
                Says your God;
2   "Speak to the heart of Jerusalem,
                And call to her—
        That her time of service is ended,
                That her guilt is paid in full,
        That she has received of the Lord's hand
                Double for her all sins."

3   Hark! one calls:
        "In the wilderness clear you the way of the Lord,
        Make straight in the desert a highway for our God.
4   Let every valley be raised up,

And every mountain and hill brought low;
Let the uneven ground become a plain,
And the rugged heights a valley.
Then shall the glory of the Lord be revealed,   5
And all flesh shall see it together;
For the mouth of the Lord has spoken."

Hark! one says, "Call!"   6
And I said, "What shall I call?"
"All flesh is grass,
And all its beauty is like the flower of the field.
The grass withers, the flower fades,   7
When the breath of the Lord blows upon it—
Truly the people is grass—
The grass withers, the flower fades,   8
But the word of our God shall stand forever."

On a high mountain get you up,   9
          O heralds of good news to Zion!
Lift your up voice with strength,
          O heralds of good news to Jerusalem!
Lift it up, fear not;
Say to the cities of Judah,
          "Behold your God!"
See! the Lord God is coming with might,   10
          His own arm having won him the kingdom;
See! his reward is with him,
          And his recompense before him.
Like a shepherd he tends his flock,   11
          With his arm he gathers them;
The lambs he carries in his bosom,
          And gently leads those who give suck.

THE MISSION OF THE SERVANT OF THE LORD, 42:1-4

See! my servant, whom I uphold;   **42**
My chosen one, in whom I delight.
I have put my spirit upon him,
He shall bring forth right to the nations.
He shall not cry, nor shout,   2
Nor make his voice heard in the streets;

3　　A bending reed shall he not break,
　　And a flickering wick shall he not quench—
　　Faithfully shall he bring forth right.
4　　He shall not flicker nor bend,
　　Till he establish right in the earth,
　　And the coast-lands wait for his teaching.

THE CALL OF CYRUS, 44:24—45:7

44　　Thus says the LORD, your Redeemer,
　　Who formed you from the womb:
　　"I, the LORD, the maker of all,
　　Who stretched out the heavens alone,
　　Who laid out the earth—who was with me?
25　　Who frustrates the omens of soothsayers,
　　And makes diviners like madmen;
　　Who turns wise men backward,
　　And makes their knowledge folly;
26　　But confirms the word of his servants,
　　And fulfils the predictions of his messengers—
　　I am he who says of Jerusalem, 'She shall be in-
　　　habited,'
　　And of the cities of Judah, 'They shall be built,
　　And their ruins will I raise up';
27　　Who says to the deep, 'Be dry!
　　And all your streams will I drain';
28　　Who says of Cyrus, 'My shepherd,
　　Who shall fulfil all my pleasure';
　　Who says of Jerusalem, 'She shall be built,'
　　And of the temple, 'Your foundations shall be
　　　laid.' "

45　　Thus says the LORD to his anointed one,
　　To Cyrus, whose right hand I have grasped,
　　To bring down nations before him,
　　And to ungird the loins of kings,
　　To open doors before him,
　　And that gates may not be closed:
2　　"I will go before you,
　　And will level the rugged heights;

The doors of bronze will I break in pieces,
And the bars of iron will I cut asunder;
I will give you treasures hidden in darkness,   3
    Hoards of secret places;
That you may know that I am the LORD,
That I who have called you by name am the God
    of Israel.
For the sake of Jacob my servant,   4
    Israel my chosen one,
I have called you by name,
I have surnamed you, though you knew me not.
I am the LORD, and there is no other—   5
Except me there is no God.
I will gird you, though you knew me not,
The men may know, from the east   6
And from the west, that apart from me there is none.
I am the LORD, and there is no other—
Who forms light, and creates darkness,   7
Who makes weal, and creates woe—
I the LORD am he who does all these things.

THE DESTINY OF THE SERVANT, 49:1–6

Listen, you coast lands, to me;   **49**
Hearken, you peoples afar!
The LORD called me from birth,
From my mother's womb he gave me my name.
He made my mouth like a sharp sword,   2
In the shadow of his hand he hid me;
He made me a polished arrow,
In his quiver he concealed me.
He said to me, "You are my servant,   3
Israel, through whom I will show forth my glory."
But I said, "In vain have I labored,   4
Idly and for nought have I spent my strength;
Nevertheless, my right is with the LORD,
And my reward with my God."
And now the LORD,   5
Who formed me from the womb to be his servant,
Says that he will bring back Jacob to himself,

And that Israel shall be gathered to him—
For I am honored in the eyes of the Lord,
And my God has become my strength—

6   He says, "It is too slight a thing for your being my
        servant
That I should but raise up the tribes of Jacob,
And restore the survivors of Israel;
So I will make you a light of the nations,
That my salvation may reach to the end of the
    earth."

THE NEARNESS OF DELIVERANCE, 51:9-11, 52:1-3, 7-12

51   "Awake, awake, put on strength,
            O arm of the Lord!
      Awake, as in days of old,
            As in generations long gone!
      Was it not thou that didst hew Rahab in pieces,
            That didst pierce the dragon?
10   Was it not thou that didst dry up the sea,
            The waters of the mighty deep—
      That didst make the depths of the sea a way
            For the redeemed to pass over?
11   And the ransomed of the Lord will return by it,
      And will come to Zion with singing,
      And with everlasting joy upon their heads;
      They will attain to joy and gladness,
      And sorrow and sighing will flee away."

52   Awake, awake, put on
            Your strength, O Zion;
      Put on your beautiful garments,
            O Jerusalem, the holy city!
      For no more shall there come to you
            An uncircumcised or unclean one.
2   Shake yourself from the dust, arise,
            O captive Jerusalem;
      Free yourself from the bonds on your neck,
            O captive daughter of Zion!
3   For thus says the Lord:

"For nought were you sold,
And without money shall you be redeemed."
How beautiful upon the mountains 7
Are the feet of the heralds,
Who bring good news of peace,
News of salvation—
Who say to Zion,
"Your God has become king."
Hark! your watchmen lift up the voice, 8
Together they sing;
For eye to eye they see
The return of the LORD to Zion.
Break into singing together, 9
You waste places of Jerusalem!
For the LORD has comforted his people,
He has redeemed Jerusalem.

The LORD has made bare his holy arm 10
In the eyes of all the nations;
And all the ends of the earth shall see
The salvation of our God.
Away! away! go out thence; 11
Touch nothing unclean!
Go out of the midst of her; keep yourselves pure,
You who bear the vessels of the LORD!
For you shall not go out in haste, 12
Nor depart in flight;
For the LORD shall go before you,
And the God of Israel shall be your rearguard.

THE SUFFERINGS AND THE TRIUMPH OF THE SERVANT,
52:13—53:12

Lo! my servant shall prosper, 52
He shall be exalted, and lifted up, and shall be very
high.
As many were amazed at him— 14
So marred was his appearance from that of a man,
And his form from that of the sons of men—

[36]

15 So shall he startle many nations,
On account of him kings shall shut their mouths;
For what has not been told them shall they see,
And what they have not heard shall they contemplate.

53 "Who could have believed what we have heard?
And the arm of the LORD—to whom has it been revealed?
2 For he grew up like a sapling before us,
Like a root out of dry ground;
He had no form nor charm, that we should look upon him,
No appearance, that we should desire him.
3 He was despised, and avoided by men,
A man afflicted by pains, and familiar with sickness;
And like one from whom men hide their faces,
He was despised, and we took no account of him.

4 "Yet it was our sicknesses that he bore,
Our pains that he carried;
While we accounted him stricken,
Smitten by God, and humbled.
5 He was pierced for our transgressions,
He was crushed for our iniquities;
The chastisement of our welfare was upon him,
And through his stripes we were healed.
6 All we like sheep had gone astray,
We had turned everyone to his own way;
And the LORD made to light upon him
The guilt of us all.
7 "When he was oppressed, he humbled himself,
And opened not his mouth—
Like a sheep that is led to the slaughter,
Or like a ewe that is dumb before her shearers,
He opened not his mouth.
8 Through violence in judgment was he taken away,
And who gave thought to his fate—
How he was cut off from the land of the living,
For our transgressions he was stricken to death?

They made his grave with the wicked,   9
His tomb with evil-doers;
Although he had done no violence,
Nor was any deceit in his mouth."

Yet the LORD was pleased to crush him by sickness,   10
That when he had made himself a guilt-offering,
He might see posterity, might prolong his life,
And the pleasure of the LORD might prosper in his
    hand.
Now through his suffering shall he see it, and be   11
    satisfied;
Through his affliction shall my servant, the
    Righteous One, bring righteousness to many,
And shall carry the burden of their guilt.
Therefore will I divide him a portion with the great,   12
And with the strong shall he share the spoil;
Because he poured out his lifeblood,
And was numbered with transgressors,
While he bore the sin of many,
And for transgressors he interposed.

A CALL TO THE NEEDY, 55:1-13

"Ho! everyone that is thirsty, come to the waters,   **55**
And he that has no money, come, buy, and eat!
Come, buy grain without money,
And wine and milk without price!
Why should you spend money for what is not bread,   2
And your earnings for what does not satisfy?
If you but listen to me, you shall eat what is good,
And shall delight yourselves with rich nourishment.

"Bend your ear, and come to me;   3
Listen, that you may live!
For an everlasting covenant will I make with you,
The covenant of love which I faithfully promised to
    David.
As once I made him a witness to peoples,   4
A leader and commander of peoples,
So you shall call nations you know not,   5

And nations that know you not shall run to you,
For the sake of the LORD your God,
The Holy One of Israel, because he has shed glory
on you.

6 "Seek the LORD while he may be found,
Call upon him while he is near!
7 Let the wicked forsake his way,
And the unrighteous man his thoughts;
And let him return to the LORD, that he may have
pity upon him,
And to our God, for he shall abundantly pardon.
8 For my thoughts are not your thoughts,
Nor are your ways my ways," is the oracle of the
LORD;
9 "But as the heavens are higher than the earth,
So are my ways higher than your ways,
And my thoughts than your thoughts.

10 "For, as the rain comes down,
And the snow from heaven,
And returns not thither,
Without having watered the earth,
And made it bring forth and sprout,
Giving seed to the sower,
And bread to the eater,
11 So shall my word be that goes out of my mouth—
It shall not return to me fruitless,
Without having done the thing that I pleased,
And accomplishing the purpose for which I sent it.

12 "For with joy shall you go out,
And in peace shall you be led;
The mountains and the hills shall break into sing-
ing before you,
And all the trees of the field shall clap their hands.
13 Instead of the thorn shall come up the cypress,
And instead of the brier shall come up the myrtle;
And they shall be to the LORD a memorial,
An everlasting sign that shall not be cut off."

[39]

LATER PROPHECIES

THE GLORY OF THE NEW JERUSALEM, 60:1–22

Arise, shine! for your light has come, 60
And the glory of the LORD has risen upon you.
For lo! darkness shall cover the earth, 2
And thick darkness the peoples;
But upon you the LORD shall rise,
And upon you his glory shall appear;
And nations shall walk by your light, 3
And kings by the brightness of your rising.

Lift up your eyes round about, and see! 4
All of them gather, they come to you—
Your sons shall come from afar,
And your daughters shall be borne on the hip.
When you see it, you shall be radiant, 5
And your heart shall throb and swell;
For the riches of the sea shall be turned to you,
The wealth of the nations shall come to you.

A flood of camels shall cover you, 6
The young camels of Midian and Ephah;
All those of Sheba shall come—
Gold and frankincense shall they bring,
And shall herald the praises of the LORD.
All the flocks of Kedar shall gather to you, 7
The rams of Nebaioth shall minister to you;
They shall mount my altar as a well-pleasing sacri-
    fice,
And my glorious house will I glorify.

Who are these that fly like a cloud, 8
Or like doves to their windows?
It is the ships which are gathering for me, 9
With the vessels of Tarshish in the van,
To bring your sons from afar,
Their silver and their gold with them,
In honor of the LORD your God,
The Holy One of Israel, because he has glorified you.

10 And aliens shall build your walls,
And their kings shall minister to you;
For though in my wrath I smote you,
In my favor will I have pity upon you.

11 And your gates shall be open continually,
Day and night shall they not be closed,
That men may bring to you the wealth of the nations,
Their kings leading the way.

12 For the nation and the kingdom that will not serve
you shall perish—
Utterly waste shall those nations be laid.

13 The glory of Lebanon shall come to you,
The cypress, the pine, and the larch together,
To glorify the place of my sanctuary,
And that I may do honor to my footstool.

14 Then the sons of those who oppressed you shall
come bending to you,
And all those who scorned you shall bow down at
the soles of your feet;
And they shall call you, "The city of the Lord,
The Zion of the Holy One of Israel."

15 Instead of your being forsaken and hated,
With none passing through you,
I will make you a pride forever,
A joy for all generations.

16 You shall suck the milk of the nations,
The breast of kings shall you suck;
And you shall know that I the Lord am your savior,
That your redeemer is the Mighty One of Jacob.

17 Instead of bronze will I bring gold,
And instead of iron will I bring silver;
And instead of wood, bronze,
And instead of stones, iron;
And Peace will I make your government,
And Righteousness your ruler.

18 No more shall news of violence be heard in your
land,

Nor of wreck and ruin within your borders,
But you shall call your walls Salvation,
  And your gates Praise.

No more shall the sun be your light by day,   19
Nor the moon by night shine upon you;
But the LORD shall be your unfailing light,
  And your God your glory.
No more shall your sun set,   20
Nor shall your moon wane;
For the LORD shall be your unfailing light,
And your days of mourning shall be ended.

Your people shall be all of them righteous, 21
And shall possess the land forever,
As the shoot of my planting, the work of my hands,
  With which I may glorify myself.
The least one shall become a tribe,   22
The smallest a mighty nation—
I the LORD will hasten it
  In its proper time.

THE YEAR OF THE LORD'S FAVOR, 61:1-9; 62:1-3

The spirit of the Lord GOD is upon me,   61
For the LORD has anointed me;
He has sent me to bring good news to the miserable,
  To bind up the broken-hearted,
To proclaim liberty to the captives,
  And release to the prisoners—
To proclaim the year of the LORD's favor,   2
And the day of our God's vengeance—
To comfort all mourners,
To provide for the mourners of Zion,   3
To give them a crown instead of ashes,
Oil of joy instead of a garment of mourning,
A song of praise instead of a drooping spirit,
That they may be called oak trees of righteousness,
The planting of the LORD, with which he may
 glorify himself.

4   Then shall they rebuild the ancient ruins,
They shall raise up the desolations of former genera-
      tions;
They shall renew the wasted cities,
The desolations of many generations.

5   And strangers shall stand and feed your flocks,
Aliens shall be your plowmen and your vinedressers;

6   But you shall be called the priests of the LORD,
The ministers of our God shall you be named.
You shall enjoy the wealth of the nations,
And in their glory shall you revel.

7   Because their shame was in double measure,
And contempt was the lot they inherited,
Therefore in their land shall they inherit a double
      measure,
Everlasting joy shall be theirs.

8   For I the LORD love justice,
I hate robbery and crime;
So I will faithfully give them their recompense,
And an everlasting covenant will I make with them.

9   Their sons shall be known among the nations,
Their offspring in the midst of the peoples;
All who see them shall acknowledge them
As a race which the LORD has blessed.

62   For Zion's sake will I not keep silent,
And for Jerusalem's sake will I not rest,
Until her vindication come forth clear as light,
And her salvation as a burning torch.

2   Then the nations shall see your vindication,
          And all kings your glory;
You shall be called by a new name,
Which the mouth of the LORD shall determine;

3   And you shall be a glorious crown in the hand of the
      LORD,
A royal diadem in the hand of your God.

THE BOOK OF ZEPHANIAH
· · ·

About 627 B.C. the Scythians were pouring into south-west Asia, and seemed likely to overwhelm not only Judah but its neighbors and oppressors. In this threatened universal destruction the young prophet Zephaniah saw the judgment of God upon these peoples, his own included, for their several sins. Zephaniah lived in Jerusalem, and was not, like Amos or Micah, a peasant, but a man of aristocratic family, being descended from King Hezekiah.

The future looked very black to Zephaniah. Even the sufferings of Judah have not led her to mend her ways. He can only repeat the warnings of doom that her false worships and disregard of God are bringing upon her. But her arrogant and supercilious neighbors are to suffer likewise. Zephaniah did not reproduce the ethical idealism and passion so characteristic of Amos and Isaiah, nor did he bring anything new to the solution of the problems of his day. He thought only of the terrible Day of the Lord, of which Amos had spoken. He looked forward to a great destructive movement, a divine judgment, which the Scythian invaders seemed to foreshadow, which should involve Assyria, Philistia, Ethiopia, and Judah in a common ruin.

The Scythian migration had no such sweeping consequences as Zephaniah at first anticipated. But the days of Assyria were numbered, and in 612 B.C., while

[44]

Zephaniah was still a young man, Nineveh fell before the Medes from the East and the rising power of Babylon.

. . .

THE SUPERSCRIPTION, 1:1

1 The word of the LORD which came to Zephaniah, the son of Cushi, the son of Gedaliah, the son of Amariah, the son of Hezekiah, in the days of Josiah, the son of Amon, king of Judah.

A DAY OF DOOM UPON THE WORLD, 1:2–6

1 "I will utterly sweep away everything
From upon the face of the ground"; it is the oracle of the LORD.

3 "I will sweep away man and beast;
I will sweep away the fowl of the heavens, and the fish of the sea.
And I will cause the wicked to stumble,
And I will cut off mankind from upon the face of the ground."
It is the oracle of the LORD.

4 "And I will stretch out my hand against Judah,
And against all the inhabitants of Jerusalem.
And from this place I will cut off Baal to the last remnant;
The name of the priestlings, with the priests;

5 And those who prostrate themselves upon the roofs
To the host of the heavens;
And those who prostrate themselves before the LORD
And swear by Milcom;

6 And those who have withdrawn from following the LORD,
And those who have not sought the LORD,
Nor inquired after him."

THE TERRORS OF THE DAY OF THE LORD, 1:7–18

7 Silence before the Lord GOD,
For the day of the LORD is near at hand!

[45]

For the Lord has prepared a sacrifice,
He has sanctified his guests!

It shall come to pass in the day of the sacrifice of the   8
    Lord,
That I will punish the princes and the king's sons,
And everyone that clothes himself in foreign gar-
    ments.
And I will punish everyone that leaps over the thresh-   9
    old in that day,
Those filling their master's house with violence and
    deceit.

"It shall come to pass in that day," it is the oracle of   10
    the Lord,
"That a voice will cry from the Fish-Gate,
And will utter a wail from the New Town;
And there will be a great crash from the hills.
Wail, O inhabitants of the Mortar!   11
For all the people of Canaan shall be ruined;
And who weigh out silver shall be cut off.

"At that time I will search Jerusalem with lamps,   12
And will punish those who are at ease,
Thickened upon their lees, who say to themselves,
'The Lord does neither good, nor bad.'
And their property shall become a ruin,   13
And their houses a desolation.
And they shall build houses, but not inhabit them;
And plant vineyards, but not drink their wine."

Near at hand is the great day of the Lord;   14
Near and speeding fast!
Near at hand is the bitter day of the Lord.
Then the warrior will cry in terror!
A day of wrath is that day;   15
A day of trouble and distress,
A day of desolation and waste,
A day of darkness and gloom,
A day of cloud and thundercloud;
A day of the trumpet and battle-cry,   16

[46]

Against the fortified cities,
And against the lofty battlements.

17 "And I will bring trouble upon mankind so that they
    shall walk like blind men";
Because they have sinned against the LORD.
And their blood shall be poured out like dust,
And their flesh like dung.

18 Neither their silver nor their gold
Will be able to rescue them.
In the day of the wrath of the LORD, and in the fire
    of his zeal,
All the earth shall be consumed;
For a complete destruction, indeed a frightful one,
    will he make
Of all the inhabitants of the earth.

DOOM UPON ETHIOPIA AND ASSYRIA, 2:12–15

2 You, too, O Ethiopians,
        Shall be slain by my sword!

13 And he will stretch out his hand against the north,
        And destroy Assyria.
And he will make Nineveh a desolation,
        A drought like the desert.

14 And herds shall lie down in the midst of her,
        Every beast of the field.
Both screech owl and porcupine
        Shall lodge in her capitals.
The owl shall hoot in the window,
        The bustard on the threshold.
For I will destroy her city.

15 This is the exultant city,
        That dwelt in security!
That said to itself,
        "I am, and there is none else."
How has she become a ruin,
        A lair for wild beasts.
Everyone that passes by her hisses,
        And shakes his fist!

SIN AND JUDGMENT, 3:1–7

Woe to the defiant and defiled one, the oppressing 3
   city!
She has listened to no voice;   2
She has accepted no correction!
In the LORD she has not trusted;
To her God she has not drawn near!

Her princes within her are roaring lions;   3
Her judges are wolves of the night,
Who long not for the morning.
Her prophets are reckless, treacherous men;   4
Her priests profane holy things;
They do violence to the law.

The LORD is righteous within her;   5
He will do no wrong.
Every morning he brings his judgment to light;
He does not fail.
But the wicked knows no shame.

I have cut off nations; their battlements are de-   6
   stroyed.
I have made their streets desolate, with none passing
   by.
Their cities have been laid waste, without a man,
   without an inhabitant.
I said, "Surely she will fear me; she will accept cor- 7
   rection;
And there shall not be cut off from her sight,
Anything which I have laid upon her.
But they have zealously made
All their doings corrupt."

THE BOOK OF NAHUM
. . .

The conquests and cruelties of the Assyrians in the century following the fall of Samaria stirred the Jewish prophet Nahum to proclaim the judgment of God upon their capital Nineveh. He looked back upon the fall of Thebes, which took place probably in 661 B.C.; and he looked forward confidently to the fall of Nineveh, which occurred in 612. His prophetic activity therefore fell in the half-century between these two events, culminating probably toward 612.

The poetry of Nahum is of a quality unsurpassed in the Old Testament. His descriptive power, realistic imagery, and picturesque phraseology combine to make his poem a great piece of literature. His battle scenes in the second and third chapters are particularly vigorous and splendid. An acrostic—that is, a poem alphabetically arranged—was afterward prefixed to his prophecy.

The spirit of Nahum's prophecy is one of exultant revenge. The prophet is completely absorbed in contemplation of the approaching downfall of Nineveh. It is significant that while Nahum's attention is wholly occupied by this coming disaster, his contemporary Jeremiah has nothing to say about it, but is absorbed in the sins and problems of his own people. Nahum's point of view is rather that of the old-fashioned, less profound nationalistic prophets. But his joy is not merely exultation over the imminent downfall of Israel's foe, but it is also the glad cry of his assured faith in the God of his fathers.

THE SUPERSCRIPTION, 1:1

An oracle on Nineveh: the book of the vision of 1
Nahum, the Elkoshite.

THREATS AND PROMISES, 1:11—2:2

Did not one go forth from you plotting evil against 1
    the Lord,
Counselling rascality?
Thus says the Lord,   12
"When many days are fulfilled,
They shall be cut off and shall pass away.
I have afflicted you, but I will never again afflict you.
And now I will break his rod from upon you,   13
And burst asunder your bonds."
For the Lord has given command regarding you,   14
"There shall be sown of your name no longer.
From the house of your gods I will cut off the graven
    and the molten images.
I will make your grave a disgrace."

Behold, upon the mountains, the feet of a herald,   15
       One proclaiming prosperity.
Celebrate your feasts, O Judah,
       Fulfil your vows,
For not again will ruin pass through you;
       He will be wholly cut off.
For the Lord will restore the vine of Jacob,   2
       Likewise, the vine of Israel;
Though devastators have devastated them,
       And laid waste their branches.

THE SACK OF NINEVEH, 2:1, 3–13

The shatterer has come up against you;   2
Keep the rampart;
Watch the road; brace your loins.
Strengthen your forces to the utmost.

The shield of his warriors is reddened.   3
The mighty men are clothed in scarlet,

Like the flame of torches.
That will make ready the chariot in that day;
And the chargers will prance.

4   The chariots will rage in the streets,
Dashing to and fro in the open spaces.
Their appearance will be like that of torches,
Darting about like lightning.

5   He summons his nobles; they stumble as they go.
They hasten to the wall,
And the battering ram is set up.

6   The gates of the rivers are opened,
And the palace melts away.

7   Its mistress is brought forth; she goes into captivity,
While her maidens mourn,
Moaning like the sound of doves,
Beating upon their breasts.

8   And Nineveh is like a pool of water,
Whose water escapes.
"Halt, halt!" they cry,
But no one turns back.

9   "Plunder silver, plunder gold;
For there is no end to the equipment,
An abundance of all sorts of valuable articles."

10   There is emptiness, and desolation, and waste,
And a melting heart and trembling knees;
And anguish is in all loins,
And the faces of all of them become livid.

11   Where is the den of the lions,
And the cave of the young lions,
Whither the lion went bringing in spoil,
The lion's cub, with none to disturb?

12   Where the lion tore enough prey for his cubs,
And rended for his lionesses,
Filling his den with prey,
And his lair with booty?

13   "Behold, I am against you";
It is the oracle of the Lord of hosts.

"And I will burn up your chariots with smoke,
And the sword shall devour your young lions,
And I will cut off your prey from the land,
And the voice of your messenger shall be heard no
    more."

THE IMMINENT AND INEVITABLE END, 3:1-19

Oh city, bloody throughout,   3
Full of lies and booty!
Prey ceases not.
The crack of the whip, and the noise of the rumbling   2
    wheel;
And the galloping horse, and the jolting chariot.
The charging horseman, and the flashing sword,   3
And the glittering spear, and a multitude of slain,
And a mass of bodies, and no end to the corpses!
They stumble over the corpses!
Because of the many harlotries of a harlot   4
Of goodly favor and a mistress of spells,
Who sells nations by her harlotries,
And clans by her spells.

"Behold, I am against you";   5
It is the oracle of the Lord of hosts,
"And I will strip off your skirts to your face,
And I will show nations your nakedness,
And kingdoms your shame.
And I will throw vile things at you,   6
And treat you with contempt, and make you a
    horror;
So that everyone that sees you will flee from you,   7
Saying, 'Nineveh is destroyed;
Who will mourn for her?
Whence can I seek comforters for her?'

"Are you any better than Thebes,   8
That sat by the great Nile,
(Water was around her)
Whose rampart was the sea,
Whose wall was water?

9   Ethiopia was her strength, and Egypt,
And there was no end.
Put and the Libyans were her help.

10   Yet even she became an exile;
She went into captivity.
Even her children were dashed in pieces at the head
    of every street;
And upon her honored ones they cast lots,
And all her great men were bound in chains.

11   "You too shall reel and swoon;
You too shall seek refuge from the foe.

12   All your fortresses shall be fig trees with the first
    ripe figs,
If they be shaken they fall into the mouth of the
    eater.

13   Behold your people shall be but women in the midst
    of you;
To your foes the gates of your land will be opened
    wide.
Fire will devour your barriers.

14   "Draw yourself waters for the siege; strengthen your
    forts.
Plunge into the mud; and trample the clay;
Lay hold of the brick-mold!

15   But there fire shall devour you,
The sword shall cut you off.
It shall devour you as the locust does.
Multiply yourselves like the locust;
Multiply yourselves like the locust-swarm.

16   "Increase your merchants more than the stars of the
    heavens!
(Locusts spread the wing and fly away!)

17   Your watchers are like locust-swarms;
Your scribes like clouds of locusts,
That settle in the hedges in the cool of the day.
When the sun arises, they flee;
And their location is unknown.

[53]

"Your shepherds slumber, O king of Assyria;   18
    Your nobles sleep!
Your people are scattered upon the hilltops,
    With none to gather them.
There is no healing for your wound;   19
    Your hurt is incurable.
Everyone who shall hear the news about you,
    Will clap his hands over you.
For against whom has your malice not continually
  gone forth?"

THE BOOK OF DEUTERONOMY
· · ·

In the eighteenth year of Josiah (621 B.C.) there was found in the temple a book which was destined to have a marked effect upon Jewish religion. It had been written by Jewish reformers a few years before, probably in the reign of Manasseh, 693–639 B.C., and sought to recodify Jewish law and worship upon a loftier basis. God is the god of the whole earth, and his will is law. But he loves his people and they must both obey and love him. Ethical and spiritual values are emphasized; religion is to permeate and elevate the whole life of the people. The unity, sovereignty, and love of God are dwelt upon, and the doctrine is advanced that only in one place (obviously Jerusalem) can he be acceptably worshiped.

This remarkable book, which embodies so many of the great prophetic religious ideals, comprises the bulk of what we know as Deuteronomy, chapters 5–26, 28:1–46; and occasioned the reforms described in II Kings, chapters 22 f. It was probably composed secretly in the half-heathen reign of Josiah's predecessor Manasseh by prophets who could not longer speak openly, but hoped by this book to purify and shape the nation's faith, life, and worship. It became the first Bible of the Jewish people, and long after, toward 350 B.C., it was developed into substantially its present form and made a part of that great survey of Jewish religion, law, and tradition which we know as the books of Genesis, Exodus, Leviticus, Numbers, Deuteronomy, and Joshua. But from 621

*on, Deuteronomy importantly and most beneficially af-
fected Jewish life, thought, and literature, in which it
marked and indeed created a new era.*

　*It takes the form of three orations by Moses before the
children of Israel, followed by two poems; the Song of
Moses and his Blessing. The first oration is a historical
retrospect; the second, 5:1—26:19, presents a system of
laws, to regulate the life and religious practices of the
Hebrews. This is the oldest extended code in the Old
Testament, but because in the arrangement of the larger
work of which it finally formed a part, another code preceded it, the Greeks called it Deuteronomy—the Second
Giving of the Law.*

• • •

THE SECOND DISCOURSE OF MOSES: THE CODE OF LAWS, 5:1—6:25

Moses summoned all Israel, and said to them,　　　**5**
　"Hear, O Israel, the statutes and ordinances which I
am delivering in your hearing today, that you may learn
them and be careful to observe them. The LORD our God　2
made a covenant with us at Horeb; it was not with our
forefathers that the LORD made this covenant, but with　3
ourselves, with those of us who are all here alive today.
The LORD talked with you face to face out of the fire at　4
the mountain, myself standing between the LORD and you　5
at the time, to communicate to you the words of the
LORD; for you stood in fear of the fire, and did not ascend
the mountain. He said,
　" 'Since I, the LORD, am your God, who brought you　6
out of the land of Egypt, out of a state of slavery, you　7
must have no other gods beside me.
　" 'You must not carve an image for yourself in the　8
shape of anything that is in the heavens above, or that is
on the earth below, or that is in the waters under the
earth; you must not pay homage to them, nor serve them;　9

for I, the LORD your God, am a jealous God, punishing children for the sins of their fathers, to the third or fourth

10 generation of those who hate me, but showing grace to the thousandth generation of those who love me and keep my commands.

11   " 'You must not invoke the name of the LORD your God to evil intent; for the LORD will not excuse anyone who invokes his name to evil intent.

12   " 'Be careful to keep the sabbath day holy, as the

13 LORD your God commanded you. Six days you are to

14 labor and do all your work, but on the seventh day, a sabbath to the LORD your God, you must not do any work at all, neither you, nor your son, nor your daughter, nor your male or female slave, nor your ox, nor your ass, nor any of your cattle, nor the alien in your employ residing in your community, that your male and female

15 slaves may rest as well as you. You must remember that you were once a slave yourself in the land of Egypt, and that the LORD your God brought you out from there by a strong hand and an outstretched arm; that is why the LORD your God has commanded you to observe the sabbath day.

16   " 'Honor your father and mother, as the LORD your God has commanded you, that you may live long and prosper in the land that the LORD your God is giving you.

17   " 'You must not commit murder.

18   " 'You must not commit adultery.

19   " 'You must not steal.

20   " 'You must not bring a false charge against your fellow.

21   " 'You must not lust after your neighbor's wife, nor covet your neighbor's home, his fields, his male or female slave, his ox, his ass, or anything at all that is your neighbor's.'

22   "These words, and nothing more, the LORD spoke to all your assemblage at the mountain with a loud voice out of the midst of the fire, cloud, and gloom; and he wrote them on two stone tablets, which he gave to me.

23 When you heard the voice out of the darkness, the moun-

tain being aflame with fire, you came up to me, that is, all the heads of your tribes and your elders, and said, "See- 24 ing that the LORD our God has let us see his glory and his greatness, and that it is his voice which we have heard out of the fire, we know now that God can speak with man, and he still live. Why then should we die? For this 25 great fire is going to consume us! If we continue to hear the voice of the LORD our God any longer, we shall die! For what mortal at all is there that has ever heard the 26 voice of the living God speak out of fire, as we have, and has still lived? Do you go near, and hear all that the 27 LORD our God has to say, and then tell us whatever the LORD our God tells you; when we hear it, we will observe it.'

"When the LORD heard your protestations when you 28 spoke to me, the LORD said to me, 'I have heard the pro-testations which this people have made to you. They have spoken quite properly. O that their present attitude 29 might lead them always to stand in awe of me and keep all my commands, that it might go well with them and with their children for all time! Go and say to them, 30 "Go home to your tents"; but do you stand here beside 31 me, that I may tell you the whole charge, the statutes and ordinances, that you are to teach them to observe in the land which I am about to give them to occupy.'

"Be careful, then, to do as the LORD your God has 32 commanded you, swerving neither to the right nor to the left. You must walk wholly in the way that the LORD 33 your God has appointed you, that you may live, and prosper, and live long in the land that you are to occupy.

"Now this is the charge, the statutes and ordinances, 6 which the LORD your God commanded that you be taught to observe in the land into which you are crossing for conquest, a land abounding in milk and honey, that 2 you, with your son and your grandson, may stand in awe of the LORD your God all your life by observing all his statutes and commands which I am giving you, and that you may live long. Therefore heed them, O Israel, 3 and be careful to observe them, that you may prosper, and multiply greatly, as the LORD, the God of your fathers, promised you.

4 "Listen, O Israel; the LORD is our God, the LORD
5 alone; so you must love the LORD your God with all your
6 mind and all your heart and all your strength. These instructions that I am giving you today are to be fixed
7 in your mind; you must impress them on your children, and talk about them when you are sitting at home, and when you go off on a journey, when you lie down
8 and when you get up; you must bind them on your hand as a sign, and they must be worn on your forehead as a
9 mark; you must inscribe them on the door-posts of your house and on your gates.

10 "When the LORD your God brings you into the land which he promised on oath to your fathers, Abraham, Isaac, and Jacob, to give you great and splendid cities
11 which you did not build, houses full of all kinds of goods with which you did not fill them, cisterns already hewn out, which you did not hew out, and vineyards and olivegroves which you did not plant, but from which
12 you may eat your fill, then take care not to forget the LORD who brought you out of the land of Egypt, out of
13 a state of slavery. You must stand in awe of the LORD your God; him you must serve; and by his name you must
14 swear. You must not run after alien gods, any of the gods
15 of the nations that surround you, lest the anger of the LORD your God blaze against you, and he wipe you off the face of the earth; for the LORD your God who is in your midst is a jealous God.

16 "You must not put the LORD your God to the test, as
17 you did at Massah. You must be sure to keep the commands of the LORD your God, as well as his decrees and
18 statutes which he commanded you. You must do what is right and good in the sight of the LORD, that you may prosper, and go in and occupy the fine land concerning
19 which the LORD swore to your fathers that he would drive all your enemies out of your way, as the LORD promised.

20 "When your son asks you in time to come, 'What is

the significance of the decrees, statutes, and ordinances which the LORD our God has commanded you?' you must say to your son, 'When we were Pharaoh's slaves in Egypt, the LORD brought us out of Egypt by a strong hand. The LORD displayed before our eyes great and ominous signs and portents against Egypt, against Pharaoh and all his court, but he brought us out from there that he might bring us into a position to give us the land which he promised on oath to our fathers. So the LORD commanded us to observe all these statutes, by standing in awe of the LORD our God for our good always, that he might keep us alive, as at this day. Hence it will stand to our credit with the LORD our God to be careful to observe this charge, as he commanded us.' "

THE BOOK OF HABAKKUK
· · ·

The Jewish prophets, zealous for mercy and justice, and keenly sensitive to right and wrong, looked forth upon a succession of cruel and brutal tyrannies as one oriental empire gave way to another as masters of their world. They could see nothing but right forever on the scaffold, wrong forever on the throne, and it sometimes almost shook their faith in God himself.

Toward the end of the seventh century, Assyria went down (612 B.C.), and Babylon began to rise threateningly upon the horizon. It seemed that the world had gotten rid of one cruel tyrant only to be oppressed by another. Why should this be? This was the question that stirred the prophet Habakkuk, sometime in the reign of Jehoiakim, king of Judah, 608–597 B.C.

The Book of Habakkuk has been much supplemented and altered. As it now stands, it presents the first formulation of the problem of evil. In the opening lines, the prophet laments the sinfulness of his people. God announces the coming of the Babylonians, 1:5–11, and describes the devastation they will create among the nations. The prophet protests against this, 1:12–17, and points out the cruelty and rapacity of the Babylonians. Why should power be committed to such a wicked people? God answers that he gets no satisfaction from the wicked but that " the righteous man lives by reason of his faithfulness."

[61]

This seems just a repetition of the old view that piety brings prosperity. But at least the question has been raised whether or not this is true. It is the beginning of a long-continued study of the problem of evil.

The third chapter of Habakkuk is a psalm, taken from some collection. It is probably of later origin than the days of Habakkuk, but it is a splendid piece of poetry, and closes with the noble resolve that no matter what misfortunes the times may bring, the psalmist will trust in God and rejoice in him.

. . .

THE SUPERSCRIPTION, 1:1

The message which Habakkuk, the prophet, proph- 1
esied.

THE PROPHET'S PROBLEM AND ITS ANSWER, 1:2—2:20

How long, O LORD, must I cry for help,   1
    And thou not hear?
And call out to thee, "Violence,"
    And thou not save?
Wherefore dost thou show me wrongdoing,   3
    And make me look upon trouble?
Destruction and violence are before me,
    And there is strife, and opposition arises.
Therefore the law is paralyzed,   4
  And judgment never goes forth.
But the wicked circumvent the innocent;
    And so judgment goes forth perverted.

"Look out upon the nations and see,   5
    And be utterly amazed!
For a deed is being done in your days
    That you would not believe, were it told you.
For behold I am raising up the Chaldeans,   6
    That savage and impetuous nation,

That marches through the breadth of the earth,
To seize habitations that are not his own.

7 "Terrible and dreadful is he;
   Judgment and destruction go forth from him.
8 Swifter than leopards are his horses,
   And keener than wolves of the desert.
   His horses prance;
   And his horsemen come from afar.
   They swoop down like a vulture hasting to devour.

9 "Wholly for violence does he come;
   Terror marches before him;
   And he gathers up captives like sand.
10 He makes scorn of kings;
   And rulers are a joke to him!
   He laughs at all fortresses;
   And heaps up dirt and captures them.
11 Then he changes like the wind and passes on.
   And he makes strength his god."

12 Art thou not from of old,
   O LORD, my holy God?
   Thou diest not!
   O LORD, thou hast made him for judgment!
   And thou, O Rock, hast established him for chas-
      tisement!
13 Too pure of eyes art thou to look upon wickedness,
   And thou canst not gaze upon wrongdoing.
   Wherefore then dost thou gaze upon faithless men,
   And keep silent when the wicked swallows up
   Him that is more righteous than himself?
14 For thou makest men like fishes of the sea,
   Like crawling things, with no ruler.

15 He brings them all up with the hook,
   He drags them away with his net,
   And he gathers them up in his seine.
   So he rejoices and exults;

So he sacrifices to his net,   16
And makes offerings to his seine;
For through them his portion is fat,
And his food is abundant.
Shall he keep on emptying his net forever,   17
And never cease slaying the nations?

I will take my stand upon my watch-tower,   2
And station myself upon the rampart;
And watch to see what he will say to me,
And what answer he will make to my complaint.
Then the LORD answered me, saying,   2
"Write the vision clearly upon the tablets,
That one may read it on the run.
For the vision is a witness for the appointed time,   3
And speaks of the end, and does not lie.
If it tarry wait for it;
For it will surely come without delay.

"Verily, the wicked man—I take no pleasure in him;   4
But the righteous lives by reason of his faithfulness.
How much less shall the faithless man live,   5
And the arrogant man who is restless,
Who enlarges his appetite like Sheol,
And is as insatiable as death;
For he gathers to himself all nations,
And assembles to himself all peoples.

"Shall not all these take up a taunt-song against him,   6
And a sharp satire against him, saying,
'Woe to him who enriches himself with what is not
    his own,—
How long?—and loads himself with debts!'
Will not your creditors rise up suddenly,   7
And those awake who will make you quake?
And you will become spoil for them.
Because you have spoiled many nations,   8
All the rest of the peoples shall spoil you;

Because of human bloodshed, and the violence done
to the land,
The city and all that dwelt therein."

9　Woe to him who acquires unjust gain for his household,
Setting his nest on high, that he may be delivered
from the power of disaster.

10　You have devised disgrace for your household,
By cutting off many peoples; so forfeiting your life.

11　For the stone from the wall cries out,
And the beam from the woodwork answers it.

12　Woe to him who builds a city by bloodshed,
And establishes a town by wrong.

13　Are not these things from the LORD of hosts,
That peoples exhaust themselves for the fire,
And nations wear themselves out for naught?

14　But the earth shall be filled with the knowledge of
the glory of the LORD,
As the waters cover the sea.

15　Woe to him who makes his friend drink
From the cup and the wineskin, till he makes him
drunk,
So as to gaze upon his shame!

16　You shall be sated with shame rather than honor.
Drink yourself and be disgraced!
The cup of the right hand of the LORD shall come
round to you,
And disgrace upon your glory.

17　For the violence done to Lebanon shall cover you;
And the destruction wrought upon Hamath shall
terrify you;
Because of human bloodshed, and the violence done
to the land,
The city and all that dwelt therein.

18　Of what use is an idol when its designer has designed it,

[65]

Or a molten image, and a teacher of lies?
For he who designed his own image trusts in it,
So that he makes dumb nonentities!

Woe to him who says to wood, "Wake up,"   10
To a dumb stone, "Arise."
Can it give oracles?
It, indeed, is encased with gold and silver;
And there is no breath within it!
But the Lord is in his holy temple;   20
Be silent before him, all the earth!

THE BOOK OF JEREMIAH
. . .

Jeremiah lived in one of the most troubled and tragic periods of Hebrew history. He was born about 650 B.C., and spent his early life in the village of Anathoth, four miles north east of Jerusalem. He was called to prophesy about 627 B.C., when the Scythian invaders appeared. He lived through this invasion, saw the adoption of the Deuteronomic law, suffered the privations of the long siege of Jerusalem, and after the second fall of the city before the Babylonians in 586 B.C., and the deportation of most of the people, was compelled to flee to Egypt, where he spent his last days.

Some of Jeremiah's earliest sermons (4:5—6:26) deal with the invasion of the Scythians, who passed over Palestine on their way to attack Egypt, between 630 and 620 B.C. The Deuteronomic Law was introduced by King Josiah about 621 B.C. Jeremiah was not active in its introduction, but his sermons reflect the change in law and ritual, chaps. 7, 8, 11, and he seems to have opposed some of the Deuteronomic positions, as to the Law, the origin of sacrifice, and the significance of the Temple. Jeremiah emphasized the importance of moral and spiritual life, and discounted the value of ritual and sacrifice.

From the time of the introduction of the Deuteronomic Law to the end of his life, Jeremiah had a hard time. He predicted the destruction of the Temple and thus aroused the opposition of the priesthood, and he foretold the fall of Jerusalem and thus antagonized the king and the court. He was a warm friend of King Josiah, who died in 608 B.C., but a stern critic of his successors, Jehoiakim, Jehoiachin, and Zedekiah. During the later years of Josiah, Jeremiah seems to have kept silent, but with the disorders following Josiah's death he resumed his prophetic activity.

The national tragedy was hastening to its climax. Josiah had met his death before Necho, Pharaoh of Egypt, at Megiddo, and his son Jehoahaz who succeeded him was carried off to Egypt as a captive. Another son of Josiah's, Jehoiakim, was left on the throne. Necho was soon after decisively defeated by the Babylonian Nebuchadrezzar, and Judah passed into the control of Babylon. But Jehoiakim underestimated the strength of the new Babylonian empire and offended it. Judah was invaded and Jerusalem besieged. Jehoiakim died in the midst of these troubles, and soon after the city capitulated. Then the people of the better class, including the new king Jehoiachin, were carried away into captivity.

The death of Josiah was a great blow to the party of religious reform. But Jeremiah was a prophet of extraordinary insight and courage. He perceived that religion is an inward, individual, spiritual experience, which does not stand or fall with sacred sites or national fortunes.

The Book of Jeremiah consists of oracles and sermons from Jeremiah himself, narratives of his life and times by Baruch, his secretary, and Exilic and post-Exilic narratives and prophecies by later hands.

INTRODUCTION, 1:1–3

1   The words of Jeremiah, the son of Hilkiah, a member of the priestly family that was at Anathoth in the land
2 of Benjamin, to whom the word of the Lord came in the days of Josiah, the son of Amon, king of Judah, in the
3 thirteenth year of his reign, and continued to come during the reign of Jehoiakim, the son of Josiah, king of Judah, till the end of the eleventh year of Zedekiah, the son of Josiah, king of Judah, when Jerusalem was carried into exile in the fifth month.

THE CALL OF THE PROPHET, 1:4–19

4   The word of the Lord came to me, saying,
5   "Before I formed you in the womb I knew you,
     And before you were born I set you apart for my service—
     I appointed you a prophet to the nations."
6   Then said I,
     "Ah, Lord God! I cannot speak;
     For I am only a boy."
7   But the Lord said to me,
     "Do not say, 'I am only a boy';
     For to all to whom I send you shall you go,
     And all that I command you shall you speak.
8   Do not be afraid of them;
     For I am with you to deliver you,"
     Is the oracle of the Lord.
9   Then the Lord stretched forth his hand, and touched my mouth. And the Lord said to me,
     "See! I put my words in your mouth;
10   This moment I give you authority over the nations and kingdoms,
     To root up and to pull down, to wreck and to ruin,
     To build and to plant."

11   The word of the Lord came to me, saying,
     "What do you see, Jeremiah?"
     I answered,
     "I see a twig of an almond tree."

Then the Lord said to me,   12
"You have seen well; for I am watching over my
word, to carry it into effect."
A second time the word of the Lord came to me, say- 13
ing,
   "What do you see?"
I answered,
"I see a boiling pot, facing from the north."
Then the Lord said to me,   14
"Out of the north shall trouble boil over all the inhabitants of the land. For behold! I am summoning all 15
the kingdoms of the north," is the oracle of the Lord;
"and they shall come and set up their several thrones at
the entrances of the gates of Jerusalem, and against all
her walls round about, and against all the cities of
Judah. And I will pronounce my judgments against them 16
for all the wickedness they have done in forsaking me,
and offering sacrifice to other gods, and worshipping the
works of their own hands. You, then, gird up your loins, 17
and arise, and speak to them all that I command you. Do
not be dismayed before them, lest I dismay you before
them. For behold! I make you this moment a fortified 18
city, an iron pillar, and a bronze wall, against the whole
land—the kings of Judah, its princes and priests, and its
common people. They shall fight against you, but they 19
shall not overcome you; for I am with you to deliver
you," is the oracle of the Lord.

THE FOE FROM THE NORTH, 4:5–18

Declare in Judah, and publish in Jerusalem, saying,   4
   "Blow the trumpet through the land,
   Proclaim aloud, saying,
   'Gather and let us go
   To the fortified cities!'
   Raise a signal toward Zion,   6
   Seek refuge, stay not;
   For trouble I bring from the north,
      Even dire destruction.

[70]

7 A lion has gone up from his thicket,
   A destroyer of nations—
 He has broken loose from his place,
 To make your land a desolation,
 That your cities may be ravaged,
 And left without inhabitant.
8 Gird on sackcloth for this,
 Lament, and wail;
 For the glowing anger of the LORD
 Has not turned back from us."

9 "On that day," is the oracle of the LORD, "the courage of the king and the princes shall fail, the priests shall stand aghast, and the prophets shall be dazed with 10 horror. They shall say, 'Ah, Lord GOD! thou hast certainly deceived this people, and Jerusalem, saying, "All shall be well with you," when the sword was reaching the heart.'

11 "At that time shall it be said of this people, and of Jerusalem, 'A scorching wind from the desert heights— 12 no wind to fan or cleanse, but one too full for this— comes at my command against the daughter of my people; for now I too pronounce judgment against them.'"

13 See! he comes up like a cloud,
   His chariots like a whirlwind;
 His horses are swifter than eagles—
   Ah me! we are ruined.
14 O Jerusalem! wash your heart of wickedness,
   That you may be saved!
 How long shall your evil thoughts
   Find a lodgment within you?
15 For hark! a messenger from Dan,
  A bearer of bad news from Mount Ephraim!
16 Make it known through the nations,
  Announce it to Jerusalem:
 "Leopards are coming from a distant land,
  They lift up their voice against the cities of Judah;
17 Like keepers of a field, they ring her about,

For she has rebelled against me," is the oracle of
  the LORD.
"Your ways and your doings have brought this upon 18
  you,
This is the fruit of your wickedness—
It is bitter, it reaches the heart."

THE PROPHET'S EXPOSTULATION, AND THE LORD'S REPLY, 12:1–6

Thou must be in the right, O LORD,   12
If I take issue with thee;
Yet would I lay my case before thee:
Why does the way of the wicked prosper?
Why do all the faithless live in comfort?
Thou plantest them, and they take root;   2
They grow, and they bring forth fruit;
Near art thou in their mouths,
But far from their thoughts.
Yet thou, O LORD, knowest me,   3
Thou seest me, and testest my mind toward thee.
Pull them out like sheep for the shambles,
And devote them to the day of slaughter!
How long must the land mourn,   4
And all the herbs of the field wither?
Through the wickedness of those who dwell in it
Beast and bird are swept away;
For they say, "God is blind to our ways."

"If you have raced with men on foot, and they have   5
  beaten you,
How will you compete with horses?
And if you take to flight in a safe land,
How will you do in the jungle of Jordan?
For even your brothers, those of your father's   6
  household—
Even they have played you false,
Even they are in full cry after you;
Trust them not, though they speak fair words to
  you!"

THE TEMPLE ADDRESS, AND ITS CONSEQUENCES, 26:1-19

26 In the beginning of the reign of Jehoiakim, the son of Josiah, king of Judah, came this word from the LORD:

2 "Thus says the LORD: Stand in the court of the house of the LORD, and speak to all the people of Judah who come to worship in the house of the LORD all the words that I command you to speak to them—keep not back

3 one word! Perhaps they may listen, and turn each from his evil way, so that I may repent of the evil which I am planning to bring upon them because of their evil doings.

4 Say to them, 'Thus says the LORD: If you do not listen to me—following my law which I have set before you,

5 and listening to the words of my servants the prophets whom I have been sending to you early and late, but to

6 whom you have not listened—I will make this house like Shiloh, and will make this city a curse to all the nations of the earth.'"

7 Now the priests and the prophets, together with all the people, heard Jeremiah speaking these words in the

8 house of the LORD. So when Jeremiah had finished speaking all that the LORD had commanded him to speak to all the people, the priests and the prophets laid hold on him, saying,

9 "You shall die! How dare you prophesy in the name of the LORD, saying, 'This house shall become like Shiloh, and this city shall become an uninhabited waste?'"

Thereupon all the people crowded round Jeremiah in the house of the LORD.

10 When the princes of Judah heard the news, they came up from the palace to the house of the LORD, and took their seats at the entrance to the new gate of the house

11 of the LORD. Then the priests and the prophets addressed the princes and all the people, saying,

"This man deserves to die; for he has prophesied against this city in the terms which you have heard."

12 Then Jeremiah addressed the princes and all the people saying,

"The LORD sent me to prophesy against this house and
this city all the words which you have heard. But now, 13
if you amend your ways and your doings, and listen to
the voice of the LORD your God, the LORD will repent of the
evil which he has pronounced against you. As for myself, 14
see! I am in your hands. Do to me as you think right
and proper. Only be well assured of this, that, if you put 15
me to death, you will bring innocent blood upon yourselves, upon this city, and upon its people; for the LORD
has truly sent me to you, to speak all these words in your
hearing."

Then the princes and all the people said to the priests 16
and the prophets,

"This man does not deserve to die; for he has spoken
to us in the name of the LORD our God."

And certain of the elders of the land rose and addressed 17
the whole assembly of the people, saying,

"Micah of Moresheth prophesied in the days of 18
Hezekiah, king of Judah; and he said to all the people of
Judah,

'Thus says the LORD of hosts:
"Zion shall be plowed like a field,
    And Jerusalem shall become a ruin,
    And the temple hill a high place in a forest." '

"Did Hezekiah king of Judah and all the people of 19
Judah go the length of putting him to death? Did they
not rather reverence the LORD, and entreat the favor of
the LORD, with the result that the LORD repented of the
evil which he had pronounced against them? We, on the
contrary, are in the act of bringing great evil upon ourselves."

THE NEW COVENANT, 31:27–34

"Behold! days are coming," is the oracle of the LORD, 31
"when I will sow the household of Israel and the household of Judah with the seed of men and with the seed of
cattle; and as once I watched over them to root up and 28
to pull down, to wreck, to ruin, and to harm, so will I

watch over them to build and to plant," is the oracle of
29 the LORD. "In those days shall they say no more,
'The fathers have eaten sour grapes,
And the children's teeth are set on edge';
30 but everyone shall die for his own guilt—everyone who
eats the sour grapes shall have his own teeth set on edge.
31 "Behold! days are coming," is the oracle of the LORD,
"when I will make a new covenant with the household
32 of Israel and with the household of Judah, not like the
covenant which I made with their fathers on the day that
I took them by the hand to lead them out of the land of
Egypt—that covenant of mine which they broke, so that
33 I had to reject them—but this is the covenant which I
will make with the household of Israel after those days,"
is the oracle of the LORD: "I will put my law within
them, and will write it on their hearts; and I will be their
34 God, and they shall be my people. And they shall teach
no more every one his neighbor, and every one his
brother, saying, 'Know the LORD'; for all of them shall
know me, from the least of them to the greatest of
them," is the oracle of the LORD; "for I will pardon their
guilt, and their sin will I remember no more."

THE CAPTURE OF JERUSALEM, 39:1-2, 4-10

39 In the ninth year of Zedekiah, king of Judah, the tenth
month, Nebuchadrezzar, king of Babylon, and all his
2 army advanced against Jerusalem and besieged it; and in
the eleventh year of Zedekiah, the fourth month, the
4 ninth day of the month, the city was breached. And
when Zedekiah, king of Judah and all the soldiers saw
what had happened, they left the city by night, and
fled by way of the king's garden, through the gate between the two walls, and made for the Jordan valley.
5 But the Chaldean army pursued them, and overtook
Zedekiah in the steppes of Jericho; and they arrested
him, and brought him up to Nebuchadrezzar, king of
Babylon, at Riblah in the land of Hamath, where he
6 pronounced judgment against him. And the king of
Babylon slew the sons of Zedekiah at Riblah before his

eyes. The king of Babylon likewise slew all the nobles
of Judah. Then he put out the eyes of Zedekiah, and   7
bound him with chains, to carry him to Babylon. The   8
Chaldeans also burned the house of the king and the
houses of the people with fire, and demolished the walls
of Jerusalem. Then Nebuzaradan, the commander of the   9
guard, carried captive to Babylon the rest of the people
that were left in the city, and the deserters who had sur-
rendered to him, together with the artisans that were
left. But Nebuzaradan, the commander of the guard, left   10
in the land of Judah a number of the poor people, who
had nothing, and at the same time gave them vineyards
and fields.

THE BOOK OF EZEKIEL

· · ·

The destruction of their capital and the extinction of their national life and temple worship put Jewish religion to a fearful test. The Jews had felt that God was peculiarly the champion of their nation, and their religion was fundamentally tied up with their national existence. Some had believed that Jerusalem could never fall; God would certainly protect his own Temple.

The national disasters gave rise to widespread despair, to meet which prophetic thinkers were driven to perceive the individual character of religion, and the personal responsibility of the individual. It was Ezekiel, more than any other prophet, who perceived and taught this (chap. 18), as he sought to serve the religious needs of his countrymen amid the discouraging experiences of the Exile.

Ezekiel was a priest. He was carried into exile in the deportation of 597 B.C. His call to prophesy came in the fifth year of the captivity of King Jehoiachin, that is, 592 B.C. He seems to have spent the rest of his life in Babylonia. In 29:17, the twenty-seventh year of the Exile, 570 B.C., is mentioned, and if the thirtieth year of 1:1 means the thirtieth year of the Exile, which is quite possible, it would bring Ezekiel's activity down to 567 B.C.

Ezekiel's priestly training appears in the code of laws, relating to the future temple and its priesthood, with which

*the book ends. A notable feature of the Book of Ezekiel
is the fact that much of it is in the form of visions: chapters 1–5; 8:1—11:25; 37:1–14; chapters 40–48. Moreover, the whole book is described as the word of God; the
oracles are constantly introduced by the statement "The
word of the Lord came to me." Of course this appears
occasionally in all the prophets, but in none of them to
such an extent as in Ezekiel.*

*Ezekiel also prophesied the return of the people to
Palestine. Chapters 37–39 present the future revival of
Israel under the figure of a resurrection from the dead,
and they portray the overthrow of the hostile nations
under the figure of an invasion of Palestine by the hosts
of Gog of Magog, which are to meet with overwhelming
defeat and destruction.*

*So the Exile, which at first threatened to destroy Jew-
ish religion altogether, actually resulted in elevating
and developing it, bringing to consciousness and expression one of the greatest and most enduring aspects of religion—its individual character and man's personal responsibility. And so great was the part Ezekiel played
in this development that he has been called the Founder
of Judaism.*

· · ·

THE CALL OF THE PROPHET, 1:1—3:15

In the thirtieth year, the fourth month, the fifth day 1
of the month, as I was among the exiles by the river
Chebar, the heavens opened, and I saw visions of God.
[It was on the fifth day of the month, in the fifth year of 2
the exile of King Jehoiachin, that the word of the LORD 3
came to Ezekiel, the son of Buzi, the priest, in the land of
the Chaldeans, by the river Chebar, and the hand of the
LORD was upon him there.]

[78]

4   I looked, and lo! there came from the north a violent
gale, accompanied by a great cloud, with fire flashing
through it, and a radiance round about it, while out of
the midst of it gleamed something with a luster like that
5   of shining metal. Out of the midst of it emerged the
semblance of four living creatures, and this was their
6   appearance: Their form was like that of a man. Each,
7   however, had four faces and four wings. Their legs, too,
were straight, while the soles of their feet resembled
the sole of a calf's foot; and they sparkled like burnished
8   bronze. Under their wings, on their four sides, were the
9   hands of a man. The wings of the four of them were
linked one to another; and their faces turned not as they
10   went, but each went straight forward. As for the form of
their faces, the four of them had the face of a man and the
face of a lion on the right, and the face of an ox and the
11   face of an eagle on the left. The wings of the four of them
were outstretched, one pair being linked to those of the
next creature, and the other pair covering the body.
12   Each went straight forward; wherever the spirit wished
13   to go, they went, not turning as they went. And in the
midst of the creatures was an appearance like burning
coals of fire, resembling torches, moving to and fro
14   among the creatures; and the fire had a radiance, while
out of the fire went lightning, running to and fro.

15   As I looked at the creatures, lo! there was a wheel on
16   the ground beside each of the four of them. The color of
the wheels was like topaz; and the four of them had the
same shape, their construction being as if one wheel were
17   within another. When they went, they went on their
18   four sides, not turning as they went. The wheels had
felloes; and as I looked at them, lo! the felloes of the four
19   of them were full of eyes round about. When the creatures went, the wheels went beside them; and when the
creatures rose from the earth, the wheels also rose.
20   Wherever the spirit wished to go, they went; for the
21   spirit of the creatures was in the wheels. When these
went, they went; and when these stood still, they stood
still; and when these rose from the earth, the wheels rose

along with them; for the spirit of the creatures was in the wheels.

Over the heads of the creatures was the semblance of a 22 firmament, glittering like transparent ice, stretched above their heads. Under the firmament one pair of their 23 wings touched those of the next creature, while the other pair covered the body. And when they went, the sound 24 of their wings sounded to me like the sound of mighty waters, or like the voice of the Almighty—it was a sound of tumult like that of an armed camp—and when they stood still, they let down their wings. Above the firma- 25 ment that was over their heads was the semblance of a 26 throne, colored like sapphire; and upon the semblance of the throne was a semblance like that of a man sitting above it. From the appearance of his loins upward I saw 27 something with a luster like that of shining metal; and from the appearance of his loins downward I saw something resembling fire, with a radiance round about it, resembling the bow that appears in the clouds on a rainy 28 day.

Such was the semblance of the glory of the LORD, as it appeared to me. And when I saw it, I fell upon my face. Then I heard the voice of someone speaking. And he said 2 to me,

"O mortal man, stand upon your feet, that I may speak with you!"

As he spoke to me, a spirit entered me, and set me 2 upon my feet. And I heard him that spoke to me saying, 3

"O mortal man, I am sending you to the household of Israel, that nation of rebels who have rebelled against me—they and their fathers have sinned against me to this very day, the children also are hard-faced and stubborn— 4 I am sending you to them, and you shall say to them, 'Thus says the Lord GOD!' And whether they listen or 5 decline to listen—for they are a rebellious household— they shall know that there is a prophet among them. And you, O mortal man, fear them not, nor be dismayed at 6 them—even when thistles and thorns are round about you, and you dwell among scorpions—fear not their words, nor

be dismayed at their looks—for they are a rebellious
7 household. You shall speak what I say to them, whether
they listen or decline to listen—for they are a rebellious
8 household. And you, O mortal man, hear what I say to
you; be not rebellious like that rebellious household.
Open your mouth, and eat what I give you!"
9   Then I looked, and lo! there was a hand stretched out
10 to me; and lo! there was in it a scroll. And he unrolled
it before me; and it was covered with writing on both
sides—words of lamentation, mourning, and woe were
3 written on it. And he said to me,
    "O mortal man, eat what you find here; eat this scroll,
then go and speak to the household of Israel!"
2   So I opened my mouth, and he gave me the scroll to
3 eat, saying to me,
    "O mortal man, eat and digest this scroll which I am
giving you!"
    And when I ate the scroll, it was as sweet as honey in
4 my mouth. Then he said to me,
    "O mortal man, go to the household of Israel, and
5 speak what I say to them. For it is not to a people of
unintelligible speech or difficult language that you are
6 sent, but to the household of Israel—not to many peoples
of unintelligible speech or difficult language, whose
words you cannot understand. If I sent you to them, they
7 would certainly listen to you. But the household of
Israel will not listen to you; for they will not listen to
me; for the whole household of Israel is hard-faced and
8 stubborn. But I will make you as hard-faced and stub-
9 born as they; I will make you like adamant harder than
flint. Fear them not, nor be dismayed before them—for
they are a rebellious household."
10   He said further to me,
    "O mortal man, all the words that I shall speak to
11 you receive and attend to. Then go to the exiles, your
fellow-countrymen, and speak to them, and say, 'Thus
says the Lord God!' whether they hear or decline to
hear."
12   Then a spirit lifted me up (and as the glory of the Lord

rose from its place, I heard behind me the sound of a 13
great rustling; it was the sound of the wings of the creatures as they touched one another, and the sound of the
wheels beside them, that caused the great rustling) a 14
spirit lifted me up and carried me away, and I went with
my spirit in the fierce glow—the hand of the LORD
pressing hard upon me—and came to the exiles who lived 15
at Tel-abib, by the River Chebar, and stayed with them
there for seven days in a state of stupor.

THE PROPHET AS WATCHMAN, 3:16-21

At the end of seven days the word of the LORD came to 3
me, saying,
"O mortal man, I appoint you a watchman to the 17
household of Israel; and whenever you hear a word from
my mouth, you shall warn them from me. If I say to the 18
wicked, 'You shall surely die,' and you fail to warn him
—if you say nothing to warn the wicked man from his
wicked way, in order to save his life—he being wicked
shall die for his iniquity, but his blood will I require at
your hand. If, however, you warn the wicked man, and 19
he turn not from his wicked conduct and his wicked way,
he shall die for his iniquity, but you will have saved
yourself. Or if a righteous man turn from his righteous- 20
ness, and do what is wrong, and I make that the occasion
for bringing about his downfall, he shall die—because
you did not warn him, he shall die for his sin, and the
righteous deeds which he has done shall not be remembered—but his blood will I require at your hand. If, 21
however, you warn the righteous man not to sin, and he
do not sin, he shall live, because he took warning; and
you will have saved yourself."

THE INEXORABLE DOOM OF JERUSALEM, 14:12-23

The word of the LORD came to me, saying, 14
"O mortal man, if a land sin against me by acting 13
faithlessly, and I stretch out my hand against it, and
break its staff of bread, and send famine upon it, and cut
off from it man and beast, even though these three men 14

were in the midst of it—Noah, Daniel, and Job—they should by their righteousness save but themselves," is the oracle of the Lord GOD.

15 "Or if I send wild beasts over the land, and they de-populate it, so that it becomes a desolation, with none
16 passing through it because of the wild beasts, even though these three men were in the midst of it, as I live," is the oracle of the Lord GOD, "they should save neither sons nor daughters—they should save but themselves alone—and the land should be left a desolation.

17 "Or if I bring a sword upon that land, saying, 'Let the sword pass through the land!' and cut off from it man and
18 beast, even though these three men were in the midst of it, as I live," is the oracle of the Lord GOD, "they should save neither sons nor daughters—they should save but themselves alone.

19 "Or if I send pestilence into that land, and pour out my fury upon it in bloodshed, cutting off from it man and
20 beast, even though Noah, Daniel, and Job were in the midst of it, as I live," is the oracle of the Lord GOD, "they should save neither son nor daughter—they should by their righteousness save but themselves.

21 "Therefore thus says the Lord GOD: How much more when I send against Jerusalem my four deadly judg-ments—sword, famine, wild beasts, and pestilence—to
22 cut off from it man and beast! Nevertheless, if there be any survivors left in it, sons and daughters who shall make good their escape to you, you shall be consoled for the trouble that I have brought upon Jerusalem—even for all that I have brought upon it—when you see their ways
23 and their doings; they shall console you when you see their ways and their doings, and you shall know that it was not without cause that I did all that I have done in it," is the oracle of the Lord GOD.

THE PRINCIPLE OF PERSONAL RESPONSIBILITY, 18:1–32

18 The word of the LORD came to me, saying,
2 "What mean you by quoting this proverb in the land of Israel:

'The fathers eat sour grapes,
    And the children's teeth are set on edge'?
As I live," is the oracle of the Lord God, "you shall have   3
no more occasion to quote this proverb in Israel. Behold!   4
all men are mine—the son is mine equally with the father
—he who sins shall die.

"If a man be righteous, and do what is lawful and   5
right—if he eat no flesh with the blood in it, nor lift up   6
his eyes to the idols of the household of Israel; if he defile
not his neighbor's wife, nor approach a woman in her
time of uncleanness; if he oppress no one, but conscien-   7
tiously restore the debtor's pledge; if he commit no robbery, but share his bread with the hungry, and cover the
naked with a garment; if he lend no money at interest,
nor take increase for himself; if he withhold his hand   8
from crime, observe strict justice between man and man,
follow my statutes, and keep my ordinances to obey them   9
—he is righteous, and shall surely live," is the oracle of
the Lord God.

"If he beget a son, a violent man, and a shedder of   10
blood, who does none of these things—but eats flesh with   11
the blood in it, defiles his neighbor's wife, oppresses the   12
poor and needy, commits robbery, does not restore the
debtor's pledge, lifts up his eyes to the idols, commits
abomination, lends on interest, and takes increase—that   13
son shall by no means live; because he commits all these
abominations, he shall surely die, and his blood shall be
upon his own head.

"But if this man beget a son who sees all the sins that   14
his father has done, and is afraid, and does not act likewise—does not eat flesh with the blood in it, nor lift up   15
his eyes to the idols of the household of Israel, does not
defile his neighbor's wife, oppresses no one, exacts no   16
pledge, commits no robbery, shares his bread with the
hungry, and covers the naked with a garment, withholds
his hand from crime, takes no interest nor increase,   17
obeys my ordinances, and follows my statutes—that son
shall not die for the iniquity of his father, but shall surely
live. His father died for his iniquity, because he prac-   18

[84]

ticed oppression, robbed his fellow-man, and did what
19 was evil among his people; and you ask, 'Why should not
the son bear the consequences of his father's iniquity?'
If the son do what is lawful and right—if he keep my
20 statutes, and do them—he shall surely live. He who sins
shall die; the son shall not bear the consequences of the
father's iniquity, nor the father bear the consequences of
the son's iniquity; the righteousness of the righteous
shall be put to his own account, and the wickedness of
the wicked shall be put to his.
21 "Or if the wicked man turn from all the sins which
he has committed, and keep all my statutes, and do what
is lawful and right, he shall surely live, and not die.
22 None of the transgressions which he has committed
shall be remembered against him; for the righteousness
23 which he has done he shall live. Have I any pleasure at
all in the death of the wicked?" is the oracle of the Lord
God; "and not rather in this, that he turn from his way
and live?
24 "But if the righteous man turn from his righteousness,
and commit iniquity, acting in accordance with all the
abominations which the wicked man practices, none of
the righteous deeds which he has done shall be remembered; for the treason which he has committed, and the
25 sin which he has done, he shall die. Yet you say, 'The
way of the Lord is not fair.' Hear, then, O household of
Israel! Is my way not fair? Is it not your ways that are
26 not fair? If a righteous man turn from his righteousness,
and commit iniquity, he shall die—for the iniquity
27 which he has committed he shall die. And if a wicked
man turn from the wickedness which he has committed,
and do what is lawful and right, he shall save his life;
28 because he is afraid, and turns from all the transgressions
which he has committed, he shall surely live, and not die.
29 Yet the household of Israel says, 'The way of the Lord
is not fair.' Are my ways not fair, O household of Israel?
30 Is it not your ways that are not fair? Therefore, O household of Israel, I will judge you each in accordance with
his ways," is the oracle of the Lord God. "Repent, then,

and turn from all your transgressions, lest your iniquity bring you to ruin. Cast away from you all the trans- 31 gressions which you have committed against me; and get you a new heart and a new spirit. Why should you die, O household of Israel? For I have no pleasure in the death 32 of anyone who dies," is the oracle of the Lord God. "Turn, then, and live!"

THE VISION OF THE VALLEY, 37:1-14

The hand of the Lord was upon me; and the Lord 37 carried me out by the spirit, and set me down in the midst of a valley which was full of bones. He led me all round 2 them, and lo! there were very many of them on the surface of the valley, and lo! they were very dry. And he 3 said to me,

"O mortal man, can these bones live?"

And I answered,

"O Lord God, thou knowest."

Then he said to me,   4

"Prophesy over these bones, and say to them, 'O dry bones, hear the word of the Lord! Thus says the Lord 5 God to these bones: Behold! I am causing breath to enter you, and you shall live. I will put sinews upon you, 6 and will clothe you with flesh, and cover you with skin; then I will put breath into you, and you shall live; and you shall know that I am the Lord.'"

So I prophesied as I had been commanded; and as I 7 prophesied, there was a sound; and lo! there followed a rustling; and the bones came together, bone to its bone. And as I looked, lo! there were sinews upon them, and 8 flesh came up, and skin covered them over; but there was no breath in them. Then he said to me,   9

"Prophesy to the breath; prophesy, O mortal man, and say to the breath, 'Thus says the Lord God: Come from the four winds, O breath, and breathe into these slain men, that they may live!'"

So I prophesied as he had commanded me; and the 10 breath came into them, and they lived, and stood upon

¹¹ their feet—an exceedingly great host. Then he said to me,

"O mortal man, these bones are the whole household of Israel. Behold! they keep saying, 'Our bones are dried ¹² up, and our hope is lost; we are clean cut off.' Therefore prophesy, and say to them, 'Thus says the Lord GOD: Behold! I am opening your graves, and will raise you out of your graves, O my people, and will bring you into the ¹³ land of Israel. And when I open your graves, and raise you out of your graves, O my people, you shall know that ¹⁴ I am the LORD. And I will put my spirit into you, and you shall live; and I will settle you on your own land; and you shall know that I am the LORD. I have spoken it, and I will do it,' is the oracle of the LORD."

THE BOOKS OF SAMUEL AND KINGS

· · ·

The bitter experience of the Exile, beginning with the deportation of 597 B.C., turned the minds of thoughtful Jews back over the centuries of the kingdom, now apparently at an end. They found satisfaction in reviewing their national past, from the days of Samuel the king-maker to the national collapse under Jehoiachin and Zedekiah.

Old chronicles and records dealing with those far-off times were still preserved among them, but have since perished: some about Samuel, Saul, and David; the Records of Solomon; the Chronicles of the Kings of Israel; the Chronicles of the Kings of Judah; besides temple annals and prophetic narratives. These were some of them of great antiquity, the oldest going back to the latter half of the tenth century before Christ, and they were sometimes quite diverse in attitude, taking opposite views as to the founding of the monarchy, for example.

With such materials a Jewish writer of this time and under the influence of Deuteronomy undertook to produce an account of the experiences of his people from Samuel, the last of the judges, to Zedekiah, the last of the kings, with all the glorious story of David and Solomon, and the golden age, as it now appeared, of Jewish history. It was a long story, covering nearly five hundred years, from about 1075 B.C. to his own days.

Half a century later, after the collapse of the national

life, and in the midst of the captivity, a Jewish exile in Babylonia revised and finished the story, bringing it down to the thirty-seventh year of the captivity of King Jehoiachin, or 561 B.C. The stories of Samuel, Saul, David, and Solomon, of Elijah and Elisha, and of the fortunes of the nation surrounded by the great empires of Egypt, Assyria, and Babylon make the book from any point of view one of the great works of ancient literature, and the influence of Deuteronomy with its noble prophetic ideal of religion led the writer to survey it all from that religious point of view.

. . .

THE FIRST BOOK OF SAMUEL

THE CALL OF SAMUEL, 3:1—4:1*a*

3   The child Samuel was ministering in the presence of the Lord before Eli. And the word of the Lord was rare
2 in those days; there was no frequent vision. Now it happened at that time, as Eli was lying down in his place
3 (his eyesight had begun to fail, so that he could not see), and the lamp of God had not yet gone out, and Samuel was lying down in the temple of the Lord, where the ark
4 of God was; that the Lord called,

"Samuel, Samuel,"
And he said,
"Here I am!"

5   And he ran to Eli, and said,
"Here I am; for you called me.
And he said,
"I did not call; go back and lie down."

6   And he went and lay down. And the Lord called yet again,
"Samuel! Samuel!"
And Samuel arose and went to Eli, and said,
"Here I am, for you called me."
And he said,

"I did not call, my son; go back and lie down."

Now Samuel did not yet know the LORD, neither was 7
the word of the LORD yet revealed to him. So when the 8
LORD called Samuel again the third time, he arose and
went to Eli, and said,

"Here I am; for you called me."

Then Eli perceived that the LORD was calling the lad. 9
Therefore Eli said to Samuel,

"Go, lie down: and it shall be, if he calls you, you
shall say, "Speak, LORD; for thy servant hears.""

So Samuel went and lay down in his place. Then the 10
LORD came, and took his stand, and called as at other
times,

"Samuel! Samuel!"

And Samuel said,

"Speak, for thy servant hears."

Then the LORD said to Samuel, 11

"Behold, I am about to do a thing in Israel, at which
both the ears of everyone that hears it will tingle. At 12
that time I will execute against Eli all that I have spoken
concerning his house, from beginning to end. And you 13
shall tell him that I am about to judge his house forever,
for the wrong-doing which he knew, because his sons
were blaspheming God, and he did not rebuke them. And 14
therefore I have sworn to the house of Eli, that the
wrong-doing of Eli's house shall not be expiated by
sacrifice nor offering forever."

And Samuel lay until morning; then he rose early in 15
the morning, and opened the double doors of the house
of the LORD. But Samuel feared to show Eli the vision.
Then Eli called Samuel, and said, 16

"Samuel, my son."

And he said,

"Here I am."

And he said, 17

"What is the thing that he spoke to you? Do not, I
beg of you, hide it from me; may God do so to you, and
worse still, if you hide anything from me of the whole
matter which he spoke to you."

18   Samuel told him everything, and concealed nothing from him. And he said,

"It was the LORD; let him do what is good in his sight."

19   Thus Samuel grew, and the LORD was with him, and
20 he let none of his words fall to the ground. And all Israel from Dan even to Beersheba knew that Samuel was one accredited as a prophet of the LORD. And the LORD
21 continued to reveal himself in Shiloh; for the LORD revealed himself to Samuel. And Eli was exceedingly old, and his sons kept right on making their conduct hateful
4 before the LORD. Thus the word of Samuel came to all Israel.

DAVID SLAYS GOLIATH, 17:1–58

17   Now the Philistines mustered their armed forces for war, and they were gathered together at Socoh, which belongs to Judah, and encamped between Socoh and
2 Azekah, in Ephes-dammim. And Saul and the men of Israel were gathered together and encamped in the valley of Elah; and they drew up in line of battle facing the
3 Philistines. And the Philistines were stationed on the mountain on one side, and the Israelites were stationed on the mountain on the other side, and the valley was
4 between them. And there came out a champion from the camp of the Philistines, named Goliath of Gath, whose
5 height was about ten feet. And he had a helmet of bronze upon his head, and he was clad with a coat of mail of bronze scales, whose weight was about five thousand
6 shekels. And he had greaves of bronze upon his legs and
7 a javelin of bronze between his shoulders. And the shaft of his spear was like a weaver's beam, and the head of his iron spear weighed six hundred shekels; and his shield-bearer went before him.

8   And he stood and shouted to the battle line of Israel and said to them,

"Why have you come out to draw up the line of battle? Am I not a Philistine and you the servants of Saul? Choose for yourselves a man and let him come down to

me. If he is able to fight with me and can kill me, then 9
we will be your servants; but if I overcome him and kill
him, then you shall be our servants and serve us."

And the Philistine said, 10

"I challenge the ranks of Israel this day; give me a
man that we may fight together."

And when Saul and all Israel heard the words of the 11
Philistine, they were terrified and panic-stricken.

Now David was the son of an Ephrathite of Bethle- 12
hem in Judah, whose name was Jesse, and he had eight
sons. And the man was old in the days of Saul, well advanced in years. And the three eldest sons of Jesse had 13
gone after Saul to the war; and the names of these three
sons who went to the war were Eliab the eldest, his second Abinadab, and the third Shammah. But David was 14
the youngest; and the three eldest had followed Saul.
Now David went to and fro from Saul to feed his 15
father's sheep at Bethlehem. And the Philistine drew 16
near morning and evening and took his stand forty days.
And Jesse said to David his son, 17

"Take now for your brothers a bushel of this parched
grain and these ten loaves and take them quickly to the
camp of your brothers. But bring these ten cheeses to the 18
captain of the thousand, and look into the welfare of your
brothers and take assurance of them."

Now Saul and they and all the men of Israel were in 19
the valley of Elah fighting with the Philistines.

So David rose up early in the morning and left the flock 20
with a keeper and took and went, as Jesse had commanded him. And he came to the intrenchment just as
the army was going forth to the battle-line, raising the
shout of battle. And Israel and the Philistines drew up 21
the battle lines facing each other. And David left his 22
supplies in care of the keeper of the baggage and ran to
the battle line and came and greeted his brothers. And 23
while he was talking with them the champion, the
Philistine of Gath, Goliath by name, was seen coming
up from the Philistine lines and he spoke the same words
as before; and David heard them. And all the men of 24

Israel, when they saw the man, fled from him and were
25 panic-stricken. And the men of Israel said,

"Have you seen this man who comes up? Surely to
taunt Israel he comes up. Whoever overcomes him, the
king will make very rich and will give him his daughter
and make his father's house free in Israel."

26 Then said David to the men standing by him as follows,

"What shall be done for the man who overcomes yonder Philistine and takes away the reproach of Israel?
For who is this uncircumcised Philistine, that he should
taunt the battle lines of the living God?"

27 And the people replied to him according to the above
words, saying,

"Thus shall it be done to the man who overcomes
him."

28 Now Eliab, his eldest brother, heard when he spoke
to the men; and Eliab's anger was roused against David,
and he said,

"Why now have you come down? And with whom
have you left those few sheep in the desert? I know your
insolence, and the wickedness of your heart; for you have
come down to look at the battle."

29 And David said,

"What have I now done? Is there not a cause?"

30 And turning away from him to another, he spoke as
before; and the people returned answer as at the first.

31 And when the words which David spoke were heard,
they reported them to Saul. And they took him and
brought him before Saul.

32 Then David said to Saul,

"Let not my lord's courage fail him; your servant will
go and fight with this Philistine."

33 And Saul said to David,

"You are not able to go against this Philistine to fight
with him, for you are but a youth and he has been a
warrior from his youth."

34 But David said to Saul,

"Your servant has been a shepherd with his father's

flock; and when a lion or a bear would come and take a sheep out of the flock, I would go out after him and attack him and deliver it from his mouth; and if he rose up against me, I would seize him by his beard and wound him and kill him. Your servant has slain both lion and bear; and this uncircumcised Philistine shall be as one of them, since he has taunted the battle lines of the living God."

And David said,

"The Lord who delivered me from the paw of the lion, and from the paw of the bear, will deliver me from the hand of this Philistine."

Therefore Saul said to David,

"Go, and may the Lord be with you."

And Saul clothed David with his garments, and put a helmet of bronze on his head, and equipped him with a coat of mail. And he girded David with his sword over his outer garments; and he struggled in vain to go, for he had not tried them. Then David said to Saul,

"I cannot go with these, for I have not tried them."

And David put them off him.

So he took his stick in his hand, and chose five smooth stones out of the brook and put them in his bag, and with his sling in his hand he advanced toward the Philistine. And the Philistine began cautiously to approach David, having the bearer of his shield directly in front of him. And when the Philistine observed and saw David, he scorned him, for he was youthful and ruddy, and of attractive appearance. And the Philistine said to David,

"Am I a dog that you come to me with sticks?"

And the Philistine cursed David by his gods. And the Philistine said to David,

"Come to me and I will give your flesh to the birds of the heavens and to the beasts of the field."

Then David said to the Philistine,

"You come to me with a sword and a spear and a javelin,
But I come to you in the name of the Lord of armies,

The God of the battle lines of Israel whom you have taunted.

46 This day the LORD will deliver you into my hand,
That I may slay you and sever your head from your body;
And I will this day give your dead body and the dead of the camp of the Philistines
To the birds of the heavens and to the wild beasts of the earth,
That all the earth may know that there is a God in Israel,

47 And that all this congregation may know
That not with sword and spear does the LORD deliver,
For the battle is the LORD's and he will give you into our hands."

48 Now when the Philistine arose and came and drew near to meet David, David also hastened and ran toward
49 the line to meet the Philistine. And David put his hand in his bag and took from it a stone and slung it and it struck the Philistine on his forehead; and the stone sank into his forehead, so that he fell on his face to the earth.
50 So David overpowered the Philistine with a sling and a stone, and he struck the Philistine, and slew him, al-
51 though there was no sword in David's hand. And David ran and stood over the Philistine, and took his sword, and drew it out of its sheath, and slew him, and cut off his head with it. And when the Philistines saw that their champion was dead, they fled.
52 And the men of Israel and Judah arose and raised a shout and pursued the Philistines to the entrance to Gath and to the gates of Ekron, so that the wounded of the Philistines fell down on the way from Shaaraim, even to
53 Gath and Ekron. And when the Israelites returned from
54 pursuing the Philistines, they plundered their camp, but David took the head of the Philistine and brought it to Jerusalem; and he put his armor in his tent.
55 When Saul saw David going out against the Philistine, he said to Abner, the commander of the army,
"Whose son is this lad, Abner?"

[95]

And Abner said,
"As you live, O king, I do not know."   56
And the king said,
"Inquire whose son the youth is."
And when David returned from slaying the Philistine,   57
Abner took him, and brought him before Saul with the
Philistine's head in his hand. And Saul said to him,   58
"Whose son are you, my lad?"
And David said,
"The son of your servant Jesse, the Bethlehemite."

THE SECOND BOOK OF SAMUEL

DAVID'S DIRGE OVER SAUL AND JONATHAN, 1:17–27

¹ Then David sang this dirge over Saul and Jonathan his
¹⁸ son; (behold it is written in the Book of the Upright to
instruct the Judeans).

And he said,

¹⁹ "Thy beauty, O Israel!
   Upon thy heights is slain.
   How have the heroes fallen!

²⁰ "Tell it not in Gath,
   Announce it not in the streets of Askelon;
   Lest the daughters of the Philistines rejoice,
   Lest the daughters of the uncircumcised exult.

²¹ "O mountains of Gilboa, let neither dew fall,
   Nor rain be upon you, O fields of death!
   For there was the shield of the mighty thrown aside,
   The shield of Saul, not anointed with oil.

²² "From the blood of the slain,
   From the fat of the mighty,
   The bow of Jonathan turned not back,
   Nor empty returned the sword of Saul.

²³ "Saul and Jonathan, beloved and lovely!
   In life and death they were not divided;
   Swifter than eagles were they,
   They were stronger than lions.

²⁴ "O daughters of Israel, weep over Saul,
   Who clothed you in scarlet daintily,
   Who adorned your garments with gold and jewels;
²⁵ How are the mighty fallen in the midst of battle!

"O Jonathan! by your death am I mortally wounded,
   I am distressed for you, my brother Jonathan!   26
   You were exceedingly dear to me,
   Your love was more marvellous to me than the love
      of women!

"How have the mighty fallen,   27
   And the weapons of war perished!"

THE FIRST BOOK OF KINGS

ELIJAH AND THE DROUGHT, 17:1–16; 18:1–2, 17–46

17 Now Elijah the Tishbite, of Tishbe in Gilead, said to Ahab,

"As the LORD, the God of Israel, lives, before whom I stand, there shall be neither dew nor rain these years, except by my word."

2 Accordingly, the word of the LORD came to him, saying,

3 "Depart from here and turn eastward, and hide your-
4 self by the Brook Cherith, that is east of Jordan, and you shall drink from the brook; and I have commanded the ravens to feed you there."

5 So he went and did according to the word of the LORD and went and dwelt by the Brook Cherith that is east of
6 Jordan. And the ravens uninterruptedly brought him bread and flesh in the morning and bread and flesh in the
7 evening, and he used to drink from the brook. But after a time the brook dried up because there was no rain in the land.

8 Then the word of the LORD came to him, saying,

9 "Arise, go to Zarephath, which belongs to Sidon, and dwell there; see, I have commanded a widow there to provide for you."

10 So he arose and went to Zarephath. And as he came into the gate of the city, there was a widow there gathering sticks, and calling to her, he said,

"Bring me, I pray you, a little water in a vessel that I may drink."

11 But as she was going to bring it, he called to her and said,

"Bring me, I pray you, a morsel of food in your hand."

12 And she said,

"As the LORD your God lives, I have nothing but a

handful of meal in the jar and a little oil in a cruse; and now I am gathering a few sticks that I may go in and prepare it for myself and my son, that we may eat it and die."

But Elijah said to her, 13

"Fear not; go and do as you have said; but first make me from it a little cake, and bring it to me, and afterward make for yourself and your son. For thus the LORD, the 14 God of Israel, has said, 'The jar of meal shall not be exhausted nor the cruse of oil spent until the day that the LORD sends rain upon the ground.' "

So she went and did according to the word of Elijah. 15 And she and he and her household did eat day after day. The jar of meal was not exhausted, neither did the cruse 16 of oil fail according to the word of the LORD which he spoke by Elijah.

Now after many days the word of the LORD came to 18 Elijah, in the third year, saying,

"Go, show yourself to Ahab; and I will bring rain 2 upon the face of the ground."

Now as soon as Ahab saw Elijah, Ahab said to him, 17 "Is it you, you troubler of Israel?"

But he said, 18

"I have not troubled Israel, but you and your father's house, in that you have forsaken the commandments of the LORD and have gone after the Baals. Now therefore 19 send and gather to me all Israel, to Mount Carmel, together with the four hundred and fifty prophets of the Baal and the four hundred prophets of the Asherah, who eat at Jezebel's table."

So Ahab sent to all the Israelites and gathered the 20 prophets together to Mount Carmel. Accordingly Elijah 21 came near to all the people and said,

"How long are you going to limp upon two diverse opinions? If the LORD be God, follow him, but if the Baal, follow him."

But the people gave him no answer. Then Elijah said 22 to the people,

"I, even I only, am left as a prophet of the LORD, but

the prophets of the Baal are four hundred and fifty men.

23 Let them therefore give us two bulls, and let them choose one bull for themselves and cut it in pieces and lay it on the wood but make no fire, and I will prepare the other bull and place it on the wood, but I will make no fire.

24 Then call you on the name of your god and I will call on the name of the LORD; and the god who answers by fire, he is God."

And all the people answered and said,

"It is a fair test!"

25 Thereupon Elijah said to the prophets of the Baal,

"Choose for yourselves a bull and prepare it first, for you are many, and call on the name of your god, but make no fire."

26 So they took the bull which he gave them and prepared it, and called on the name of the Baal from morning until noon, saying,

"O Baal, answer us."

But there was no voice and none answered. And they

27 limped about the altar which they had made. But at noon Elijah mocked them, and said,

"Cry with a loud voice; for he is a god; either he is meditating, or he has gone aside, or he is on a journey, or perhaps he is asleep and needs to be awakened!"

28 Then they cried with a loud voice, and proceeded to slash one another according to their custom, with swords and with lances until the blood gushed out upon them.

29 And when midday had passed they worked themselves into a prophetic frenzy until the offering of the oblation; but there was no voice, nor answer, and none regarded.

30 Then Elijah said to all the people,

"Come near to me."

So all the people drew near to him; and he repaired the

31 altar of the LORD which had been torn down. Accordingly Elijah took twelve stones, corresponding to the number of the tribes of the sons of Jacob to whom the word of the LORD came, saying,

"Israel shall be your name."

32 And with the stones he made an altar in the name of

the Lord. Then he made a trench about the altar of the
capacity of two measures of seed. He also laid the pieces 33
of wood in order, cut up the bull, and laid it upon the
wood. And he said,

"Fill four jars with water and pour it on the burnt-
offering and on the wood."

He also said,

"Do it a second time";

And they did it a second time.

Again he said, 34

"Do it a third time."

And they did it a third time, so that the water ran 35
around the altar; and he also filled the trench with water.

Then when it was time to offer the oblation, Elijah 36
the prophet came near and said,

"O Lord, God of Abraham, of Isaac, and of Israel, let
it be known today that thou art God in Israel and that
I am thy servant, and that at thy command I have done
all these things. Answer me, O Lord, answer me, that 37
this people may know that thou, O Lord, art God, and
that thou hast turned their heart back again."

Then the fire of the Lord fell and consumed the burnt- 38
offering and the wood, the stones and the dust, and licked
up the water that was in the trench. So when all the 39
people saw it, they fell upon their faces and said,

"The Lord, he is God; the Lord, he is God."

But Elijah said to them, 40

"Seize the prophets of the Baal; let not a man of them
escape."

So they seized them and Elijah brought them down to
the Brook Kishon and slew them there.

Then Elijah said to Ahab, 41

"Go up, eat and drink; for there is the rushing sound
of rain."

So Ahab went up to eat and drink, but Elijah went up 42
to the top of Carmel, and crouched down upon the earth,
with his face between his knees. And he said to his serv- 43
ant,

"Go up now, look toward the sea."

So he went up, and looked and said,
"There is nothing."
But he said,
"Go back seven times."

44 So the servant went back seven times. However, the seventh time he said,
"There is a cloud as small as a man's hand, rising out of the sea."
And he said,
"Go up, say to Ahab, 'Harness your steeds and go down that the rain stop you not.'"

45 Moreover, in a very short time the heavens grew black with clouds and wind, and there was a great downpour.

46 But Ahab rode on and arrived at Jezreel. The hand of the Lord also was on Elijah so that he girded up his loins and ran before Ahab to the entrance of Jezreel.

ELIJAH ON MOUNT HOREB, 19:1–18

19 Now when Ahab told Jezebel all that Elijah had done, and how that he had slain all the prophets with the
2 sword, Jezebel sent a messenger to Elijah saying,
"As surely as you are Elijah and I am Jezebel, so may God do to me and more also, if I do not make your life as the life of one of them by tomorrow about this time."

3 Then he was afraid and arose and went for his life, and came to Beersheba that belongs to Judah; and there he
4 left his servant. But he himself went into the desert a day's journey, and came and sat down under a broom tree, and he requested for himself that he might die, and he said,
"It is enough; now, O Lord, take away my life, for I am no better than my fathers."

5 Then he lay down and slept under a broom tree. Suddenly an angel was touching him, and he said to him,
"Arise, eat."

6 And when he looked, behold there was at his head a cake baked on hot stones, and a cruse of water. So he ate
7 and drank and lay down again. But the Messenger of the Lord returned a second time and touched him and said,

"Arise, eat, for the journey is too great for you."

So he arose and ate and drank and went in the strength 8 of that food forty days and forty nights to Horeb, the Mount of God. And he came there to a cave and lodged 9 there.

And behold the word of the Lord came to him, and he said to him,

"What are you doing here, Elijah?"

Then he said, 10

"I have been very jealous for the Lord, the God of hosts; for the Israelites have forsaken the covenant with thee, thrown down thine altars, and slain thy prophets with the sword; and I, even I only, am left, and they are seeking to take away my life."

But he said, 11

"Go forth, and stand upon the mount before the Lord."

And behold, the Lord was passing by, and a great and mighty wind was rending the mountain and shattering the rocks before the Lord; but the Lord was not in the wind. After the wind came an earthquake, but the Lord was not in the earthquake. After the earthquake a fire; 12 but the Lord was not in the fire. And after the fire a sound of gentle stillness. Now as soon as Elijah per- 13 ceived it, he wrapped his face in his mantle and went out and stood at the entrance of the cave. Then behold there came a voice to him and said,

"What are you doing here, Elijah?"

And he said, 14

"I have been very jealous for the Lord, the God of hosts, because the Israelites have forsaken the covenant with thee, thrown down thine altars, and slain thy prophets with the sword, and I, even I only, am left, and they are seeking to take away my life."

But the Lord said to him, 15

"Go, return on your way to the desert of Damascus, and when you arrive anoint Hazael to be king over Syria. And Jehu, the son of Nimshi, you shall anoint to be king 16 over Israel, and Elisha, the son of Shaphat of Abel-

meholah, you shall anoint to be prophet in your place.
17 And it shall be that whoever escapes the sword of Hazael shall Jehu slay; and whoever escapes the sword of Jehu,
18 shall Elisha slay. Yet will I spare seven thousand in Israel—all the knees which have not bowed to the Baal and every mouth which has not kissed him.''

THE CALL OF ELISHA, 19:19–21

19 Now when he departed from there he found Elisha, the son of Shaphat, as he was plowing behind twelve yoke of oxen, he being with the twelfth. Then Elijah came over to him and threw his mantle upon him.
20 Thereupon he left the oxen and ran after Elijah, and he said,

"Let me, I pray you, kiss my father and my mother, and then I will follow you."

And he said to him,

"Go back again, for what have I done to you?"

21 So he returned from following him and took a yoke of oxen and sacrificed them, and using the ox-yoke to boil their flesh, he gave it to the people and made them a feast; then he arose and went after Elijah and became his attendant.

THE SECOND BOOK OF KINGS

THE TRANSLATION OF ELIJAH, 2:1-15

Now when the Lord took up Elijah by a whirlwind 2 to the heavens, Elijah and Elisha were on their way from Gilgal. And Elijah said to Elisha, 2

"I pray you, remain here, for the Lord has sent me as far as Bethel."

But Elisha said,

"As the Lord lives and as you yourself are alive, I will not leave you."

So they went down to Bethel. Then the members of 3 the prophetic group who were at Bethel came out to Elisha and said to him,

"Do you know that today the Lord is about to take away your master from being your leader?"

And he said,

"Yes, I know it; hold your peace."

Again Elijah said to him, 4

"Elisha, tarry here, I pray you, for the Lord has sent me to Jericho."

But he said,

"As the Lord lives and as you yourself are alive, I will not leave you."

So they entered Jericho. And the members of the 5 prophetic group who were in Jericho came near Elisha and said to him,

"Do you know that the Lord is about to take away your master from being your leader today?"

And he said,

"Yes, I know it. Hold your peace."

Elijah again said to him, 6

"Remain here, I pray you, for the Lord has sent me to the Jordan."

But he said to him,

"As the Lord lives and as you yourself are alive, I will not leave you."

So the two of them went on.

7 Now fifty men of the prophetic group went and stood opposite them at a distance, while they two stood by the
8 Jordan. Then Elijah took his mantle and rolled it up and struck the waters; thereupon they were divided on either side so that the two of them passed over on dry ground.
9 Now as soon as they had crossed over, Elijah said to Elisha,

"Ask what I shall do for you, before I am taken from you."

Then Elisha said,

"Let there be now a twofold share of your spirit upon me!"

10 But he said,

"You have asked a hard thing; still, if you see me as I am being taken from you, so shall it be with you; but if not, it shall not be so."

11 Now as they were going along conversing, suddenly a chariot of fire and horses of fire separated the two of them; and Elijah went up by a whirlwind to heaven.
12 And as Elisha looked, he cried out,

"My father, my father! the chariots of Israel and its horsemen!"

But he saw him no more, and he took hold of his own
13 garments and tore them in two pieces. He also took up the mantle of Elijah that had fallen from him and re-
14 turned and stood by the brink of the Jordan. Then he took the mantle of Elijah that had fallen from him and struck the waters and said,

"Where now is the Lord, the God of Elijah?"

And when he had struck the waters they were divided on either side so that Elisha passed over.

15 And when the members of the prophetic group who were at Jericho opposite him saw him, they said,

"The spirit of Elijah is upon Elisha."

THE BOOK OF JUDGES

. . .

For two centuries or more of that long dark period which followed the invasion and conquest of Canaan by the Hebrews, their history was little more than the story of one tribal champion after another, who appeared in response to some pressing situation, and for a time commanded some degree of obedience and support. It was a shadowy, half-legendary interval between the conquest and the kingdom. Stories and memories of it lingered among the people, some of them, like the Song of Deborah, perhaps going back to the twelfth century before Christ.

These adventurous stories were gathered into a book as early as the seventh century, but it was during the Exile, under the influence of the religious ideas of Deuteronomy, that the book received substantially its present form, in which the ancient episodes are given a moralizing cast: the Hebrews sin, and in punishment God brings affliction from the neighboring peoples. Then the Hebrews repent, and he raises up a champion who delivers them and judges them through an interval of peace. But they sin again; and the process is repeated. The narrative was later completed with the short ancient account of the conquest at the beginning, 1:1—2:5, and the addition of chapters 17–21 at the end, by some priestly hand, toward the end of the fifth century before Christ.

The work of the judges was local and tribal rather than national, but these stories are many of them very

*ancient, and present vivid pictures of the old heroes of
Israel—Gideon, Jephthah, Samson—and one notable
heroine, Deborah, whose song has been called the oldest
piece of literature in the Old Testament, and the most
important source in existence for the history of Israel.*

. . .

THE VICTORY OF DEBORAH AND BARAK OVER THE CANAANITES, 5:1–31

5   Then sang Deborah and Barak, the son of Abinoam,
on that day, saying:

2   "When locks were worn loose in Israel,
       When the people volunteered;
           bless the Lord!

3   Hear, O kings; give ear, O princes!
       I—to the Lord I will sing,
       I will praise the Lord, the God of Israel.

4   "O Lord, when thou camest forth from Seir,
       When thou marchedst from the land of Edom,
       The earth quaked, the heavens also shook,
       The clouds, too, dripped water,

5   The mountains rocked at the presence of the Lord
       (that is, Sinai),
       At the presence of the Lord, the God of Israel.

6   "In the time of Shamgar, the son of Anath,
       In the time of Jael, caravans had disappeared,
       And travelers kept to the by-roads;

7   The peasantry had disappeared, they had disap-
       peared in Israel,
       Until you arose, O Deborah, arose as a mother in
       Israel.

8   "Armorers had they none;
       Armed men failed from the city.
       Was shield to be seen or lance,
       Among forty thousand in Israel?

9   My heart is with the commanders of Israel,

Who volunteered among the people;
    bless the Lord!

"O riders on tawny asses, sitting on robes;   10
    And you who travel on the road, attend!
To the noise of musicians at the watering-places,   11
There the triumphs of the Lord will be recounted,
The triumphs of his peasantry in Israel."

Then the people of the Lord went down to the gates.

"Awake, awake, Deborah;   12
Awake, awake, strike up the song!
Up, Barak, and take your captives,
O son of Abinoam!

"Then the remnant went down like nobles;   13
The people of the Lord went down like heroes.
Ephraim surged into the valley;   14
Following you came Benjamin among your clansmen.
From Machir came down commanders,
And from Zebulun those who carry the marshal's
    staff.
The chieftains of Issachar were with Deborah and 15
    Barak;
In like manner Barak rushed into the valley among
    his foot-soldiers.

"In the clans of Reuben great were the debates.
Why did you lounge among the ravines,   16
Listening to the bleating of the flocks?
In the clans of Reuben great were the debates.
Gilead remained beyond the Jordan;   17
And Dan, why did he take service on alien ships?
Asher stayed by the sea-coast,
And remained by his creeks.

"Zebulun was a people who exposed themselves to 18
    death,
And Naphtali, on the heights of the field.
The kings came, they fought;   19

Then fought the kings of Canaan;
At Taanach, by the brooks of Megiddo,
They won no booty of silver.
20   From the heavens fought the stars;
From their courses they fought with Sisera.

21   "The river Kishon swept them away;
A river barring the way was the river Kishon.
Bless thou, my soul, the might of the LORD!
22   Then the hoofs of the horses struck down
Their warriors by their furious plunging.
23   'Curse Meroz,' said the angel of the LORD,
'Curse utterly its inhabitants;
For they came not to the help of the LORD,
To the help of the LORD like heroes.'
24   Most blessed of women may Jael be,
The wife of Heber, the Kenite;
Of bedouin women most blessed!
25   Water he asked; milk she gave;
In a lordly bowl she brought him curds.
26   She put her hand to the tent-pin,
And her right hand to the workman's mallet;
And she struck down Sisera, she crushed his head;
She shattered and smashed his temple.
27   At her feet he sank, he fell, he lay prone;
At her feet he sank, he fell;
Where he sank, there he fell slain.

28   "Out of the window she peered, and exclaimed,
The mother of Sisera, out of the lattice:
'Why is his chariot so long in coming?
Why is the clatter of his chariots so delayed?'
29   The wisest of her princesses replies;
She it is who makes answer to her:
30   'Are they not finding, dividing booty?
A maid or two for each warrior;
Booty of dyed stuffs for Sisera,
Booty of dyed stuffs embroidered:
A couple of pieces of dyed embroidery for his neck
as booty.'

"Thus may all thy enemies perish, O Lord;   31
But let thy friends be like the rising of the sun in
his might."

So the land enjoyed security for forty years.

THE MIDIANITES AND GIDEON, 7:1–25

So Jerubbaal (that is, Gideon) and all the people that   7
were with him rose early, and encamped near En-harod,
while the camp of Midian was north of Gibeah-moreh
in the valley. Then the Lord said to Gideon,   2
"The people that are with you are too many for me to
deliver Midian into their power, lest Israel should glory
over me, saying, 'My own power has saved me.' Now   3
then, proclaim in the hearing of the people, 'Whoever is
afraid and timid must go home.' "
So Gideon put them to the test, and twenty-two
thousand of the people went home, but ten thousand
were left. Then the Lord said to Gideon,   4
"The people are still too many. Bring them down to
the water, and let me test them there for you; he of whom
I say to you, 'This one is to go with you,' shall go with
you; but everyone of whom I say to you, 'This one is not
to go with you,' must not go."
So he brought the people down to the water, and the   5
Lord said to Gideon,
"Everyone who laps up the water with his tongue as
a dog laps, put off by himself; and likewise everyone who
kneels down to drink."
The number of those who lapped with their tongues   6
was three hundred, while all the rest of the people knelt
down to drink water. Then the Lord said to Gideon,   7
"With the three hundred men who lapped I will save
you, and will deliver Midian into your power; but let
all the rest of the people go each to his home."
Then they took the pitchers of the people in their   8
hands, together with their trumpets; and he sent all the
rest of the Israelites home, each to his tent, keeping only

the three hundred men. Now the camp of Midian was beneath him in the valley.

9 That very night the LORD said to him,

"Rise, go down into the camp; for I am delivering it
10 into your power. But if you are afraid to go down alone,
11 go down with your servant Purah to the camp, and hear what they are saying; and after that you will have the courage to descend on the camp."

So he went down with his servant Purah to the out-
12 posts of the warriors that were in the camp. Now the Midianites, Amalekites, and all the Kedemites were lying along the valley like locusts for number, and their camels were innumerable, being like the sands on the sea-
13 shore for number. Just as Gideon came, a man was telling his comrade a dream.

"I just had a dream," he said, "that a crust of barley bread came tumbling into the camp of Midian, and coming to a tent, struck it so that it fell, and turned it upside down, so that the tent lay flat."

14 "That," his comrade responded, "is nothing other than the sword of Gideon, the son of Joash, an Israelite. God is delivering Midian and all the camp into his power."

15 As soon as Gideon heard the telling of the dream and its interpretation, he bowed in reverence; and returning to the camp of Israel, he said,

"Up! for the LORD is delivering the camp of Midian into your power."

16 Then he divided the three hundred men into three companies, and put trumpets into the hands of all of them, and empty pitchers, with torches inside the pitchers.

17 "Watch me," he said to them, "and do likewise; as I reach the outskirts of the camp, see that you do just as I
18 do; when I blow the trumpet, I and all those accompanying me, you also must blow your trumpets all around the camp, and say, 'For the LORD and for Gideon!'"

19 When Gideon and the hundred men that accompanied

him reached the outskirts of the camp at the beginning
of the middle watch, the guards having just been posted,
they blew their trumpets, and smashed the pitchers that
were in their hands; whereupon the three companies 20
blew their trumpets, and shattered their pitchers,
holding the torches in their left hands and the trumpets
in their right to blow them, and they cried, "For the
Lord and for Gideon!" Then they stood each in his place 21
around the camp, and all the camp ran; they cried out,
and fled. When the three hundred trumpets were blown, 22
the Lord set them to fighting with one another all
through the camp; and the camp fled as far as Beth-
shittah in the direction of Zererah, as far as the edge of
Abel-meholah, near Tabbath. Israelites were mustered 23
from Naphtali, Asher, and all Manasseh to pursue
Midian; and Gideon sent messengers all through the 24
highlands of Ephraim, saying,

"Come down against Midian, and seize the streams
against them as far as Bethbarah, and also the Jordan."

So all the Ephraimites were mustered, and seized the
streams as far as Bethbarah, and also the Jordan. Captur- 25
ing Midian's two chieftains, Oreb and Zeeb, they killed
Oreb at Zur-Oreb, and Zeeb they killed at Jekel-Zeeb.
They pursued Midian, and the heads of Oreb and Zeeb
they brought to Gideon on the other side of the Jordan.

THE STORY OF SAMSON, 16:4-31

Afterwards he fell in love with a woman in the valley 16
of Sorek, whose name was Delilah. Then the Philistine 5
tyrants came to her, and said to her,

"Coax him, and find out why his strength is so great,
and how we can overpower him and bind him helpless,
and we will give you each eleven hundred shekels of
silver."

So Delilah said to Samson, 6

"Do tell me why your strength is so great, and how
you can be bound helpless?"

Samson said to her, 7

"If I were to be bound with seven fresh bowstrings

that have not been dried, I should become weak, and be like any other man."

8 Then the Philistine tyrants brought her seven fresh bowstrings that had not been dried, and she bound him 9 with them. Then, having men lie in wait in the inner room, she said to him,

"The Philistines are on you, Samson!"

But he snapped the bowstrings, as a strand of tow is snapped when it comes near fire. So the source of his strength was not discovered.

10 Then Delilah said to Samson,

"There, you have trifled with me, and told me lies! Do tell me now how you can be bound."

11 So he said to her,

"If I were but bound with new ropes that have not been used, I should become weak, and be like any other man."

So Delilah took new ropes, and bound him with 12 them. Then she said to him,

"The Philistines are on you, Samson!"

(Meanwhile men were lying in wait in the inner room.)

But he snapped them off his arms like thread.

13 Then Delilah said to Samson,

"Up to now you have trifled with me, and told me lies. Tell me how you can be bound."

So he said to her,

"If you were to weave the seven locks of my head into the web, and beat them in with the pin, I should become weak, and be like any other man."

So, when he was asleep, Delilah took the seven locks of his head and wove them into the web, and beat them 14 in with the pin. Then she said to him,

"The Philistines are on you, Samson!"

But he awoke from his sleep, and pulled up both the loom and the web.

15 Then she said to him,

"How can you say, 'I love you,' when you do not confide in me? Three times already you have trifled with me, and have not told me why your strength is so great."

At last, after she had pressed him with her words 16 continually, and urged him, he got tired to death of it, and told her his whole secret. 17

"A razor has never been used on my head," he said to her; "for I have been a Nazarite to God from conception. If I were to be shaved, my strength would leave me; I should become weak, and be like any other man."

When Delilah saw that he had told her his whole 18 secret, she sent for the Philistine tyrants, saying,

"Come up this once; for he has told me his whole secret."

So the Philistine tyrants came to her, and brought the money in their hands. Then she put him to sleep on her 19 knees, and summoning a man, she had him shave off the seven locks of his head, so that he became quite helpless, and his strength left him. Then she said, 20

"The Philistines are on you, Samson!"

He awoke from his sleep, and thought, "I shall get off as I have done over and over again, and shake myself free"—not knowing that the LORD had left him. Then 21 the Philistines seized him, and gouged out his eyes, and bringing him down to Gaza, they bound him with bronze shackles, and he spent his time grinding in the prison. But the hair of his head began to grow again as soon as 22 it had been shaved off.

Now the Philistine tyrants gathered to offer a great 23 sacrifice to their god Dagon, and for merry-making, saying, "Our god has delivered our enemy Samson into our power!"

When the people saw him, they praised their god; 24 "For," said they, "our god has delivered our enemy into our hands, the devastator of our lands, and him who slew us in bands."

When they were in high spirits, they said, 25

"Summon Samson, that he may make sport for us!"

So Samson was summoned from the prison, and made sport before them. When they had stationed him be- 26 tween the pillars, Samson said to the attendant who was holding his hand,

"Put me so that I can feel the pillars on which the building is supported, that I may lean against them."

27 Now the building was full of men and women, and all the Philistine tyrants were there; and on the roof there were about three thousand men and women, looking on

28 while Samson made sport. Then Samson cried to the LORD, saying,

"O Lord GOD, pray remember me, and give me strength just this one time, O God, to wreak vengeance but once upon the Philistines for my two eyes!"

29 Then Samson grasped the two middle pillars on which the building was supported, one with his right hand and the other with his left, and braced himself against them.

"Let me die with the Philistines!" said Samson.

30 Then he pulled with all his might, so that the building fell in upon the tyrants and all the people that were in it. So those that he killed at his death were more than those that he had killed during his life.

31 Then his kinsmen and all his father's household came down, and took him up; and bringing him away, they buried him between Zorah and Eshtaol, in the tomb of his father Manoah, He had governed Israel for twenty years.

THE BOOKS OF HAGGAI AND ZECHARIAH

. . .

The rise of _Cyrus the Persian_, so commended in the forty-fourth and forty-fifth chapters of Isaiah, brought the long years of the Jewish exile officially to an end in 538 B.C., when he captured Babylon and set about the humane policy of liberating the peoples she had carried into exile. To that period belong those exultant lyrics that form the second part of Isaiah, chapters 40–55. The exiles began to return to Jerusalem, and to rebuild the houses which had lain in ruins for fifty years. But eighteen years passed and the Temple had not been rebuilt. It was this situation that in 520 B.C. challenged the attention of two prophets.

The sermons of Haggai that have come down to us were all preached in Jerusalem, in that year. His first sermon was addressed to Zerubbabel, the governor of Judah. He urged him to undertake at once the rebuilding of the Temple, which the Babylonians had destroyed in 586 B.C. His preaching was successful and Zerubbabel undertook the work. In subsequent sermons, two months and four months later, he encouraged Zerubbabel to carry on the enterprise.

Two months after Haggai's first sermon, in 520 B.C., Zechariah began his preaching, pointing out to the people of Jerusalem that God had tried to win over their fathers but they had refused to heed him, and now all that he had threatened through the prophets had overtaken them.

Zechariah's preaching is apocalyptic in character. It takes the form of visions of symbolic scenes—the four horns, the lamp and the olive trees, the flying roll, the woman in the measure, the four chariots. Like Haggai, he seeks to encourage the people to rebuild the Temple and restore the ancient worship. He calls upon the Jews still in exile to return to Jerusalem, and promises that the Messiah will come and the land be prosperous and happy.

This apocalyptic way of preaching shows the influence of Egyptian literary forms and of Babylonian symbolism, and later became very popular among Jewish and Christian writers, as the Book of Daniel and the Revelation of John show.

The closing chapters of Zechariah, 9–14, are anonymous and are generally acknowledged to be very late. A mention of Greece, 9:13, combined with references to the captivity and the Dispersion, allusions to the Jewish monarchy as past, and frequent dependence upon older prophecies, all point to a date long after the Exile for these chapters.

· · ·

THE BOOK OF HAGGAI

THE BEGINNING OF THE REBUILDING OF THE TEMPLE, 1:1–15a

1 In the second year of Darius, the king, in the sixth month, on the first day of the month, the word of the LORD came through Haggai, the prophet, to Zerubbabel, the son of Shealtiel, governor of Judah, and to Joshua, the son of Jehozadak, the chief priest, saying:

2 "Thus says the LORD of hosts, namely, 'This people say, "The time has not yet come to rebuild the house of the LORD."'"

[119]

The word of the Lord came through Haggai, the 3
prophet, saying,

"Is it a time for you yourselves to live in your panelled 4
houses, while this house lies waste?"

"But now," thus says the Lord of hosts, "Give 5
thought to your ways. You have sown much, but reaped 6
little; you have eaten, but not to repletion; you have
drunk, but not your fill; you have put on clothes, but
there was no warmth in them; and he who earned wages
put it into a bag with a hole in it."

Thus says the Lord of hosts,   7

"Give thought to your ways. Go up to the hills, and 8
fetch lumber, and rebuild the house, that I may be 9
pleased with it and be honored"; says the Lord. "You
expected much, and it was but little; and you brought it
home, and I blew it away! For what reason?" It is the
oracle of the Lord of hosts. "Because of my house which
lies waste, while you yourselves run each one to his own
house. Therefore, the heavens above you withhold their 10
dew, and the earth withholds its increase. For I called 11
for a drought upon the land, and upon the hills, upon the
corn and the wine and the oil, and upon everything that
the ground yields; and upon man and beast, and every
product of labor."

So Zerubbabel, the son of Shealtiel, and Joshua, the 12
son of Jehozadak, the chief priest, and all the remnant of
the people, listened to the voice of the Lord, their God,
and to the words of the prophet Haggai, inasmuch as
the Lord, their God, had sent him; and the people were
afraid because of the Lord. Whereupon, Haggai, the 13
messenger of the Lord, with the message of the Lord to
the people, spoke, saying,

"'I am with you'; it is the oracle of the Lord."

So the Lord aroused the spirit of Zerubbabel, the son 14
of Shealtiel, governor of Judah, and the spirit of Joshua,
the son of Jehozadak, the chief priest, and the spirit of
all the remnant of the people, so that they came and went 15a
to work upon the house of the Lord of hosts, their God,
on the twenty-fourth day of the sixth month.

WORDS OF ENCOURAGEMENT TO THE BUILDERS,
1:15*b*—2:1–9

1, 2 In the second year of Darius, the king, in the seventh month, on the twenty-first day of the month, the word of the LORD came through Haggai, the prophet, saying,

2 "Say, now, to Zerubbabel, the son of Shealtiel, the governor of Judah, and to Joshua, the son of Jehozadak, the chief priest, and to the remnant of this people, thus:

3 'Who is there left among you that saw this house in
4 its ancient splendor? And how it looks to you now! Does it not seem to you like nothing at all? But now, be strong, O Zerubbabel,' it is the oracle of the LORD, 'and be strong, O Joshua, the son of Jehozadak, the chief priest, and be strong, all the people of the land,' it is the
5 oracle of the LORD, 'and work; for I am with you,' says the LORD of hosts; 'it is the promise I made you when you came forth from Egypt; and my spirit is standing in the midst of you; fear not.' "

6 For thus says the LORD of hosts,
"Yet a little while, and I will shake the heavens and
7 the earth, the sea and the dry land. And I will shake all the nations, and the treasures of all the nations shall come in, and I will fill this house with splendor"; says
8 the LORD of hosts. "Mine is the silver and mine is the
9 gold," says the LORD of hosts. "The future splendor of this house shall be greater than the past," says the LORD of hosts; "and upon this place I will bestow prosperity." It is the oracle of the LORD of hosts.

THE BOOK OF ZECHARIAH

A LESSON FROM THE PAST, 1:1-6

In the eighth month in the second year of Darius, the 1
word of the LORD came to Zechariah, the son of Berechiah, the son of Iddo, the prophet, saying,

"The LORD was very angry at your fathers. Say to 2
them, 'Thus says the LORD of hosts: "Return to me," 3
it is the oracle of the LORD of hosts, "that I may return
to you"; says the LORD of hosts.' Be not like your 4
fathers, to whom the former prophets preached, saying,
'Thus says the LORD of hosts: "Turn now from your
wicked ways and from your wicked deeds." ' But they
did not hearken, nor did they give heed to me"; it is the
oracle of the LORD. "Your fathers—where are they? 5
And the prophets—do they live forever? Yet did not my 6
words and my statutes with which I charged my servants,
the prophets, overtake your fathers? So they turned and
said, 'Even as the LORD of hosts had purposed to do to
us, in accordance with our ways and our deeds, so has he
treated us.' "

A VISION OF RESTORATION, 1:7-17

On the twenty-fourth day of the eleventh month 1
(namely, the month of Shebat), in the second year of
Darius, the word of the LORD came to Zechariah, the son
of Berechiah, the son of Iddo, the prophet, saying,

"I saw by night, and there was a man riding upon a 8
red horse, and he was standing among the myrtle trees
which are in the hollow, and behind him were red, sorrel,
and white horses. And I said, 'What are these, sir?' 9
Then the angel that was talking to me said to me, 'I will 10
show you what these are.' And the man who was standing among the myrtles answered, saying, 'These are those
whom the LORD sent forth to patrol the earth.' Then 11

they answered the angel of the L<small>ORD</small>, who was standing among the myrtle trees, saying, 'We have patrolled the earth; and lo, the whole earth is resting peacefully.'

12 Then the angel of the L<small>ORD</small> spoke, saying, 'O L<small>ORD</small> of hosts, for how long wilt thou have no mercy upon Jerusalem and the cities of Judah, with which thou hast

13 been angry now for seventy years?' Then the L<small>ORD</small> answered the angel who was talking with me, with

14 gracious words, comforting words. So the angel who was talking with me said to me, 'Proclaim as follows, "Thus says the L<small>ORD</small> of hosts, 'I am very greatly moved with

15 reference to Jerusalem and Mount Zion. And I am exceedingly angry at the easy-going nations. For while I was angry but a little, they furthered the disaster.'

16   "Therefore," thus says the L<small>ORD</small>,
      "I will return to Jerusalem in mercy;
       My house shall be rebuilt therein";
       It is the oracle of the L<small>ORD</small> of hosts;
      "And a line shall be stretched over Jerusalem."

17   "Again proclaim, saying,
      Thus says the L<small>ORD</small> of hosts,
      "My cities shall again overflow with prosperity,
       And the L<small>ORD</small> will again have pity upon Zion
       And again choose Jerusalem." ' "

A SUMMONS TO THE EXILES, 2:6–13

2   "Ho, ho, flee from the land of the north."
      It is the oracle of the L<small>ORD</small>.
    "For like the four winds of the heavens, I will make you fly."
      It is the oracle of the L<small>ORD</small>.

7   "Ho! O Zion! Escape, O inhabitants of Babylon."

8   For thus says the L<small>ORD</small> of hosts (hereafter he will send me forth with honor) regarding the nations that have plundered you (he who touches you touches the apple of his eye!),

9   "Verily I will wave my hand over them, and they shall become plunder for their slaves."

And you shall know that the LORD of hosts has sent
me.

"Shout with joy, and rejoice, O daughter of Zion!   10
   For lo, I am coming to dwell in the midst of you."
It is the oracle of the LORD.
   Many nations will attach themselves to the LORD,   11
      in that day;
   And they will become his people,
   And he will dwell in the midst of you;
   And you will know that the LORD of hosts has sent
      me unto you.
   And the LORD will take possession of Judah,   12
   His portion upon the holy land;
   And he will again choose Jerusalem.
   Silence, all flesh, in the presence of the LORD!   13
   For he arouses himself from his holy dwelling.

SPIRITUAL DELIVERANCE, 4:6*b*–10

This is the word of the LORD to Zerubbabel, saying,   4
"Not by arms, nor by force, but by my spirit," says
the LORD of hosts.
   "What are you, O great mountain?   7
   Before Zerubbabel, become a plain!
   And he shall bring forth the top-stone
   With shouts of 'Grace, grace, to it.'"

The word of the LORD came to me thus,   8
"The hands of Zerubbabel founded this house, and his   9
hands shall complete it."
So you shall know that the LORD of hosts has sent me
unto you. For who has despised a day of small things?   10
They shall rejoice when they see the plummet in the
hand of Zerubbabel.

THE BOOK OF JOEL

. . .

In the later years of the Persian domination, the Jewish community in Judea had little influence in international affairs. At its head were the high priest and the elders, and its interests were chiefly religious, economic, and social rather than political. A plague of locusts and a severe drought, probably toward 400 B.C., led the prophet Joel to voice the distress of his people and call them to repentance. The scarcity was so acute that even the daily offering in the Temple was curtailed.

Other troubles beset the little community. The slave-dealers of Philistia were selling Jewish boys and girls into slavery in the Greek west. Even today desperate necessity sometimes drives Asiatic parents to sell their children. Judah was also being distressed by Egypt, which was struggling about this time to shake off the dominion of Persia.

In the midst of these trials Joel, with sublime faith in God, assured his countrymen of deliverance from their enemies and oppressors, and predicted a glorious future for the Jewish people and the Jewish religion.

. . .

THE LOCUST PLAGUE AND THE DROUGHT, 1:1–19

1 The word of the LORD, which came to Joel, the son of Pethuel:

2   Hear this, O elders;
      And listen, all you dwellers in the land!
      Has such a thing ever been in your days,

Or in the days of your fathers?
Tell of it to your sons; 3
And your sons to their sons in turn;
And their sons to the next generation.

What the shearer left, the locust ate; 4
And what the locust left, the hopper ate;
And what the hopper left, the destroyer ate.
Rouse yourselves, you topers, and weep; 5
And wail, all you drinkers of wine,
For the new wine; because it is cut off from your
    mouth.

For a nation has come up against my land, 6
Strong and innumerable;
His teeth are a lion's teeth,
And the fangs of a lioness are his.
He has made my vine a waste, 7
And blighted my fig tree;
He has stripped off its bark and thrown it away;
Its branches are whitened.

Wail, like a virgin girded with sackcloth, 8
For the bridegroom of her youth.
Cut off are the sacrifice and the libation, 9
From the house of the LORD.
The priests mourn,
The ministers of the LORD.

The field is devastated; 10
The ground mourns;
Because the grain is laid waste,
The new wine is dried up,
The fresh oil fails.
The farmers are disappointed, 11
The vine-dressers lament,
For the wheat and the barley;
Because the harvest of the field is lost.
The vine withers, 12
And the fig tree wilts.

The pomegranate, palm, and apple—
All the trees of the field dry up;
So that mirth has withered away
From the sons of men.

13   Gird yourselves with sackcloth and mourn, O
          priests;
      Wail, O ministers of the altar!
      Come, spend the night in sackcloth,
      O ministers of my God!
      Because the sacrifice and libation are withheld
      From the house of your God.

14   Sanctify a fast;
      Call a convocation!
      Gather, O elders,
      All the inhabitants of the land
      Into the house of the LORD your God;
      And cry unto the LORD.

15   Alas for the day!
      For the day of the LORD is near,
      And as destruction from the Almighty it comes.

16   Has not food been cut off
      From before our eyes?
      From the house of our God,
      Gladness and joy?

17   The mules stamp at their stalls;
      The granaries are devastated;
      The barns are ruined;
      Because the grain has failed.

18   What can we put in them?
      The herds of cattle wander about,
      Because they have no pasture.
      The flocks of sheep, also, are dismayed.

19   Unto thee, O LORD, do I cry,
      Because fire has consumed
                the pastures of the wilderness,
      And flame has scorched
                all the trees of the field.

The beasts of the field, also,
    cry out unto thee;
Because the streams of water are dry,
And fire has consumed the pastures of the steppe.

THE DAY OF THE LORD AND ITS MANIFESTATIONS, 2:28-32

"It shall come to pass afterward,   2
That I will pour out my spirit upon all flesh;
Your sons and your daughters shall prophesy;
Your old men shall dream dreams;
And your young men shall see visions.
Furthermore, upon the menservants and the hand-   29
    maids,
In those days I will pour out my spirit.

"And I will set portents in the heavens and on the   30
    earth,
Blood, and fire, and columns of smoke.
The sun shall be changed to darkness and the moon   31
    to blood,
Before the coming of the day of the LORD, great and
    terrible.
But everyone that calls upon the name of the LORD   32
    shall be delivered;
For in Mount Zion and in Jerusalem there shall be
    those that escape;"
As the LORD has said.
And the escaped will be those whom the LORD
    proclaims.

JUDGMENT UPON THE NATIONS, 3:1-8

"For behold, in those days and at that time, when I   3
restore the fortunes of Judah and Jerusalem, then I will
gather all the nations, and bring them down to the valley
of Jehoshaphat; and I will enter into judgment with
them there, on account of my people and my heritage,
Israel, whom they have scattered among the nations.
They have divided my land, and cast lots upon my   3

people, and given a boy for a harlot, and sold a girl for wine, and drunk it.

4 "Moreover, what are you to me, O Tyre, and Sidon, and all the districts of Philistia? Are you paying me back for something I have done? Or are you doing something to me? Right speedily will I requite your deed upon 5 your own head! For you have taken my silver and my gold; and my goodly treasures you have brought into 6 your palaces. The people of Judah, and the people of Jerusalem, you have sold to the Greeks, so as to remove 7 them far from their own territory. Behold, I am going to rouse them up from the place into which you have sold them; and I will bring back your deed upon your own 8 head. For I will sell your sons and your daughters into the hand of the people of Judah, and they will sell them to the Sabeans, to a distant nation." For the Lord has spoken.

THE BOOK OF RUTH

. . .

Early in the fourth century before Christ strict Jews like Ezra sought to explain the worldliness of the people as caused by their intermarriage with persons not of Jewish descent. Ezra called upon such Jews to put away their foreign wives and to disown their children. This, of course, led to much unhappiness and bitterness in the community.

The short story of Ruth is a protest against this narrow-minded policy. In it, Ruth, the woman of Moab, is presented as a shining example of what a foreign woman can be. Moreover, the child of her marriage with Boaz, who from Ezra's point of view should have been disowned, became the grandfather of David the king. The simple, vivid story becomes a withering protest against national intolerance and exclusiveness.

The old story of a strain of Moabite blood in the national hero David was thus skilfully used to counteract a narrow policy, and became an idyl of interracial goodwill.

. . .

THE ANTECEDENTS OF RUTH, 1:1–22

In the time when the judges were in power a famine 1 occurred in the land; so a certain man from Bethlehem in Judah emigrated to the country of Moab, along with his wife and two sons. The man's name was Elimelech, his 2 wife's Naomi, and the names of his two sons Mahlon and Chilion—Ephrathites from Bethlehem in Judah. So they came to the country of Moab, and remained there. Then 3

Elimelech, the husband of Naomi, died; and she was left
4 a widow, with her two sons. These married Moabite
women, the name of one being Orpah, and the name of
the other Ruth. They lived there for about ten years,
5 and then both Mahlon and Chilion died. Then, being
6 bereft of her two children as well as of her husband, the
woman, with her daughters-in-law, prepared to return
from the country of Moab; for she had heard in the country of Moab that the LORD had taken note of his people
7 by giving them food. So she left the place where she was,
accompanied by her two daughters-in-law, and they set
8 out on the road to return to the land of Judah. But
Naomi said to her two daughters-in-law,

"Go, return each of you to her mother's house. May
the LORD deal as kindly with you as you have dealt with
9 the dead and with me! May the LORD enable you to find
a home, each of you, in the house of her husband!"

Then she kissed them good-bye; but they lifted up
10 their voices in weeping, and said to her,

"No, we will go back with you to your people."
11 But Naomi said,

"Turn back, my daughters. Why should you go with
me? Have I any more sons in my womb to become hus-
12 bands for you? Turn back, my daughters; go your way;
for I am too old to get married. If I should say that I
have hopes both of getting married tonight and of bear-
13 ing sons, would you wait for them until they were grown
up? Would you forego marriage for them? No, my
daughters; but I am very sorry for your sakes that the
hand of the LORD has been raised against me."
14 Then they lifted up their voices again in weeping, and
Orpah kissed her mother-in-law good-bye, but Ruth
clung to her.
15 "See," she said, "your sister-in-law has turned back
to her own people and her own gods; turn back after
your sister-in-law."
16 But Ruth said,

"Do not press me to leave you, to turn back from following you; for wherever you go, I will go; and wherever

you lodge, I will lodge; your people shall be my people, and your god my god; wherever you die, I will die, and there will I be buried. May the Lord requite me and worse, if even death separate me from you." 17

When she saw that she was determined to go with her, she ceased arguing with her. So the two of them went on until they came to Bethlehem. Upon their arrival in Bethlehem the whole city became agitated over them, and the women said, 18 19

"Is this Naomi?"

But she said to them, 20

"Do not call me Naomi [pleasant]; call me Mara [bitter]; for the Almighty has dealt very bitterly with me. I went away full, but the Lord has brought me back destitute. Why should you call me Naomi, seeing that the Lord has afflicted me, and the Almighty has brought evil upon me?" 21

So Naomi returned from the country of Moab, accompanied by her daughter-in-law, Ruth, the Moabitess. They reached Bethlehem at the beginning of the barley harvest. 22

THE MEETING OF RUTH AND BOAZ, 2:1-23

Now Naomi had a kinsman of her husband, a man of great wealth, belonging to the family of Elimelech, whose name was Boaz. 2

One day Ruth, the Moabitess, said to Naomi, 2

"Let me go to the fields and glean among the ears of grain after him with whom I may find favor."

"Go, my daughter," she said to her.

So off she went, and came and gleaned in the fields after the harvesters; and it was her fortune to come upon the part of the field belonging to Boaz, who belonged to the family of Elimelech. Just then Boaz himself came from Bethlehem. 3 4

"The Lord be with you!" he said to the harvesters.

"The Lord bless you!" they replied.

"Whose girl is this?" said Boaz to his overseer in charge of the harvesters. 5

6   "It is a Moabite girl who came back with Naomi from the country of Moab," the overseer in charge of the
7 harvesters answered. "She said, 'Let me glean, if you please, and gather among the sheaves after the harvesters.' So she came, and has remained since morning until now, without resting even a little."
8   The Boaz said to Ruth,
   "Now listen, my girl. Do not go to glean in another field, nor leave this one, but stay here close by my
9 women. Note the field that they are reaping, and follow them. Have I not charged the servants not to molest you? And, when you are thirsty, go to the water jars, and drink some of what the servants draw."
10   Then she fell on her face, bowing to the ground, and said to him,
   "Why have I found such favor with you that you should take notice of me, when I am a foreigner?"
11   Boaz in reply said to her,
   "I have been fully informed of all that you have done for your mother-in-law since the death of your husband, and of how you left your father and mother, and the land of your birth, and came to a people that you did not
12 know before. May the LORD reward your conduct, and may you receive full recompense from the LORD, the God of Israel, under whose wings you have come for shelter!"
13   "I thank you, sir," she said; "for you have cheered me, and have spoken comfortingly to your maidservant, even though I do not belong to your maidservants."
14   At mealtime Boaz said to her,
   "Come here, and eat some of the bread, and dip your piece in the sour wine."
   So she seated herself beside the harvesters, and he
15 handed her roasted grain. She ate until she was satisfied, and had some left over. When she got up to glean, Boaz gave orders to his servants,
   "Let her glean right among the sheaves, and do not
16 be rude to her. Indeed pull out some bunches for her, and leave them for her to glean, and do not hinder her."
17   So she gleaned in the field until evening; then she beat

out what she had gleaned, and it amounted to about
an ephah of barley. She took it up, and coming into the 18
city, showed her mother-in-law what she had gleaned.
Then she brought out and gave her what she had left over
after being satisfied.

"Where did you glean today," her mother-in-law said 19
to her. "Where did you work? Blessed be he who took
such notice of you!"

So she told her mother-in-law with whom she had
worked.

"Boaz is the name of the man with whom I worked
today," she said.

Then Naomi said to her daughter-in-law, 20
"May he be blessed by the LORD, whose goodness has
failed neither the living nor the dead!"

"The man is a relation of ours," Naomi said to her;
"he is one of our close relatives."

"Furthermore," said Ruth, the Moabitess, "he said 21
to me, 'You must stay close by my servants until they
have finished all my harvest.' "

"It is best, my daughter," Naomi said to her daugh- 22
ter-in-law, Ruth, "that you should go out with his
women, so as not to be molested in another field."

So she stayed close by the women working for Boaz, 23
gleaning until the end of both the barley and wheat
harvests; then she returned to her mother-in-law.

THE BOOK OF JOB

. . .

The Book of Job is perhaps the greatest piece of literature in the Old Testament. It deals with the meaning of suffering. The Jews believed that it was a punishment for sin, and was a mark of the divine displeasure. This crude, harsh understanding of it the Book of Job proves to be false and unjust.

The book tells the story of Job, a man perfectly upright yet the victim of every kind of misfortune, and tries to find the explanation of such an experience. The story is told in a Prologue and an Epilogue. Apart from them the book is a series of speeches forming a debate. It may be described as a drama without action. The discussion is taken up by Job's three friends, whom Job answers. It is continued by Elihu, with no answer from Job. Finally, God himself speaks to Job, and Job admits the imperfection of his own understanding of it all.

The earliest part of the book is represented by the Prologue, 1:1–2:13, and the Epilogue, 42:7–16, which were written some time in the period before Deuteronomy.

Into this was afterward introduced the debate between Job and his three friends, chapters 3–31. This is arranged in three cycles, in each of which each friend speaks once, and Job answers him immediately. The friends formulate the old traditional views regarding the cause of suffering—that Job had sinned against God and that his afflictions were the punishments sent upon him by God because of his sins. Job, on the other hand, strenu-

ously defends his own integrity and denies the correctness of his friends' view of his case.

The third section of the book consists of four addresses by a new speaker, named Elihu, 32:1–37:24. This is a later addition made by someone who sympathized with the friends and sought to strengthen their case by his own presentation of the facts. But his argument adds very little to what has already been said, and his style is in every way inferior to that of the main part of the book.

The fourth section of the book is the interview between Job and the Lord, 38:1—40:14, which has been separated from the original debate by the later insertion of the Elihu speeches. The Lord overwhelms Job by citing his own mighty deeds and by implication asking Job what basis he has for questioning the wisdom and justice of so mighty a God. The voice of God reconciles Job to his lot, and makes him content to leave his destiny to God's wisdom and mercy.

A poem in praise of Wisdom (chap. 28) has been appended to Zophar's last speech, and 40:15—41:26 is a later expansion of the interview between Job and the Lord. This passage contains a description of the hippopotamus and the crocodile, written by someone who had lived in Egypt and was familiar with the monsters of the Nile. The book is in the main a product of the fourth century before Christ.

. . .

JOB'S CALAMITIES, 1:1—3:1

There was a man in the land of Uz whose name was 1
Job; and that man was perfect and upright, and he feared 2
God and shunned wickedness. Now there were born to 3

him seven sons and three daughters. And his property
was seven thousand sheep and three thousand camels
and five hundred yoke of oxen and five hundred she-asses
4 and a very large number of slaves. So that man was the
greatest of all the people of the East. His sons would go
and hold a feast in the house of each one on his day; and
they would send and invite their three sisters to eat and
5 drink with them. When the days of feasting had gone
round, Job would send and sanctify them, and he would
get up early in the morning and offer sacrifices according
to the number of them all; for Job said,
"Perhaps my children have sinned,
And cursed God in their thoughts."
Thus would Job do always.
6   Now one day when the heavenly beings had come to
7 stand in the presence of the LORD, and the Satan too had
come among them, the LORD said to the Satan,
"Whence do you come?"
And the Satan answered the LORD, saying,
"From roaming in the earth and from going to and fro
therein."
8   And the LORD said to the Satan,
"Have you noticed my servant Job,
That there is none like him in the earth,
A man perfect and upright, who fears God and
shuns wickedness?"
9   But the Satan answered the LORD, saying,
"Has Job feared God for nothing?
10   Hast thou not hedged him round about,
And his house and all that belongs to him?
Thou hast blessed the labor of his hands;
And his wealth has spread abroad in the land.
11   But now, put forth thy hand,
And touch whatsoever he has:
He will curse thee to thy face!"
12 And the LORD said to the Satan,
"Well, all that he has is in your power;
Only upon himself you shall not lay your hand."
Then the Satan went out from the presence of the LORD.

Now one day when his sons and daughters were eating 13
and were drinking wine in the house of their oldest
brother, a messenger came to Job, saying, 14
  "While the oxen were plowing,
    And the she-asses grazing close by,
    The Sabeans fell upon them and seized them; 15
    They smote the servants with the edge of the sword;
    And I only have escaped alone to tell you."
While he was yet speaking, another came, saying, 16
  "The fire of God fell down from the heavens,
    And burned up the flocks and the servants and con-
      sumed them;
    And I only have escaped alone to tell you."
While he was yet speaking, another came, saying, 17
  "The Chaldeans formed three divisions,
    And swooped down upon the camels and seized
      them,
    And smote the servants with the edge of the sword;
    And I only have escaped alone to tell you."
While he was yet speaking, another came, saying, 18
  "As your sons and your daughters were eating
    And were drinking wine in the house of their oldest
      brother,
    A mighty wind came from beyond the wilderness, 19
    And smote the four corners of the house,
    So that it fell upon the young folks and they died.
    And I only have escaped alone to tell you."
Then Job arose and tore his mantle and shaved his head 20
and fell to the earth and worshipped; and he said, 21
  "Naked did I come forth from my mother's womb,
    And naked shall I return thither.
    The LORD gave and the LORD has taken away;
    Blessed be the name of the LORD."
Notwithstanding all this, Job did not sin; nor did he 22
charge anything unseemly against God.
One day when the heavenly beings had come to present 2
themselves before the LORD, and when the Satan too had
come among them to present himself before the LORD,
the LORD said to the Satan, 2

"Whence do you come?"
The Satan answered the Lord, saying,
"From roaming in the earth and from going to and fro
therein."

3   And the Lord said to the Satan,
"Have you noticed my servant Job,
That there is none like him in the earth,
A perfect and upright man, who fears God and
shuns wickedness?
He still holds fast to his integrity,
Though you incited me against him, to ruin him
without cause."

4   Then the Satan answered the Lord, saying,
"Skin for skin!
All that a man has will he give for his life.

5   Now, just put forth thy hand,
And touch his bone and his flesh:
He will curse thee to thy face!"

6   And the Lord said to the Satan,
"Behold, he is in your power; but preserve his life."

7   Then the Satan went forth from the presence of the
Lord, and smote Job with a bad leprosy from the sole of

8   his foot to the crown of his head; so that he took a pots-
herd with which to scrape himself as he sat in the midst

9   of the ash-heap. So his wife said to him,
"Do you yet hold fast to your integrity?
Curse God and die!"

10   But he said to her,
"You speak as one of the foolish women might speak.
Should we, indeed, receive good from God,
And should we not receive evil?"
Notwithstanding all this, Job did not sin with his lips.

11   When the three friends of Job heard all this disaster
that had befallen him, they came each from his place,
Eliphaz the Temanite, Bildad the Shuhite, and Zophar

12   the Naamathite; for they had arranged together to come
to condole with him and to comfort him. When they
lifted up their eyes from afar, they did not recognize him;

13   so they raised their voices and wept. Then they tore,

[139]

each one, his mantle, and they cast dust over their heads
toward the heavens. Then they sat down with him upon
the ground for seven days and seven nights; and no one
spoke a word to him, for they saw that his affliction was
very severe. Afterwards Job opened his mouth and cursed   3
his day.

JOB'S LAMENT THAT HE WAS EVER BORN, 3:2–26

Then Job spoke, saying,   3
   "Perish the day wherein I was born,   3
      And the night which said, 'A man is conceived.'
   May that day be darkness;   4
   May God on high not search for it;
   May light not shine upon it;
   May the blackest darkness reclaim it;   5
   May a cloud drop down thereon;
   May the blackening of the day terrify it.
   That night—may blackness seize it;   6
   May it not rejoice among the days of the year;
   Into the number of the months may it not come.
   So, that night—may it be barren;   7
   May no sound of joy enter it.
   May they curse it who curse the day,   8
   Who are skilled in arousing Leviathan.
   May the stars of its twilight be darkened;   9
   May it wait for light and there be none;
   And may it not see the eyelids of the dawn.
   Because it did not shut the doors of my mother's   10
      womb,
   And so conceal trouble from my eyes.

   "Why did I not die at birth,   11
   Come forth from the womb and expire?
   Why did the knees receive me?   12
   Or why the breasts, that I should suck?
   For then I had lain down and been quiet,   13
   I had slept; then were I at rest
   With kings and counsellors of the earth,   14
   Who rebuild ruins for themselves;

[140]

15   Or with nobles who have gold,
      Who fill their houses with silver.
16   Or like a hidden untimely birth I should not be,
      Like babes that never saw light.
17   There the wicked cease from troubling;
      There the tired out are at rest.
18   The prisoners also are at ease;
      They hear not the voice of the overseer.
19   The small and the great are there,
      And the slave is free from his master.

20   "Why is light given to the wretched,
      And life to the bitter of spirit;
21   Who long for death, but it comes not,
      And hunt for it more than for buried treasures,
22   Those who would rejoice exultingly,
      And would be glad, if they could find the grave?
23   To a man whose way is hidden,
      Whom God has fenced in?
24   For my sighing comes in place of my food,
      And my groans are poured forth like water.
25   If I entertain a fear, then it comes upon me;
      And what I was afraid of befalls me.
26   I am not at ease, nor am I quiet,
      Nor am I at rest; for trouble keeps coming."

JOB'S INTERVIEW WITH THE LORD, 38:1—42:6

THE FIRST ADDRESS OF THE LORD, 38:1—39:30

38   Then the LORD answered Job from the whirlwind,
      saying,
2   "Who is this that obscures counsel
          By words without knowledge?
3   Gird up, now, your loins like a man,
          That I may question you, and do you instruct me.

4   "Where were you when I laid the foundations of
              the earth?
          Declare, if you have insight.
5   Who fixed its measurements, for you should know?

Or who stretched a line over it?
Upon what were its bases sunk,   6
Or who laid its cornerstone,
When the morning stars sang together,   7
And all the gods shouted for joy?

"Who enclosed the sea with doors,   8
When it burst forth issuing from the womb,
When I made the cloud its covering,   9
And dense darkness its swaddling-band;
When I imposed upon it my decree,   10
And established its barrier and doors;
And said, 'Thus far shalt thou come and no farther,   11
And here shall thy proud waves be stayed'?

"Have you ever in your life commanded the morning?   12
Or assigned its place to the dawn,
That it should lay hold of the corners of the earth,   13
And the wicked should be shaken out of it?
It changes like clay under the seal,   14
And is dyed like a garment.
Their light is withdrawn from the wicked,   15
And the arm of the proud is broken.

"Have you gone to the sources of the sea,   16
Or walked in the hollows of the deep?
Have the gates of death been revealed to you,   17
Or can you see the gates of darkness?
Have you considered the breadth of the earth?   18
Tell, if you know all this.

"Which is the way where light dwells,   19
And which is the place of darkness,
That you may take it to its border,   20
And that you may perceive the paths to its house?
You know, for you were born then,   21
And the number of your days is great!

"Have you been to the storehouses of snow,   22
Or do you see the storehouses of hail,
Which I have reserved against the time of distress,   23
Against the day of war and battle?

24 Which is the way to where light is distributed?
Where does the east wind spread itself over the earth?
25 Who cleaved its channel for the torrent,
And a way for the thunderbolts,
26 To send rain on a land without people,
On the steppe where there is no man;
27 To satisfy the waste ground and desolate,
And to cause the blade of grass to spring up?

28 "Has the rain a father?
Or who brought forth the dew drops?
29 From whose womb did the ice come forth?
And who gave birth to the hoarfrost of the skies,
30 When the waters congeal like a stone,
And the surface of the deep is frozen solid?

31 "Can you bind the chains of the Pleiades,
Or loosen the girdle of Orion?
32 Can you send forth Mazzaroth in its season,
And lead forth the Bear with its satellites?
33 Do you know the laws of the heavens?
Or do you appoint the arrangements of the earth?
34 Can you lift your voice up to the clouds,
That a flood of waters may cover you?

35 "Can you send forth the lightnings that they may go
And say to you, 'Here we are!'
36 Who put wisdom in the inner parts,
Or who gave insight to the mind?
37 Who counts the clouds by wisdom?
And who tilts the waterskins of the heavens,
38 When the dust runs into a mass,
And the clods stick together?

39 "Do you hunt prey for the lioness,
Or satisfy the hunger of young lions,
40 When they crouch in dens,
Or lie in wait in the thicket?
41 Who provides its prey for the raven,
When its young ones cry unto God,
And wander without food?

"Do you know the time when the mountain-goats **39**
  bear young?
Do you watch the travail of the does?
Do you number the months that they fulfill,   2
And know the time that they bear,
When they kneel down, bring forth their young,   3
Deliver their offspring?
Their young are robust, they grow up in the open,   4
They go forth, and do not return to them.

"Who sent forth the wild ass free?   5
And who loosened the bonds of the mustang,
Whose range I made the steppe,   6
And his dwellings the salt-marshes?
He laughs at the roar of the city;   7
The shouts of the driver he does not hear.
He explores the mountains, his pasture,   8
And searches after everything green.

"Is the wild-ox willing to serve you?   9
Or will he pass the night at your crib?
Can you bind the wild-ox to the furrow with cords,   10
Or will he harrow the valleys after you?
Do you trust in him because his strength is great?   11
And do you leave your hard-won gains to him?
Do you believe in him, that he will return your grain,   12
And gather it to the threshing-floor?

"Is the wing of the ostrich joyful,   13
Or has she a kindly pinion and feathers,
That she leaves her eggs on the ground,   14
And warms them on the dust,
And forgets that the foot may crush them,   15
Or the beast of the field trample them?
She is hard to her young as though not her own;   16
For nothing is her labour; she has no anxiety.
For God has made her oblivious of wisdom,   17
And has not given her a share in understanding.
When she flaps her wings aloft,   18
She laughs at the horse and his rider.

19   "Can you give strength to the horse?
            Can you clothe his neck with power?
20   Do you make him leap like the locust,
            With majesty and terrible snorting?
21   They paw in the valley and exult in strength;
            Going forth to meet the battle.
22   He laughs at terror and is not frightened;
            Nor does he turn back from the sword.
23   Against him rattles the quiver,
            The flashing spear and the javelin.
24   In quivering excitement he devours the ground,
            And does not stand firm when there is the sound of
                the trumpet.
25   As often as the trumpet sounds he says 'Aha';
            And smells the battle from afar,
            The thunder of the captains and the war-cry.

26   "Is it by your understanding that the hawk soars,
            And spreads his wings toward the south?
27   Or does the vulture fly high at your order,
            When he sets his nest aloft?
28   He occupies the cliff and makes a lodging
            Upon the peak of the cliff and the rocky hold.
29   Thence he searches for food,
            His eyes look afar off.
30   His brood gorge themselves with blood;
            And wherever the slain are, there are they."

JOB'S RETRACTION, 42:1–6

42   Then Job replied to the LORD, saying:
2   "I know that thou canst do all things;
            And no plan is too difficult for thee.
3   [Who is this who hides counsel without knowl-
                edge?]
            Therefore I have declared, without understanding,
            Things too wonderful for me, without knowing."
4   [Listen now, while I speak;
            I will question you, and do you instruct me.]
5   I had heard of thee by the hearing of the ear;

But now my eye has seen thee.
Therefore I retract and repent,
In dust and ashes. 6

THE EPILOGUE, 42:7–16

After the LORD had spoken these words to Job, then **42**
the LORD said to Eliphaz, the Temanite,
"My anger is hot against you and your two friends, because you have not spoken regarding me what is true, as
my servant Job has. So now take for yourselves seven 8
bullocks and seven rams, and go to my servant Job, and
offer up a burnt-offering for yourselves, and my servant
Job will pray for you; for his plea will I accept, that I
deal not harshly with you, because you have not spoken
regarding me what is true, as my servant Job has."
Then Eliphaz, the Temanite, and Bildad, the Shuhite, 9
and Zophar, the Naamathite, went and did as the LORD
had told them; and the LORD accepted the plea of Job.
Then the LORD turned the fortune of Job when he inter- 10
ceded for his friends; and the LORD doubled all Job's
possessions. And all his brothers and all his sisters and 11
all his friends came to him as of old, and they did eat
food with him in his house; and they consoled him and
comforted him for all the misfortune that the LORD had
brought upon him. And they gave him each a piece of
gold and each a golden ring.
So the LORD blessed the end of Job more than his be- 12
ginning; for he had fourteen thousand sheep, and six
thousand camels, and a thousand yoke of oxen, and a
thousand she-asses. And he had seven sons and three 13
daughters. He named the first Jemimah, the second 14
Kezia, and the third Keren-happuch. There were not 15
found women as fair as the daughters of Job in all the
land. And their father gave them a heritage among their
brothers.
Thereafter Job lived one hundred and forty years; and 16
he saw his sons and his sons' sons, four generations. So
Job died, old and sated with age.

GENESIS TO JOSHUA

. . .

The first six books of the Old Testament, from Genesis to Joshua, really form a single work of extraordinary range and power, upon the beginnings of Hebrew life, institutions, and religion, traced back not simply to the dawn of history, but to creation itself and the origins of the material universe, and comprehending not only the backgrounds of other nations known to the Hebrews, but the beginnings as they were then understood, of arts and crafts and social institutions—in short, of civilized life in general. So regarded, the Hexateuch, as it is called, is, in the mere matter of its conception, one of the most remarkable works of the human mind. Into it are woven masterpieces of oriental story-telling, often fraught with the profoundest moral lessons, and with these are combined the romantic traditions of the nation's past—its patriarchal ancestry, its Egyptian bondage, its conquest of Canaan, its laws, customs, institutions, and above all its religion. It would be difficult to find in ancient or modern literature any parallel to the stupendous scope of the undertaking into which some great Hebrew of the post-Exilic age toward 350 B.C. wrought the literary inheritance of his people.

He had learned much from Babylonian laws, cosmogonies, and deluge stories, but built his work around the law book found in Josiah's day that we know as Deuteronomy. But for generations the Jews had been interested in recording their history and traditions, and in both the Northern and the Southern kingdoms accounts of their common beginnings had long been in circulation. When the Northern Kingdom was destroyed by Assyria, the Southern Kingdom fell heir to its literature, and the old Ephraimitic stories came to be combined with the Judean. In this combination, Hebrew prose style reached its highest level. The secret work of the prophets at about the same time produced the early form of the Book of Deuteronomy (probably about 650 B.C.) and this and the Judean-Ephraimitic record were in time united into one.

In the days of the Exile, priestly leaders found the explanation of the nation's disasters in its unholiness, and to prevent such lapses in the future formed the Holiness Code, Leviticus, chapters 17–26. And a century after the Exile the priests, with old sources and documents to draw upon, retold the story of the nation's origin and early history from their priestly point of view.

Out of these varied materials, amassed and partly organized by preceding generations, sprang the Hexateuch, a work of such range and power as to seem to most people the supreme and characteristic creation of the Hebrew genius. For the variety of the materials used in it must not distract us from the commanding use it has made of them. The clearest evidence of this is the fact that five of the six books into which it was afterward divided soon came to be held sacred by the Jews, and formed the nucleus of the Old Testament and indeed of the Bible. These five were translated into Greek about the middle of the third century before Christ, and then received the names by which we know them: Genesis (Beginning),

*Exodus (Going Out), Leviticus (the Levitical Book),
Numbers (from the numbering of the people, chaps. 1–4,
26), Deuteronomy (the Second Giving of the Law).*

. . .

THE BOOK OF GENESIS

THE STORY OF CREATION, 1:1—2:3

1   When God began to create the heavens and the earth,
the earth was a desolate waste, with darkness covering
the abyss and a tempestuous wind raging over the sur-
3 face of the waters. Then God said,
"Let there be light!"
4   And there was light; and God saw that the light was
good. God then separated the light from the darkness.
5 God called the light day, and the darkness night. Evening came, and morning, the first day.
6   Then God said,
"Let there be a firmament in the middle of the waters
to divide the waters in two!"
7   And so it was. God made the firmament, dividing the
waters that were below the firmament from those that
8 were above it; and God called the firmament sky. Evening came, and morning, the second day.
9   Then God said,
"Let the waters below the sky be gathered into one
place so that the dry land may appear!"
10 And so it was. God called the dry land earth, and the
gathered waters seas. God saw that it was good.
11 Then God said,
"Let the earth produce vegetation, seed-bearing
plants and the various kinds of fruit-trees that bear fruit
containing their seed!"
12 And so it was. The earth brought forth vegetation,
the various kinds of seed-bearing plants and the various
kinds of trees that bear fruit containing their seed. God
13 saw that it was good. Evening came, and morning, the
third day.

Then God said, 14
"Let there be luminaries in the firmament of the sky
to separate day from night; let them serve as signs and as
indicators of times, days, and years; and let them serve 15
as luminaries in the firmament of the sky to shed light on
the earth!"

And so it was. God made the two great luminaries, the 16
greater luminary to rule the day and the smaller one to
rule the night—and the stars also. God set them in the 17
firmament of the sky to shed light on the earth, to rule by 18
day and by night, and to separate the light from the darkness. God saw that it was good. Evening came, and 19
morning, the fourth day.

Then God said, 20
"Let the waters teem with shoals of living creatures,
and let birds fly over the earth across the firmament of
the sky!"

And so it was. God created the great sea-monsters and 21
all the various kinds of living, gliding creatures with
which the waters teem, and all the various kinds of
winged birds. God saw that it was good, and God blessed 22
them saying,
"Be fruitful, multiply, and fill the waters in the seas;
and let the birds multiply on the earth!"

Evening came, and morning, the fifth day. 23

Then God said, 24
"Let the earth bring forth the various kinds of living
creatures, the various kinds of domestic animals, reptiles,
and wild beasts!"

And so it was. God made the various kinds of wild 25
beasts, the various kinds of domestic animals, and all the
various kinds of land reptiles; and God saw that it was
good.

Then God said, 26
"Let us make man in our image, after our likeness, and
let him have dominion over the fish of the sea, the birds
of the air, the domestic animals, the wild beasts, and all
the land reptiles!"

So God created man in his own image; in the image of 27

God he created him; he created both male and female.
28 Then God blessed them, and God said to them,
"Be fruitful, multiply, fill the earth, and subdue it;
have dominion over the fish of the sea, the birds of the
air, the domestic animals, and all the living things that
crawl on the earth!"
29   Further, God said,
"See, I give you all the seed-bearing plants that are
found all over the earth, and all the trees which have
30 seed-bearing fruit; it shall be yours to eat. To all the wild
beasts of the earth, to all the birds of the air, and to all
the land reptiles, in which there is a living spirit, I give
all the green plants for food."
31   And so it was. God saw that all that he had made was
very good. Evening came, and morning, the sixth day.
2   Thus the heavens and the earth were finished, and all
2 their host. On the seventh day God brought his work to
an end on which he had been engaged, desisting on the
seventh day from all his work in which he had been en-
3 gaged. So God blessed the seventh day, and consecrated
it, because on it he had desisted from all his work, in doing which God had brought about creation.

THE CREATION AND FALL OF MAN, 2:4—3:24

4   The following are the origins of the heavens and the
earth in their creation.
At the time when the LORD God made the earth and
the heavens, there were as yet no field shrubs on the
5 earth, and no field plants had as yet sprung up; for the
LORD God had sent no rain on the earth, and there was
6 no man to till the soil—although a mist used to rise from
7 the earth and water all the surface of the ground. Then
the LORD God molded man out of the dust of the ground,
and breathed into his nostrils the breath of life, so that
8 man became a living being. Then the LORD God planted
a garden in Eden, to the east, and put there the man
9 whom he had molded. Out of the ground the LORD God
made all sorts of trees grow that were pleasant to the
sight and good for food, as well as the tree of life in the

middle of the garden, and the tree of the knowledge of good and evil.

There was a river flowing out of Eden to water the 10 garden, and leaving there it divided into four branches; the name of the first being Pishon (the one which encir- 11 cles all the land of Havilah, where there is gold—the gold 12 of that land is fine—and bdellium and onyx stone); the 13 name of the second river, Gihon (the one which encircles all the land of Cush); the name of the third river, the 14 Tigris (the one which flows east of Ashur); and the name of the fourth river, the Euphrates.

The Lord God took the man and put him in the gar- 15 den of Eden to till it and look after it; and the Lord God 16 laid this command upon the man:

"From any tree in the garden you are free to eat; but 17 from the tree of the knowledge of good and evil you must not eat; for the day that you eat of it you shall certainly die."

Then the Lord God said, 18

"It is not good for the man to be alone; I must make a helper for him who is like him."

So the Lord God molded out of the ground all the wild 19 beasts and all the birds of the air, and brought them to the man to see what he would call them; whatever the man should call each living creature, that was to be its 20 name. So the man gave names to all the domestic animals, the birds of the air, and all the wild beasts; but for man himself no helper was found who was like him. 21 Then the Lord God had a trance fall upon the man; and when he had gone to sleep, he took one of his ribs, closing up its place with flesh. The rib which he took from 22 the man the Lord God built up into a woman, and 23 brought her to the man, whereupon the man said,

"This at last is bone of my bone,
And flesh of my flesh;
She shall be called woman,
For from man was she taken."

(That is why a man leaves his father and mother, and 24 clings to his wife, so that they form one flesh.)

25   Both of them were naked, the man and his wife, but they felt no shame.

3   Now the serpent was the most clever of all the wild beasts that the LORD God had made.

"And so God has said that you are not to eat from any tree in the garden?" he said to the woman.

2   "From the fruit of the trees of the garden we may eat,"
3   the woman said to the serpent; "it is only concerning the fruit of the tree which is in the middle of the garden that God has said, 'You may not eat any of it, nor touch it, lest you die.'"

4   But the serpent said to the woman,
5   "You would not die at all; for God knows that the very day you eat of it, your eyes will be opened, and you will be like gods who know good from evil."

6   So when the woman realized that the tree was good for food and attractive to the eye, and further, that the tree was desirable for its gift of wisdom, she took some of its fruit, and ate it; she also gave some to her husband with
7   her, and he ate. Then the eyes of both of them were opened, and they realized that they were naked; so they sewed fig-leaves together, and made themselves girdles.

8   But when they heard the sound of the LORD God taking a walk in the garden for the breezes of the day, the man and his wife hid themselves from the LORD God among
9   the trees of the garden. The LORD God called to the man.

"Where are you?" he said to him.

10   "I heard the sound of you in the garden," he replied, "and I was afraid, because I was naked; so I hid myself."

11   "Who told you that you were naked?" he said. "Have you eaten from the tree from which I commanded you not to eat?"

12   The man said,

"The woman whom you set at my side, it was she who gave me fruit from the tree; so I ate it."

13   Then the LORD God said to the woman,

"What have you done?"

The woman said,

"It was the serpent that misled me, and so I ate it."

So the LORD God said to the serpent,   14
"Because you have done this,
    The most cursed of all animals shall you be,
    And of all wild beasts.
    On your belly you shall crawl, and eat dust,
    As long as you live.
    I will put enmity between you and the woman,   15
    And between your posterity and hers;
    They shall attack you in the head,
    And you shall attack them in the heel."
To the woman he said,   16
"I will make your pain at child-birth very great;
    In pain shall you bear children;
    And yet you shall be devoted to your husband,
    While he shall rule over you."
And to the man he said,   17
"Because you followed your wife's suggestions, and
ate from the tree from which I commanded you not to
eat,
    Cursed shall be the ground through you,
    In suffering shall you gain your living from it as
        long as you live;
    Thorns and thistles shall it produce for you,   18
    So that you will have to eat wild plants.
    By the sweat of your brow shall you earn your liv- 19
        ing,
    Until you return to the ground,
    Since it was from it that you were taken;
    For dust you are,
    And to dust you must return."
The man called his wife's name Eve [mother], because 20
she was the mother of all living beings.
The LORD God made skin tunics for the man and his   21
wife, and clothed them.
Then the LORD God said,   22
"See, the man has become like one of us, in knowing
good from evil; and now, suppose he were to reach out
his hand and take the fruit of the tree of life also, and
eating it, live forever!"

²³ So the Lᴏʀᴅ God expelled him from the garden of Eden, to till the ground from which he had been taken;
²⁴ he drove the man out, and stationed the cherubs east of the garden of Eden, with the flaming, whirling sword to guard the way to the tree of life.

THE STORY OF THE FLOOD, 6:5—9:17

⁶ When the Lᴏʀᴅ saw that the wickedness of man on the earth was great, and that the whole bent of his thinking
⁶ was never anything but evil, the Lᴏʀᴅ regretted that he had ever made man on the earth, and he was grieved to
⁷ the heart. So the Lᴏʀᴅ said,
"I will blot the men that I have created off the face of the ground, both men and animals, reptiles, and birds of the air; for I regret that I ever made them."
⁸ Noah, however, had found favor with the Lᴏʀᴅ.
⁹ The following are the descendants of Noah. Noah alone among his contemporaries was a pious and exceed-
¹⁰ ingly good man; Noah walked with God. Noah had
¹¹ three sons born to him, Shem, Ham, and Japheth. Now in God's sight, the earth was corrupt; the earth was full
¹² of wrong-doing; God saw that the earth was corrupt; for
¹³ every mortal on the earth had corrupted his life. So God said to Noah,
"I have resolved on the extermination of all mortals; for the earth is full of wrong-doing through them; I am
¹⁴ going to exterminate them from the earth. Make yourself an ark of oleander wood; make the ark with cabins,
¹⁵ and smear it with bitumen inside and out. This is how you are to make it: the length of the ark is to be three hundred cubits, its breadth fifty cubits, and its height
¹⁶ thirty cubits; you are to make a roof for the ark, finishing it off on top to the width of a cubit; and the doorway of the ark you are to put in its side; you are to make it
¹⁷ with lower, second, and third decks. I on my part am about to bring a flood upon the earth, to destroy every mortal from under the heavens, who has the breath of life in him; everything that is on the earth shall perish.
¹⁸ But with you I will make a covenant; you shall enter the

ark, accompanied by your sons, your wife, and your sons' wives. Also, of all living creatures, of all animals, you 19 must have two of every kind enter the ark, to keep them alive with you; they are to be a male and a female. Of 20 the various kinds of birds, the various kinds of animals, and all the various kinds of reptiles, two of every kind are to join you, that you may keep them alive. Take also 21 some of every kind of edible food, and store it by you, to be food for yourself and them."

Noah did so; he did just as God had commanded him. 22

The LORD said to Noah,   7

"Enter the ark, with all your household; for you alone of the present age have I found righteous. Of all 2 clean animals, you are to take seven pairs, a male with its mate; but of the animals that are not clean a pair, a male with its mate; likewise, of the birds of the air seven pairs, 3 a male and a female—to keep their kind alive all over the earth. For in seven days' time I am going to make it 4 rain for forty days and nights on the earth, to blot off the face of the earth every living thing that I have made."

Noah did just as God had commanded him.   5

Noah was six hundred years old when the flood came 6 on the earth.

Noah, with his sons, his wife, and his sons' wives, 7 went into the ark to escape the waters of the flood. Of 8 the clean animals and of those that were not clean, of the birds, and of all the reptiles, a pair of each, a male 9 and a female, joined Noah in the ark, as God had commanded Noah. Then, at the end of the seven days the 10 waters of the flood came on the earth.

In the six hundredth year of Noah's life, on the seven- 11 teenth day of the second month, on that very day the fountains of the great abyss were all broken open, and the windows of the heavens were opened. (The rain fell 12 on the earth for forty days and nights.) That same day 13 Noah, with Shem, Ham, and Japheth, Noah's sons, and Noah's wife, and the three wives of his sons accompany- ing them, went into the ark, together with all the vari- 14 ous kinds of domestic animals, all the various kinds of

land reptiles, and all the various kinds of birds, every-
15 thing with feathers and wings; of all creatures in which
there was the breath of life, a pair of each joined Noah in
16 the ark. Those that entered were a male and a female of
every kind of animal, as God had commanded him. Then
the LORD shut him in.

17 The flood continued for forty days upon the earth.
The waters mounted, and lifted the ark so that it rose
18 above the earth. The waters rose and increased greatly
on the earth, so that the ark floated on the surface of the
19 waters. The waters rose higher and higher on the earth,
until the highest mountains everywhere under the heav-
20 ens were all covered. Fifteen cubits above them the waters
21 rose, so that the mountains were covered. Every creature
that moved on the earth perished, including birds, domestic animals, wild beasts, all the land reptiles, and all
22 mankind. Of all that was on the land, everything in
23 whose nostrils was the breath of life died; every living
thing was blotted off the face of the earth, both men and
animals and reptiles and birds; they were blotted off the
earth, so that Noah alone was left, and those that were
24 with him in the ark. The waters rose on the earth for
one hundred and fifty days.

8 Then God remembered Noah, and all the wild and
domestic animals that were with him in the ark; so God
made a wind blow over the earth, and the waters sub-
2 sided. Likewise, the fountains of the abyss and the
windows of the heavens were closed. The rain from the
heavens ceased, and the waters abated steadily from the
3 earth. At the end of one hundred and fifty days the
4 waters subsided, so that on the seventeenth day of the
seventh month the ark grounded on the mountains of
5 Ararat. The waters subsided steadily until the tenth
month; and on the first day of the tenth month the tops
of the mountains became visible.

6 At the end of forty days Noah opened the window
7 that he had made in the ark, and released a raven, which
went flying back and forth until the waters had dried off
8 the earth. Then he released a dove, so see whether the

waters had subsided from the surface of the land; but the 9
dove could find no resting-place for the sole of her foot,
so she came back to him into the ark; for there was water
all over the earth. He put out his hand, and catching her,
drew her into the ark with him. After waiting another 10
seven days, he again released the dove from the ark; in 11
the evening the dove came back to him, and there, in her
beak, was a freshly picked olive leaf! So Noah knew
that the waters had subsided off the earth. After waiting 12
another seven days, he released the dove, but she never
came back to him. By the first day of the first month of 13
the six hundred and first year of Noah's life the waters
had dried off the earth. So Noah removed the covering
of the ark and found that the surface of the ground was
quite dry. By the twenty-seventh day of the second 14
month the earth was dry.

Then God said to Noah, 15
"Come out of the ark, your wife, your sons, and your 16
sons' wives accompanying you; bring out with you every 17
animal of every sort that is with you, birds, quadrupeds,
and all land reptiles, that they may breed freely on the
earth, and be fruitful and multiply on the earth."

So Noah came out, his sons, his wife, and his sons' 18
wives accompanying him. Every animal, every reptile, 19
and every bird, everything that moves on the earth came
out of the ark by their species.

Then Noah built an altar to the LORD, and taking some 20
clean animals and birds of every kind, he offered them as
burnt-offerings on the altar. When the LORD smelled the 21
soothing odor, the LORD said to himself,
"I will never again curse the soil because of man,
though the bent of man's mind may be evil from his very
youth; nor will I ever again destroy all life, as I have just
done. As long as the earth endures, seedtime and harvest, 22
cold and heat, summer and winter, day and night, shall
never cease."

God blessed Noah and his sons, and said to them, 9
"Be fruitful, multiply, and fill the earth. The fear and 2
dread of you shall be on every beast of the earth and on

every bird of the air; as in the case of all the reptiles on the ground and all the fish of the sea, they have been de-
3 livered into your power. Everything that moves, that is alive, is to be food for you; as I once gave you the green
4 plants, I now give you everything. Only, you must never
5 eat flesh with the life (that is, the blood) in it. For your own life-blood, however, I will require an account; I will hold every animal accountable for it, and I will hold men
6 accountable for one another's lives; whoever sheds the blood of man, by man shall his blood be shed; for God
7 made man in his own image. As for you then, be fruitful, and multiply; be prolific in the earth and multiply in it.''
8   God then said to Noah and to his sons with him,
9   ''As for me, I do hereby establish my covenant with
10 you and your descendants, and with every living creature that is with you, the birds, the domestic animals, and all the wild beasts with you, as many of them as came out of
11 the ark; I establish my covenant with you, that never again shall all flesh be destroyed by the waters of a flood, and never again shall there be a flood to ravage the earth.''
12   Further, God said,
''This shall be the symbol of the covenant which I am making between myself and you and every living crea-
13 ture that is with you, to endless generations: I put my rainbow in the clouds, and it shall be a symbol of the
14 covenant between myself and the world. Whenever I bring clouds over the earth, the rainbow will appear in
15 the clouds, and then I will remember my covenant, which obtains between myself and you and every living creature of every sort, and the waters shall never again become a
16 flood to destroy all flesh. When the rainbow appears in the clouds, I will see it, and remember the everlasting covenant between God and every living creature of every sort that is on the earth.''
17   God said to Noah,
''This shall be the symbol of the covenant which I am making between myself and all flesh that is on the earth.''

THE TOWER OF BABEL, 11:1–9

Now the whole earth used only one language, with 11
few words. On the occasion of a migration from the east, 2
men discovered a plain in the land of Shinar, and settled
there. Then they said to one another, 3
"Come, let us make bricks, burning them well."
So they used bricks for stone, and bitumen for mortar. 4
Then they said,
"Come, let us build ourselves a city with a tower
whose top shall reach the heavens (thus making a name
for ourselves), so that we may not be scattered all over
the earth."
Then the LORD came down to look at the city and 5
tower which human beings had built. The LORD said, 6
"They are just one people, and they all have the same
language. If this is what they can do as a beginning,
then nothing that they resolve to do will be impossible
for them. Come, let us go down, and there make such a 7
babble of their language that they will not understand
one another's speech."
Thus the LORD dispersed them from there all over the 8
earth, so that they had to stop building the city. That 9
was why its name was called Babel, because it was there
that the LORD made a babble of the language of the whole
earth, and it was from there that the LORD dispersed them
all over the earth.

THE STORY OF ABRAHAM, 12:1–9; 17:1–8; 18:17–33; 22:1–19

The LORD said to Abram, 12
"Leave your land, your relatives, and your father's
home, for the land that I will show you; and I will make 2
a great nation of you; I will bless you, and make your
name so great that it will be used for blessings. I will 3
bless those who bless you, and anyone who curses you
I will curse; through you shall all the families of the
earth invoke blessings on one another."
So Abram departed, as the LORD had told him, and 4
Lot went with him. Abram was seventy-five years old

5 when he left Haran. Abram took his wife Sarai and his nephew Lot, with all the property that they had accumulated, and the persons that they had acquired in Haran, and they started out for the land of Canaan; and to the land of Canaan they came.

6 Abram travelled through the land as far as the sanctuary of Shechem at the terebinth of Moreh, the Canaan-
7 ites being then in the land. Then the Lord appeared to Abram, and said,

"To your descendants I am going to give this land."

So he built an altar there to the Lord, who had ap-
8 peared to him. From there he moved on to the hills east of Bethel, and pitched his tent, with Bethel on the west and Ai on the east. There he built an altar to the Lord,
9 and called upon the name of the Lord. Then Abram set out, continuing on his way to the Negeb.

17 When Abram was ninety-nine years old, the Lord appeared to Abram, and said to him,

"I am God Almighty; conduct yourself before me so
2 as to be blameless, and then I will establish my covenant between you and me, and will make you grow more and more numerous."

3 Thereupon Abram fell on his face; and God said to him,

4 "This is my covenant with you: you shall be the an-
5 cestor of a company of nations. Accordingly, your name shall no longer be called Abram, but your name shall be Abraham; for I am making you the ancestor of a
6 company of nations. I will make you more and more prolific, and will make nations of you, and kings shall
7 spring from you. Between myself and you and your descendants, for generation after generation in perpetuity, I am establishing my covenant, to be God to you and
8 your descendants. I will give you and your descendants the land in which you are now only an immigrant, the whole of the land of Canaan, as a possession for all time, and I will be their God."

18 Then the Lord thought,
18 "Shall I hide what I am about to do from Abraham,

seeing that Abraham is bound to become a great and
powerful nation, and through him all the nations of the
earth will invoke blessings on one another? No, I will   19
make it known to him, in order that he may give instructions to his sons and his family after him to keep to the
way of the Lord by doing what is good and right, so that
the Lord may fulfil for Abraham what he promised him."

So the Lord said,   20

"Because the outcry against Sodom and Gomorrah is
great, and their sin very grave, I must go down and see   21
whether or not their conduct entirely answers to the outcry against them that has reached me; I would know."

So the men departed from there, and went off to   22
Sodom, while the Lord remained standing before Abraham. Abraham then went up to him, and said,   23

"Wilt thou really sweep away good along with bad?   24
Suppose there are fifty good men in the city, wilt thou
really sweep it away, and not spare the place for the sake
of the fifty good men that are in it? Far be it from thee   25
to do such a thing as this, to make the good perish with
the bad, so that good and bad fare alike! Far be it from
thee! Shall not the judge of the whole earth himself act
justly?"

So the Lord said,   26

"If I find in Sodom fifty good men within the city,
I will spare the whole place for their sake."

Abraham rejoined,   27

"Here I am venturing to speak to the Lord, and I
mere dust and ashes! Suppose there are five short of the   28
fifty good men; wouldst thou destroy the whole city by
reason of the five?"

"I will not destroy it, if I find forty-five there," he
replied.

Once more he said to him,   29

"Suppose only forty are to be found there?"

"I will not do it for the sake of the forty," he replied.

Then he said,   30

"Pray, let not my Lord be angry if I should say: suppose only thirty are to be found there?"

"I will not do it, if I find thirty there," he said.

31   "Here I am venturing to speak to the Lord; suppose only twenty are to be found there?" he said.

"I will not destroy it for the sake of the twenty," he said.

32   Then he said,

"Pray, let not my Lord be angry if I should speak just once more; suppose only ten are to be found there?"

"I will not destroy it for the sake of the ten," he said.

33   As soon as he finished speaking to Abraham, the LORD went away, while Abraham returned home.

22   Some time after this God put Abraham to the test.

"Abraham!" he said to him.

"Here am I," he said.

2   "Take your son," he said, "your only son, whom you love, Isaac, and go to the land of Moriah, and there offer him as burnt-offering on one of the hills which I shall designate to you."

3   So next morning Abraham rose early, and harnessing his ass, he took two of his servants with him and his son Isaac, and having cut wood for the burnt-offering, he started off for the sanctuary which God had designated to

4   him. On the third day, when Abraham raised his eyes,

5   he saw the sanctuary in the distance. So Abraham said to his servants,

"Stay here with the ass, while I and the boy go yonder to perform our devotions, after which we shall return to you."

6   So Abraham took the wood for the burnt-offering and put it on the back of his son Isaac, while he carried in his own hand the fire and the knife. So the two of them went off together.

7   "Father!" said Isaac to his father Abraham.

"Yes, my son," he responded.

"Here are the fire and the wood," he said, "but where is the sheep for a burnt-offering?"

8   "God will provide himself with the sheep for a burnt-offering, my son," said Abraham.

Thereupon the two of them proceeded on their way together.

When they arrived at the sanctuary which God had 9 designated to him, Abraham built the altar there, arranged the wood, and binding his son Isaac, laid him on the altar on top of the wood. But as Abraham put out 10 his hand to grasp the knife to slay his son, the angel of 11 the LORD called to him from the heavens,

"Abraham, Abraham!"

"Here I am," he replied.

"Do not lay hands on the boy," he said, "do nothing 12 of the sort to him; for I know now that you revere God, in that you have not withheld your son, your only son, from me."

When Abraham raised his eyes, he saw behind him a 13 ram caught in the brushwood by its horns! So Abraham went and took the ram, and offered it up as a burnt-offering in place of his son. Then Abraham called the name 14 of that sanctuary Yahweh-jireh, which is today interpreted as "At the hill of the LORD provision is made."

A second time the angel of the LORD called to Abraham 15 from the heavens,

"I swear by myself"—it is the oracle of the LORD— 16 "that since you have done this, and have not withheld your son, your only son, I will indeed bless you, and will 17 surely make your descendants as numerous as the stars of the sky, or the sands that are on the seashore, so that your descendants shall take possession of the cities of their enemies, and through your descendants all the na- 18 tions of the earth shall invoke blessings on one another —just because you heeded my injunction."

Abraham then returned to his servants, and together 19 they started off for Beersheba; and in Beersheba Abraham made his home.

THE STORY OF JACOB, 27:1–41; 28:10—29:20; 35:9–15

One day, after Isaac had become old and his eyes so 27 dim that he could not see, he called his older son Esau.

"My son!" he said to him.

"Here I am," he replied.

2   He said,

3   "Here I am an old man, not knowing what day I may die. Get your weapons, then, your quiver and bow, and

4   go out into the fields, and hunt some game for me. Then make me a tasty dish, such as I like, and bring it to me to eat, that I may give you my blessing before I die."

5   Now Rebekah was listening when Isaac spoke to his son Esau; so when Esau went off to the fields to hunt

6   game for his father, Rebekah said to her son Jacob,

7   "I have just heard your father say to your brother Esau, 'Bring me some game, and make me a tasty dish to eat, that I may bless you before the LORD before I die.'

8   Now then, my son, obey me in the charge that I am giv-

9   ing you. Go to the flock and get two fat kids for me there, that I may make them into a tasty dish for your

10   father, such as he likes. Then you shall take it to your father to eat, that he may bless you before he dies."

11   But Jacob said to his mother Rebekah,

"Ah, but my brother Esau is a hairy man, while I am

12   smooth. Suppose my father were to feel me? I should look like an impious person to him, and bring a curse on myself, and not a blessing."

13   "Let any curse for you, my son, fall on me!" his mother replied. "Only obey me, and go and get them for me."

14   So he went and got them, and brought them to his mother. His mother then made a tasty dish, such as his

15   father liked; and taking the best clothes of her older son Esau, which she had in the house, Rebekah dressed her

16   younger son Jacob in them; she put the skins of the

17   kids on his hands and on the smooth parts of his neck, and committed the tasty dish and bread which she had

18   made into the hands of her son Jacob. Then he went in to his father, and said,

"Father!"

"Yes," he said. "Who are you, my son?"

19   Jacob said to his father,

"I am Esau, your first-born; I have done as you told

me; now sit up and eat once more of my game, that you
may give me your blessing."

But Isaac said to his son,   20

"How ever did you come to find it so quickly, my
son?"

"Because the Lord your God brought it in my path,"
he said.

Isaac then said to Jacob,   21

"Come up close that I may feel you, my son, to see
whether you really are my son Esau or not."

So Jacob went up to his father Isaac, who felt him, and   22
said,

"The voice is Jacob's voice, but the hands are those of
Esau."

Hence he did not detect him, because his hands were   23
hairy, like those of his brother Esau; so he blessed him.

"Are you really my son Esau?" he said.   24

"I am," he replied.

So he said,   25

"Bring me some of your game to eat, my son, that I
may give you my blessing."

So he brought it to him, and he ate; he also brought
him wine, and he drank. Then his father Isaac said to   26
him,

"Come here and kiss me, my son."

So he went up and kissed him; and when he smelt his   27
clothes, he blessed him, saying,

"Ah, my son's smell is like that of a field that the
Lord has blessed.

May God give you of the heaven's dew,   28
Of earth's fatness, with plenty of grain and wine!
Nations shall serve you,   29
And peoples bow down to you.
Be master of your brothers,
And let your mother's sons bow down to you!
Cursed be they who curse you,
And blessed be they who bless you!"

No sooner had Isaac finished blessing Jacob, indeed Ja-   30
cob had just left the presence of his father Isaac, when his

31 brother Esau came in from his hunt. He too made a tasty dish, and brought it to his father.

"Let my father sit up," he said to his father, "and eat some of his son's game, that you may give me your blessing."

32 "Who are you?" his father Isaac said to him.

"I am your son," he said, "your first-born, Esau."

33 Thereupon Isaac was very greatly agitated, and said, "Who was it then who got some game and brought it to me? I ate heartily of it before you came, and blessed him, so that he is indeed blessed."

34 On hearing his father's words, Esau cried loud and bitterly, and said to his father,

"Bless me also, my father!"

35 But he said,

"Your brother came under false colors, and stole your blessing."

36 "Is it because he is named Jacob that he has twice now got the better of me?" he said. "He stole my birthright, and now he has stolen my blessing! Have you not kept a blessing for me?" he added.

37 But Isaac in reply said to Esau,

"Since I have made him master over you, and have made all his brothers his slaves, and have provided grain and wine for his sustenance, what then is there that I can do for you, my son?"

38 Esau said to his father,

"Have you only one blessing, my father? Bless me too, my father."

39 Whereupon Esau lifted up his voice in weeping. So his father Isaac complied, and said to him,

"Away from the fat of the earth shall your dwelling be,
Away from the dew of the heavens on high.

40 By your sword you shall live,
And your brother you shall serve;
But when you become restive,
You shall break his yoke off your neck."

41 So Esau had a grudge against Jacob because of the blessing which his father had bestowed on him.

"It will soon be time to mourn for my father," Esau said to himself, "and then I will slay my brother Jacob."

Leaving Beersheba, Jacob set out for Haran. Reaching 28 a certain sanctuary, he spent the night there; for the sun had set. He took one of the stones of the sanctuary, and using it for a pillow, he lay down in that sanctuary. He had a dream in which he saw a ladder set up on the 12 earth, with its top reaching the sky, and angels of God were ascending and descending on it. Then the Lord 13 stood over him, and said,

"I am the Lord, the God of your father Abraham and of Isaac. The land on which you are lying, I am going to give to you and your descendants. Your descendants shall 14 be like the dust on the ground; you shall spread to the west, to the east, to the north, and to the south, so that all races in the earth will invoke blessings on one another through you and your descendants. I will be with 15 you, and guard you wherever you go, and bring you back to this land; for I will never forsake you, until I have done what I have promised you."

When Jacob woke from his sleep, he said, 16

"The Lord must surely be in this place—and I did not know it!"

He was awe-struck, and said, 17

"What an awesome place this is! This can be nothing other than the house of God, and that the gate of the sky."

Accordingly, he called the name of that sanctuary 19 Bethel [house of God], whereas the earlier name of the city had been Luz.

So when Jacob rose in the morning, he took the stone 18 which he had used as a pillow, and setting it up as a sacred pillar, he poured oil on its top. Jacob then made 20 this vow:

"If God will go with me, and watch over me on this journey that I am making, and give me food to eat and 21 clothes to wear, so that I come home safely to my father's house, then the Lord shall be my God, and this stone 22 which I have set up as a sacred pillar shall be God's house, and I will give to thee a portion of everything that thou givest me."

29 Jacob then continued his journey, and came to the
2 land of the Kedemites. Looking round, he saw a well in the open, with three flocks of sheep lying beside it; for it was from this well that the flocks were watered, but the
3 stone over the mouth of the well was so large that it was only after all the shepherds had collected there that they could roll the stone off the mouth of the well, and water the sheep, after which they would replace the stone over the mouth of the well.

4 "My friends, where do you come from?" Jacob said to them.

"We come from Haran," they said.

5 "Do you know Laban, the son of Nahor?" he said to them.

"We do," said they.

6 "Is he well?" he said to them.

"He is," they said, "and here is his daughter Rachel coming with his sheep!"

7 "Why," said he, "the day has still long to run! It is not yet time for the live stock to be gathered in; water the sheep, and go on pasturing them."

8 But they said,

"We cannot until all the shepherds assemble, and roll the stone off the mouth of the well so that we can water the sheep."

9 While he was still talking with them, Rachel arrived
10 with her father's flock; for she was a shepherdess. As soon as Jacob saw Rachel, the daughter of Laban, his mother's brother, with the flock of Laban, his mother's brother, Jacob went up, and rolling the stone off the mouth of the well, watered the flock of Laban, his
11 mother's brother. Then Jacob kissed Rachel, and lifted up his voice in weeping.

12 When Jacob told Rachel that he was a relative of her father and the son of Rebekah, she ran and told her
13 father. As soon as Laban heard about Jacob, his sister's son, he ran to meet him, embraced him, kissed him, and

brought him home. Jacob then told Laban his whole
story, whereupon Laban said to him,   14
   "You are my very own flesh and blood!"
So he stayed with him for a whole month.
Then Laban said to Jacob,   15
   "Should you, just because you are a relative of mine,
work for me for nothing? Let me know what your wages
should be."
   Now Laban had two daughters, the name of the older   16
being Leah, and that of the younger Rachel; Leah had   17
weak eyes, while Rachel was beautiful and lovely. Jacob   18
had fallen in love with Rachel, so he said,
   "I will work seven years for you in return for Rachel,
your youngest daughter."
   Whereupon Laban said,   19
   "It is better for me to give her to you than to anyone
else; stay with me."
So Jacob worked seven years for Rachel, and they   20
seemed to him but a few days, because he loved her.
   On his journey from Paddan-aram, God again ap-   35
peared to Jacob, and blessed him. God said to him,   10
   "Your name has been Jacob; you shall no longer be
called Jacob, but Israel is to be your name."
So he came to be named Israel.
Further, God said to him,   11
   "I am God Almighty; be fruitful and multiply; a nation, or rather a company of nations shall come from
you, and kings shall spring from you. The land which I   12
gave to Abraham and Isaac, I will give to you, and to
your descendants after you I will give it."
   God then left him at the place where he spoke with   13
him, whereupon Jacob erected a sacred pillar at the place   14
where he spoke with him, a pillar of stone, poured a libation on it, and anointed it with oil. So Jacob called   15
the name of the place where God spoke with him Bethel.

THE STORY OF JOSEPH, 37:2–36; 39:1—45:28

The following are the descendants of Jacob.   37
At the age of seventeen Joseph used to accompany his

brothers in looking after the flocks, being a mere lad alongside the sons of Bilhah and Zilpah, his father's wives; and Joseph brought a bad report of them to their father.

3 Now Israel loved Joseph more than any of his other sons, because he was the son of his old age; so he made a 4 long cloak for him. When his brothers saw that their father loved him more than any of his brothers, they hated him, and could not say a good word about him.

5 Joseph had a dream, which he told to his brothers, so 6 that they hated him all the more. He said to them,

7 "Listen to this dream that I have had. While we were binding sheaves in the field, my sheaf rose up and remained standing, while your sheaves gathered round it, and made obeisance to my sheaf!"

8 His brothers said to him,

"Are you indeed to be king over us; would you actually rule us?"

So they hated him all the more for his dream and for his words.

9 Then he had another dream which he recounted to his brothers.

"I have just had another dream," he said, "and the sun, moon, and eleven stars made obeisance to me!"

10 When he recounted it to his father and his brothers, his father reproved him, saying to him,

"What is this dream that you have had? Am I actually to come with your mother and your brothers, and make obeisance to the earth to you?"

11 But while his brothers became jealous of him, his father kept the matter in mind.

12 After his brothers had gone off to pasture their 13 father's flocks at Shechem, Israel said to Joseph,

"Are not your brothers pasturing the flocks at Shechem? Come, let me send you to them.

"I am ready," he replied.

14 So he said to him,

"Go and see how your brothers are, and the flocks; and bring me back word."

So he despatched him from the valley of Hebron; and he arrived at Shechem. But a man found him wandering 15 about the country; so the man asked him,

"What are you looking for?"

"I am looking for my brothers," he said; "do tell me 16 where they are pasturing the flocks."

The man said, 17

"They have moved from here; for I heard them say, 'Let us go to Dothan.' "

So Joseph followed his brothers, and found them at 18 Dothan. But they saw him in the distance, and before he could reach them, they plotted against him to kill him.

"There comes the dreamer yonder!" they said to one 19 20 another. "Come now, let us kill him, and throw him into one of the pits. We can say that a wild beast devoured him. Then we shall see what his dreams will come to."

But when Reuben heard this, he tried to save him from 21 their hands; so he said,

"Let us not take his life."

"Do not shed any blood," Reuben said to them; 22 "throw him into the pit here in the wilderness, but do not lay hands on him"; (his idea being to save him from their hands, and restore him to his father).

As soon as Joseph reached his brothers, they stripped 23 him of his cloak (the long cloak that he was wearing), and seizing him, they threw him into the pit. The pit, 24 however, was empty, with no water in it.

Then they sat down to eat a meal; but raising their 25 eyes, they saw a caravan of Ishmaelites coming from Gilead, with their camels carrying gum, balm, and laudanum, which they were engaged in taking down to Egypt. Thereupon Judah said to his brothers, 26

"What is the good of killing our brother and covering up his blood? Come, let us sell him to the Ishmaelites, 27 and not lay hands on him; for after all he is our brother, our own flesh."

His brothers agreed. Some Midianite traders passed 28 by, so pulling Joseph up, they lifted him out of the pit.

They sold Joseph to the Ishmaelites for twenty shekels of silver; and they took him to Egypt.

29 So when Reuben went back to the pit, there was no
30 Joseph in the pit! Then he tore his clothes, and returning to his brothers, said,

"The boy is gone! And I, how can I go home?"

31 Then they took Joseph's cloak, and killing a goat,
32 they dipped the cloak in the blood. So they soiled the long cloak, and then they brought it to their father, saying,

"We found this; see whether it is your son's cloak or not."

33 Examining it, he said,

"It is my son's cloak! Some wild beast has devoured him; Joseph must be torn to pieces."

34 Then Jacob tore his clothes, and girded himself with
35 sackcloth, and mourned for his son for a long time. His sons and daughters all tried to console him, but he would not be consoled.

"No," he said, "I will go down mourning to my son to Sheol."

Thus did his father weep for him.

36 Meanwhile the Midianites had sold him in Egypt to Potiphar, an officer of Pharaoh, his head steward.

39 When Joseph was taken down to Egypt, Potiphar, an Egyptian, an officer of Pharaoh, his head steward, bought him from the Ishmaelites who had taken him down
2 there. The Lord was with Joseph, so that he became a prosperous man. He lived in the house of his master, the
3 Egyptian; and his master noticed that the Lord was with him and that the Lord made everything prosper with him
4 that he undertook; so Joseph found favor with him, and was made his personal attendant; then he made him superintendent of his household, and put him in charge
5 of all his property. From the time that he made him superintendent of his household and all his property, the Lord blessed the house of the Egyptian for Joseph's sake, the Lord's blessing resting on everything that belonged
6 to him, both indoors and outdoors. So he left every-

thing that he had to Joseph's charge, and having him, gave no concern to anything, except the food that he ate.

Now Joseph was so handsome and good-looking that 7 some time later the wife of his master took a fancy to Joseph, and said,

"Lie with me."

But he refused, saying to his master's wife, 8

"Having me, my master is giving no concern to anything in the house, but has committed all his property to my charge; there is no one in this house greater than I; 9 he has kept nothing from me except yourself, and that because you are his wife. How then can I commit this great crime, and sin against God?"

Though she spoke to Joseph day after day, he would 10 not listen to her solicitations to lie with her, or be with her. One day, however, when he went into the house to 11 do his work, none of the household servants being anywhere in the house, she caught hold of his coat, saying, 12

"Lie with me."

But he fled, leaving the coat in her hands, and went outdoors. When she saw that he had fled outdoors, 13 leaving his coat in her hands, she called her household 14 servants, and said to them,

"See how he has brought this Hebrew fellow into our house to violate us! He came into my room to lie with me, but I screamed; and as soon as he heard me scream 15 and call, he fled, leaving his coat beside me, and went outdoors."

So she left the coat beside her until his master came 16 home, and then told him this same story, 17

"The Hebrew slave whom you brought into our house came into my room to violate me, but as soon as I 18 screamed and called, he fled outdoors, leaving his coat beside me."

When Joseph's master heard the statements of his wife 19 who said to him, "This is the way your slave treated me," his anger blazed, and Joseph's master took him and 20 threw him into the prison where state prisoners were confined. So he lay there in prison.

21 The LORD, however, was with Joseph and was kind to
22 him, and got him into the good graces of the jailer, so
that the jailer put Joseph in charge of all the prisoners
who were in the jail, and he looked after everything that
23 was done there. The jailer exercised no oversight over
anything in his charge, because the LORD was with him,
and the LORD made whatever he undertook prosper.

40 Some time after these events the butler and the baker
of the king of Egypt offended their lord, the king of
2 Egypt, so that Pharaoh became angry with his two offi-
3 cers, the chief butler and the chief baker, and put them in
custody in the head steward's house, in the prison where
4 Joseph was confined. The head steward entrusted Joseph
with them, and he waited on them. After they had been
in custody some time, they both had dreams on the same
5 night, each having a dream of different meaning—the
butler and the baker of the king of Egypt who were con-
6 fined in the prison. When Joseph came to them in the
7 morning, he saw that they were worried, so he asked
Pharaoh's officers who were in custody with him in his
master's house,

"Why do you look so gloomy today?"

8 "We have had dreams," they replied, "and there is
no one to interpret them."

Joseph said to them,

"Does not dream interpretation belong to God? Pray
recount them to me."

9 So the chief butler recounted his dream to Joseph.

"In my dream," he said to him, "there was a vine in
10 front of me, and on the vine were three branches. As
soon as it budded, its blossoms shot up, its clusters ri-
11 pened into grapes. With Pharaoh's cup in my hand, I
took the grapes, and squeezing them into Pharaoh's cup,
I placed the cup in Pharaoh's hand."

12 Joseph said to him,

"This is its interpretation: the three branches repre-
13 sent three days; within three days Pharaoh shall summon
you, and restore you to your position, so that you shall
place Pharaoh's cup in his hand as you used to do when

you were his butler; so, if you will be good enough to 14
keep me in mind when prosperity comes to you, do me
the kindness of mentioning me to Pharaoh, and so liber-
ate me from this house; for I was really kidnapped from 15
the land of the Hebrews, and further, I have done nothing
here that I should be put into a dungeon."

When the chief baker found that the interpretation 16
was favorable, he said to Joseph,

"I too had a dream; in mine there were three open-
work baskets on my head, and in the top basket was some 17
of every kind of baked food for Pharaoh, but the birds
were eating it out of the basket on my head."

Joseph answered, 18

"This is its interpretation: the three baskets represent three days; within three days Pharaoh shall summon 19
you, and hang you on a tree, and the birds shall eat the
flesh off you."

On the third day, which was Pharaoh's birthday, he 20
held a feast for all his officials; and among his officials he
summoned the chief butler and the chief baker. The chief 21
butler he restored to his duties, so that he again placed
the cup in Pharaoh's hand; but the chief baker he hanged, 22
as Joseph had told them in his interpretation. The chief 23
butler, however, did not keep Joseph in mind, but forgot
him.

Two whole years later Pharaoh dreamed that he was 41
standing beside the Nile, when seven beautiful, fat cows 2
came up out of the Nile, and browsed in the sedge. After 3
them seven other cows came up out of the Nile, ugly and
thin, and stood beside the other cows on the bank of the
Nile. Then the thin, ugly cows ate up the seven beauti- 4
ful, fat cows, whereupon Pharaoh awoke. When he fell 5
asleep again, he had a second dream: there were seven
ears of grain growing on a single stalk, fine and plump,
and after them there sprouted seven other ears, thin and 6
blasted by the east wind. Then the thin ears swallowed 7
up the seven fine, full ears, whereupon Pharaoh awoke,
only to find it a dream!

Next morning he was so perturbed that he sent for all 8

the magicians and wise men of Egypt. To them Pharaoh recounted his dreams, but no one could interpret them for

9 Pharaoh. Then the chief butler said to Pharaoh,

10 "I would today recall my offence, how Pharaoh became angry with his servants, and put them in custody in the house of the head steward, myself and the chief

11 baker. On the same night we had dreams, he and I, each

12 of us having a dream of different meaning. With us there was a Hebrew youth, a slave belonging to the head steward, and when we recounted our dreams to him, he interpreted them for us, giving each the proper interpretation

13 of his dream. And it fell out just as he had indicated in the interpretation; I was restored to my position, while the other was hanged."

14 Thereupon Pharaoh sent for Joseph, and he was brought hurriedly from the dungeon. When he had shaved and changed his clothes, he came into Pharaoh's presence.

15 "I have had a dream," Pharaoh said to Joseph, "but there is no one to interpret it. However, I have heard it said of you that you know how to interpret dreams."

16 "Apart from God can Pharaoh be given a favorable response?" Joseph answered Pharaoh.

17 Then Pharaoh said to Joseph,

18 "I dreamed that I was standing on the bank of the Nile, when seven fat and beautiful cows came up out of

19 the Nile, and browsed in the sedge. After them there came up seven other cows, thin and very ugly and lean— I have never seen such poor cows in all the land of

20 Egypt. Then the lean, ugly cows ate up the first seven

21 fat cows; they passed right into them, but no one would have known that they had done so—they looked just as bad as before. Then I awoke.

22 "In another dream I saw seven ears of grain growing

23 on a single stalk, full and plump, and after them there sprouted seven other ears, withered, thin, and blasted by

24 the east wind. Then the thin ears swallowed up the seven plump ears. I told this to the magicians, but there was no one to explain it to me."

Joseph said to Pharaoh, 25
"Pharaoh's dream is simple; God would reveal to
Pharaoh what he is about to do. The seven fat cows rep- 26
resent seven years, and the seven plump ears represent
seven years—it is a single dream. The seven lean and 27
ugly cows that came up after them represent seven years,
and so do the seven empty ears blasted by the east wind;
there are to be seven years of famine. It is as I told Pha- 28
raoh, God would show Pharaoh what he is about to do.
Seven years of great plenty are coming throughout all 29
the land of Egypt, but following them there will be seven 30
years of famine, so that the plenty will all be forgotten
in the land of Egypt; the famine will devastate the land, 31
and the plenty will become quite unknown in the land
because of that famine which is to follow; for it will be
very severe. The fact that the dream was sent twice to 32
Pharaoh in two forms means that the matter is absolutely
settled by God, and that God will soon bring it about.
Now then, let Pharaoh find a shrewd and prudent man, 33
and put him in control of the land of Egypt. Let Pharaoh 34
proceed to appoint officials over the land to forearm the
land of Egypt during the seven years of plenty; let them 35
collect all the food of these good years that are coming,
and under the authority of Pharoah store up grain for
food in the cities, and hold it there. The food shall serve 36
as a reserve for the land against the seven years of famine
that are to befall the land of Egypt, so that the land may
not perish from the famine."

The proposal commended itself to Pharaoh and all his 37
courtiers, and Pharaoh said to his courtiers, 38
"Can we find a man with the spirit of God in him like
this one?"

So Pharaoh said to Joseph, 39
"Since God has made all this known to you, there is
no one so shrewd and prudent as you; you shall be in 40
charge of my palace, and all my people shall be obedient
to your commands; it is only in the matter of the throne
itself that I shall be your superior."

Thereupon Pharaoh said to Joseph, 41

"I hereby put you in charge of the whole land of Egypt."

42 And taking the signet ring from his finger, Pharaoh put it on Joseph's finger; he dressed him in linen robes,

43 put a gold chain round his neck, and had him ride in the second of his chariots, with people shouting "Bow down!" before him, thus putting him in charge of the whole land of Egypt.

44 "Although I continue as Pharaoh," said Pharaoh to Joseph, "yet without your consent shall no one stir hand or foot in all the land of Egypt."

45 Then Pharaoh called Joseph's name Zaphenath-paneah, and married him to Asenath, the daughter of Potiphera, priest of On; and Joseph's fame spread throughout the land of Egypt.

46 Joseph was thirty years old when he entered the service of Pharaoh, king of Egypt.

47 After leaving the presence of Pharaoh, Joseph made a tour through the whole land of Egypt. During the seven

48 years of plenty the land produced abundant crops; so he collected all the food of the seven years when there was plenty in the land of Egypt, and thus stored food in the cities, storing in each city the food from the fields around

49 it. Joseph stored up grain like the sands of the sea, in great quantities, until he ceased to keep account of it; for it was past measuring.

50 Before the years of famine came, two sons were born to Joseph by Asenath, the daughter of Potiphera, priest

51 of On. Joseph called the name of the first-born Manasseh [forgetfulness]; "For," said he, "God has made me for-

52 get all about my hardships and my father's home." The name of the second he called Ephraim [fruitfulness]; "For God has made me fruitful in the land of my misfortune."

53 When the seven years of plenty that had prevailed in

54 the land of Egypt came to an end, the seven years of famine set in, as Joseph had said.

There was famine in all lands, but throughout all the land of Egypt there was food.

When all the land of Egypt became famished, the 55
people cried to Pharaoh for food; so Pharaoh announced
to all Egypt,

"Go to Joseph, and do what he tells you."

The famine spread all over the land, so Joseph threw 56
open all that he had locked up, and sold grain to the
Egyptians, since the famine was severe in the land of
Egypt. People from all lands came to Joseph in Egypt 57
to buy grain; for the famine was severe all over the earth.

When Jacob learned that there was grain to be had **42**
in Egypt, he said to his sons,

"Why do you stare at one another? I have just heard," 2
he said, "that there is grain to be had in Egypt; go down
there, and buy some for us there, that we may live and
not die."

So ten of Joseph's brothers went down to buy grain in 3
Egypt, since Jacob would not let Joseph's brother Benja- 4
min go with his other brothers; "Lest," thought he,
"harm should befall him." Thus the Israelites came with 5
the rest to buy grain; for the famine was in the land of
Canaan.

Now Joseph was the vizier of the land; it was he who 6
sold the grain to all the people of the land. So Joseph's
brothers came and prostrated themselves before him,
with their faces to the ground. When Joseph saw his 7
brothers, he recognized them, but he treated them as if
he were a stranger, and spoke harshly to them.

"Where have you come from?" he said to them.

"From the land of Canaan to buy food," they said.

Joseph recognized his brothers, but they did not rec- 8
ognize him. Remembering the dreams that he had had 9
about them, Joseph said to them,

"You are spies; you have come to find out the condition of the land!"

"No, my lord," they said to him, "your servants have 10
come to buy food. We are all sons of one man; we are 11
honest men; your servants are not spies."

"Not so," he said to them; "but you have come to 12
find out the condition of the land."

13   But they said,

"Your servants are brothers, twelve in all; we are sons of a certain man in the land of Canaan; the youngest is at present with our father, while the other is no more."

14   But Joseph said to them,

15   "It is as I told you; you are spies. By this you shall be put to the proof: as Pharaoh lives, you shall not leave

16   this place unless your youngest brother comes here. Send one of your number to fetch your brother, while the rest of you remain in custody. Thus shall your statements be put to the proof as to whether you are truthful or not. As Pharaoh lives, you are spies!"

17
18   So he bundled them off to prison for three days, but on the third day Joseph said to them,

"Since I am one who fears God, you may save your

19   lives, if you do this: if you are honest men, let one of you brothers remain confined in your prison, and then the rest of you, go and take grain home to your starving

20   households; but you must bring me your youngest brother. Thus shall your words be verified, and you shall not die."

21   They proceeded to do so, saying to one another,

"Unfortunately, we were to blame about our brother, upon whose distress, when he pleaded with us for mercy, we gazed unmoved; that is why this distress has come to us."

22   Then Reuben spoke up and said to them,

"Did I not say to you, 'Do not sin against the lad'? But you paid no attention; so now comes a reckoning for his blood!"

23   They did not know that Joseph heard them; for the
24   intermediary was between them. He turned from them, and wept. On coming back to them, he spoke to them, took Simeon from them, and imprisoned him in their

25   presence. Joseph then ordered their receptacles to be filled with grain, the money of each of them to be replaced in his sack, and provisions to be given them for

26   the journey. This was done for them. Then they loaded their asses with their grain, and departed.

At the camping-place for the night one of them opened 27
his sack to give his ass some fodder, and there he saw his
money in the mouth of his sack!

"My money has been put back! It is right here inside 28
my sack!" he said to his brothers.

Thereupon their hearts sank, and they turned to one
another in fear, saying,

"What is this that God has done to us?"

On reaching their father Jacob in the land of Canaan, 29
they told him all that had befallen them:

"The man who is lord of the land talked harshly to us, 30
making us out to be spies of the land. But we said to 31
him, 'We are honest men; we are not spies. We are 32
brothers on our father's side, twelve in all; one is no
more, and the youngest is at present with our father in
the land of Canaan.' Then the man who is lord of the 33
land said to us, 'By this I shall find out whether you are
honest men: leave one of your brothers with me, and
taking something for your famishing households, be off;
and then bring me your youngest brother. Thus shall I 34
know that you are not spies, but honest men. I will restore your brother to you, and you will be free to trade in
the land.' "

When they came to empty their sacks, there was 35
the money-packet of each in his sack! On seeing their
money-packets, both they and their father were dismayed, and their father Jacob said to them, 36

"It is I that you bereave. Joseph is no more, Simeon
is no more, and now you would take Benjamin! It is on
me that all this falls."

Reuben said to his father, 37

"You may kill my two sons if I do not bring him home
to you! Put him in my charge, and I will bring him back
to you."

But he said, 38

"My son shall not go down with you; for his brother
is dead, and he alone is left. If harm were to befall
him on the journey that you make, you would bring my
gray hairs down to Sheol in sorrow."

43   The famine continued severe in the land, so when they
had finished eating all the grain which they had brought
from Egypt, their father said to them,

      "Go again, and buy us a little food."

3   But Judah said to him,

      "The man strictly warned us: 'You cannot have audi-
4   ence with me unless your brother is with you.' If you are
ready to let our brother go with us, we will go down and
5   buy food for you; but if you are not ready to let him go,
we cannot go down; for the man said to us, 'You cannot
have audience with me unless your brother is with you.'"

6   "Why did you bring this trouble on me," said Israel,
"by telling the man that you had another brother?"

7   They said,

      "The man persisted in asking about ourselves and our
family—'Is your father still living? Have you another
brother?' We only gave him the information demanded
by these questions of his. How could we possibly know.
that he would say, 'Bring your brother down'?"

8   "Let the lad go with me," said Judah to his father
Israel; "but we must go at once, if we would save our
9   lives and not die, both we, you, and our dependents. I
will be surety for him; you may hold me responsible for
him. If I do not bring him back to you and set him be-
10 fore you, you may blame me for it all my life; in fact if
we had not wasted so much time, we could have made a
second trip by now."

11   Then their father Israel said to them,

      "If it must be so, then do this: take some of the coun-
try's best in your receptacles, and take it down to the
man as a present—a little balm, a little honey, gum,
12 laudanum, pistachio nuts, and almonds. Also take double the money with you, and so take back with you the
money that was replaced in the mouths of your sacks—
13 perhaps there was a mistake. Take your brother too, and
14 go, return to the man. May God Almighty grant you
such kindness with the man that he will release your other
brother for you, as well as Benjamin. As for me, as I have
already suffered bereavement, I may have to do so again."

So the men took this present, and taking double the 15
money with them, as well as Benjamin, they started off,
went down to Egypt, and stood in the presence of Joseph.
When Joseph saw Benjamin with them, he said to his 16
house-steward,

"Take the men home, kill an animal, and get it ready;
for the men are to dine with me at noon."

The man did as Joseph said, and brought the men 17
to Joseph's house. On being brought to Joseph's house 18
the men became frightened, saying,

"It is because of the money which reappeared in our
sacks the first time that we are being brought in, in
order that he may devise some pretext against us, and
falling upon us, take us into slavery, together with our
asses."

So they went up to Joseph's house-steward, and spoke 19
to him at the doorway of the house.

"If you please, sir," they said, "we came down the 20
first time specially to buy food, but when we reached the 21
camping-place for the night, and opened our sacks, there
was each man's money in the mouth of his sack—our
money in full. Accordingly we have brought it back
with us, and we have brought other money down with us 22
to buy food. We do not know who put our money in our
sacks."

"Be at ease," he said, "do not be afraid! It must have 23
been your God, the God of your fathers, who put treasure in your sacks for you. I received your money."

Then be brought Simeon out to them.

After bringing the men into Joseph's house, the man 24
gave them water to wash their feet, and he gave them 25
fodder for their asses. Then they set out the present
in anticipation of Joseph's arrival at noon; for they
had heard that they were to dine there. When Jo- 26
seph came home, they brought him the present that they
had carried into the house, and bowed to the ground before him. He asked after their health. 27

"Is your father well," he said, "the old man of whom
you spoke? Is he still living?"

28 "Your servant, our father, is well; he is still living," they said, bowing in homage to him.

29 Raising his eyes, he saw his brother Benjamin, the son of his own mother, and said,

"Is this your youngest brother, of whom you told me?" "May God be gracious to you, my son!" he said.

30 Thereupon Joseph hastily sought a place to weep; for his heart was deeply stirred at sight of his brother; he

31 retired to his room, and wept there. Then he bathed his face, and came out, and controlling himself, said,

"Serve the meal."

32 The meal was served, separately for him, for them, and for the Egyptians that were dining with him; for the Egyptians could not eat with the Hebrews, because that

33 would be abhorrent to the Egyptians. They were seated in his presence in order of age, from the oldest to the youngest, so that the men stared at one another in amaze-

34 ment. Portions were carried from his own table to them, but Benjamin's portion was five times as much as any other's. So they feasted, and drank with him.

44 He then gave orders to his house-steward,

"Fill the men's sacks as full as they will hold with food, and put each man's money in the mouth of his sack;

2 in the mouth of the sack belonging to the youngest put my cup, the silver cup, along with his money for the grain."

He followed the instructions which Joseph gave.

3 With the dawn of morning the men with their asses

4 were sent on their way. Although they had left the city, they had not gone far, when Joseph said to his house-steward,

"Run at once after the men, and when you overtake them, say to them, 'Why have you returned evil for

5 good? Why have you stolen my silver cup? Is not this the one from which my lord drinks, which in fact he uses for divination? It is a wicked thing that you have done.'"

6 So he overtook them, and addressed these words to

7 them; but they said to him,

"Why should my lord speak like this? Your servants would never think of doing such a thing! Why, we even 8 brought you back from the land of Canaan the money that we found in the mouths of our sacks. How then could we steal silver or gold from your master's house? That one of your servants in whose possession it is found 9 shall die, and the rest of us will become slaves to my lord."

"Although it may indeed be just as you say," he said, 10 "yet the one in whose possession it is found shall become my slave, but the rest of you shall be held blameless."

Then each of them quickly lowered his sack to the 11 ground, and opened it, and search being made, beginning 12 with the oldest and ending with the youngest, the cup was found in Benjamin's sack. Thereupon they tore their 13 clothes, and each having reloaded his ass, they returned to the city.

Judah and his brothers arrived at the house of Joseph, 14 while he was still there, so they flung themselves on the ground before him.

"What is this that you have done?" Joseph said to 15 them. "Did you not know that a man like me would be sure to use divination?"

Judah said, 16

"What can we say to my lord? What can we urge? How can we prove our innocence? God has discovered the crime of your servants; here we are, the slaves of my lord, both we and he in whose possession the cup has been found."

"I could not think of doing such a thing," he said; 17 "only the man in whose possession the cup has been found shall be my slave; the rest of you are free to go back to your father."

Then Judah went up to him, and said, 18

"If you please, my lord, let your servant speak a word in the ear of my lord, and your anger not blaze against your servant; for you are the equal of Pharaoh himself. My lord asked his servants, 'Have you a father or a 19 brother?' And we said to my lord, 'We have an aged 20

father, and a young brother, the child of his old age; his brother is dead, so that he alone is left of his mother's
21 children, and his father loves him.' Then you said to your servants, 'Bring him down to me that I may see
22 him.' But we told my lord, 'The boy cannot leave his father; his father would die if he were to leave him.'
23 Whereupon you said to your servants, 'Unless your youngest brother comes down with you, you cannot have audience with me again.'

24   "When we went back to your servant, my father, we
25 reported to him the words of my lord. Then our father
26 said, 'Go again and buy a little food for us.' But we said, 'We cannot go down; if our youngest brother accompanies us, we can go down; for we shall not be allowed to have audience with the man unless our youngest
27 brother is with us.' Then your servant, my father, said to us, 'You know that my wife bore me only two chil-
28 dren; then one of them left me, and I think he must surely have been torn to pieces; for I have never seen him since.
29 If then you take this one from me too, and harm befall him, you will bring down my gray hairs to Sheol in trouble.'

30   "And now, when I rejoin your servant, my father, and
31 the boy not with us, his life is so bound up with the boy's that he will die when he sees that there is no boy, and your servants will bring down the gray hairs of your
32 servant, our father, to Sheol in sorrow; for your servant went surety for the boy to my father, saying, 'If I do not bring him back to you, you may blame me for it all my
33 life.' Now then, pray let your servant remain in the boy's place as my lord's slave, but let the boy go back
34 with his brothers; for how can I go back to my father unless the boy is with me, and witness the agony that would come to my father?"

45   Joseph could no longer control himself before all his attendants, so he cried out,
    "Have everyone withdraw from me."
    So there was no one with Joseph when he made him-
2 self known to his brothers; but he wept so loudly that

the Egyptians heard it, and Pharaoh's household heard
it. Joseph said to his brothers,   3

"I am Joseph. Is my father still living?"

But his brothers could not answer him, because they
were so dismayed at being in his presence. So Joseph said   4
to his brothers,

"Come nearer to me."

When they came nearer, he said,

"I am your brother Joseph whom you sold into Egypt.   5
Now do not be distressed nor angry with yourselves that
you sold me here; for it was to save life that God sent me
ahead of you; for it is two years now that the famine has   6
prevailed in the land, but there are still five years in
which there will be no ploughing or reaping. God sent   7
me ahead of you to insure you a remnant in the earth, and
to be the means of a remarkable escape for you. So then   8
it was not you, but God who sent me here, and made me
a father to Pharaoh, lord of all his house, and ruler over
all the land of Egypt. Hurry back to my father and say   9
to him, 'Thus speaks your son Joseph: "Since God has
made me lord of all Egypt, come down to me without delay. You shall live in the land of Goshen, and be near   10
me, you, your sons, your grandsons, your flocks, your
herds, and all that belong to you; and there I will pro-   11
vide for you, lest you, your household and all that belong to you come to want; for there are still five years of
famine to come." ' You can see for yourselves and my   12
brother Benjamin for himself that it is I who speak to
you. You must tell my father all about my splendor in   13
Egypt, and all that you have seen; hurry and bring my
father here."

Then he fell on the neck of his brother Benjamin and   14
wept, while Benjamin wept on his neck. He kissed all his   15
brothers, and wept on their shoulders, after which his
brothers talked with him.

When the news was received at Pharaoh's palace that   16
Joseph's brothers had arrived, Pharaoh was delighted, as
were also his courtiers. Pharaoh said to Joseph,   17

"Say to your brothers, 'Do this: load your animals,

18 go back to the land of Canaan, and taking your father and
your households, come to me, and I will give you the
best of the land of Egypt, so that you shall eat the fat of
19 the land. Also, carry out this order: take wagons from
the land of Egypt for your little ones and your wives;
20 convey your father in them, and come back. Never mind
your goods; for the best of the whole land of Egypt will
be yours.' "

21   The sons of Israel did so. Joseph gave them wagons in
accord with the command of Pharaoh, and he also gave
22 them provisions for the journey. To each of them he
gave a festal garment, but to Benjamin he gave three hun-
23 dred shekels of silver and five festal garments. To his
father he sent likewise ten asses loaded with the best
products of Egypt, and ten she-asses loaded with grain,
24 bread, and provisions for his father on the journey. Then
he sent his brothers away; and as they left, he said to
them,
    "Do not get too excited on the way."
25   So they went up from Egypt, and came to the land of
Canaan, to their father Jacob.
26   "Joseph is still living, and he is ruler over all the land
of Egypt," they told him.
27   But he was so stunned that he would not believe them.
However, when they told him all that Joseph had said to
them, and he saw the wagons that Joseph had sent to
convey him, their father Jacob recovered.
28   "Enough!" said Israel; "my son Joseph is still living;
I will go and see him before I die."

THE BLESSING OF JACOB, 49:1-28

49 Then Jacob summoned his sons, and said,
    "Come together that I may tell you what is to befall
you in days to come:

2   Gather round and listen, you sons of Jacob;
        Listen to Israel, your father.

3   Reuben, you are my first-born,
        My strength and the first issue of my manly vigor;

Excessively proud and excessively fierce,
Turbulent as water—you shall no longer excel;   4
For you went up to your father's bed;
So I degraded him who went up to my couch.

Simeon and Levi are brothers;   5
Ruthless weapons are their daggers.
I will never enter their circle;   6
I will never join in their assembly;
For in their anger they slay men,
And in their normal mood they hamstring oxen.
Cursed be their anger, for it is fierce,   7
And their wrath, for it is cruel!
I will disperse them throughout Jacob,
And scatter them throughout Israel.

Your brothers shall praise you, O Judah;   8
With your hand on the necks of your foes,
Your father's sons shall bow down to you.
A lion's whelp is Judah;   9
On prey you have grown up, my son.
He crouches, he couches as a lion,
As an old lion; who dare disturb him?
The sceptre shall never depart from Judah,   10
Nor the staff from between his feet,
Until his ruler comes,
To whom the peoples shall be obedient.
He tethers his ass to the vine,   11
And his ass's colt to the choicest vine;
He washes his garments in wine,
And his robes in the blood of grapes;
His eyes are darker than wine,   12
And his teeth whiter than milk.

Zebulun shall dwell by the seashore;   13
He shall be a haven for ships,
With his flank at Sidon.

Issachar is a sturdy ass,   14
Lounging among the ravines;

15   He saw that settled life was good,
      And that the land was pleasant;
      So he offered his shoulder to bear burdens,
      And became a gang-slave.

16   Dan shall judge his people,
      As any other of the tribes of Israel.
17   May Dan be a serpent by the roadside,
      A viper beside the path,
      That bites the horse's hoofs,
      So that its rider tumbles backward.

18   For succor from thee, O LORD, I wait!

19   As for Gad, raiders shall raid him,
      But he shall raid their rear.

20   As for Asher, his food shall be rich,
      And he shall yield royal dainties.

21   Naphtali is a free-ranging deer,
      That bears beautiful fawns.

22   Joseph is a young bull,
      A young bull at a spring,
      A wild-ass at Shur.
23   Shooting at him in enmity,
      The archers fiercely assailed him;
24   But their bow was broken by the Eternal,
      And their arms and hands trembled,
      At the might of the Mighty One of Jacob,
      At the name of the Shepherd, the Rock of Israel,
25   At your father's God, who helps you,
      And God Almighty, who blesses you
      With the blessings of the heavens above,
      The blessings of the abyss couching below;
      The blessings of breast and of womb,
26   The blessings of fatherhood, yea of man and child;
      The blessings of the ancient mountains,
      The dainties of the eternal hills—
      May these rest on the head of Joseph,

And on the brow of him who was cursed by his
brothers!

Benjamin is a ravenous wolf; 27
Devouring prey in the morning,
And dividing spoil at evening."

All these constituted the twelve tribes of Israel, and 28
this was what their father said to them. He blessed them,
bestowing on each the blessing suited to him.

THE BOOK OF EXODUS

1   The following are the names of the sons of Israel who came to Egypt in the company of Jacob, each with his
2
3 household: Reuben, Simeon, Levi, and Judah, Issachar,
4 Zebulun, and Benjamin, Dan and Naphtali, Gad and
5 Asher. The total number of persons that were direct de-
6 scendants of Jacob was seventy, Joseph being already in Egypt. Then Joseph died, and likewise all his brothers
7 and all that generation; but the Israelites were fruitful and prolific; they increased in numbers, and grew greater and greater, so that the land was filled with them.

8   Then a new king rose over Egypt, who knew nothing
9 about Joseph; he said to his people,

    "See, the Israelite people have become too numerous
10 and too strong for us; come, let us take precautions against them lest they become so numerous that in the case of a war they should join forces with our enemies and fight against us, and so escape from the land."

11   Accordingly, gang-foremen were put in charge of them, to oppress them with their heavy labor; and they built Pithom and Rameses as store-cities for Pharaoh.
12 But the more they oppressed them, the more they multiplied and expanded, so that they became apprehensive about the Israelites.

13   The Egyptians reduced the Israelites to rigorous
14 slavery; they made life bitter for them in hard work with mortar and bricks, and in all kinds of work in the fields, all the work that they exacted of them being rigorous.

22   So Pharaoh commanded all his people,

    "Every boy that is born to the Hebrews, you must throw into the Nile, but you are to let all the girls live."

THE RISE OF THE DELIVERER, MOSES, 2:1—3:14; 4:18–20,
27—6:1

Now a man belonging to the house of Levi went and 2
married the daughter of Levi. The woman conceived and 2
bore a son, and seeing that he was robust, she hid him for
three months. When she could no longer hide him, she 3
procured an ark of papyrus reeds for him, and daubing it
with bitumen and pitch, she put the child in it, and
placed it among the reeds beside the bank of the Nile.
His sister posted herself some distance away to see what 4
would happen to him.

Presently Pharaoh's daughter came down to bathe at 5
the Nile, while her maids walked on the bank of the
Nile. Then she saw the ark among the reeds and sent her
maid to get it. On opening it, she saw the child, and it 6
was a boy crying! She took pity on him, and said,
"This is one of the Hebrews' children."

Thereupon his sister said to Pharaoh's daughter, 7
"Shall I go and summon a nurse for you from the
Hebrew women, to nurse the child for you?"

"Go," said Pharaoh's daughter to her. 8

So the girl went and called the child's mother, to 9
whom Pharaoh's daughter said,

"Take this child away and nurse it for me, and I will
pay the wages due you."

So the woman took the child and nursed him; and 10
when the child grew up, she brought him to Pharaoh's
daughter, and he became her son. She called his name
Moses [drawn out]; "For," said she, "I drew him out
of the water."

It was in those days that Moses, now grown up, went 11
out to visit his fellow-countrymen and noted their heavy
labor. He saw an Egyptian kill a Hebrew, one of his own
countrymen; so, looking this way and that, and seeing 12
that there was no one in sight, he killed the Egyptian,
and hid him in the sand. Another day, when he went 13
out, there were two Hebrews fighting! So he said to him
that was in the wrong,

"Why do you strike your companion?"

14   He replied,
      "Who made you ruler and judge over us? Are you
thinking of murdering me as you did the Egyptian?"
      Then Moses was afraid. "The incident must surely be
known," he thought.

15   When Pharaoh heard about the matter, he tried to kill
Moses, but Moses fled from Pharaoh and went to the land
of Midian, and sat down beside a well.

16   Now the priest of Midian had seven daughters, who
came to draw water, and fill the troughs to water their
17 father's flock, but some shepherds came and drove them
off. So Moses went to their rescue and watered their
18 flock. When they came home to their father Reuel, he said,
      "How did you come to get home so soon today?"
19   They said,
      "An Egyptian protected us against the shepherds; he
even drew water for us, and watered the flock."
20   "Then where is he?" he said to his daughters. "Why
did you leave the man behind? Invite him to have a
meal."
21   When Moses agreed to live with the man, he gave
22 Moses his daughter Zipporah in marriage; and she bore
a son whom he named Gershom [immigrant]; "For,"
said he, "I am an immigrant in a foreign land."
23   In the course of this long time the king of Egypt died.
The Israelites, groaning under their bondage, cried for
help, and their cry because of their bondage came up to
24 God. God heard their moaning, and God remembered
25 his covenant with Abraham, Isaac, and Jacob; God saw
the plight of Israel, and took cognizance of it.
3   While Moses was tending the flock of his father-in-
law, Jethro, the priest of Midian, he led the flock to the
western side of the desert, and came to the mountain of
2   God, Horeb. Then the angel of the LORD appeared to
him in a flame of fire, rising out of a bush. He looked,
and there was the bush burning with fire without being
3   consumed! So Moses said,
      "I will turn aside and see this great sight, why the
bush is not burned up."

When the LORD saw that he had turned aside to look 4 at it, God called to him out of the bush.

"Moses, Moses!" he said.

"Here I am!" said he.

"Do not come near here," he said; "take your sandals 5 off your feet; for the place on which you are standing is holy ground." "I am the God of your father," he said, 6 "the God of Abraham, Isaac, and Jacob."

Then Moses hid his face; for he was afraid to look at God.

"I have indeed seen the plight of my people who are in 7 Egypt," the LORD said, "and I have heard their cry under their oppressors; for I know their sorrows, and I have 8 come down to rescue them from the Egyptians and bring them up out of that land to a land, fine and large, to a land abounding in milk and honey, to the country of the Canaanites, Hittites, Amorites, Perizzites, Hivvites, and Jebusites. Now the cry of the Israelites has reached me, 9 and I have also seen how the Egyptians are oppressing them; so come now, let me send you to Pharaoh, that 10 you may bring my people, the Israelites, out of Egypt."

But Moses said to God, 11

"Who am I, to go to Pharaoh and bring the Israelites out of Egypt?"

"I will be with you," he said; "and this shall be the 12 sign for you that I have sent you. When you bring the people out of Egypt, you shall serve God at this mountain."

"But," said Moses to God, "in case I go to the Israel- 13 ites and say to them, 'The God of your fathers has sent me to you,' and they say to me, 'What is his name?' what am I to say to them?"

"I am who I am," God said to Moses. Then he said, 14 "This is what you are to say to the Israelites: ' "I am" has sent me to you.' "

Then Moses went off, and returning to his father-in- 4 law Jethro, said to him,

"Pray let me go back to my relatives in Egypt, to see whether they are still living."

"Go in peace," said Jethro to Moses.

19 The LORD said to Moses in Midian,
"Go, return to Egypt; for all the men who sought your
life are dead."

20 So Moses took his wife and sons, and mounted them
on an ass, to return to the land of Egypt; Moses also took
the staff of God in his hand.

27 The LORD said to Aaron,
"Go into the desert to meet Moses."

So he went; and he met him at the mountain of God
28 and kissed him. Then Moses told Aaron all that the
LORD had commissioned him to say and all the signs that
29 he had commanded him to perform. So Moses and Aaron
30 went and assembled all the elders of the Israelites, and
Aaron spoke all the words that the LORD had spoken to
Moses, and performed the signs in the sight of the people,
31 so that the people believed. When they heard that the
LORD had taken note of the Israelites and had marked
their plight, they bowed their heads in homage.

5 Following this, Moses and Aaron came and said to
Pharaoh,
"Thus says the LORD, the God of Israel: 'Let my
people go, that they may hold a feast for me in the
desert.'"

2 But Pharaoh said,
"Who is the LORD that I should heed his plea to let
Israel go? I know nothing about the LORD, and besides,
I will not let Israel go."

3 They said,
"The God of the Hebrews has paid us a visit; pray let
us make a three days' journey into the desert to offer
sacrifices to the LORD our God, lest he strike us with
pestilence or sword."

4 "Moses and Aaron," said the king of Egypt to them,
"why would you draw the people from their work?
Mind your own business."

5 "The people of the land are lazy as it is," said
Pharaoh, "and yet you would relieve them of their
burdens!"

[197]

So that same day Pharaoh commanded the taskmasters 6
in charge of the people and their foremen,

"You must no longer provide the people with straw 7
for making bricks as previously; let them go and gather
straw for themselves. But you must require of them the 8
same quantity of bricks that they have been making in
the past, without diminishing it at all; for they are lazy;
that is why they are crying, 'Let us go and offer sacrifices
to our God.' Let heavier work be loaded on the men, 9
that they may give their attention to it and not to lying
words."

So the taskmasters and foremen of the people departed, 10
and said to the people,

"Thus says Pharaoh: 'I am not going to provide you
with straw; go and get straw for yourselves wherever 11
you can find it; but there is to be no reduction in your
output."

So the people scattered all over the land of Egypt in 12
search of stubble for straw, while the taskmasters urged 13
them on, saying,

"Complete your daily quota of work, as when the
straw was provided for you."

The Israelite foremen were beaten, and Pharaoh's task- 14
masters took them to task, saying,

"Why have you not completed your prescribed
amount of brickmaking as usual, today just as previously?"

Then the Israelite foremen came and appealed to 15
Pharaoh,

"Why do you treat your servants like this? There is no 16
straw provided for your servants, and yet we are told to
make bricks, and your servants get beaten, whereas the
fault lies with you."

But he said, 17

"You are lazy, lazy; that is why you say, 'Let us go
and offer sacrifices to the LORD.' Be off now to your 18
work; straw shall not be provided for you, but you must
deliver the set quantity of bricks."

Then the Israelite foremen saw that they were in an 19

evil plight in having to say, "You must make no reduction in your daily quota of bricks."

20   On leaving the presence of Pharaoh they met Moses
21 and Aaron who were waiting for them, and said to them,
"May the LORD turn his attention to you, and punish
you for giving us an unsavory reputation with Pharaoh
and his courtiers, by putting a sword into their hands to
slay us!"

22   Then Moses turned again to the LORD, and said,
"O Lord, why hast thou brought evil on this people?
23 Why didst thou ever send me? Ever since I came to
Pharaoh to speak in thy name, he has ill-treated this
people; and thou hast done nothing to deliver thy
people!"

6   The LORD said to Moses,
"Now you shall see what I will do to Pharaoh; compelled by a mighty power he will not only let them go,
but will drive them out of his land."

THE EXODUS FROM EGYPT, 12:29–42; 13:20—14:31; 15:20, 21

12   At midnight the LORD struck down all the first-born in
the land of Egypt, from Pharaoh's first-born who was to
sit on his throne to the first-born of the captive in the dungeon, as well as all the first-born of the live stock. Then
30 Pharaoh rose in the night, he and all his courtiers and
all the Egyptians, and there arose a loud cry in Egypt;
for there was not a house where there was not someone
31 dead. So he summoned Moses and Aaron in the night,
and said,
"Withdraw at once from my people, both you and the
Israelites, and go, serve the LORD as you suggested.
32 Take both your flocks and herds as you suggested, and
begone; also ask a blessing on me."

33   The Egyptians became urgent with the people in their
hurry to get them out of the land; "For," said they, "we
34 shall all be dead." So the people snatched up their
dough before it was leavened, and shouldered their
kneadingbowls, wrapped up in their cloaks.

35   The Israelites followed the instructions of Moses; they

asked the Egyptians for articles of silver and gold and for clothing, and the LORD had put the people in such 36 favor with the Egyptians that they granted them their requests, and thus they despoiled the Egyptians.

So the Israelites set out from Rameses for Succoth, 37 about six hundred thousand men on foot, besides the dependants; a great crowd went up with them, as well as 38 very much live stock, both flocks and herds. With the 39 dough that they brought out of Egypt they baked unleavened cakes; for it was not leavened, because they had been driven out of Egypt and could not wait, nor had they prepared any provisions for themselves.

The length of time that the Israelites lived in Egypt 40 was four hundred and thirty years; and at the end of the 41 four hundred and thirty years, on that very day all the hosts of the LORD left the land of Egypt; that was a night 42 of vigil on the part of the LORD to bring them out of the land of Egypt, and so this night shall be one of vigil for the LORD on the part of all the Israelites from one generation to another.

Setting out from Succoth, they camped at Etham on 13 the edge of the desert. The LORD used to go in front of 21 them, in a column of cloud by day to guide them along the road, and in a column of fire by night to give them light, in order that they might travel by day and night; the column of cloud by day and the column of fire by 22 night never moved from the head of the people.

Then the LORD said to Moses, 14

"Tell the Israelites to turn back and camp in front of 2 Pi-hahiroth, between Migdol and the sea, in front of Baal-zephon; you must camp opposite it, beside the sea. Pharaoh will say of the Israelites, 'They are wandering 3 aimlessly in the land; the desert has shut them in.' Then I will make Pharaoh obstinate, so that he will 4 pursue them, and thus I will gain honor through Pharaoh and all his army, and the Egyptians shall know that I am the LORD."

They did so.

When the news was brought to the king of Egypt that 5

the people had fled, Pharaoh and his courtiers changed their minds about the people.

"What have we done," they said, "to let Israel leave our service?"

6 7 So he hitched the horses to his chariot, and took his people with him; he took six hundred chariots, picked from all the chariots of Egypt, with charioteers in charge 8 of them all. The LORD made Pharaoh, king of Egypt, obstinate, so that he pursued the Israelites, as they were 9 going triumphantly out; the Egyptians pursued them, all of Pharaoh's horses and chariots, his cavalry and infantry, and overtook them, camping by the sea, near Pi-10 hahiroth, in front of Baal-zephon. As Pharaoh drew near, the Israelites raised their eyes, and there were the Egyptians setting out in pursuit of them! The Israel-11 ites were terribly afraid, and cried to the LORD. And they said to Moses,

"Was it because there were no graves in Egypt that you have taken us away to die in the desert? What a way 12 to treat us, bringing us out of Egypt! Isn't this what we told you in Egypt would happen, when we said, 'Leave us alone and let us serve the Egyptians; for it is better for us to serve the Egyptians than to die in the desert.'"

13 But Moses said to the people,

"Do not be afraid; stand by and see how the LORD is going to save you today; for although you see the 14 Egyptians today, you shall never see them again. The LORD will fight for you, while you have only to keep still."

15 Then the LORD said to Moses,

16 "Why do you cry to me? Tell the Israelites to set forth; and then raise your staff and stretch out your hand over the sea, and thus divide it in two, so that the Israel-17 ites may proceed on dry ground right into the sea. Then I will make the Egyptians obstinate, so that they will go in after them, and thus I will gain honor through Pha-18 raoh and all his infantry, chariotry, and cavalry, so that the Egyptians may know that I am the LORD, when I

have gained honor through Pharaoh, his chariotry and cavalry."

Then the angel of God who was accustomed to go in 19 front of the army of Israel left his position and went behind them; the column of cloud also left its position in front of them and took its place behind them, and came between the army of Egypt and that of Israel, so that the 20 cloud was there with its darkness, and the night passed by without the one coming near the other all night.

Then Moses stretched out his hand over the sea, and 21 the LORD moved the sea away by means of a strong east wind all night, and turned the sea into dry land. The 22 waters were divided, so that the Israelites proceeded on dry ground right into the sea, the waters forming a wall for them to right and left of them. Pursuing them, the 23 Egyptians followed them right into the sea, all of Pharaoh's horses, his chariotry and cavalry. At the morn- 24 ing watch the LORD lowered himself toward the Egyptian army in the column of fire and cloud, and threw the Egyptian army into a panic. He clogged their chariot- 25 wheels, and caused them to proceed with such difficulty that the Egyptians said,

"Let us flee from the Israelites; for the LORD is fighting for them against the Egyptians."

Then the LORD said to Moses, 26

"Stretch out your hand over the sea, that the water may flow back upon the Egyptians, upon their chariotry and cavalry."

So Moses stretched out his hand over the sea, and as 27 morning broke, the sea returned to its steady flow; and as the Egyptians fled before it, the LORD shook the Egyptians right into the sea. The water returned, and covered 28 the chariotry and cavalry belonging to the whole army of Pharaoh that had followed them into the sea, not so much as one being left. But the Israelites had walked 29 through the middle of the sea on dry ground, the water forming a wall for them to right and left of them.

Thus did the LORD save Israel that day from the power 30 of the Egyptians. So Israel saw the Egyptians lying dead

31 on the seashore; and when Israel saw the mighty act which the LORD had performed against the Egyptians, the people stood in awe of the LORD and trusted the LORD and his servant Moses.

15 .Then the prophetess Miriam, the sister of Aaron, took a tambourine in her hand, and all the women went out
21 after her with tambourines and dancing, while Miriam responded to them in song,

"Sing to the LORD, for he has completely triumphed; The horse and its rider he has hurled into the sea."

THE GIVING OF THE LAW, 19:16-25

19 On the third day, when morning came, there was thunder and lightning, with a heavy cloud over the mountain, and a very loud trumpet-blast, so that all the people
17 that were in the camp trembled. Then Moses brought the people out of the camp to meet God, and they
18 took their stand at the foot of the mountain. Mount Sinai was completely enveloped in smoke, because the LORD had descended upon it in fire; its smoke ascended like the smoke from a kiln, so that the people all trem-
19 bled violently. As the blast of the trumpet grew louder and louder, Moses spoke, and God answered him with a
20 thunderpeal. The LORD descended upon Mount Sinai, to the top of the mountain; the LORD then summoned
21 Moses to the top of the mountain, and when Moses went up, the LORD said to Moses,

"Go down and warn the people not to break through
22 to the LORD to see him, or many of them will fall. The priests, also, whose place it is to approach the LORD, are to sanctify themselves, lest the LORD break loose upon them."

23 Moses said to the LORD,

"The people may not ascend Mount Sinai; for thou thyself didst charge us, saying, 'Mark off the mountain, and make it taboo.'"

24 The LORD said to him,

"Go down, and then come up again, accompanied by Aaron; but the priests and the people are not to break through to come up to the Lord, lest he break loose upon them."

So Moses went down to the people, and told them.   25

THE TEN COMMANDMENTS, 20:1–17

God spoke all these words, saying,   20

"Since I, the Lord, am your God, who brought you   2
out of the land of Egypt, out of a state of slavery, you   3
must have no other gods beside me.

"You must not carve an image for yourself in the shape   4
of anything that is in the heavens above, or that is on the
earth below, or that is in the waters under the earth; you   5
must not pay homage to them, nor serve them; for I, the
Lord your God, am a jealous God, punishing children
for the sins of their fathers, to the third or fourth generation of those who hate me, but showing grace to the   6
thousandth generation of those who love me and keep
my commands.

"You must not invoke the name of the Lord your God   7
to evil intent; for the Lord will not excuse anyone who
invokes his name to evil intent.

"Remember to keep the sabbath day holy. Six days   8
                                                                            9
you are to labor and do all your work, but on the seventh   10
day, a sabbath to the Lord your God, you must not do
any work at all, neither you, nor your son, nor your
daughter, nor your male or female slave, nor your cattle,
nor the alien in your employ residing in your community;
for in six days the Lord made the heavens, the earth, and   11
the sea, together with all that is in them, but rested on
the seventh day; that is how the Lord came to bless the
seventh day and to hallow it.

"Honor your father and mother, that you may live   12
long in the land that the Lord your God is giving you.

"You must not commit murder.   13

"You must not commit adultery.   14

"You must not steal.   15

"You must not bring a false charge against your   16
fellow.

"You must not **covet your neighbor's home**; you must   17

[204]

not covet your neighbor's wife, nor his male or female slave, nor his ox, nor his ass, nor anything at all that is your neighbor's."

THE BOOK OF THE COVENANT, 20:18—23:19

20 As the people all perceived the thunder and lightning, the blast of the trumpet, and the mountain smoking, the people became afraid, and fell back, standing off at a distance.

19 "If you yourself will speak to us," they said to Moses, "we will listen; but do not let God speak to us, lest we die."

20 "Fear not," said Moses to the people; "for it is only to test you that God has come, and in order that the fear of him may be present with you so that you may not sin."

21 The people, however, stood off at a distance, while Moses approached the dense darkness where God was.

22 Then the LORD said to Moses,

"Thus shall you say to the Israelites: 'You have seen for yourselves that I have talked with you out of the 23 heavens. Gods of silver, and gods of gold you must 24 not make for yourselves. You must construct an altar of earth for me, and sacrifice on it your burnt-offerings, your thank-offerings, your sheep, and your oxen; at every sanctuary where I record my name, I will come to you 25 and bless you. If, however, you construct an altar of stones for me, you must not build it of dressed stones; for if you were to use your tools on it, you would pollute it. 26 Further, you must never ascend my altar on steps, so that your nakedness may not be exposed on it.'

21 "The following are the ordinances which you are to lay before them:

2 "'When you buy a Hebrew slave, he is to work for you for six years, but in the seventh year he is to go free without paying anything. If he came in single, he shall 3 go out single; if he was married, his wife shall go out 4 with him. If his master gives him a wife, and she bears him sons or daughters, the wife with her children shall

belong to her master, while he shall go out alone. But   5
if the slave declares, "I am fond of my master, my wife,
and my children; I will not go free," his master shall   6
bring him up to God; he shall bring him up to the door or
the door-post, and his master shall pierce his ear with an
awl; he shall then be his slave permanently.

" 'If a man sells his daughter as a slave, she shall not   7
go free as the male slaves do. If she is displeasing to her   8
master, who acquired her for himself, he shall let her be
redeemed; he shall have no right to sell her to a foreign
people, since he has treated her unfairly. If he acquires   9
her for his son, he must treat her like a daughter. If he   10
marries another, he must not diminish her food, nor her
clothes, nor her conjugal rights; if he does not observe   11
these three duties to her, she shall go free without any
money payment whatsoever.

" 'Whoever strikes another, so that he dies, must be   12
put to death; if, however, he did not lie in wait for him,   13
but God let him fall into his hands, I will designate a
place for you to which he may flee. If a man wilfully   14
plans to murder another treacherously, even from my
altar you must take him, that he may be put to death.

" 'Whoever strikes his father or mother must be put   15
to death.

" 'Whoever kidnaps a man, and sells him, or if he is   16
found in his possession, must be put to death.

" 'Whoever reviles his father or mother must be put   17
to death.

" 'If men get into a quarrel, and one strikes the other   18
with a stone or with his fist, so that he does not die, but
is laid up in bed, if he gets up again, and can go out   19
walking on his staff, the one who struck him shall be let
off, except that he must pay for his loss of time, and
have him thoroughly restored to health.

" 'If a man strikes his male or female slave with a   20
stick, so that he dies under his hand, he must be avenged.
If, however, he survives a day or two, he is not to be   21
avenged; for he is his own property.

" 'If men get into a fight, and hurt a pregnant woman   22

so that she has a miscarriage, without further harm, he must pay such fine as the woman's husband imposes on

23 him, and so pay for the miscarriage; but if there is further

24 harm, you must give life for life, eye for eye, tooth for

25 tooth, hand for hand, foot for foot, burn for burn, wound for wound, lash for lash.

26 " 'If a man strikes the eye of his male or female slave, and destroys it, he must let him go free in compensation

27 for his eye; if he knocks out the tooth of his male or female slave, he must let him go free in compensation for his tooth.

28 " 'If an ox gores a man or a woman to death, the ox must be stoned to death, but its flesh is not to be eaten;

29 the owner of the ox is blameless. If, however, the ox has been in the habit of goring, and its owner has been warned, but still does not keep it in, and it kills a man or a woman, the ox must be stoned, and its owner must also

30 be put to death. If only a fine is imposed on him, he must pay in redemption of his life whatever amount is im-

31 posed on him. Whether it is a free man or a free woman that it gores, he is to be dealt with in accordance with

32 this same ordinance. If the ox gores a male or a female slave, he must pay their master thirty shekels of silver, and the ox must be stoned.

33 " 'If a man opens a cistern, or a if man digs a cistern

34 and does not cover it, and an ox or an ass falls into it, the owner of the cistern must make restitution by reimbursing its owner with money, but the carcass is to be his.

35 " 'If a man's ox hurt another's ox, so that it dies, they shall sell the live ox and divide its price between them,

36 and the dead animal as well. Or, if the ox is known to have been in the habit of goring, and its owner has not been keeping it in, he must make restitution with an ox for the ox, but the dead animal is to be his.

22 " 'If a man steals an ox or a sheep, and kills it or sells it, he must pay an indemnity of five oxen for the ox, and

3b four sheep for the sheep; he must surely make restitution; if he has nothing, he must be sold to pay for what he

4 stole. If the stolen animal is found alive in his pos-

session, whether it is an ox, an ass, or a sheep, he must make two-fold restitution.

" 'If the thief is caught in the act of breaking in, and is struck a fatal blow, there is no guilt of blood in his case; if the sun has risen on him, then there is guilt of blood.

" 'If a man in burning over a field or vineyard lets the fire spread so that it burns in another man's field, he must make restitution with the very best of his own field or vineyard. If fire breaks out and catches in a thorn-hedge, so that the shocks of grain or the standing grain or the field itself is consumed, he who lit the fire must make restitution.

" 'If a man gives money or other articles to another to keep, and it is stolen from the latter's house, if the thief is found, he must make two-fold restitution; if the thief is not found, the owner of the house must be brought into the presence of God to determine whether he himself has not laid hands on the other's property.

" 'In every case of dispute, whether it concerns ox, or ass, or sheep, or clothing, or any article at all that has disappeared, concerning which claim is made, "This is it," the case of both parties shall come before God; he whom God convicts must make two-fold restitution to the other.

" 'If a man gives an ass, or an ox, or a sheep, or any kind of animal to another to keep, and it dies, or is injured, or is taken as booty when no one was looking, there must be an oath by the Lord between the two of them as to whether one did not lay hands on the other's property; the owner must then accept it, and no restitution shall be made. But if it is really stolen from him, he must make restitution to its owner. If it is torn in pieces, let him bring it as evidence; he need not make good what has been torn.

" 'If a man borrows an animal from another, and it is injured or dies, its owner not being employed with it, he must make restitution; if the owner is employed with it,

15 he need not make restitution; if it was hired, the owner is to receive the price of its hire.

16   " 'If a man seduces a virgin who is not betrothed, and lies with her, he must pay the marriage-price for her, and

17 marry her; if her father absolutely refuses to give her to him, he must pay money equivalent to the marriage-price of virgins.

18   " 'You must not let a sorceress live.

19   " 'Whoever lies with an animal must be put to death.

20   " 'He who sacrifices to any god except the Lord alone must be destroyed.

21   " 'You must not ill-treat a resident alien, nor oppress him; for you were once resident aliens yourselves in the

22 land of Egypt. You must not wrong any widow or

23 orphan. If you ever wrong them and they cry aloud to

24 me, I will be sure to hear their cry, and my anger will blaze, and I will slay you with the sword; thus shall your own wives become widows and your children orphans.

25   " 'If you lend money to my people, to any poor person among you, you must not behave like a creditor toward

26 him; you must not charge him any interest. If you ever take another's cloak in pledge, you must return it to him

27 by sunset; for that is his only covering; it is his cloak for his body. What else could he sleep in? And if he should cry to me, I would respond; for I am kind.

28   " 'You must not revile God, nor curse a ruler of your people.

29   " 'You must not be dilatory with your offering, whether much or little. You must give me the first-born

30 of your sons; you must do the same with your oxen and your sheep; for seven days it may remain with its dam; on the eighth day you must give it to me.

31   " 'Since you are men sacred to me, you must not eat flesh that has been torn in the field; you must throw it to the dogs.

23   " 'You must not give false, hearsay evidence; do not join hands with a wicked person by being a malicious

2 witness. You must not follow the majority by doing wrong, nor give evidence in a suit so as to pervert justice,

by turning aside with the majority. Neither must you ₃
favor a poor man in his case.

 " 'If you come across your enemy's ox or ass going ₄
astray, you must be sure to take it home to him.

 " 'If you see the ass of one who hates you lying pros- ₅
trate under its load, you must refrain from deserting him;
you must be sure to help him get it up.

 " 'You must not pervert the justice due your poor in ₆
his case. Avoid false charges; do not have innocent and ₇
guiltless persons put to death, nor acquit the wicked. You ₈
must never take a bribe; for a bribe blinds the open-eye,
and subverts even a just case.

 " 'You must not oppress a resident alien, since you ₉
know the feelings of an alien; for you were once aliens
yourselves in the land of Egypt.

 " 'For six years you may sow your land and gather in ₁₀
its crops, but during the seventh year you must leave it ₁₁
alone and let it lie fallow, so that the poor of your people
may eat of it, and what they leave the wild animals may
eat. You must do the same with your vineyards and
olive groves.

 " 'Six days you are to do your work, but on the ₁₂
seventh day you must desist, in order that your ox and
ass may rest, and that your slave and the resident alien
may refresh themselves.

 " 'Give heed to all that I have told you; never mention ₁₃
the names of alien gods; do not let them be heard on your
lips.

 " 'Three times a year you are to hold a festival for me. ₁₄
You must keep the festival of unleavened cakes, eating ₁₅
unleavened cakes for seven days, as I commanded you, at
the appointed time, the new moon of Abib (for it was
then that you came out of Egypt); none may come to see
me empty-handed. There is also the harvest festival, ₁₆
that of the first-fruits of your labor, of what you sowed in
the field; and the festival of ingathering at the end of the
year, when you gather in the fruit of your labor from the
field. Three times a year all your males must appear be- ₁₇
fore the Lord GOD.

18   " 'You must not offer the blood of any sacrifice to me with leaven, nor may the fat of my festivals be left over night until morning.

19   " 'The very first of the first-fruits of your soil you must bring to the house of the LORD your God.

" 'You must not boil a kid in its mother's milk.' "

THE TABLES OF STONE, 34:1–28

34   The LORD said to Moses,

"Cut two stone tablets like the former ones, and I will write on the tablets the words that were on the former

2 tablets which you broke. Be ready by morning, and in the morning ascend Mount Sinai, and present yourself

3 there to me on the top of the mountain. No one is to ascend with you, nor is anyone to be seen anywhere on the mountain, nor must the flocks and herds graze in front of that mountain."

4   So Moses cut two stone tablets like the former ones, and rising early next morning, he ascended Mount Sinai, as the LORD had commanded him, taking the two stone

5 tablets in his hand. Then the LORD descended in a cloud, and took up a position with him there, while he called

6 upon the name of the LORD. The LORD passed in front of him, proclaiming,

"The LORD, the LORD, a God compassionate and gra-

7 cious, slow to anger, rich in grace and fidelity, showing grace to the thousandth generation, forgiving iniquity, transgression, and sin, without leaving it unpunished however, but avenging the iniquity of fathers upon their children and grandchildren down to the third or even the fourth generation."

8   Then Moses quickly bowed his head to the ground, and made obeisance.

9   "If I have really found favor with thee, O Lord," he said, "pray let the Lord go with us; for this is a stiff-necked people; but do thou pardon our iniquity and our sin, and make us thy very own."

10   So he said,

"I hereby make a covenant: before all your people I

will perform such wonders as have never occurred anywhere on the earth nor in any nation, so that all the people among whom you are living shall see that it is an awful deed that I, the Lord, am going to do along with you. Mark what I command you today. I am going to 11 drive the Amorites, Canaanites, Hittites, Perizzites, Hivvites, and Jebusites out of your way; so you must 12 take care not to make a covenant with the inhabitants of the land which you are about to enter, lest they become a snare among you; but you must tear down their altars, 13 smash their sacred pillars, and cut down their sacred poles (for you must not pay homage to any other god, 14 because the Lord, being jealous by nature, is a jealous God), lest in making a covenant with the inhabitants of 15 the land you run wantonly after their gods, sacrificing to their gods, and whenever anyone invites you, partaking of his sacrifice, and you marry your sons to their daugh- 16 ters, which daughters will run wantonly after their gods, and make your sons run wantonly after their gods.

"You must not make any molten gods for yourself. 17

"You must keep the festival of unleavened cakes, eat- 18 ing unleavened cakes for seven days, as I commanded you, at the appointed time, the new moon of Abib; for it was on the new moon of Abib that you came out of Egypt.

"Whatever first opens the womb belongs to me, in the 19 case of all your live stock that are male, the firstlings of oxen and sheep; a firstling ass, however, you may redeem 20 with a sheep, but if you do not redeem it, you must break its neck; any first-born son of yours you may redeem.

"None may come to see me empty-handed.

"Six days you are to labor, but on the seventh day you 21 must rest, resting at ploughing-time and at harvest.

"You must observe the festival of weeks, that of the 22 first-fruits of the wheat harvest, and also the festival of ingathering at the close of the year; three times a year 23 must all your males come to see the Lord God, the God of Israel. For I will drive nations out of your way, and 24 enlarge your territory; and no one shall covet your land

[212]

when you go up to see the LORD your God three times a year.

25 "You must not offer the blood of a sacrifice to me with leavened bread. The sacrifice of the passover festival must not be left over night until morning.

26 "The very first of the first-fruits of your land you must bring to the house of the LORD your God.

"You must not boil a kid in its mother's milk."

27 Then the LORD said to Moses,

"Write down these words; for it is on the basis of these words that I have made a covenant with you and Israel."

28 So he remained there with the LORD for forty days and nights, without eating bread or drinking water; and he wrote on the tablets the terms of the covenant, the decalogue.

THE BOOK OF LEVITICUS

The LORD said to Moses, **19**

"Speak to the whole Israelite community, and say to ₂ them, 'You must be holy; for I, the LORD your God, am holy. You must each revere his father and mother, and ₃ you must keep my sabbaths, since I, the LORD, am your God. Do not turn to unreal gods, nor make yourselves ₄ molten gods, since I, the LORD, am your God.

"'When you offer a thanksgiving sacrifice to the ₅ LORD, sacrificing it so as to make you acceptable, you ₆ must eat it on the day that you sacrifice it, or on the next day; any left over until the third day must be burned up. If it should ever be eaten on the third day, it would be ₇ mere refuse; it would not be acceptable; anyone eating ₈ it shall answer for his iniquity, because he has profaned what is sacred to the LORD; so that person shall be cut off from his people.

"'When you reap the harvest of your land, you must ₉ not reap your field to the very corners, nor gather the gleanings of your harvest; you must not glean your vine- ₁₀ yards bare, nor gather the fallen fruit of your vine- yard; you must leave them for the poor and the resident alien, since I, the LORD, am your God.

"'You must not steal, nor cheat, nor lie to one an- ₁₁ other. You must not take a false oath in my name, and so ₁₂ profane the name of your God, of me, the LORD.

"'You must not defraud your fellow, nor rob him; ₁₃ the wages of a hired laborer are not to remain all night with you until morning.

"'You must not curse a deaf person, nor place an ₁₄ obstacle in the way of a blind person; you must stand in awe of your God, of me, the LORD.

"'You must do no injustice in a case, neither showing ₁₅

[214]

partiality to the poor, nor deferring to the powerful, but judging your fellow fairly.

16   " 'You must not play the part of a talebearer against your people; you must not secure yourself by the life of another, since I am the LORD.

17   " 'You must not cherish hate against your fellow-countryman; you must be sure to reprove your fellow, but not incur sin because of him. You must not avenge 18 yourself, nor bear a grudge against the members of your own race, but you must love your fellow, since he is the same as yourself, for I am the LORD.

19   " 'You must keep my statutes; you must not let your cattle breed with a different species; you must not sow your field with two kinds of seed, nor put on a garment made of two kinds of material.

30   " 'You must keep my sabbaths, and stand in awe of my sanctuary, since I am the LORD.

31   " 'Do not turn to mediums or magicians; do not defile yourselves with them by consulting them, since I, the LORD, am your God.

32   " 'You must rise in the presence of the hoary-headed, and defer to the aged, and so stand in awe of your God, of me, the LORD.

33   " 'If a proselyte is residing with you in your land, you 34 must not mistreat him; you must treat the proselyte who resides with you like the native born among you, and love him as one of your own race, since I, the LORD, am your God; for you were once aliens yourselves in the land of Egypt.

35   " 'You must do no injustice in a case, with rule, or 36 weight, or measure; you must have just balances, just weights, a just ephah, and a just hin, since it was I, the LORD your God, who brought you out of the land of 37 Egypt. So you must be careful to observe all my statutes and ordinances, since I am the LORD.' "

THE BOOK OF NUMBERS

Then God came to Balaam in the night, and said to 22 him,

"If it is to summon you that the men have come, be off and go with them; but it is only the message that I give you that you are to give."

So, when Balaam rose next morning, he harnessed his 21 ass, and went off with the chieftains of Moab.

The anger of God blazed at his going, and the angel of 22 the LORD stationed himself on the road to obstruct him, as he rode on his ass, accompanied by his two slaves. When the ass saw the angel of the LORD standing on the 23 road with his drawn sword in his hand, the ass turned out of the road, and went into the fields; but Balaam struck the ass to turn her back into the road. Then the 24 angel of the LORD took his stand on a lane between vineyards, with a wall on either side; and when the ass saw 25 the angel of the LORD, she pressed herself against the wall, and crushed Balaam's foot against the wall, so that he struck her again. Then the angel of the LORD passed 26 on further, and took his stand at a narrow place where there was no room to turn either to the right or to the left; and when the ass saw the angel of the LORD, she lay 27 down under Balaam, so that Balaam's anger blazed, and he struck the ass with his staff. Then the LORD opened 28 the mouth of the ass, and she said to Balaam,

"What have I done to you that you should have struck me three times now?"

"Because you have made a toy of me," said Balaam to 29 the ass. "Would that there had been a sword in my hand, for then I would have killed you."

The ass said to Balaam, 30

"Am I not your own ass, upon which you have ridden

all your life long until this day? Have I ever been accustomed to deal thus with you?"

"No," he said.

31   Then the Lord opened Balaam's eyes completely, and he saw the angel of the Lord standing on the road, with his drawn sword in his hand, whereupon he bowed his head, and fell on his face.

32   "Why have you struck your ass these three times now?" the angel of the Lord said to him. "See, it was I who came forth to obstruct you; for your errand is displeasing

33 to me. The ass saw me, and swerved from me these three times; unless she had swerved from me, I would surely have slain you just now, but would have spared her."

34   "I have sinned," said Balaam to the angel of the Lord; "for I did not know that it was you who stationed yourself on the road against me. Now then, if it is displeasing to you, I will go back."

35   But the angel of the Lord said to Balaam,

"Go with the men; but it is only the message that I give you that you are to give."

24   Then Balak's anger blazed against Balaam, and he struck his fists together.

"It was to curse my enemies that I summoned you," said Balak to Balaam; "and here you have actually blessed them three times now. So then, hurry back to

11 your home! I intended to honor you greatly, but, as it is, the Lord has held you back from honor."

12   But Balaam said to Balak,

"Was it not indeed to the messengers whom you sent

13 to me that I said, 'If Balak were to give me his house full of silver and gold, I could not violate the instructions of the Lord to do either good or bad of my own accord'?

14 It is only what the Lord tells me that I can say. Now then, I leave at once for my own people; come, let me advise you what this people will do to your people in days to come."

15   Whereupon he gave utterance to his oracle, saying,

"The oracle of Balaam, the son of Beor,
    The oracle of the man who had evil designs,

The oracle of him who hears the words of God, 16
And is acquainted with the knowledge of the Most
  High,
Who has a vision of the Almighty,
Prostrate, but with eyes opened:
I see them, but not as they are now, 17
I behold them, but not as they are at present;
A star has come forth from Jacob,
A comet has risen from Israel,
He has shattered the temples of Moab,
And the skulls of all the sons of Seth;
Edom has become a possession, 18
Seir has become a possession;
Israel has performed valiantly,
Jacob has conquered his enemies, 19
And has exterminated any survivors from Ar."
Then he looked at Amalek, and gave utterance to his 20
oracle, saying,
    "The first of the nations was Amalek,
    But in the end he shall perish forever."
Then he looked at the Kenites, and gave utterance to 21
his oracle, saying,
    "Though your dwelling-place is enduring,
    And your nest set on a rock,
    Nevertheless it shall be annihilated, O Kain; 22
    How long will Ashur make captives of you?"
Then he gave utterance to his oracle, saying, 23
    "Alas, who can live longer than God has appointed
      him?
    Ships shall come from the coast of Kittim, 24
    They shall harass Ashur, they shall harass Eber,
    So that he in turn shall perish forever."
Then Balaam rose, and departing, returned home; 25
while Balak also went his way.

THE BOOK OF DEUTERONOMY

See pp. 55–60

THE BOOK OF JOSHUA

10 So the five Amorite kings, the king of Jerusalem, the king of Hebron, the king of Jarmuth, the king of Lachish, and the king of Eglon, mustered their forces, and coming up with all their armies, they invested

6 Gibeon, and attacked it. Then the Gibeonites sent this message to Joshua at the camp at Gilgal:

"Do not abandon your servants; come up quickly to our rescue, and help us; for all the Amorite kings inhabiting the highlands have gathered against us."

7 So Joshua went up from Gilgal, accompanied by all the warriors, as well as all the seasoned troops.

8 "Do not be afraid of them," the Lord said to Joshua; "for I am delivering them into your power; not one of them shall hold his own against you."

9 So Joshua made a surprise attack upon them, by march-
10 ing all night from Gilgal; and the Lord threw them into a panic before Israel, so that they inflicted great slaughter on them at Gibeon, and pursuing them in the direction of the slope of Beth-horon, they harried them all the way
11 to Azekah and Makkedah. After they had fled from the Israelites, while they were at the descent of Beth-horon, the Lord cast great stones from the sky upon them all the way to Azekah, so that they died, more dying from the hailstones than the Israelites slew with the sword.

12 It was on the day that the Lord put the Amorites at the mercy of the Israelites that Joshua spoke to the Lord, and in the presence of Israel said,

"O sun, stop at Gibeon;
And thou moon, at the valley of Aijalon!"

13 So the sun came to a stop, and the moon stood still, until the nation took vengeance on their foes. (Is this

not written in the Book of Jashar?) The sun stood still at the zenith, and delayed its setting for about a whole day. Never before or since has there been a day like that, when the LORD heeded the cry of a man; for the LORD fought for Israel. Then Joshua, accompanied by all Israel, returned to the camp at Gilgal.

THE BOOKS OF CHRONICLES, NEHE-
MIAH, AND EZRA

. . .

*Alexander's conquest of the east was not unwelcome
to the Jews, for it overthrew the empire of their old masters the Persians. They did not, of course, become inde-
pendent, but after Alexander's death in 323 B.C. they
found themselves subject to the Greek monarchs of Egypt.
In these times of national insignificance and humiliation the Jews found solace in reviewing the glories of the
past and magnifying the great days of old. The age of
the prophets was past. Jewish religion had become fundamentally priestly; the religious life of the nation now
centered in the priesthood and the temple worship, and
Jewish writers naturally viewed their whole national
past from a priestly and ritualistic point of view.*

*In such a spirit a Jewish chronicler soon after the
death of Alexander re-wrote the history of his people,
from the death of Saul seven hundred years earlier (ca.
1000 B.C.) to the work of Nehemiah and Ezra, 444–397
B.C. Most of this story had already been told in what
we know as II Samuel and I and II Kings. But those
narratives were now freely supplemented and exagger-
ated. The colors of the earlier narratives are deepened,
the glories of the past are heightened, and the whole is
viewed in the light of the priestly legislation, which had
now come to dominate Jewish life. Thus the Jewish
mind, at this low ebb in the national fortunes, finds
satisfaction in repainting the splendors of its distant*

past, and glorifying and magnifying its heroic periods. The book is an imaginative priestly recast of Jewish history, prefaced with genealogical lists, chapters 1–9, and has been termed an ecclesiastical chronicle of Jerusalem.

The work was later divided into the four books known to us as I and II Chronicles, Ezra, and Nehemiah. But modern study has shown that Nehemiah's work, which began in 444 B.C., preceded that of Ezra, which cannot have been earlier than 397 B.C.

. . .

THE BOOK OF NEHEMIAH
NEHEMIAH SENT TO JERUSALEM AS ROYAL COMMISSIONER, 2:1–10

Now I was cupbearer to the king. Accordingly it was 2 in the month Nisan in the twentieth year of Artaxerxes, the king, when the wine was served, that I took up the wine and gave it to the king. And I had not formerly been sad. Therefore the king said to me, 2

"Why is your countenance sad, since you are not ill? This is nothing else but sorrow of heart."

Then I was exceedingly frightened, and I said to the 3 king,

"Let the king live forever: Why should not my countenance be sad, when the city, the place of my fathers' sepulchre is desolate, and its gates have been destroyed by fire."

Thereupon the king said to me, 4

"For what then do you make request?"

So I prayed to the God of the heavens. And I said to 5 the king,

"If it please the king, and if your servant is acceptable in your sight, that you would send me to Judah to the city of my fathers' sepulchres, that I may rebuild it."

Then the king said to me, the queen also being seated 6 beside him,

"For how long will your journey be? And when will you return?"

7 However it pleased the king to let me go; for I proposed to him a time limit. Moreover I said to the king, "If it please the king, let letters be given me to the governors of the provinces beyond the River, that they

8 may let me pass through until I come to Judah, and a letter to Asaph, the keeper of the king's park, that he may give me timber to furnish the beams for the gates of the citadel, which belongs to the temple, and for the walls of the city, and for the house that I shall enter."

And the king granted my request, according to the good hand of my God that was upon me.

9 Then I came to the governors of the provinces beyond the River, and gave them the king's letters. Moreover the king had sent with me army officers and horsemen.

10 But when Sanballat the Horonite and Tobiah the Ammonite slave heard of it, it caused them great irritation that a man had come to seek the welfare of the Israelites.

NEHEMIAH BEGINS REBUILDING THE CITY WALLS, 2:11-20

2 So I came to Jerusalem and was there three days. Then I arose in the night, I and a few men with me, and I told no man what my God had put in my heart to do for Jerusalem, neither was there any beast with me except the

13 beast on which I rode. Accordingly I went out by night through the Valley Gate, even toward the Serpent's Well and to the Refuse Gate, and I examined in detail the walls of Jerusalem, which were broken down, and its

14 gates destroyed by fire. So I passed on to the Fountain Gate and to the King's Pool, but there was no place for

15 the beast that was under me to pass. Then I went on up in the night by the valley carefully examining the wall, whereupon I turned back and entered by the Valley Gate

16 and so returned. And the rulers did not know whither I had gone or what I had been doing, neither had I as yet told it to the Jews nor to the priests nor to the nobles, nor to the rulers nor to the rest who did the work.

17 Then I said to them,

"You see the serious condition in which we are, how Jerusalem is desolate and its gates are destroyed by fire. Come and let us rebuild the wall of Jerusalem, that we be no longer an object of reproach."

Then I told them of the good hand of my God that was 18 with me, and also of the king's words that he said to me. Thereupon they said,

"Let us arise and build."

So they took courage for the good work. But when 19 Sanballat the Horonite, and Tobiah the Ammonite slave, and Geshem the Arabian heard it they derided and despised us, and said,

"What is this thing that you are doing? Are you about to rebel against the king?"

Then I answered and said to them, 20

"The God of the heavens, he will prosper us, therefore we his servants will arise and build; but you have no portion nor right nor memorial in Jerusalem."

NEHEMIAH'S REFORM MEASURES, 13:1–3, 15–31

On that day they read in the book of Moses in the 13 hearing of the people, and it was found written therein that no Ammonite or Moabite should ever enter into the assembly of God; for they did not meet the Israelites with 2 bread and water, but hired Balaam against them to curse them; but our God turned the curse into a blessing. Accordingly when they heard the law they separated from 3 Israel all the mixed multitude.

In these days I saw in Judah men treading wine presses 15 on the sabbath and bringing in heaps of grain loaded on asses, also wine, grapes, figs, and all kinds of burdens which they brought into Jerusalem on the sabbath day; and I protested on the day when they sold provisions. Tyrians also dwelt therein, who brought in fish and all 16 kinds of wares, and sold them on the sabbath to the Judeans and in Jerusalem. Then I contended with the no- 17 bles of Judah and said to them,

"What evil thing is this that you are doing, and thereby profaning the sabbath day? Did not your fathers do 18 this and did not our God bring all this misfortune upon us and upon this city? Yet you are bringing more wrath upon Israel by profaning the sabbath.''

19 Accordingly when the gates of Jerusalem began to be in darkness, before the sabbath, I commanded and the gates were shut; and I gave orders that they should not be opened until after the sabbath. And I put some of my servants in charge of the gates, that none should bring in
20 a burden on the sabbath day. So the traders and sellers of all kinds of wares lodged outside Jerusalem once or twice.
21 Then I warned them and said to them,

"Why do you lodge before the wall? If you repeat it, I shall arrest you.''

22 From that time on they came no more on the sabbath. Moreover I gave orders to the Levites that they should purify themselves and that they should come and guard the gates, to keep the sabbath day holy. Remember, O my God, this also to my account and have compassion upon me according to the greatness of thy grace.
23 In those days also I saw the Jews who had married
24 women of Ashdod, of Ammon, and of Moab, and their children spoke half in the language of Ashdod, and none of them could speak in the Jews' language, but according
25 to the language of each people. Therefore I contended with them and cursed them and beat some of them and pulled out their hair and made them swear by God, saying,

"You shall not give your daughters to their sons nor take their daughters as wives for your sons or for your-
26 selves. Did not Solomon, king of Israel, sin by these means? Yet among many nations there was no king like him, and he was beloved by his God, and God made him king over all Israel; nevertheless foreign wives were the
27 cause of his sin; and shall it be reported of you that you do all this great evil, and break faith with our God in marrying foreign women?''
28 Now one of the sons of Joiada, the son of Eliashib, the high priest, was the son-in-law of Sanballat, the Horon-
29 ite; therefore I chased him from me. Remember them, O

my God, because they have defiled the priesthood and the covenant of the priesthood and of the Levites. Thus I 30 cleansed them from all foreigners and established the duties for the priests and the Levites, each for his own task, and for the wood-offering at appointed times, and 31 the firstfruits. Remember it, O my God, to my credit.

THE BOOK OF EZRA

. . .

THE RENEWAL OF WORSHIP AT JERUSALEM, 3:1-6

3 Now when the seventh month arrived, and the Israelites were in their cities, the people gathered themselves
2 together as one man to Jerusalem. Then Jeshua, the son of Jozadak, and his kinsmen the priests, and Zerubbabel, the son of Shealtiel, and his kinsmen arose and built the altar of the God of Israel to offer burnt-offerings on it, as
3 prescribed in the law of Moses, the man of God. So they set up the altar in its place, for fear was upon them, because of the peoples of the lands, and they offered upon it burnt-offerings to the LORD, even burnt-offerings morn-
4 ing and evening. Moreover they kept the feast of booths as it is written and offered the fixed number of burnt-offerings day by day according to the direction for each
5 day; and afterward the continual burnt-offerings and the offerings at the new moons, and of all the sacred festivals of the LORD, that were consecrated, and for everyone
6 who offered a voluntary offering to the LORD. From the first day of the seventh month they began to offer burnt-offerings to the LORD; although the foundation of the temple of the LORD was not yet laid.

THE FOUNDATION OF THE TEMPLE LAID, 3:7-13

3 But they gave money to the masons and to the carpenters, and food, and drink, and oil to the Sidonians and the Tyrians to bring cedar trees from Lebanon by sea to Joppa, according to the grant that they had from Cyrus, king of Persia.
8 Now in the second year of their coming to the house of God at Jerusalem, in the second month, Zerubbabel, the son of Shealtiel, and Jeshua, the son of Jozadak, and the rest of their kinsmen the priests and the Levites, and all

who came from the captivity of Jerusalem, made a beginning and appointed the Levites from twenty years old and upward to have the oversight of the work of the house of the LORD. Then Jeshua stood up with his sons 9 and his kinsmen, Kadmiel and his sons, Judeans, to have together the direction over the execution of the work in the house of God; the sons of Henadad, with their sons and their kinsmen the Levites. Now when the builders 10 had laid the foundation of the temple of the LORD, they stationed the priests in their official robes with trumpets and the Levites, the sons of Asaph, with cymbals to praise the LORD according to the directions of David, king of Israel. And they sang responsively in praising and 11 giving thanks to the LORD, saying,

"For he is good, for his grace is forever over Israel."

And all the people raised a great shout when they praised the LORD because the foundation of the house of the LORD had been laid. But many of the priests and the 12 Levites and heads of families and the old men, who had seen the first house, when the foundation of this house was laid before their eyes, wept with a loud voice, while many shouted aloud for joy, so that the people could not 13 distinguish the sound of the shout of joy from the sound of weeping of the people, for the people shouted with a great shout, and the sound was heard a great distance away.

THE TEMPLE REBUILT AND DEDICATED, 5:1–2; 6:16–22

Now the prophets Haggai and Zechariah, the son of 5 Iddo, prophesied to the Jews who were in Judah and Jerusalen, in the name of the God of Israel who was over them. Then Zerubbabel, the son of Shealtiel, and Jeshua, 2 the son of Jozadak, arose and began to build the house which is at Jerusalem; and with them were the prophets of God supporting them.

Then the Israelites, the priests, the Levites, and the 6 rest of the returned exiles, celebrated the dedication of this house of God with joy. Moreover they offered at the 17 dedication of this house of God a hundred bulls, two hun-

dred rams, four hundred lambs, and twelve he-goats for
a sin-offering for all Israel, according to the number of
the tribes of Israel. They also set the priests in their divi- 18
sions and the Levites in their courses, for the service of
God at Jerusalem, as it is prescribed in the book of Moses.

Moreover the returned exiles kept the passover upon 19
the fourteenth day of the first month. For the priests and 20
the Levites had purified themselves to a man, all of them
were ceremonially clean. And they slaughtered the passover for all the returned exiles, both for their kinsmen
the priests and for themselves. Then the Israelites who 21
had returned from the captivity, and everyone who separated himself from the uncleanness of the peoples of the
land to join them in order to seek the LORD, the God of
Israel, ate, and kept the feast of unleavened bread seven 22
days with gladness; for the LORD had made them joyful,
and had turned the heart of the king of Persia to them, to
strengthen their hands in the work of the house of God,
the God of Israel.

THE BOOK OF JONAH

. . .

The Book of Jonah is a prophetic message in the form of a story. Jonah is not its author but its hero. It was told at a time when the Jews were for the most part intensely narrow-minded and self-centered. But there was an element of the Jewish people that thought of their God as God of the Universe and lover of all mankind, and this is the view of him embodied in the book. It is not a piece of history but of religious fiction, and it constitutes the first real missionary document in religious literature. The story was written probably some time in the third century before Christ. The unknown prophet who wrote it had grasped something of the wideness of God's mercy. He realized that the love of God is broader than the measure of man's mind, and he cast his message in forms of such vividness and power that his little story is among the masterpieces of the world.

. . .

THE GREAT REFUSAL, 1:1-16

The word of the LORD came to Jonah, the son of 1
Amittai, as follows:

"Arise, go to Nineveh, that great city, and preach 2
against it; for their wickedness has come up before me."

Then Jonah arose to flee to Tarshish, from the presence 3
of the LORD. So he went down to Joppa, where he found
a ship, bound for Tarshish. He paid his fare, and went
aboard, to go with them to Tarshish, from the presence
of the LORD.

But the LORD hurled a great wind upon the sea, so that 4

5 there was a great storm on the sea; and it was thought that the ship would be broken up. Then the sailors were frightened, and they cried each one to his god; and they threw overboard the stuff that was in the ship, in order to lighten her.

6 But Jonah had gone down into the hold of the ship, and was lying fast asleep. So the captain approached him, and said to him,

"Why are you sleeping? Get up; call upon your god. Perhaps that god will bethink himself of us, that we perish not."

7 Then they said, one to another,

"Come, let us cast lots, that we may know upon whose account this disaster has befallen us."

8 So they cast lots; and the lot fell upon Jonah. Then they said to him,

"Tell us, now, for what reason this disaster has befallen us. What is your business? Whence do you come? What is your country? And from what people are you?"

9 So he said to them,

"I am a Hebrew; and I stand in awe of the Lord, the God of the heavens, who made both the sea and the dry land."

10 Then the men were exceedingly terrified, and said to him,

"What a wicked thing you have done!"

For the men knew that he was fleeing from the pres-
11 ence of the Lord; because he had told them. Whereupon, they said to him,

"What shall we do with you, that the sea may become calm for us?"

12 For the sea was running higher and higher. Then he said to them,

"Pick me up, and cast me into the sea, so that the sea may be calm for you; for I know that this great storm is upon you because of me."

13 But the men rowed hard to bring the ship back to the dry land, yet could not; for the sea was running higher

and higher against them. Wherefore, they cried unto the 14
Lord, saying,

"O Lord, we beseech thee, let us not perish for this
man's life; and lay not up against us innocent blood; for
thou, O Lord, dost do as thou dost please."

Then they picked up Jonah and threw him overboard; 15
and the sea ceased from its raging.

Thereupon the men feared the Lord profoundly; and 16
they sacrificed to the Lord and made vows.

JONAH'S REPENTANCE, 1:17—2:10

Now, the Lord had assigned a great fish to swallow 17
up Jonah; and Jonah was in the belly of the fish three 2
days and three nights. Then Jonah prayed to the Lord, 2
his God, from the belly of the fish, saying,

"Out of my trouble I called unto the Lord, and he
    answered me.
From the heart of Sheol I called for help; thou didst
    hear my voice.
For thou hadst cast me into the depths, into the 3
    heart of the sea,
And a flood encompassed me.
All thy breakers and thy waves passed over me.
And I said, 'I am cast out of thy sight; 4
How shall I ever again look upon thy holy temple?'
The waters closed in over my life; the deep sur- 5
    rounded me.
Sea-weed was wound around my head.
To the roots of the hills I went down. 6
The earth with its bars was against me forever.
But thou didst bring up my life from the pit, O
    Lord, my God!
When I was losing consciousness, I remembered the 7
    Lord;
And my prayer unto thee entered thy holy temple.
Those who heed false futilities forsake their piety, 8
But I will sacrifice to thee with the voice of thanks- 9
    giving.
What I have vowed, I will pay.

[232]

Deliverance belongs to the LORD."

10   Then the LORD commanded the fish, and it vomited Jonah forth upon the dry land.

JONAH'S MISSION AND ITS RESULT, 3:1–10

3   Then the word of the LORD came to Jonah a second time, as follows:

2   "Arise, go to Nineveh, that great city, and proclaim unto it the proclamation which I shall tell you."

3   So Jonah arose, and went to Nineveh, as the LORD had said. Now Nineveh was an exceedingly great city, the

4 walk through it requiring three days. And Jonah had gone a day's journey into the city, when he made proclamation, saying,

"Yet forty days, and Nineveh shall be overthrown."

5   Whereupon the men of Nineveh believed God, and proclaimed a fast, and clothed themselves in sackcloth,

6 from the greatest unto the least of them. When the thing reached the King of Nineveh, he rose from his throne, put off his robe, put on sackcloth, and sat upon the ash

7 heap. He also sent messengers through Nineveh, saying, "By decree of the king and his nobles, namely, let neither man nor beast, cattle nor sheep, taste a thing; let

8 them not feed, and let them not drink water. But let them put on sackcloth, both man and beast, and let them call aloud unto God; and let each one turn from his wicked

9 way, and from whatsoever violence he has in hand. Who knows but that God will turn and relent, turning from his fierce anger, so that we perish not."

10   Then God saw their actions, that they had turned from their wicked way. So God relented of the evil which he had said he would do unto them, and he did it not.

JONAH REBUKED, 4:1–11

4   But Jonah was greatly displeased and very angry. So he prayed to the LORD, saying,

"O LORD, is not this what I said while I was still upon my own soil? Therefore, I hastened to flee to Tarshish. For I knew that thou wast a gracious God,

and merciful, slow to anger, and abounding in grace, and
relenting of evil. Now, therefore, O LORD, take my life,   3
I pray thee, from me. For I am better off dead, than
alive!"

Then the LORD said,   4
"Are you so very angry?"

Then Jonah went forth from the city, and sat down to   5
the east of the city; and he made a booth for himself
there, and sat under it in the shade, until he should see
what would happen in the city. So the LORD, God, gave   6
orders to a gourd, and it grew up above Jonah so as to be
a shade over his head, to save him from his discomfort;
and Jonah was very glad over the gourd. Then God   7
ordered a worm, when the dawn came up on the morrow,
to smite the gourd, so that it wilted. And when the sun   8
arose, God ordered a burning east wind; and the sun
smote down upon Jonah's head so that he fainted, and
asked that he might die, and said,
"I am better off dead than alive!"

Then God said to Jonah,   9
"Are you so very angry over the gourd?"

And he replied,
"I am angry enough to die!"

Then the LORD said,   10
"You have had pity on the gourd, for which you did
not toil; nor did you raise it; which grew in a night, and
perished in a night! And should not I, indeed, have pity   11
on Nineveh, that great city, wherein are more than a
hundred and twenty thousand infants, that cannot distinguish between their right hand and their left, and
much cattle?"

THE BOOK OF PROVERBS

. . .

A proverb may be described as a social axiom. The first proverbs embodied obvious practical truths about morals and conduct. This kind of homely wisdom probably existed among the Hebrews from the beginning, but the cultivation of it as something like a fine art came to be the work of the Wise—the Sages of Israel, who in time came to rank almost with the prophets and the priests as guides of the nation's life. These practical philosophers cast in crisp, engaging forms the national ideals of behavior, and these were gradually gathered into groups. The Book of Proverbs contains two principal collections of this kind, 10:1—22:16 and chapters 25–29. But the oldest part of the book, 22:17—24:22, is based upon an Egyptian work, the Wisdom of Amen-em-ope, from which many of its proverbs are taken almost word for word. The Jews probably became acquainted with it in the time of Jeremiah or soon after, when some of them took refuge in Egypt.

Solomon had come to be regarded as the Sage among the ancients, and most proverbs were credited to him, very much as most psalms were ascribed to David; indeed, he was said to have uttered three thousand proverbs, I Kings 4:32. But the Proverbs were the work of many minds and periods. Our present book is evidently a collection of collections, and reached its present proportions probably not long after 300 B.C., for it belongs to the later stage of Hebrew literature.

*Most proverbs are brief, but the Sages sometimes de-
veloped single themes into little poems of a dozen or
twenty lines. The description of the Ideal Wife, Proverbs, chapter 31, is an acrostic, like some of the psalms,
the lines beginning with the successive letters of the Hebrew alphabet. Erasmus' "Adages" and "Poor Rich-
ard's Almanac" illustrate the popularity of proverbs in
more recent times. But the Hebrew proverbs, in particular chapters 1–9, along with their shrewd worldly wisdom are deeply tinged with religious faith.*

· · ·

THE APPEAL OF WISDOM, 1:20-33

Wisdom cries aloud in the streets,   1
She lifts up her voice in the squares;
At the head of noisy thoroughfares she calls,   21
At the openings of the city gates she utters her
   words:
"How long, you simple ones, will you love simplic-   22
   ity,
And scoffers delight in scoffing,
And fools hate knowledge?
If you but turn and pay heed to my admonition,   23
Lo! I will open my mind to you,
I will acquaint you with my thoughts:
Because I called and you refused to listen,   24
I stretched out my hand and no one paid heed;
You ignored all my counsel,   25
And would not have my admonition—
I in my turn will laugh in the hour of your doom,   26
I will mock when your terror comes;
When your terror comes like a storm,   27
And your doom descends like a whirlwind,
When distress and anguish befall you.
Then they may call me, but I will not answer;   28
They may seek me, but they shall not find me.
Because they hated knowledge,   29

[236]

And chose not reverence for the LORD;
30   They would not have my counsel,
   They spurned all my admonition—
31   Now shall they eat of the fruit of their conduct,
   And shall have their fill of what they purposed.
32   For the waywardness of the simple shall slay them,
   And the complacency of fools shall destroy them;
33   While he who listens to me shall live in security,
   And shall enjoy peace of mind unruffled by dread of
      evil."

PROVERBS OF SOLOMON, 14:34—15:4, 15–17

14   Righteousness exalts a nation;
   But sin is a people's ruin.

35   A capable servant will enjoy the king's favor,
   But a worthless one will incur his wrath.

15   A gentle answer turns away wrath;
   But harsh words stir up anger.

2   The tongue of the wise drops knowledge;
   But the mouth of fools pours out folly.

3   The eyes of the LORD are in every place,
   Keeping watch on the bad and the good.

4   A soothing tongue is a tree of life;
   But wild words break the spirit.

15   For the miserable man every day is unhappy;
   But the cheerful man enjoys a continual feast.

16   Better a little, with reverence for the LORD,
   Than much treasure, and anxiety with it.

17   Better a dish of herbs, where love is,
   Than a fatted ox, and hatred with it.

WORDS OF THE WISE, 23:29–35

23   Who have woe? who have pain?
   Who have strifes? who complaints?

Who have wounds without cause?
Who have redness of eyes?
Those who stay long over wine, 30
Who go often to test the mixture!
Look not on wine when it is red, 31
When it sparkles in the cup.
It may go down smoothly;
But at the end it bites like a serpent, 32
And stings like an adder.
You will see strange sights, 33
And will utter weird words;
You will be like a man asleep at sea, 34
Asleep in the midst of a violent storm.
"They may strike me, but I feel no pain; 35
They may beat me, but I know it not.
When shall I awake from my wine,
That I may seek it again?"

THE GOOD WIFE, 31:10-31

If one can find a good wife, 31
She is worth far more than corals.

Her husband puts his trust in her, 11
And finds no lack of gain.

She brings him good, and not harm, 12
All the days of his life.

She sorts out wool and flax, 13
And works it up as she wills.

She is like the ships of the merchant— 14
She brings her food from afar.

She rises while yet it is night, 15
And gives her household food,
With a portion for her maidens.

She examines a field, and buys it— 16
With her earnings she plants a vineyard.

17   She girds her loins with strength,
      And she braces her arms.

18   She perceives that her work is profitable,
      So her lamp goes not out at night.

19   She lays her hand on the distaff,
      Her fingers grasp the spindle.

20   She stretches her hand to the poor,
      She extends her arms to the needy.

21   She is not afraid of the snow for her household,
      For her household are all clothed in doublets.

22   She makes coverlets for herself,
      Her clothing is linen and purple.

23   Her husband is known at the gates,
      As he sits among the elders of the land.

24   She makes linen vests, and sells them,
      She supplies the merchants with girdles.

25   She is clothed with strength and dignity,
      And she laughs at the days to come.

26   She opens her mouth in wisdom,
      And kindly counsel is on her tongue.

27   She looks well after her household,
      And eats not the bread of idleness.

28   Her children rise up, and bless her—
      Her husband also, and praises her:

29   "Many women have done well,
      But you have excelled them all."

30   Charms are deceptive, and beauty is a breath;
      But a woman who reveres the Lord—she will be
          praised.

31   Give her the due reward of her work;
      And let her deeds bring her praise at the gates.

[239]

THE BOOK OF DANIEL
. . .

*Alexander the Great was a great apostle of Greek
speech and culture, and the men who inherited his empire in Egypt and Syria carried on his efforts to spread
Greek civilization among their subjects. The pious Jews
of Palestine steadily resisted such efforts to hellenize
them, and toward the middle of the second century before
Christ especial efforts to impose Greek practices upon
them were made by Antiochus Epiphanes, the king of
Syria, to whom they were then subject. The Jews were in-
furiated by the attack upon their cultus and ideals and
a rebellion broke out under the leadership of Mattathias
and his warlike son Judas Maccabaeus. But it had little prospect of success and the struggle seemed hopeless.*

*But the heroes of the Hebrews had gone through greater
trials than these and come out of them triumphant, and
to remind the Jewish rebels of this the Book of Daniel
was written. It is Antiochus who is referred to as a little horn in 8:9 and as a contemptible person in 11:21.
The revolt was successful, and Jewish independence was
reestablished in Judea in 165 B.C.*

*The Book of Daniel is the climax of that form of Jew-
ish literature called apocalyptic, which put the message
intended for its own day into the mouth of some heroic
figure of the past, and employed the Babylonian symbolism of beasts and monsters to represent kings and empires, thus stimulating its Jewish readers to find the
great messages of comfort and courage that lay hidden in*

*its mysteries, while at the same time effectually conceal-
ing them from gentile persecutors. Egyptian literature
had also developed the apocalypse, so that both Babylonian and Egyptian influences lie back of the literary
form of Daniel.*

*The book is written partly in Hebrew and partly in
Aramaic (2:4—7:28). It is clear that when it was composed Aramaic had begun to displace Hebrew.*

*It is perhaps an open question whether or not some of
the material in the first half of Daniel was written at an
earlier time than the Maccabean period. But the book as
a whole in its present form is clearly a product of the
Maccabean age, and its stories did much to brace the
courage of the Jews in that struggle, enabling them to
face a most serious situation with unshrinking faith.*

. . .

NEBUCHADNEZZAR'S DREAM, 2:1-49

2   In the second year of the reign of Nebuchadnezzar,
Nebuchadnezzar dreamed a dream; and his spirit was dis-
2 turbed, and his sleep left him. Then the king gave orders
to summon the magicians, the enchanters, the sorcerers,
and the Chaldeans, that they might tell the king his
3 dream. So they came and stood before the king. And the
king said to them,

"I have dreamed a dream; and my spirit is disturbed,
till I know the dream."

4   Then the Chaldeans spoke to the king in Aramaic,

"O king, live forever! Tell your servants the dream,
and we will give the interpretation."

5   The king answered the Chaldeans, saying,

"I am fully resolved that, if you do not make known to
me the dream and its interpretation, you shall be hewn
limb from limb, and your houses shall be made a dung-
6 hill. But if you tell me the dream and its interpretation,

[241]

you shall receive from me gifts and rewards and great
honor. So tell me the dream and its interpretation."

A second time they answered, saying,   7
"Let the king tell his servants the dream, and we will
give the interpretation."

The king answered, saying,   8
"I know quite well that you are trying to gain time,
because you see how fully resolved I am that, if you do   9
not make known to me the dream, there is but one fate
for you; and you have conspired together to speak false
and deceitful words to me, hoping that a change may
come. So tell me the dream, and I shall know that you
can give me its interpretation."

The Chaldeans answered the king, saying,   10
"There is not a man on the earth who can tell the king
what he asks; for no king, however great and mighty,
has asked such a thing of any magician, enchanter, or
Chaldean. The king is asking a hard thing, and none can   11
tell the king what he asks, except the gods whose dwelling is not with mortal flesh."

At this answer the king became so angry and so very   12
furious that he gave orders to destroy all the wise men of
Babylon. So the decree went forth that the wise men   13
were to be slain; and Daniel and his companions would
have been slain.

Then Daniel made a wise and tactful answer to Arioch,   14
the captain of the king's guard, who had gone to slay the
wise men of Babylon; he answered Arioch, the king's   15
captain, saying,
"Why is the king's decree so harsh?"

When Arioch had explained the matter to Daniel,   16
Daniel went in, and asked the king to grant him time,
and he would give the king the interpreation. Then   17
Daniel went home, and explained the matter to his companions, Hananiah, Mishael, and Azariah, in order that   18
they might ask mercy of the God of the heavens concerning this secret, and so Daniel and his companions might
not perish with the rest of the wise men of Babylon.
Then the secret was revealed to Daniel in a vision of the 19

night. Then Daniel blessed the God of the heavens.
20 Daniel spoke, saying,

"Blessed be the name of God from everlasting to everlasting,
For wisdom and might are his!

21 He changes the seasons and times,
He removes kings, and he sets up kings;
He gives wisdom to the wise,
And knowledge to those who are endowed with
understanding.

22 He reveals things deep and secret,
He knows what is in the darkness,
And with him dwells the light.

23 I thank thee, and praise thee, O God of my fathers,
Who hast given me wisdom and might,
And hast now made known to me what we asked
of thee,
For thou hast made known to me the concern of the
king."

24 So Daniel went to Arioch, whom the king had appointed to destroy the wise men of Babylon; he went and
spoke to him as follows,

"Do not destroy the wise men of Babylon; bring me
before the king, that I may give the king the interpretation."

25 Then Arioch brought Daniel before the king in haste,
and spoke to him as follows,

"I have found a man, among the exiles of Judah, who
can make known the interpretation to the king."

26 The king spoke to Daniel, whose name was Belteshazzar, saying,

"Are you able to make known to me the dream that I
have seen, and its interpretation?"

27 Daniel answered the king, saying,

"No wise men, enchanters, magicians, or astrologers
are able to tell the king the secret which the king has
28 asked; but there is a GOD in the heavens who reveals
secrets, and he makes known to King Nebuchadnezzar

what shall be in the end of the days. Your dream, and the
visions of your head on your bed, were as follows:

"You, O king, lay in bed, wondering what should be 29
in the future; and he who reveals secrets makes known to
you what shall be. As for myself, this secret has not been 30
revealed to me by virtue of any wisdom that I possess
more than any other living man, but in order that the
interpretation may be made known to the king, and that
you may understand the thoughts of your mind.

"You, O king, looked, and lo! there was a great 31
image. This image, which was of vast size and surpassing
brightness, stood before you; and its appearance was
terrible. As for that image, its head was of fine gold, its 32
breast and arms were of silver, its belly and thighs of
bronze, its legs of iron, its feet partly of iron, and partly
of clay. You looked till you saw a stone hewn from a 33
mountain without hands, which smote the image on its 34
feet of iron and clay, breaking them in pieces. Then the 35
iron, the clay, the bronze, the silver, and the gold were
broken in pieces together, and became like chaff from
summer threshing-floors, and were carried away by the
wind, so that no trace of them could be found; while the
stone that smote the image became a great mountain,
filling all the earth. This was the dream, and we will 36
tell the king the interpretation of it.

"You, O king, the king of kings, to whom the God 37
of the heavens has given the kingdom, the power, the
strength, and the glory, and into whose hand he has put 38
the children of men, the beasts of the field, and the birds
of the air, wheresoever they dwell, making you rule over
them all—you are the head of gold. After you shall arise 39
another kingdom, inferior to you; then a third kingdom,
of bronze, which shall rule over all the earth. And the 40
fourth kingdom shall be strong as iron; for as iron breaks
in pieces and beats down all things, and as iron crushes
all things, so shall it break in pieces and crush. And as
you saw the feet and toes partly of potter's clay, and partly 41
of iron, it shall be a divided kingdom: there shall be
something of the firmness of iron in it, as you saw iron

42 mixed with muddy clay; but as the toes of the feet were partly iron, and partly clay, the kingdom shall be partly
43 strong, and partly brittle. As you saw iron mixed with muddy clay, they shall mix together in marriage; but they
44 shall not hold together, as iron does not mix with clay. In the days of those kings the God of the heavens shall set up a kingdom which shall never be destroyed, nor shall the kingdom be left to another people; it shall break in pieces and annihilate all these kingdoms, but it shall
45 stand forever, as you saw how a stone was hewn from a mountain without hands, which broke in pieces the iron, the bronze, the clay, the silver, and the gold. A great God makes known to the king what shall be in the future; the dream is certain, and its interpretation sure."
46 Then King Nebuchadnezzar fell upon his face, and prostrated himself before Daniel, and commanded sacri-
47 fice and sweet odors to be offered to him. And the king spoke to Daniel, saying,

"Truly, your God is the God of gods, and the Lord of kings; and he is a revealer of secrets, inasmuch as you have been able to reveal this secret."
48 Then the king promoted Daniel, and gave him many great gifts; he made him ruler over the whole province of Babylon, and chief prefect over all the wise men of
49 Babylon. At Daniel's request, the king appointed Shadrach, Meshach, and Abednego in charge of the affairs of the province of Babylon; but Daniel remained at the gate of the king.

THE FURNACE OF FIRE, 3:1–30

3   King Nebuchadnezzar made an image of gold, sixty cubits in height, and six cubits in breadth, which he set up on the plain of Dura, in the province of Babylon.
2 Then King Nebuchadnezzar sent to assemble the satraps, the prefects, the governors, the councillors, the treasurers, the judges, the justices, and all the officials of the provinces, to come to the dedication of the image which
3 King Nebuchadnezzar had set up. And when the satraps, the prefects, the governors, the councillors, the treas-

urers, the judges, the justices, and all the officials of the provinces were assembled for the dedication of the image which King Nebuchadnezzar had set up, the herald called aloud, 4

"To you is given a command, O peoples, nations, and 5 tongues, that as soon as you hear the sound of the horn, the pipe, the lyre, the trigon, the harp, the bagpipe, and every other kind of musical instrument, you shall fall down and prostrate yourselves before the image of gold which King Nebuchadnezzar has set up; and whosoever 6 does not fall down and prostrate himself shall forthwith be cast into the midst of a furnace of flaming fire."

As soon, then, as all the peoples heard the sound of the 7 horn, the pipe, the lyre, the trigon, the harp, and every other kind of musical instrument, all the peoples, nations, and tongues fell down and prostrated themselves before the image of gold which King Nebuchadnezzar had set up. Thereupon certain Chaldeans came forward, 8 and laid an accusation against the Jews, saying to King 9 Nebuchadnezzar,

"O king, live for ever! You, O king, have made a 10 decree that every man who hears the sound of the horn, the pipe, the lyre, the trigon, the harp, the bagpipe, and every other kind of musical instrument, shall fall down and prostrate himself before the image of gold; and who- 11 soever does not fall down and prostrate himself shall be cast into the midst of a furnace of flaming fire. Now 12 there are certain Jews whom you have appointed in charge of the affairs of the province of Babylon, Shadrach, Meshach, and Abednego; these men, O king, pay no regard to you—they do not serve your gods, nor do they prostrate themselves before the image of gold which you have set up."

Then Nebuchadnezzar, in rage and fury, ordered Shad- 13 rach, Meshach, and Abednego to be brought; and when these men were brought before the king, Nebuchadnezzar 14 addressed them, saying,

"Is it true, O Shadrach, Meshach, and Abednego, that you do not serve my gods, nor prostrate yourselves before

15 the image of gold which I have set up? If, then, you are ready, as soon as you hear the sound of the horn, the pipe, the lyre, the trigon, the harp, the bagpipe, and every other kind of musical instrument, to fall down and prostrate yourselves before the image which I have made, well and good; but if you will not prostrate yourselves, you shall forthwith be cast into the midst of a furnace of flaming fire; and what god is there who shall deliver you out of my hands?"

16 Shadrach, Meshach, and Abednego answered the king, saying,

"O Nebuchadnezzar, we need not waste any words in 17 discussing this matter with you. If our God, whom we serve, is in a position to deliver us, he will deliver us out of the furnace of flaming fire, and out of your hand, O 18 king; but if not, be it known to you, O king, we will not serve your gods, nor prostrate ourselves before the image of gold which you have set up."

19 At these words Nebuchadnezzar was filled with fury, and his face was distorted with rage against Shadrach, Meshach, and Abednego. He ordered the furnace to be heated seven times more than it was usual for it to be 20 heated; then he ordered certain of the strongest men in in his army to bind Shadrach, Meshach, and Abednego, 21 and to cast them into the furnace of flaming fire. Thereupon, these men were bound in their cloaks, their tunics, their hats, and their other clothes, and were cast into the 22 midst of the furnace of flaming fire. So sharp was the king's order, and so very hot was the furnace, that the flame of the fire slew the men who took up Shadrach, 23 Meshach, and Abednego. But these three men, Shadrach, Meshach, and Abednego, fell down bound into the midst of the furnace of flaming fire.

24 Then King Nebuchadnezzar became alarmed; and he rose up hastily, and addressed his ministers, saying,

"Did we not cast three men bound into the midst of the fire?"

They answered the king, saying,

"Certainly, O king."

He answered, saying,   25
"Well, I see four men loose, walking in the midst of
the fire, quite unscathed; and the appearance of the
fourth resembles one of the gods."

Then King Nebuchadnezzar approached the mouth   26
of the furnace of flaming fire, and spoke, saying,
"O Shadrach, Meshach, and Abednego, servants of
the Most High God, come out, and come here!"

Then Shadrach, Meshach, and Abednego came out of
the midst of the fire; and when the assembled satraps,   27
prefects, governors, and king's ministers saw that the
fire had had no effect on the persons of these men, that
the hair of their heads had not been singed, nor their
cloaks damaged, and that no smell of burning had settled
on them, Nebuchadnezzar spoke, saying,   28
"Blessed be the God of Shadrach, Meshach, and Abednego, who has sent his angel to deliver his servants who
trusted in him, and frustrated the king's order, by sur-
rendering their own persons, rather than serve and worship any god, except their own God! Therefore I make a   29
decree that any people, nation, or tongue, that speaks a
word against the God of Shadrach, Meshach, and
Abednego, shall be hewn limb from limb, and their
houses made a dunghill; for there is no other god who is
able to deliver in this manner."

Then the king promoted Shadrach, Meshach, and   30
Abednego in the province of Babylon.

BELSHAZZAR'S FEAST, 5:1-31

King Belshazzar made a great feast for a thousand of   5
his lords, and drank wine before the thousand. Inflamed   2
by the taste of the wine, Belshazzar gave orders to bring
in the vessels of gold and silver, which his father Nebuchadnezzar had taken away from the temple at Jerusalem,
that the king and his lords, his consorts and his concubines, might drink out of them. So they brought in the   3
vessels of gold and silver, which had been taken away
from the temple at Jerusalem; and the king and his lords,
his consorts and his concubines, drank out of them. As   4

[248]

they drank the wine, they praised the gods of gold and
5 silver, bronze, iron, wood, and stone. Forthwith there
appeared the fingers of a man's hand, which wrote on the
plaster of the wall of the king's palace, opposite the
lampstand; and the king saw the palm of the hand as it
6 wrote. Then the king's face changed color, as his
thoughts upset him; the joints of his loins relaxed, and
7 his knees knocked one against another. The king called
aloud for the enchanters, the Chaldeans, and the astrologers to be brought in; and the king addressed the wise
men of Babylon, saying,

"Whosoever reads this writing, and gives me the interpretation of it, shall be clothed with purple, and shall
have a chain of gold round his neck, and shall be third
ruler in the kingdom."

8 But when all the king's wise men came in, they could
not read the writing, nor make known to the king the
9 interpretation of it. Then was King Belshazzar greatly
upset, and he changed color; his lords also were thrown
10 into consternation. At the cries of the king and his lords,
the queen-mother came into the banquetting-hall; and
the queen-mother addressed him, saying,

"O king, live forever! Let not your thoughts upset
11 you, nor your face change color. There is in your kingdom a man in whom is the spirit of the holy gods. In the
days of your father there was found in him light, and
understanding, and wisdom, like the wisdom of the gods,
so that King Nebuchadnezzar, your father, made him
chief of the magicians, enchanters, Chaldeans, and as-
12 trologers, because there was found in this Daniel, whom
the king named Belteshazzar, surpassing ability, knowledge, understanding, and skill in interpreting dreams,
solving riddles, and unravelling knots. Let Daniel be
called in, then, and he will give the interpretation."

13 So Daniel was brought in before the king; and the king
addressed Daniel, saying,

"You are Daniel, of the exiles of Judah, whom my
14 father the king brought from Judah! I have heard of you,
that the spirit of the gods is in you, and that light, and

[249]

understanding, and surpassing wisdom are found in you. Now the wise men, the enchanters, have been brought in 15 before me, that they might read this writing, and make known to me the interpretation of it; but they could not give the interpretation of the thing. I have heard of you, 16 however, that you can give interpretations, and unravel knots. Now, if you can read the writing, and make known to me the interpretation of it, you shall be clothed with purple, and shall have a chain of gold round your neck, and shall be third ruler in the kingdom."

Then Daniel answered the king, saying,   17

"Keep your gifts for yourself, and give your rewards to another; but I will read the writings to the king, and make known to him the interpretation of it. O king, the 18 Most High God gave Nebuchadnezzar your father the kingdom, with its greatness, its glory, and its majesty; and because of the greatness that he gave him, all the 19 peoples, nations, and tongues trembled in fear before him —whom he would he slew, and whom he would be kept alive, whom he would he raised up, and whom he would he put down. But when his mind was lifted up, and his 20 spirit became obstinate, so that he bore himself proudly, he was deposed from his kingly throne, and deprived of his glory, he was driven from among men, and his mind 21 was made like that of the beasts, his dwelling was with the wild asses, he was given grass to eat like an ox, and his person was drenched by the dew of the heavens, till he learned that the Most High God rules the kingdom of men, setting over it whom he will. And you his son, O 22 Belshazzar, have not humbled yourself, though you knew all this, but have lifted yourself up against the 23 Lord of the heavens, in that you have had the vessels of his house brought in before you, and have drunk wine out of them—you and your lords, your consorts and your concubines—and have praised the gods of silver and gold, bronze, iron, wood, and stone, which can neither see nor hear nor understand, and have not glorified the God in whose hand your breath is, and to whom belong all your ways. From him, then, has the palm of the hand been 24

25 sent, and this writing inscribed. This is the writing that
26 has been inscribed: *Mene, Tekel,* and *Peres.* And this is
the interpretation of the thing: *Mene*—God has num-
27 bered your kingdom, and brought it to an end; *Tekel*—
you have been weighed in the scales, and found wanting;
28 *Peres*—your kingdom is divided, and given to the Medes
and Persians."

29 Then Belshazzar gave orders, and Daniel was clothed
with purple, and had a chain of gold put round his neck,
while a proclamation was made concerning him, that he
should be third ruler in the kingdom.

30 That night Belshazzar, the king of Chaldea, was slain;
31 and Darius, the Mede, received the kingdom, being then
about sixty-two years of age.

THE DEN OF LIONS, 6:1–28

6 It pleased Darius to set over the kingdom a hundred
and twenty satraps, to administer the whole kingdom,
2 and over them three presidents, of whom Daniel was one,
that the satraps might be responsible to them, and the
3 king might suffer no loss. And Daniel distinguished himself above all the presidents and satraps, because surpassing ability was in him; and the king was disposed to set
him over the whole kingdom.

4 Then the presidents and satraps sought to find some
ground of complaint against Daniel in connection with
his administration of the kingdom; but they could find
no ground of complaint or fault, because he was faithful,
5 and no error or fault was to be found in him. So these
men said,

"We shall find no ground of complaint against this
Daniel, unless we find it in connection with the law of
his God."

6 Then these presidents and satraps thronged to the
king, and addressed him as follows:

7 "O King Darius, live forever! All the presidents of the
kingdom, the prefects and the satraps, the ministers and
the governors, have agreed in council that the king
should lay down a statute, and pass a strict interdict, to

the effect that whosoever shall offer a petition to any
god or man for thirty days, except to you, O king, shall
be cast into the den of lions. Now, O king, lay down the   8
interdict, and sign the document, so that it may not be
changed, in accordance with the law of the Medes and
Persians, which is unalterable."

Accordingly, King Darius signed the document con-   9
taining the interdict. Now, when Daniel learned that the   10
document had been signed, he went to his house—which
had windows in its upper chamber open toward Jerusalem—and three times a day he continued kneeling upon
his knees, praying, and giving thanks before his God,
as he used formerly to do. Then these men thronged in,   11
and found Daniel offering petitions and supplications before his God. So they approached the king, and ques-   12
tioned him concerning the king's interdict,

"Did you not sign an interdict, to the effect that whosoever should offer a petition to any god or man for thirty
days, except to you, O king, should be cast into the den
of lions?"

The king answered, saying,

"The thing stands fast, in accordance with the law of
the Medes and Persians, which is unalterable."

Then they answered the king, saying,   13

"This Daniel, of the exiles of Judah, pays no regard to
yourself, O king, nor to the interdict which you have
signed, but three times a day he continues offering his
own petitions."

When the king heard these words, he was deeply   14
grieved, and applied his mind to saving Daniel; till sunset he exerted himself to rescue him. Then these men   15
thronged to the king, and said to the king,

"You are aware, O king, that it is a law of the Medes
and Persians that no interdict or statute which the king
lays down can be changed."

So the king gave orders, and Daniel was brought   16
forward, and cast into the den of lions. And the king addressed Daniel, saying,

"May your God, whom you worship consistently, save you!"

17 Then a stone was brought forward, and laid upon the mouth of the den; and the king sealed it with his own signet, as well as with the signet of his lords, so that no 18 change might be made in respect to Daniel. Then the king went to his palace, and spent the night fasting; no diversions were brought to him, and his sleep fled from 19 him. Then at dawn, as soon as it was light, the king 20 arose, and went in haste to the den of lions. When he came near the den, where Daniel was, the king cried out with a sorrowful voice, and spoke to Daniel, saying.

"O Daniel, servant of the living God, has your God, whom you worship consistently, been able to save you from the lions?"

21 Then Daniel answered the king, saying,

22 "O king, live forever! My God has sent his angel, and has shut the mouths of the lions, so that they have not injured me; because I was found innocent before him, and before you also, O king, have I done no injury."

23 At these words the king was exceedingly glad, and gave orders that Daniel should be taken out of the den. And when Daniel was taken out of the den, no kind of injury was found on him, because he had trusted in his 24 God. Then the king gave orders, and the men who had accused Daniel were brought forward—they, and their children, and their wives—and cast into the den of lions; and before they had reached the bottom of the den the lions fell upon them, and crushed all their bones to pieces.

25 Then King Darius wrote as follows to all the peoples, nations, and tongues, that live in all the earth:

26 "Peace be multiplied to you! I hereby make a decree that throughout all the kingdom which I rule men shall tremble in reverence before the God of Daniel;

> For he is the living God,
> Immutable forever;
> His kingdom is one that shall never be overthrown,
> And his dominion is one that shall endure to the
> end;

He saves, and he delivers,   27
He does signs and wonders
    In the heavens and in the earth;
It is he who has saved Daniel
    From the power of the lions."
So this Daniel prospered during the reign of Darius, 28
and during the reign of Cyrus the Persian.

THE PSALMS
. . .

The Psalms are the hymnbook of the Jewish faith. They reflect various religious attitudes, and come, like our own hymns, from widely different periods. Some of them were written in the days of the kingdom, some in the times of the Exile, some are post-Exilic. Some have been altered in the course of time and use, like so many of of our hymns. Some may go back in their earliest forms to David himself, or further, while others may be as late as the time of the Maccabean struggle against Syria.

The Psalter was of course a growth. Collections of hymns were doubtless formed as early as the Exile, and very likely earlier. Smaller collections like the psalms of the sons of Korah, 42–49, or those of the sons of Asaph, 73–83, have been absorbed in this grand collection. Some psalms were in different collections which were taken up into the Psalter, and so these appear twice in it: 14=53; 40:13–17=70; 57:7–11+60:5–12=108. Some memory of David's musical gifts caused an increasing number of psalms to be ascribed to him. At the end of Book Two—for the Psalms are divided into five books —we read that the prayers of David the son of Jesse are ended; yet eighteen other psalms are assigned to David in the remaining books of the Psalter, and the Greek version of the Psalter (the Septuagint) adds fifteen more to the seventy-three assigned to him in the Hebrew text. It is clear that Jewish piety felt justified in ascribing its favorite hymns to its idolized national hero.

The Psalter is for the most part the product of the period after the Exile, when the national life came more and more to center in ritual and liturgy. Such psalms as survived from earlier days underwent revision, just as hymns do now, to adjust them to contemporary beliefs and needs. The collection must have assumed this final form very late, probably not far from 150 B.C., for it is simply the latest edition of the collected classics of Jewish devotion.

In all the wide range of the Old Testament nothing lives today like the great Psalms. Translations and adaptations of them enrich our hymnbooks, and the words of the Twenty-third, the Ninetieth, and many others still speak profoundly to the religious heart. For the whole great gamut of Jewish religious life, prophet and priest, for a thousand years is echoed in the poetry of the Psalms.

.   .   .

THE PROSPERITY OF THE PIOUS

How happy is the man who has not walked in the   1
   counsel of the wicked,
Nor stood in the way of sinners,
Nor sat in the seat of scoffers!
But his delight is in the law of the LORD,   2
And in his law does he study day and night.
For he is like a tree planted by streams of water,   3
That yields its fruit in its season,
And its leaf does not wither;
And whatsoever he does he brings to success.

The wicked are not so;   4
But are like the chaff which the wind drives away.
Therefore the wicked will not stand in the judgment,   5
Nor sinners in the assembly of the righteous.
For the LORD knows the way of the righteous;   6
But the way of the wicked will perish.

THE DIGNITY OF MAN AND THE GLORY OF GOD
[TO THE DIRECTOR: UPON *Gittith*. A PSALM OF DAVID]

8 O LORD, our Lord,
How glorious is thy name in all the earth!
I will sing thy praise to the heavens,
2 From the mouths of babes and infants.
Thou hast established strength because of thine
enemies,
To still the enemy and the revengeful.

3 When I see thy heavens, the work of thy fingers,
The moon and the stars which thou hast formed;
4 What is man that thou shouldst think of him,
And the son of man that thou shouldst care for him?

5 Yet thou hast made him but little lower than God,
And dost crown him with glory and honor!
6 Thou makest him ruler over the works of thy hands,
Thou hast put all things under his feet;

7 All sheep and oxen
And also the beasts of the field;
8 The birds of the heavens and the fish of the sea,
That traverse the paths of the seas.

9 O LORD, our Lord,
How glorious is thy name in all the earth.

GOD'S PRAISE IN THE PHYSICAL AND MORAL UNIVERSE
[FOR THE DIRECTOR: A PSALM OF DAVID]

19 The heavens are telling the glory of God,
And the sky shows forth the work of his hands.
2 Day unto day pours forth speech,
And night unto night declares knowledge.

3 There is no speech, nor are there words;
Their voice is not heard;
4 Yet their voice goes forth through all the earth,
And their words to the ends of the world.

In them he has pitched a tent for the sun
5 Who is like a bridegroom coming forth from his
chamber,

[257]

And rejoices like a strong man to run the course;
From one end of the heavens is his starting-point,   6
And his circuit is to the other end;
And nothing is hid from the heat thereof.

The law of the LORD is perfect,   7
    renewing the life;
The testimony of the LORD is trustworthy,
    making wise the simple;
The precepts of the LORD are right,   8
    rejoicing the heart;
The commandment of the LORD is pure,
    enlightening the eyes;
The fear of the LORD is clean,   9
    enduring forever.
The judgments of the LORD are true,
    and they are also right;
They are more valuable than gold,   10
    and much fine gold;
And sweeter than honey,
    and the droppings of the honeycomb.
Thy servant also is instructed by them,   11
In keeping them there is great reward.
Who can discern his errors?   12
Of unconscious ones, hold me guiltless!
Moreover, restrain thy servant from wilful ones,   13
May they not rule over me!
Then I shall be blameless, and I shall be acquitted of
    much transgression.
May the words of my mouth and the meditation of   14
    my heart
Be acceptable before thee.
O LORD, my rock and my avenger!

THE GOOD SHEPHERD

[A PSALM OF DAVID]

The LORD is my shepherd; I shall not want;   23
In green meadows he makes me lie down;   2
To refreshing waters he leads me.

3   He gives me new life.
He guides me in safe paths, for his fame's sake.

4   Even though I walk in the darkest valley,
I fear no harm; for thou art with me.
Thy rod and thy staff—they comfort me.

5   Thou layest a table before me in the presence of my
       enemies.
Thou anointest my head with oil; my cup overflows.

6   Only goodness and grace shall follow me all the
       days of my life;
And I shall dwell in the house of the LORD down to
       old age.

THE GLORY OF GOD AND THE GOOD MAN
[A PSALM OF DAVID]

24   The earth is the LORD's and its fulness,
The world and those who dwell therein.

2   For he founded it upon the seas,
And established it upon the ocean-currents.

3   Who can ascend into the hill of the LORD?
And who can stand in his holy place?

4   He who has clean hands and a pure heart,
Who has had no desire for falsehood,
And has not sworn to a lie.

5   He will receive a blessing from the LORD,
And justification from the God of his deliverance.

6   This is the generation of those who search for him,
Who seek the face of the God of Jacob.

7   Lift up your heads, O gates!
And lift up yourselves, O ancient doors,
That the king of glory may come in!

8   Who, then, is the king of glory?
The LORD strong and mighty,
The LORD mighty in battle!

9   Lift up your heads, O gates!
And lift up yourselves, O ancient doors,
That the king of glory may come in!

10   Who, then, is the king of glory?

The Lord of hosts,
He is the king of glory!

A SONG OF ASSURANCE

[for the director: a *maskil* of the sons of
korah]

As a deer longs for the water-courses,   **42**
So my whole being longs for thee, O God.
My whole being thirsts for God, for the living God: **2**
How long till I come and see the face of God?
My tears have been my food day and night,   **3**
While men say to me all day long, "Where is your
  God?"

These things I ponder upon and pour out my very self: **4**
That I went in the company of the nobles to the
  house of God,

With the sound of jubilation and praise—a festal
  crowd.
Why art thou brought low, O my spirit?   **5**
And why dost thou murmur within me?
Wait thou for God; for I shall again praise him,
The salvation of my countenance and my God.

My spirit is brought low within me;   **6**
Therefore do I think of thee from the land of the
  Jordan,
And the Hermons, from the hill Mizar.
Deep calls to deep to the sound of thy waterfalls;   **7**
All thy waves and thy billows pass over me.
By day the Lord orders his grace,   **8**
And by night his song is with me,
A prayer to the God of my life.

I say to God, my rock, "Why hast thou forgotten me?   **9**
Why do I go mourning because of oppression by the
  foe?"
With piercing pain my enemies reproach me,   **10**
While they say unto me all day long, "Where is your
  God?"

11 Why art thou brought low, O my spirit,
And why dost thou murmur within me?
Wait thou for God; for I shall again praise him,
The salvation of my countenance and my God.

THE JOY OF THE GODLY
[FOR THE DIRECTOR: ON *Gittith;* OF THE SONS
OF KORAH; A PSALM]

84 How lovely is thy dwelling-place, O LORD of hosts!
2 My spirit longs and pines
for the courts of the LORD.
My heart and my flesh give a shout of joy
for the living God!

3 Even the wren has found a house,
And the swallow a nest for herself,
Where she may put her young,
Thy altars, O LORD of hosts,
My king, and my God.

4 How happy are those who dwell in thy house,
Ever praising thee!
5 How happy the man whose strength is in thee!
The highways are in their minds!
6 Those who pass through the valley of Baca
Make it a region of springs;
The early rain covers it with blessings.
7 They go from strength to strength.
The God of gods is seen in Zion.

8 O LORD, God of hosts, hear my prayer;
Give heed, O God of Jacob!
9 O God, our shield, behold
And look upon the face of thy anointed!
10 For better is one day in thy courts than a thousand
elsewhere;
I would rather stand outside the door of the house
of my God
Than dwell in the tents of wickedness.
11 For the LORD God is a sun and shield.
Favor and honor the LORD bestows;

He does not withhold prosperity from them that
walk in integrity.

O Lord of hosts,   12
How happy the man who trusts in thee!

A PLEA FOR GOD'S MERCY

[A PRAYER OF MOSES, THE MAN OF GOD]

O Lord, thou hast been our dwelling-place in all **90**
generations.
Before the mountains were born,   2
Or ever thou hadst brought forth the earth and the
world,
Even from everlasting to everlasting thou art, O God.

Thou turnest man back to dust,   3
And sayest, "Return, O sons of man."
For a thousand years in thy sight   4
Are but as yesterday when it is past,
And as a watch in the night.

Thou cuttest them off; they are as a dream;   5
They are like grass which renews itself in the morn-
ing;
In the morning it flourishes and shoots up,   6
At evening it is cut down and withers.

For we are destroyed by thy anger,   7
And by thy wrath we are ruined.
Thou dost place our crimes before thee,   8
Our unconscious sins in the light of thy face.

For all our days vanish in thy wrath;   9
We come to an end; our years are like a cobweb
wiped away.
The length of our life is seventy years,   10
Perchance through strength eighty years;
And their whole extent is trouble and travail.
For it is quickly cut off and we fly away.

Who knows the power of thy anger?   11
Or thy wrath according to the fear due thee?

12 So teach us to number our days
    That we may obtain an understanding heart.

13 Return, O LORD; how long?
    And relent thyself as to thy servants.

14 Satisfy us in the morning with thy mercy,
    That we may shout with joy and be glad through-
    out our days.

    Gladden us in proportion to the days wherein thou
15 hast afflicted us,
    And the years wherein we have seen disaster.

16 May thy work appear unto thy servants,
    And thy spendor be upon their children.

17 May the favor of the Lord our God be upon us,
    And the work of our hands do thou establish upon us;
    The work of our hands establish thou it.

THE FAVOR OF GOD UPON THE FAITHFUL

91 He who dwells under the shelter of the Most High,
    Who abides under the shadow of my Mountain,
2   Says of the LORD, "My refuge and my fortress,
    My God, in whom I trust."

3   For he rescues you from the snare of the fowler,
    From the deadly pestilence;
4   With his pinions he covers you,
    And under his wings you find refuge.
    His faithfulness is a shield and buckler.

5   You will not be afraid of the terror by night,
    Nor the arrow that flies by day,
6   Nor the pestilence that stalks in darkness,
    Nor the plague that wastes at noonday.

7   A thousand may fall at your side,
    And ten thousand at your right hand;
    But it will not come near you.
8   You will but gaze upon with your eyes
    And see the reward of the wicked.

9   Because you have made the LORD your refuge,
    And the Most High your habitation,

No disaster will befall you, 10
Nor calamity come near your tent.

For he will give his angels charge over you, 11
To guard you in all your ways.
They will bear you up upon their hands, 12
Lest you strike your foot upon a stone.
Upon the lion and the adder you may tread; 13
Upon the young lion and the dragon you may tram-
ple.

Because he clings fast to me in love, I will deliver 14
him;
I will set him on high because he knows my name.
When he calls upon me, I will answer him; 15
I will be with him in trouble;
I will set him free and honor him,.
With long life will I satisfy him, 16
And show him my salvation.

A SONG OF TRIUMPH

[A PSALM]

Sing to the LORD a new song, **98**
For he has done wonderful things!
His right hand and his holy arm have brought him
victory.
The LORD has made known his victory; 2
In the sight of the nations he has revealed his
righteousness.
He has remembered his grace and his faithfulness 3
to the house of Israel.
All the ends of the earth have seen the triumph of
our God.

Shout aloud to the LORD, all the earth; 4
Rejoice, be jubilant, and sing praises;
Sing praises to the LORD with the lyre, 5
With the lyre and sound of song.
With trumpets and the sound of the horn, 6
Shout aloud before the king, the LORD!

7 Let the sea roar and all that is in it;
The world and those living in it!
8 Let the rivers clap their hands;
Let the mountains also sing,
9 Before the Lord, for he is coming to judge the earth!
He will judge the world with righteousness,
And the peoples with equity.

THE GUARDIAN GOD

[A SONG FOR THE ASCENTS]

121 I raise my eyes to the hills;
Whence does my help come?
2 My help is from the Lord,
Who made the heavens and earth.

3 He will not let your foot slip,
your guardian will not slumber.
4 He will neither slumber, nor sleep,
that guards Israel.

5 The Lord is your guardian;
The Lord is your shade upon your right hand.
6 By day the sun will not smite you,
nor the moon by night.

7 The Lord will guard you from all evil;
the Lord will guard your life.
8 The Lord will guard your goings and comings
henceforth and forever.

A PRAYER FOR JERUSALEM

[THE SONGS OF ASCENTS. OF DAVID]

122 I was glad when they said to me,
"Let us go to the house of the Lord."
2 Our feet are standing
within your gates, O Jerusalem;
3 Jerusalem that is rebuilt like a city,
with which, moreover, the law of Israel is
united;
4 Whither the tribes go up,
the tribes of the Lord,

[265]

To give thanks to the name of the Lord;
For there were set thrones of judgment,   5
The thrones of the house of David.

Pray for the peace of Jerusalem;   6
They will prosper who love you.
Peace be within your walls,   7
Tranquillity in your palaces!
For the sake of my brothers and my friends,   8
I will say, "Peace be with you!"
For the sake of the house of the Lord, our God,   9
I will seek your good.

UNSHAKABLE FAITH

[THE SONGS OF ASCENTS]

They who trust in the Lord   **125**
Are like Mount Zion which cannot be moved,
But abides forever.
Even as the mountains encircle Jerusalem,   2
So the Lord encircles his people,
From henceforth and forever.

For the wicked scepter will not rest upon the lot of   3
    the righteous,
That the righteous may not put forth their hands
    unto wrong.
Do good, O Lord, to the good,   4
And to them that are upright in heart.
But those who make their ways crooked—   5
May the Lord make them go with malefactors!
Peace be upon Israel!

SHOUTS OF JOY

[THE SONGS OF ASCENTS]

When the Lord brings back captive Zion   **126**
We shall be like dreamers!
Then will our mouth be filled with laughter,   2
And our tongue with shouts of joy.
Then will they say among the nations,

"The Lord has done great things for them."
3   The Lord has done great things for us;
We are glad.

4   Restore our fortune, O Lord,
Like torrents in the southland.
5   May those who sow in tears
Reap with shouts of joy!
6   He who goes forth weeping, bearing seed for sow-
ing,
Will indeed come back with joyful shouts, bearing
his sheaves.

DE PROFUNDIS

[THE SONGS OF ASCENTS]

130   Out of the depths I cry to thee, O Lord!
2   O Lord, hear my voice!
Let thine ears be attentive
To my supplicating voice.
3   If thou, O Lord, shouldst record iniquities,
O Lord, who could stand?
4   But with thee there is forgiveness,
That thou mayest be revered.

5   I wait for the Lord, my whole being waits,
And for his word I hope.
6   I wait for the Lord,
More than watchmen for the dawn,
Watchmen for the dawn.

7   Hope, O Israel, in the Lord,
For with the Lord is grace,
And with him is plenteous redemption.
For he will redeem Israel
From all its guilt.

THE BOOK OF ESTHER

· · ·

The Book of Esther is the romantic story of a Jewish girl who became the wife and queen of Xerxes, king of Persia, and when the Jews were in great danger of massacre and extinction declared her nationality to the king and saved her people. The writer's lack of information about Persian practices shows that he wrote far from the scenes he describes and long after the Persian period, and his bitter and vengeful attitude toward the Gentiles gives him a low place among the religious teachers of the Old Testament. The book was written not far from 150 B.C., to explain the origin of the Feast of Purim, the latest of the Jewish feasts, which it seeks to push back into the beginning of the fifth century. Its religious and historical value is certainly slight, but it lives in literature as a vivid oriental story of a brave and beautiful Jewish girl, who attained the highest possible position but did not forget her people, and in an hour of extreme crisis risked everything to save them.

· · ·

MORDECAI'S APPEAL TO ESTHER, 4:1-17

Now when Mordecai knew all that had been done, 4 Mordecai tore his garments and put on sackcloth with ashes, and went out into the midst of the city and cried out with a loud and bitter lamentation. And he came 2 even before the king's gate; for none might enter the king's gate clothed with sackcloth. Moreover in every 3 province wherever the king's command and his decree came, there was great mourning among the Jews, and

fasting, weeping and wailing; and many lay in sackcloth
4 and ashes. And Esther's maidens and her eunuchs came
and told her; and the queen was exceedingly distressed.
And she sent garments to clothe Mordecai that he might
5 take off his sackcloth; but he did not accept them. Then
Esther called for Hathach, one of the king's eunuchs,
who had been appointed to attend her, and ordered him
to go to Mordecai, to learn what this was and why it
6 was. So Hathach went forth to Mordecai to the broad
7 place of the city which was before the king's gate. Then
Mordecai told him all that had happened to him and the
exact sum of money that Haman had promised to pay to
8 the king's treasuries for the destruction of the Jews. He
also gave him a copy of the writing of the decree that was
given out in Shushan to destroy them, that he might show
it to Esther and inform her and charge her to go in to the
king to implore him and to make request before him for
her people.

9   So Hathach came and told Esther the words of Morde-
10 cai. Then Esther spoke to Hathach, and gave him a message to Mordecai, saying,
11   "All the king's servants and the people of the king's
provinces know that whoever, whether man or woman,
comes to the king into the inner court who is not summoned, there is one law for him, that he be put to death,
except those to whom the king shall hold out the golden
scepter, that he may live; but I have not been summoned
to come to the king these thirty days."
12   Accordingly they told Mordecai Esther's words.
13   Then Mordecai bade them return answer to Esther,
"Think not to yourself that you will escape inside the
14 royal palace any more than all the rest of the Jews. For
if you altogether remain silent at this time, then relief
and deliverance will rise up for the Jews from another
quarter, but you and your father's house will perish; and
who knows whether you have not come to the kingdom
for such a time as this?"
15   Thereupon Esther bade them return answer to Mordecai,

"Go, gather together all the Jews that are to be found 16
in Shushan and fast for me, and neither eat nor drink for
three days, night or day. I also and my maidens will likewise fast and so will I go to the king, which is not according to the law; and if I perish, I perish."

So Mordecai went his way and did just as Esther com- 17
manded him.

HAMAN'S RISE AND FALL, 5:1—7:10

So it came about on the third day that Esther put on 5
her royal robes, and stood in the inner court of the king's
palace directly opposite the king's apartment. And the
king was sitting upon his royal throne in the royal palace
opposite the entrance of the palace. And when the king 2
saw Esther the queen standing in the court she met with
favor in his sight, and the king extended to Esther the
golden scepter that was in his hand. So Esther drew near
and touched the top of the scepter.

Thereupon the king said to her, 3
"What is your wish, Queen Esther, and what is your
request? It shall be given you even to the half of the
kingdom."

And Esther said, 4
"If it please the king, let the king and Haman come
today to a banquet that I have prepared for him."

Then the king said, 5
"Bring Haman in haste that he may fulfil Esther's
wish."

So the king and Haman came to the banquet that
Esther had prepared.

Accordingly the king said to Esther at the banquet 6
of wine,
"What is your petition? And it shall be granted you;
and what is your request, even to the half of the kingdom? And it shall be performed."

Accordingly Esther answered and said, 7
"My petition and my request is: If I have found favor 8
in the sight of the king, and if it please the king to grant
my petition, and to perform my request, let the king and

Haman come to my banquet that I shall prepare for them, and tomorrow I will do as the king has said."

9   Then Haman went out that day joyful and glad of heart. But when Haman saw Mordecai in the king's gate, and he neither stood up nor moved for him, Haman

10 was filled with wrath against Mordecai. Nevertheless Haman restrained himself and returned home, and sent

11 and brought in his friends and Zeresh his wife. Thereupon Haman recounted to them the glory of his riches and the multitude of his children and every instance where the king had promoted him, and how he had advanced him above the princes and the servants of the

12 king. Haman also said,

    "Even Esther the queen has permitted no man to come in with the king to the banquet that she has prepared but me, and tomorrow also I am invited by her together with

13 the king. Yet all this suffices me not so long as I see Mordecai the Jew sitting at the king's gate."

14   Then Zeresh his wife and all his friends said to him,

    "Let a gallows fifty cubits high be erected and in the morning speak to the king that Mordecai may be hanged thereon. Then go in merrily with the king to the banquet."

    And the idea pleased Haman; and he had the gallows made.

6   On that night sleep forsook the king, and he commanded to bring the book of records of the chronicles,

2 and they were read before the king. And there was found written what Mordecai had told concerning Bigthana and Teresh, two of the king's eunuchs, of those who guarded the threshold, who had sought to lay hands on

3 King Xerxes. Whereupon the king said,

    "What honor and dignity have been bestowed on Mordecai for this?"

    Then the king's servants who ministered to him said,

    "Nothing has been done for him."

4   At this juncture the king said,

    "Who is in the court?"

    Now Haman had entered the outer court of the king's

house to request the king to hang Mordecai on the gallows that he had prepared for him. Accordingly the 5 king's servants said to him,

"Behold, Haman is standing in the court."

And the king said,

"Let him enter."

So Haman came in. And the king said to him, 6

"What shall be done to the man whom the king delights to honor?"

Now Haman said to himself,

"Whom would the king delight to honor more than myself?"

Therefore Haman said to the king, 7

"For the man whom the king delights to honor, let 8 royal garments be brought, which the king has worn, and a horse which the king has ridden, and on the head of which a royal crown is set. And let the garments and the 9 horse be delivered to one of the king's most noble princes, and let them clothe the man whom the king delights to honor and cause him to ride on horseback through the streets of the city, and proclaim before him, 'Thus shall it be done to the man whom the king delights to honor.'"

Then the king said to Haman, 10

"Make haste, and take the garments and the horse, as you have said, and do even so to Mordecai the Jew who sits in the king's gate. Let nothing fail of all that you have spoken."

So Haman took the garments and the horse and 11 clothed Mordecai and caused him to ride through the streets of the city and proclaimed before him,

"Thus shall it be done to the man whom the king delights to honor."

Then Mordecai returned to the king's gate. But Ha- 12 man hurried home, mourning and with his head covered. Haman also related to Zeresh his wife and to all his 13 friends all that had befallen him. Then his wise men and Zeresh his wife said to him,

"If Mordecai before whom you have begun to fall be

of the Jewish race, you will make no headway against
him but will surely fall before him."

14   While they were still speaking with him, the king's
eunuch arrived and hurriedly brought Haman to the
banquet that Esther had prepared.

7   So the king and Haman went in to drink with Esther
2 the queen. And the king said again to Esther on the second day of the banquet of wine,

    "What is your petition, Queen Esther? And it shall be
granted you. Indeed what is your request even to the
half of the kingdom? And it shall be performed."

3   Then Esther the queen answered, saying,

    "If I have found favor in the sight of the king, and if
it please the king, let my life be given me at my petition
4 and my people at my request; for we are sold, I and my
people, to be destroyed, to be slain, and to perish. But if
we had been sold as male and female slaves, I would have
held my peace since the distress would not have been
worthy of disturbing the king."

5   Then King Xerxes spoke and said to Esther the queen,

    "Who is he and where is he who dares presume in his
heart to do so?"

6   Thereupon Esther said,

    "An adversary and an enemy, this wicked Haman."

7   Then Haman was terrified before the king and queen.
And when the king arose in his wrath from the banquet
of wine and went into the palace garden, Haman stood up
to beg for his life from Esther the queen; for he saw that
8 evil was determined against him by the king. Accordingly when the king returned from the palace garden to
the apartment of the banquet of wine, Haman was prostrate upon the couch upon which Esther was. Then the
king said,

    "Will he violate the queen in my presence in the
house?"

9   And as the words left his lips they covered Haman's
face. Then Harbonah, one of the eunuchs who was before the king, said,

    "There is also the gallows fifty cubits high, which

Haman has made for Mordecai, who spoke good for the king, standing in the house of Haman."

And the king said,

"Hang him thereon."

So they hanged Haman on the gallows that he had 10 prepared for Mordecai. Then the king's wrath abated.

THE BOOK OF ECCLESIASTES
· · ·

*By the second century before Christ the great prophetic
spirit which had been the glory of Israel's religion had
almost disappeared. Men still believed in God, but the
problems of history and even of existence sometimes
seemed hopeless and insoluble. In such a mood the body
of the Book of Ecclesiastes was written. It reflected the
writer's belief in God, but boldly stated the numerous
problems that confronted him for which he could find no
solution. His name, or his pen-name, was Koheleth,
and he wrote his brief essay about 180 B.C.*

*Into these reflections was not long afterward gath-
ered a series of proverbs and wise sayings of the Sages,
which somewhat offset and counteracted what Koheleth
had originally written. Still later, but still in the second century, the whole was supplemented by a Jew of the
pious and unimaginative type, with views quite opposed
to those of Koheleth and more in line with the prevalent
Judaism of the day.*

*This is why expressions of pessimism, fatalism, and
apathy stand side by side in Ecclesiastes with admoni-
tions to fear God and keep his commandments. Three
types of mind are in fact represented in the book: the
man who frankly fronts the problems of life and longs for
light upon them; the Sage, with his homely maxims of
practical wisdom; and the pious upholder of the old religion—all are brought together here, in one of the latest
books of the Hebrew scriptures.*

THE ENDLESS ROUND OF NATURE, 1:1–11

The sayings of Koheleth, the son of David, who was 1
king of Jerusalem.
"Futility of futility," says Koheleth, 2
"Futility of futilities, all is futility!
What does a man gain from all his toil 3
Wherein he toils beneath the sun?
One generation goes, and another comes, 4
While the earth endures perpetually.
The sun rises and the sun sets, 5
And hastens to the place where he arose.
The wind blows toward the south 6
And returns to the north.
Turning, turning, the wind blows,
And returns upon its circuit.
All rivers run to the sea, 7
But the sea is never full;
To the spot where the rivers flow,
There they continue to flow.
All cases would weary; 8
One may not tell them;
Lest the eye be sated with seeing,
And the ear be filled with hearing.
Whatsoever has been is that which will be; 9
And whatsoever has been done is that which will
be done;
And there is nothing new under the sun.
Is there a thing of which it is said, 'Lo, this is new'? 10
It was already in existence in the ages
Which were before us;
But there is no record of former things; 11
Likewise of future things there will be no record
For those who live later still."

AN ORDERLY WORLD, 3:1–8

"For everything there is an appointed time; 3
And there is a time for every purpose under the
heavens:

2   A time to be born, and a time to die;
    A time for planting, and a time for uprooting;
3   A time to slay, and a time to heal;
    A time to tear down, and a time to rebuild;
4   A time to weep, and a time to laugh;
    A time to mourn, and a time to dance;
5   A time to scatter stones, and a time to gather stones;
    A time to embrace, and a time to refrain from embracing;
6   A time to seek, and a time to count as lost;
    A time to keep, and a time to throw away;
7   A time to tear, and a time to sew;
    A time to keep quiet, and a time to talk;
8   A time to love, and a time to hate;
    A time for war, and a time for peace."

ADVICE TO THE YOUNG, 11:9—12:8

11 "Rejoice, O young man, in your youth,
    And let your mind be glad in the days of your vigor,
    And walk in the ways of your mind and in the sight
        of your eyes;
    But know that for all these things God will bring
        you into judgment.
10 And put away worry from your mind,
    And remove evil from your flesh;
    For youth and the prime of life are futility.
12 Remember your Creator in the days of your vigor,
    Before the evil days come
    And the years approach of which you will say,
    'I have no pleasure in them;'
2   Before the sun become dark,
    And the light, and the moon, and the stars;
    And the clouds return after the rain;
3   In the day when the guardians of the house tremble,
    And the strong men are bent,
    And the grinding-maids cease because they are few,
    And the ladies peering through the windows be
        darkened,
4   And the doors into the street are closed;

When the sound of the mill is low,
And one rises at the sound of the bird,
And all songs sound low even when in high tones;
They fear and terrors are on the road;   5
And the almond tree blossoms, and the grasshopper
   is burdensome,
And the caper-berry becomes ineffectual;
Because man goes to his final home,
And the mourners go around in the street;
While the silver cord is not severed,   6
Nor the golden bowl broken,
Nor the jar shattered at the spring,
Nor the wheel broken at the cistern;
Nor the dust return to the earth as it was,   7
Nor the spirit return to God who gave it.
Futility of futilities,'' says Koheleth, ''all is futil-   8
   ity.''

CONCLUDING COMMENTS, 12:9–13

In addition to the fact that Koheleth was wise, he still 12
taught the people knowledge, and he composed, and
sought out, and arranged many proverbs. Koheleth   10
sought to find pleasing words, and what is written correctly, namely, true things. The words of the wise are   11
like goads; but collections which are given by one
teacher are like nails driven with a sledge. Furthermore,   12
my son, take warning; of the making of many books
there is no end, and much study is weariness of the flesh.

The conclusion of the matter. Let us hear all: Fear   13
God and keep his commandments; for this concerns every
man, that God brings every work into judgment with
regard to everything concealed, whether it be good or
bad.

THE APOCRYPHA

ECCLESIASTICUS, OR THE WISDOM
OF SIRACH
. . .

*While the early church from the beginning accepted as
its scripture the Greek Bible, including such books as
Tobit, Judith, and I and II Maccabees, and these con-
sequently passed into the Latin Bible, Jerome, when he
came to revise the Latin version, could find no Hebrew
texts for them extant. He did not go so far as to
exclude them from his Bible, but he grouped them together under the name Apocrypha. From his revision,
the so-called Vulgate, they passed into the English Bibles, from Coverdale (1535) to King James (1611).
They were distasteful to the Puritans, however, and
nowadays are more often omitted even from the King
James Bible than included in it. They were certainly
not accepted as scripture by the Jews of Palestine, but
they were by the Jews out in the Greek world.*

*One of the most notable of these books is the Wisdom of
Jesus, son of Sirach, composed in Hebrew early in the
second century before Christ by a Jewish sage, Jesus of
Jerusalem, and translated into Greek by his grandson
while on a visit to Alexandria, not long after 132 B.C.
Fragments of the original Hebrew have come to light in
recent years.*

*Ecclesiasticus, as the book came to be called in Greek,
is the longest of the Jewish books of wisdom, and contains many profound and appealing reflections.*

IN PRAISE OF FAMOUS MEN, 44:1–15

44 Let me now praise distinguished men,
  our fathers, before us;

2 They are a great glory to the Lord who created them,
  They show his majesty from of old;

3 Men who exercised authority in their reigns,
  and were renowned for their might.
  They gave their counsel with understanding,
  and brought men tidings through their prophecy;

4 Leaders of the people in deliberation and understanding,
  men of learning for the people, wise in their words
    of instruction;

5 Composers of musical airs,
  authors of poems in writing,

6 Rich men, endowed with strength,
  who lived in peace upon their lands;—

7 All these were honored in their generation,
  and were a glory in their day.

8 There are some of them who have left a name,
  so that men declare their praise;

9 And there are some who have no memorial,
  and have perished as though they had not lived,
  And have become as though they had not been,
  with their children after them.

10 Yet these were merciful men,
  and their uprightness has not been forgotten.

11 With their descendants it will remain,
  a good inheritance for their posterity.

12 Their descendants stand by the Covenants,
  and their children also, for their sakes.

13 Their posterity shall endure for ever,
  and their glory shall not be blotted out.

14 Their bodies are buried in peace,
  but their name lives to all generations.

15 Peoples will recite their wisdom,
  and the congregation declares their praise.

THE NEW TESTAMENT

THE LETTERS TO THE THESSALONIANS

. . .

*About the middle of the first century A.D. a Christian
missionary named Paul sat down in the city of Corinth
to write a letter. He was a Jew, of strict pharisaic training, born in Tarsus in Cilicia, and inheriting from his
father the rights of Roman citizenship. He had become
a Christian early in the development of the movement,
and brought to it such energy, understanding, and
imagination as made him for the rest of his life its foremost champion.*

*He was also its greatest missionary and for years had
been devoting himself to spreading his gospel of Jesus
as the messianic deliverer and judge of Jewish expectation, among the Greeks of Syria and Asia Minor. More
recently he had crossed into Europe and preached in
Macedonia and Greece. The little church he had established in Thessalonica he had had to leave so soon that
he feared they might have been led after his departure to
give up their new faith, and he had sent Timothy, one of
his young lieutenants, back to find out about them and
encourage them in their Christian life. He had waited
anxiously for Timothy's coming, and when at last he
came it was with good news. The Thessalonians are
still loyal to Christ and strong in their new faith. Paul
is overjoyed at the news and writes a letter of overflowing
relief, assuring the Thessalonians of his continued affection and interest, comforting them for the loss of friends
and giving them further moral instruction. Certain*

members of the group are idling, and becoming a charge upon the generosity of the more industrious. Paul tells them they must go to work and support themselves.

Not long after, when this situation has grown worse, Paul writes a second letter, correcting the view that the Day of the Lord had already come, and pointing out that this cannot be, for the Antichrist has not yet made his appearance, which must, according to Jewish messianic ideas, precede that of the Messiah. He corrects the idlers in the church more sharply than before, and points to his own sturdy example of self-support.

With these two short letters Paul began Christian literature, and before he ceased to write he had written one-fifth of all that the New Testament contains. In these first letters we see the difficulties that were already besetting the small new Christian groups, and the keen personal interest Paul felt in their moral and religious welfare.

. . .

THE FIRST LETTER TO THE THESSALONIANS

. . .

PAUL'S JOYFUL MEMORIES OF THEM AND RELIEF AT TIMOTHY'S NEWS, 1:1–10; 2:17–3:13

Paul, Silvanus, and Timothy to the Thessalonian church in union with God the Father and the Lord Jesus Christ; God bless you and give you peace. 1

We always thank God for you all when we mention you in our prayers, for we can never forget before our God and Father your energetic faith, your loving service, and your unwavering expectation of our Lord Jesus Christ. For we know, brothers whom God so loves, that he has chosen you, for our preaching of the good news did not come to you as mere words but with power and the holy Spirit and full conviction—you know the kind of life we 2 3 4 5

6 lived among you for your good. And you followed the example set by us and by the Lord, for though our message brought you great trouble, you welcomed it with 7 joy inspired by the holy Spirit, so that you set an example 8 to all the believers in Macedonia and Greece. For the Lord's message has rung out from you not only over Macedonia and Greece, but the story of your belief in God has gone everywhere, so that we never need to men- 9 tion it. For when people speak of us, they tell what a welcome you gave us, and how you turned from idols to 10 God, to serve a true and living God, and to wait for the coming from heaven of his Son, whom he raised from the dead—Jesus, our deliverer from God's coming wrath.

2   For our part, brothers, when we were separated from you for a little while—in person, though not in spirit— we were extremely eager and longed intensely to see you. 18 For we resolved to come to see you—I, Paul, did so again 19 and again—but Satan held us back. For what hope or happiness shall we have or what prize to be proud of in the presence of our Lord Jesus when he comes, except 20 you? You are our pride and our joy.

3   So when I could not bear it any longer, I made up my 2 mind to stay behind alone at Athens, and I sent my brother Timothy, a servant of God in preaching the good 3 news of the Christ, to strengthen you in your faith and encourage you not to be led astray, any of you, in all these troubles. You know yourselves that this is what 4 we must expect, for when we were with you, we told you beforehand that we were going to have trouble, and it 5 came true, as you know. That was why, when I could not bear it any longer, I sent to find out about your faith, for I was afraid that the tempter might have tempted 6 you and all our labor might be lost. But now that Timothy has just come back to me from you, and brought me good news of your faith and love, and told me how kindly you think of me and that you long to see me just 7 as much as I long to see you, I feel encouraged, brothers, 8 about you, in spite of all my distress and trouble, at your faith, for now I can really live, since you are standing

firm in the Lord. For how can I thank God enough 9
for you, for all the happiness you make me feel in the
presence of our God, as I pray night and day with intense 10
earnestness that I may see your faces and supply what is
lacking in your faith?

May our God and Father himself and our Lord Jesus 11
open my way to you! May the Lord make your love for 12
one another and for all men wide and full like my love
for you, so that your hearts may be strong and faultlessly 13
pure in the sight of our God and Father, when our Lord
Jesus appears with all his saints!

THEY MUST BE BENEVOLENT, INDUSTRIOUS, HOPEFUL, PREPARED, 4:9—5:22

You do not need to have anyone write to you about 4
brotherly love, for you have yourselves been taught by
God to love one another, and you are doing it to all the 10
brothers all over Macedonia.

But we do entreat you, brothers, to surpass yourselves 11
in striving to live quietly and mind your own affairs, and
work with your hands, as we directed you, so that you 12
may have the respect of the outsiders, and not be de-
pendent upon anybody.

We do not want you to be under any misapprehension, 13
brothers, about those who are falling asleep. You must
not grieve for them, as others do who have no hope. For 14
if we believe that Jesus died and rose again, then by
means of Jesus God will bring back with him those who
have fallen asleep. For we can assure you, on the Lord's 15
own authority, that those of us who will still be living
when the Lord comes will have no advantage over those
who have fallen asleep. For the Lord himself, at the 16
summons, when the archangel calls and God's trumpet
sounds, will come down from heaven, and first those who
died in union with Christ will rise; then those of us who 17
are still living will be caught up with them on clouds into
the air to meet the Lord, and so we shall be with the Lord
forever. Therefore, encourage one another with this 18
truth.

5   But as to times and dates, brothers, you do not need
2   to have anyone write to you, for you yourselves know
perfectly well that the Day of the Lord is to come like a
3   thief in the night. When people say, "What peace and
security!" then suddenly destruction will be upon them,
like birth-pains upon a woman about to give birth to a
4   child, and there will be no escape. But you are not in
darkness, brothers, so that that Day should surprise you
5   like thieves. You all belong to the light and the day. We
6   have nothing to do with night or with darkness. So we
must not sleep like other men, but we must be vigilant and
7   composed. For those who sleep, sleep at night and those
8   who get drunk do so at night, but we who belong to the
day must be composed, wearing faith and love for a coat
9   of mail, and helmeted with the hope of salvation. For
God has not destined us for his wrath, but to gain sal-
10   vation through our Lord Jesus Christ, who died for us
so that whether we are still alive or fall asleep we may
11   live with him. Therefore encourage one another and
strengthen one another, just as you are doing.
12   We beg you, brothers, to respect those who work with
you and who lead you in the service of the Lord, and
13   teach you. Hold them in the highest esteem and affection
14   for what they do. Live at peace with one another. We
beg you, brothers, warn the idlers, cheer up the de-
spondent, keep hold of the weak, be patient with every-
15   body. Take care that none of you ever pays back evil for
evil, but always try to treat one another and everybody
16   with kindness. Always be joyful. Never give up pray-
17
18   ing. Thank God whatever happens. For this is what
19   God through Christ Jesus wants you to do. Do not stifle
20   the Spirit. Do not disregard the utterances it inspires,
21
22   but test them all, retaining what is good and avoiding
every kind of evil.

THE SECOND LETTER TO THE THESSALONIANS

THE DAY OF THE LORD IS STILL TO COME, 2:1-17

As to the coming of our Lord Jesus Christ, brothers, 2
and our assembling to meet him, we beg you not to let 2
your minds be too easily unsettled or wrought up, by any
message of the Spirit or any utterance or letter purporting
to be from me, to the effect that the Day of the Lord has
already come. You must not let anyone deceive you at 3
all. For that is not until the rebellion takes place and the
embodiment of disobedience makes his appearance—he
who is doomed to destruction, the adversary of every 4
being that is called a god or an object of worship, and so
overbearing toward them as to enter God's sanctuary and
take his seat there, proclaiming himself to be God—do 5
you not remember that when I was with you, I used to
tell you this? So now you know what it is that is holding 6
him back from making his appearance before the appointed time arrives. For disobedience is already secretly 7
at work, but only until he who is now holding it in check
is gotten out of the way. Then the embodiment of dis- 8
obedience will make his appearance, and the Lord Jesus
will destroy him with the breath of his mouth and
annihilate him by his appearance and arrival. The 9
other's appearance, by the contrivance of Satan, will be
full of power and pretended signs and wonders, and full 10
of wicked deception for men who are going to destruction, because they refused to love the truth and be saved.
This is why God sends upon them a misleading influence, 11
to make them believe what is false, so that all who have 12
refused to believe the truth but have preferred disobedience may be condemned.

We always have to thank God for you, brothers whom 13
the Lord so loves, because God chose you from the beginning to be saved through consecration by the Spirit

14 and through faith in the truth, and called you to it
through our preaching of the good news, so that you
15 may share in the glory of our Lord Jesus Christ. So stand
firm, brothers, and hold fast to the instructions you have
received from us, whether by letter or by word of mouth.
16 May our Lord Jesus Christ himself and God our Father,
who has loved us and kindly given us unfailing encourage-
17 ment and a well-founded hope, encourage you and
strengthen you to do and say everything that is right.

THE LETTER TO THE GALATIANS

· · ·

Paul had hardly returned to the shores of Syria after what is commonly called his second missionary journey when an enemy appeared in his rear. He had preached the gospel a few years before in the cities of Galatia— probably Antioch, Derbe, Lystra and Iconium—and it had been warmly welcomed. But now teachers of a highly Jewish type of Christianity had appeared in Galatia and called upon the Galatian Christians to adopt the practices of Jewish proselytes, if they hoped to share in the blessings of the agreement made between God and Abraham long before. As for Paul, these new teachers declare he is no apostle at all and in no position to modify the terms of admission to the church to suit heathen tastes. The salvation secured through Christ belongs to the Jewish people and only such others as may secure adoption into that race. For God's promise was to Abraham and his posterity alone.

This narrow national conception of the work of Christ and the legalistic implications of such a conception stirred Paul very deeply. He wrote a blazing letter of indignation and protest to the Galatians. He was an apostle, commissioned by Christ himself, through inward experience and conviction. These Judaizers are striking at the heart of Christianity, which is essentially an inward life of faith and dependence upon God, a life to which the external formalities of legalism can contribute nothing, and in which they can have no place.

Galatians is, in fact, a charter of religious freedom. Its noble ideal of the religious life, so far from being outgrown, still beckons us forward, as it did the Galatians long ago. Paul knew its dangers, but he knew its promise too, and saw that for those who would sincerely accept it, it opened possibilities of spiritual development which could never be reached by the lower path. The Christian had received the spirit of God. By that he must regulate his life. If he did so he would be in no danger of gross and vulgar sin but would find freely springing up in his life the fruits of the spirit: love, joy, peace, patience, kindness, goodness, faithfulness, gentleness, self-control.

. . .

THE SALUTATION, 1:1-5

1   Paul, an apostle not from men nor sent by any man, but by Jesus Christ and God the Father who raised him
2   from the dead—and all the brothers who are here with
3   me, to the churches of Galatia; blessing and peace to you
4   from God our Father and the Lord Jesus Christ, who to save us from the present wicked world gave himself for
5   our sins at the will of our God and Father. To him be glory forever and ever! Amen.

PAUL REBUKES THEM AND CONDEMNS THEIR TEACHERS, 1:6-9

1   I am amazed that you are so quickly turning away from him who called you by the mercy of Christ, to some
7   different good news—not that there is any other, only that there are some people who are trying to unsettle you
8   and want to turn the good news of the Christ around. But even if we or an angel from heaven preach to you good news that contradicts the good news we have preached to
9   you, a curse upon him! We have said it before, and I repeat it now—if anyone is preaching to you good news

[293]

that contradicts the good news you have already received, a curse upon him!

IT IS FAITH, NOT LAW, THAT BRINGS UPRIGHTNESS, 2:15—3:9

We who are Jews by birth, and not sinful heathen, but 2 who know that a man is not made upright by doing what the Law commands, but by faith in Christ Jesus— even we believed in Christ Jesus, so as to be made upright by faith in Christ and not by doing what the Law commands—for by doing what the Law commands no one can be made upright. If through our efforts to be made 17 upright through Christ, we have ourselves been proved as much "sinners" as the heathen, does that make Christ encourage sin? By no means. I really convict myself of 18 wrongdoing when I start to rebuild what I tore down. For it is through the Law that I have become dead to the 19 Law, so that I may live for God. I have been crucified 20 with Christ, and it is no longer I that live, but Christ that lives in me. The life I am now living in the body I am living by faith in the Son of God who loved me and gave himself for me. I refuse to nullify the mercy of God. 21 For if uprightness could be secured through law, then Christ died for nothing!

You senseless Galatians! Who has bewitched you, 3 when you had Jesus Christ shown crucified right before your eyes? This is all I want to ask you: Did you receive 2 the Spirit through doing what the Law commands, or through believing the message you heard? Are you so 3 senseless? Did you begin with the Spirit only to end now with the flesh? Have you gone through so much, all for 4 nothing?—if it really is for nothing! When he supplies 5 you with the Spirit and works wonders among you, is it because you do what the Law commands, or because you believe the message you heard? Just as Abraham had faith 6 in God and it was credited to him as uprightness.

So you see, the real descendants of Abraham are the 7 men of faith. The Scripture foresaw that God would ac- 8 cept the heathen as upright in consequence of their faith, and preached the good news in advance to Abraham in the words, "All the heathen will be blessed through you." So the men of faith share the blessing of Abraham and his faith.

9

FAITH MAKES US SONS OF GOD, 3:23—4:7

3   But before this faith came, we were kept shut up under the Law, in order to obtain the faith that was to be revealed. So the Law has been our attendant on our way to Christ, so that we might be made upright through faith. But now that faith has come, we are no longer in the charge of the attendant.

24

25

26   For in Christ Jesus you are all sons of God through your faith. For all of you who have been baptized into union with Christ have clothed yourselves with Christ. There is no room for "Jew" and "Greek"; there is no room for "slave" and "freeman"; there is no room for "male" and "female"; for in union with Christ Jesus you are all one. And if you belong to Christ, then you are true descendants of Abraham and his heirs under the promise.

27

28

29

4   I mean this: As long as the heir is a minor, he is no better than a slave, although he is the owner of all the property, but he is under guardians and trustees until the time fixed by his father. So when we were minors, we were slaves to material ways of looking at things, but when the proper time came, God sent his Son, born of a woman, and made subject to law, to ransom those who were subject to law, so that we might receive adoption. And because you are sons, God has sent into our hearts the spirit of his Son, with the cry, "Abba!" that is, Father. So you are no longer a slave, but a son; and if a son, then an heir, made so by God.

2

3

4

5

6

7

CHRIST HAS FREED US TO LIVE BY THE SPIRIT, 5:1, 13—6:5

5   This is the freedom with which Christ has freed us. So stand firm in it, and do not get under a yoke of slavery again.

For you, brothers, have been called to freedom; only 13 do not make your freedom an excuse for the physical, but in love be slaves to one another. For the whole Law is 14 summed up in one saying: "You must love your neighbor as you do yourself." But if you bite one another and eat 15 one another, take care, or you will be destroyed by one another.

I mean this: Live by the Spirit, and then you will not 16 indulge your physical cravings. For the physical crav- 17 ings are against the Spirit, and the cravings of the Spirit are against the physical; the two are in opposition, so that you cannot do anything you please. But if you are 18 guided by the Spirit, you are not subject to law. The 19 things our physical nature does are clear enough—im- 20 morality, impurity, licentiousness, idolatry, sorcery, en- mity, quarreling, jealousy, anger, selfishness, dissension, party-spirit, envy, drunkenness, carousing, and the like. 21 I warn you as I did before that people who do such things will have no share in the Kingdom of God. But what the 22 Spirit produces is love, joy, peace, patience, kindness, 23 goodness, faithfulness, gentleness, self-control. There is 24 no law against such things! Those who belong to Jesus the Christ have crucified the physical nature with its propensities and cravings.

If we live by the Spirit, let us be guided by the Spirit. 25 Let us not in our vanity challenge one another or envy 26 one another. But if a man is caught doing something 6 wrong, brothers, you are spiritual, and you must set him right, in a spirit of gentleness. Think of yourself, for you may be tempted too. Bear one another's burdens, and in 2 that way carry out the law of the Christ. For if anyone 3 thinks he is somebody when he is really nobody, he is deceiving himself. Every man ought to test his own 4 work, and then whatever satisfaction he has will be with reference to himself, and not in comparison with some- one else. For everyone will have to carry his own load. 5

THE LETTERS TO THE CORINTHIANS
· · ·

Settled in Ephesus, and engaged upon the greatest ministry of his life, Paul was kept informed by visitors and letters of conditions in the church in Corinth, just across the Aegean. He had written one letter to Corinth, telling them not to permit people of bad character to remain in the church, but his visitors from Corinth brought him word of other problems there. His own prestige there was being undermined. People were criticizing his Greek style as rough and unfinished, and disparaging him in comparison with other teachers. The Corinthians were getting into lawsuits with one another, and immoral practices were still being tolerated.

As Paul was pondering over these things, messengers arrived from Corinth with a letter for him, the only one we know of his receiving. It bristled with questions. Was it right to marry? Was it right to buy meat at the idol sanctuaries, where the best meat was to be had? Must women wear veils in Christian meetings? What was to be done about the ecstatic speaking which was creating such confusion in their meetings? How were they to understand the resurrection?

Our I Corinthians is the answer to this letter. In it Paul took up first the bad reports that had reached him about the situation at Corinth, and then discussed with them with extraordinary patience the problems they had laid before him in their letter. The effect of his answer, however, was far from successful. The faction opposed

[297]

to him became more numerous and clamorous than ever, and he was in danger of losing his hold upon the Corinthian church altogether.

To meet this situation he sent a third letter to Corinth, written in great distress of mind and with many tears, and regretted after it was sent. It is probably the closing part of our II Corinthians, chapters 10–13, which constitutes the most vehement defense of himself in the whole Pauline literature. This letter was sent to Corinth by the hand of Titus, and Paul stayed on in Ephesus to finish his work. From Ephesus he went north to Troas, where he hoped to meet Titus, but he was not there. Full of anxiety, Paul crossed into Macedonia, and there to his immeasurable relief he found Titus, who brought him the good news that the Corinthians had at last responded to his advances and returned to their old loyalty and devotion to him.

To express his relief and joy Paul wrote a final letter, the fourth letter of the series,—our II Corinthians, chapters 1–9, in which he reviewed the causes of difference with the Corinthians in a gentler strain, and gave an account of the motives and methods of his ministry.

It has been said that Paul's letters take the roofs off the early Christian meeting places and let us look inside, and this is peculiarly true of the letters to Corinth. In them we see Paul as a great and understanding teacher, patiently taking up the most commonplace and trivial matters in a way so searching and profound that before he has finished he has worked out some deep enduring principle of Christian living that can never be outgrown.

THE FIRST LETTER TO THE CORINTHIANS

THE BUILDERS AND THE BUILDING, 3:10–23

3 Like an expert builder, I laid a foundation, as God commissioned me to do, and now someone else is building upon it. But let everyone be careful how he does so. **11** For no one can lay any other foundation than the one that **12** is laid, that is, Jesus Christ himself. And whether one uses gold or silver or costly stone in building on the foun- **13** dation, or wood or hay or straw, the quality of every- one's work will appear, for the Day will show it. For the Day will break in fire, and the fire will test the quality of **14** everyone's work. If what a man has built on the founda- **15** dation stands the test, he will have his pay. If a man's work is burned up, he must stand the loss, though he himself will be saved, but as one who has passed through the fire.

16 Do you know that you are God's temple and that **17** God's Spirit makes its home in you? If anyone destroys the temple of God, God will destroy him. For the tem- ple of God is sacred, and that is what you are.

18 Let no one of you deceive himself. If any one of you imagines that he is wiser than the rest of you, in what this world calls wisdom, he had better become a fool, so **19** as to become really wise. For this world's wisdom is foolishness to God. For the Scripture says, "He who **20** catches the wise with their own cunning," and "The Lord knows that the deliberations of the wise are fruit- **21** less." So no one should boast about men. For it all be- **22** longs to you—Paul, Apollos, Cephas, the world, life, death, the present, the future—all of it belongs to you. **23** But you belong to Christ and Christ belongs to God.

THE CHRISTIAN USE OF RIGHTS, 9:1–23

9 Am I not free? Am I not an apostle? Have I not seen Jesus our Lord? Are you not the product of my work in **2** the Lord's service? If I am not an apostle to other people, I certainly am one to you, for you yourselves, in your re- lation to the Lord, are the certificate of my apostleship.

My answer to those who want to investigate me is ₃
this: Have we not a right to our food and drink? Have ₄
we not a right to take a Christian wife about with us, ₅
like the rest of the apostles and the Lord's brothers and
Cephas? Or is it only Barnabas and I that have no right ₆
to give up working for a living? What soldier ever pays ₇
his expenses out of his own pay? Who plants a vineyard
and does not eat any of the grapes? Who tends a flock and
does not get any of the milk? Am I saying only what men ₈
say? Does not the Law say so too? For in the Law of ₉
Moses it reads, "You shall not muzzle an ox that is treading out the grain." Is it about the oxen that God is concerned? Is he not clearly speaking in our interest? Of ₁₀
course this law was written in our interest, because the
plowman ought to plow, and the thresher to thresh, in
the expectation of sharing in the crop. If it was we who ₁₁
sowed the spiritual seed among you, is it too much if we
reap material benefits from you? If others enjoy such ₁₂
rights over you, have we not a still better claim? But, you
say, we have never availed ourselves of this right. No,
we will stand anything rather than put any hindrance in
the way of the good news of the Christ. Do you not ₁₃
know that those who do the work about the Temple get
their living from the Temple, and those who attend to
the altar divide the sacrifices with the altar? In just that ₁₄
way the Lord directed that those who preach the good
news should get their living from it. But I have not ₁₅
availed myself of any of these rights. And I am not writing this now so that I may become an illustration of this;
I had rather die than do that. No one shall deprive me of
this boast of mine. As far as preaching the good news is ₁₆
concerned, that is nothing for me to boast of, for I cannot
help doing it. For I am ruined if I do not preach. For if I ₁₇
do it of my own accord, I have my pay, but if I do it because I must, it is still a responsibility that I am charged
with. What pay then do I get? Why, that in my preach- ₁₈
ing I can offer the good news without cost, and so not
take full advantage of my rights as a preacher.

Though I am free from anyone's control, I have made ₁₉

myself everyone's slave, so as to win over all the more.
20 To the Jews I have become like a Jew, to win Jews over; to men under the Law I have become like a man under the Law, though I am not myself under the Law, so as to win
21 over those who are under the Law. To those who have no law I have become like a man without any law— though I am not without the law of God, but under the law of Christ—so as to win over those who are without
22 any law. To the overscrupulous I have become overscrupulous, so as to win the overscrupulous; I have become everything to everybody, so as by all means to save some
23 of them. And I do it all for the sake of the good news, so that I may share in its blessings along with the rest.

WE ARE PARTS OF ONE ANOTHER, 12:12–31

12   For just as the body is one and yet has many parts, and all the parts of the body, many as they are, form one
13 body, so it is with Christ. For we have all—Jews or Greeks, slaves or free men—been baptized in one spirit to form one body, and we have all been saturated with one
14 Spirit. For the body does not consist of one part but of
15 many. If the foot says, "As I am not a hand, I am not a part of the body," that does not make it any less a part of
16 the body. And if the ear says, "As I am not an eye, I am not a part of the body," that does not make it any less a
17 part of the body. If all the body were eye, how would we hear? If it were all ear, how could we have a sense of
18 smell? As it is, God has arranged the parts, every one of
19 them in the body as he wished them to be. If they were
20 all one part, where would the body be? As it is, there are
21 many parts, but one body. The eye cannot say to the hand, "I do not need you," or the head to the feet, "I do
22 not need you." On the contrary, the parts of the body
23 that are considered most delicate are indispensable, and the parts of it that we think common, we dress with
24 especial care, and our unpresentable parts receive especial attention which our presentable parts do not need. God has so adjusted the body and given such especial distinction to its inferior parts that there is no clash in the body,

but its parts all alike care for one another. If one part 25
suffers, all the parts share its sufferings. If a part has 26
honor done it, all the parts enjoy it too. Now you are 27
Christ's body, and individually parts of it. And God has 28
placed people in the church, first as apostles, second as inspired preachers, third as teachers, then wonder-work-
ers; then come ability to cure the sick, helpfulness, administration, ecstatic speaking. Is everyone an apostle? 29
Is everyone an inspired preacher? Is everyone a teacher?
Is everyone a wonder-worker? Is everyone able to cure 30
the sick? Can everyone speak ecstatically? Can everyone
explain what it means? But you must cultivate the 31
higher endowments.

THE PLACE OF LOVE, 13:1—14:5

I will show you a far better way. If I can speak the 13
languages of men and even of angels, but have no love, I
am only a noisy gong or a clashing cymbal. If I am in- 2
spired to preach and know all the secret truths and possess all knowledge, and if I have such perfect faith that I
can move mountains, but have no love, I am nothing.
Even if I give away everything I own, and give myself 3
up, but do it in pride, not love, it does me no good. Love 4
is patient and kind. Love is not envious or boastful. It 5
does not put on airs. It is not rude. It does not insist on
its rights. It does not become angry. It is not resentful.
It is not happy over injustice, it is only happy with truth. 6
It will bear anything, believe anything, hope for any- 7
thing, endure anything. Love will never die out. If 8
there is inspired preaching, it will pass away. If there is
ecstatic speaking, it will cease. If there is knowledge, it
will pass away. For our knowledge is imperfect and our 9
preaching is imperfect. But when perfection comes, what 10
is imperfect will pass away. When I was a child, I talked 11
like a child, I thought like a child, I reasoned like a
child. When I became a man, I put aside my childish
ways. For now we are looking at a dim reflection in a 12
mirror, but then we shall see face to face. Now my
knowledge is imperfect, but then I shall know as fully as

[302]

13 God knows me. So faith, hope, and love endure. These are the great three, and the greatest of them is love.

14 You must pursue love, while you are cultivating the spiritual endowments, and especially inspired preach-
2 ing. For anyone who speaks ecstatically is speaking not to men but to God, for no one can understand him,
3 though he is uttering secret truths. But the inspired preacher does his fellow-men good and encourages and
4 comforts them. Anyone who speaks ecstatically does himself good, but the inspired preacher does a congrega-
5 tion good. I want you all to speak ecstatically, but I especially want you to be inspired to preach. The man who is inspired to preach is more useful than the one who speaks ecstatically—unless he can explain what he says so that it may do the church some good.

THE RESURRECTION, 15:12–28, 35–58

15 Now if what we preach about Christ is that he was raised from the dead, how can some of you say that there
13 is no such thing as a resurrection of the dead? If there is no resurrection of the dead, then Christ was not raised,
14 and if Christ was not raised, there is nothing in our mes-
15 sage; there is nothing in our faith either, and we are found guilty of misrepresenting God, for we have testi-fied that he raised Christ, when he did not do it, if it is
16 true that the dead are never raised. For if the dead are
17 never raised, Christ was not raised; and if Christ was not raised, your faith is a delusion; you are still under the
18 control of your sins. Yes, and those who have fallen
19 asleep in trust in Christ have perished. If we have cen-tered our hopes on Christ in this life, and that is all, we are the most pitiable people in the world.

20 But the truth is, Christ was raised from the dead, the
21 first to be raised of those who have fallen asleep. For since it was through a man that we have death, it is through a man also that we have the raising of the dead.
22 For just as because of their relation to Adam all men die, so because of their relation to Christ they will all be
23 brought to life again. But each in his own turn; Christ

first, and then at Christ's coming those who belong to him. After that will come the end, when he will turn 24 over the kingdom to God his Father, bringing to an end all other government, authority, and power, for he 25 must retain the kingdom until he puts all his enemies under his feet. The last enemy to be overthrown will be 26 death, for everything is to be reduced to subjection and 27 put under Christ's feet. But when it says that everything is subject to him, he is evidently excepted who reduced it all to subjection to him. And when everything is reduced 28 to subjection to him, then the Son himself will also become subject to him who has reduced everything to subjection to him, so that God may be everything to everyone.

But someone will say, "How can the dead rise? What 35 kind of a body will they have when they come back?" You foolish man, the very seed you sow never comes to 36 life without dying first; and when you sow it, it has not 37 the form it is going to have, but is a naked kernel, perhaps of wheat or something else; and God gives it just 38 such a form as he pleases, so that each kind of seed has a form of its own. Flesh is not all alike; men have one kind, 39 animals another, birds another, and fish another. There 40 are heavenly bodies, and there are earthly bodies, but the beauty of the heavenly bodies is of one kind, and the beauty of the earthly bodies is of another. The sun has 41 one kind of beauty, and the moon another, and the stars another; why, one star differs from another in beauty. It 42 is so with the resurrection of the dead. The body is sown 43 in decay, it is raised free from decay. It is sown in humiliation, it is raised in splendor. It is sown in weakness, it is raised in strength. It is a physical body that is sown, 44 it is a spiritual body that is raised. If there is a physical body, there is a spiritual body also. This is also what the 45 Scripture says: "The first man Adam became a living creature." The last Adam has become a life-giving Spirit. It is not the spiritual that comes first, but the physi- 46 cal, and then the spiritual. The first man is of the dust of 47 the earth; the second man is from heaven. Those who are 48 of the earth are like him who was of the earth, and those who are of heaven are like him who is from heaven, and 49 as we have been like the man of the earth, let us also try 50 to be like the man from heaven. But I can tell you this, brothers: flesh and blood cannot share in the Kingdom of God, and decay will not share in what is imperishable. 51 I will tell you a secret. We shall not all fall asleep, but 52 we shall all be changed, in a moment, in the twinkling of an eye, at the sound of the last trumpet. For the trumpet will sound, and the dead will be raised free from de- 53 cay, and we shall be changed. For this perishable nature must put on the imperishable, and this mortal nature 54 must put on immortality. And when this mortal nature puts on immortality, then what the Scripture says will come true—"Death has been triumphantly destroyed. 55 Where, Death, is your victory? Where, Death, is your 56 sting?" Sin is the sting of death, and it is the Law that 57 gives sin its power. But thank God! He gives us victory 58 through our Lord Jesus Christ. So, my dear brothers, be firm and unmoved, and always devote yourselves to the Lord's work, for you know that through the Lord your labor is not thrown away.

THE SECOND LETTER TO THE CORINTHIANS

Blessed be the God and Father of our Lord Jesus Christ, 1
the merciful Father, and the God always ready to comfort! He comforts me in all my trouble, so that I can comfort 4
people who are in any trouble with the comfort with
which I myself am comforted by God. For if I have a lib- 5
beral share of Christ's sufferings, through Christ I have a
liberal share of comfort too. If I am in trouble, it is to 6
bring you comfort and salvation, and if I am comforted,
it is for the sake of the comfort which you experience
when you steadfastly endure such sufferings as I also have
to bear. My hopes for you are unshaken. For I know 7
that just as surely as you share my sufferings, just so surely you will share my comfort. For I do not want you, 8
brothers, to misunderstand the distress that I experienced
in Asia, for I was so utterly and unendurably crushed,
that I actually despaired of life itself. Why, I felt in my
heart that the end must be death. That was to keep me 9
from relying on myself instead of on God, who can even
raise the dead. So deadly was the peril from which he 10
saved me, as he will save me again! It is on him that I
have set my hope that he will save me again. You must 11
help me by your prayers, so that many will give thanks
to God on my behalf for the blessing granted me in answer to many prayers.

MOTIVES AND METHODS OF HIS MINISTRY,
4:1—5:5, 20—6:10

So since by the mercy of God I am engaged in this 4
service, I never lose heart. I disown disgraceful, under- 2
handed ways. I refuse to practice cunning or to tamper
with God's message. It is by the open statement of the
truth that I would commend myself to every human con-

3 science in the sight of God. If the meaning of my preaching of the good news is veiled at all, it is so only in the
4 case of those who are on the way to destruction. In their case, the god of this world has blinded the minds of the unbelievers, to keep the light of the good news of the glorious Christ, the likeness of God, from dawning upon
5 them. For it is not myself but Christ Jesus that I am proclaiming as Lord; I am only a slave of yours for Jesus'
6 sake. For God who said, "Let light shine out of darkness," has shone in my heart, to give me the light of the knowledge of God's glory, that is on the face of Christ.
7 But I have this treasure in a mere earthen jar, to show that its amazing power belongs to God and not to me.
8 I am hard pressed on every side, but never cut off: per-
9 plexed, but not driven to despair; routed, but not aban-
10 doned; struck down, but not destroyed; never free from the danger of being put to death like Jesus, so that in my
11 body the life of Jesus also may be seen. For every day I live I am being given up to death for Jesus' sake, so that
12 the life of Jesus may be visible in my mortal nature. So it is death that operates in my case, but life that operates in
13 yours. In the same spirit of faith as his who said, "I be-
14 lieved, and so I spoke," I too believe, and so I speak, sure that he who raised the Lord Jesus from the dead will raise me also like Jesus, and bring me side by side with
15 you into his presence. For it is all for your benefit, in order that as God's favor reaches greater and greater numbers, it may result in more and more thanksgiving in praise of God.
16 So I never lose heart. Though my outer nature is wast-
17 ing away, my inner is being renewed every day. For this slight, momentary trouble is piling up for me an eternal
18 blessedness beyond all comparison, because I keep my
5 eyes not on what is seen but what is unseen. For what is seen is transitory, but what is unseen is eternal. For I know that if this earthly tent that I live in is taken down, God will provide me a building in heaven to live in, not
2 built by human hands but eternal. This makes me sigh
3 with longing to put on my heavenly dwelling, for if I

[307]

do, I shall never find myself disembodied. For I who   4
am still in my tent sigh with anxiety, because I do not
want to be stripped of it, but to put on the other over it,
so that what is only mortal may be absorbed in life. It is   5
God himself who has prepared me for this change, and he
has given me the Spirit as his guaranty.

It is for Christ, therefore, that I am an envoy, seeing   20
that God makes his appeal through me. On Christ's behalf I beg you to be reconciled to God. He made him who   21
knew nothing of sin to be sin, for our sake, so that
through union with him we might become God's uprightness.

As God's fellow-worker, I appeal to you, too, not to   6
accept the favor of God and then waste it. For he says,   2
    "I have listened to you at a welcome time,
    And helped you on a day of deliverance!"
Now the welcome time has come! This is the day of
deliverance! I put no obstacles in anyone's path, so that   3
no fault may be found with my work. On the contrary,   4
as a servant of God I try in every way to commend myself to them, through my great endurance in troubles,   5
difficulties, hardships, beatings, imprisonments, riots,
labors, sleepless nights, and hunger, through my purity   6
of life, my knowledge, my patience, my kindness, my   7
holiness of spirit, my genuine love, the truth of my teaching, and the power of God; with the weapons of upright-   8
ness for the right hand and the left, in honor or dishonor, in praise or blame; considered an impostor, when   9
I am true, obscure, when I am well known, at the point
of death, yet here I am alive, punished, but not dead yet,   10
pained, when I am always glad, poor, when I make many
others rich, penniless, when really I own everything.

HARDSHIPS ENDURED IN HIS MISSIONARY WORK,
11:16-33

I repeat, no one should think me a fool, but if you do,   11
show me at least the patience you would show a fool, and
let me have my little boast like the others. When I boast   17
in this reckless way, I do not say what I am saying for

18 the Lord, but as a fool would talk. Since many are so hu-
19 man as to boast, I will do it also. For you like to put
20 up with fools, you are so wise yourselves! For you put up with it if a man makes you his slaves, or lives on you, or takes you in, or puts on airs, or gives you a slap in the
21 face. To my shame I must admit that I was too weak for that sort of thing. But whatever anyone else dares to boast of—I am playing the part of a fool—I will dare to
22 boast of too. If they are Hebrews, so am I! If they are Israelites, so am I! If they are descended from Abraham,
23 so am I! If they are Christian workers—I am talking like a madman!—I am a better one! with far greater labors, far more imprisonments, vastly worse beatings, and in fre-
24 quent danger of death. Five times I have been given one
25 less than forty lashes, by the Jews. I have been beaten three times by the Romans, I have been stoned once, I have been shipwrecked three times, a night and a day I
26 have been adrift at sea; with my frequent journeys, in danger from rivers, danger from robbers, danger from my own people, danger from the heathen, danger in the city, danger in the desert, danger at sea, danger from false
27 brothers, through toil and hardship, through many a sleepless night, through hunger and thirst, often without
28 food, and exposed to cold. And besides everything else, the thing that burdens me every day is my anxiety about
29 all the churches. Who is weak without my being weak? Whose conscience is hurt without my being fired with in-
30 dignation? If there must be boasting, I will boast of the
31 things that show my weakness! The God and Father of the Lord Jesus Christ, he who is forever blessed, knows
32 that I am telling the truth. When I was at Damascus, the governor under King Aretas had the city gates watched
33 in order to catch me, but I was lowered in a basket from an opening in the wall, and got out of his clutches.

THE LETTER TO THE ROMANS
. . .

*For twenty-five years Paul had been preaching the
gospel of Christ among the eastern provinces of the empire, from Syria to Macedonia. He felt that his work in
that eastern world was done, and he turned his eyes toward the west, and fixed upon Spain as the next field
for his pioneer evangelism. On his way there he wished
to visit Rome, where Christianity had already found a
foothold. He is temporarily deterred from both these
steps by the collection he has long been making among
his churches for the poor Christians in Jerusalem, which
is now complete and must be delivered, he feels, by himself in person.*

*But standing once more in Corinth, where he might so
easily take ship for Brundisium and there take the Ap-
pian Way for Rome, his mind turns to the Eternal
City which he may never see, and to insure reaching the
Christian congregation there with his own great conception of the gospel, he writes a letter, to safeguard the
Christians of Rome against the dangers he had already
encountered in Galatia and Corinth, and to present the
great features of the Christian faith as he sees them.*

*Jew and Greek alike have fallen short of the truest
uprightness, but a way to such uprightness has now
been revealed through Christ. It is the way of faith—
that inner attitude of trust and dependence upon God
which must be the germ of any real achievement in character. God has forgiven the world, and man has only*

[310]

to accept that forgiveness through faith and live the life of the spirit.

Nowhere is Paul so clearly the missionary statesman as in Romans. His interests embrace east and west, Jerusalem, Rome, Spain, and while he looks to Spain and writes to Rome, he turns back to Jerusalem to make a final effort to unite Jew and Greek in the service of Christ.

. . .

THE SALUTATION, 1:1–7

1 Paul, a slave of Jesus Christ, called as an apostle, set
2 apart to declare God's good news which he promised long ago through his prophets in the holy Scriptures,
3 about his Son, who was physically descended from
4 David, and decisively declared Son of God in his holiness of spirit, by being raised from the dead—Jesus Christ our
5 Lord, through whom we have received God's favor and been commissioned in his name to urge obedience and
6 faith upon all the heathen, including you who have been
7 called to belong to Jesus Christ—to all those in Rome whom God loves, who are called to be his people; God our Father and the Lord Jesus Christ bless you and give you peace.

PAUL'S CONCERN FOR THE CHRISTIANS OF ROME, 1:8–17

1 First I thank my God through Jesus Christ about you all, because the news of your faith is spreading all over
9 the world. As God is my witness, whom I serve in my spirit in spreading the good news of his Son, I never fail
10 to mention you when I pray, and to ask that somehow by God's will I may some day at last succeed in reaching
11 you. For I long to see you, to convey to you some
12 spiritual gift that will strengthen you; in other words, that you and I may be mutually encouraged by one an-
13 other's faith. I want you to understand, brothers, that I have often intended to come to see you (though thus far

I have been prevented) in order to produce some results among you, as well as among the rest of the heathen. I 14 owe a debt both to Greeks and to foreigners, to the cultivated and the uncultivated. So, for my part, I am eager 15 to preach the good news to you at Rome also. For I am 16 not ashamed of the good news, for it is God's power for the salvation of everyone who has faith, of the Jew first and then of the Greek. In it God's way of uprightness is 17 disclosed through faith and for faith, just as the Scripture says, "The upright will have life because of his faith."

THE IMPARTIALITY OF GOD, 2:1–11

Therefore you have no excuse, whoever you are, if you 2 pose as a judge, for when you pass judgment on someone else, you are condemning yourself, for you, who sit in judgment, do the very same things yourself. We know 2 that God's judgment rightfully falls upon those who do such things as these. And do you suppose, when you sit 3 in judgment upon those who do such things and yet do them yourself, that you will escape the judgment of God? Do you think so lightly of his wealth of kindness, 4 forbearance, and patience, and fail to see that God's kindness ought to induce you to repent? But in your 5 obstinacy and impenitence you are storing up wrath for yourself on the Day of Wrath, when the justice of God will burst forth. For he will pay every man for what he 6 has done. Those who by persistently doing right strive 7 for glory, honor, and immortality will have eternal life, but self-seeking people who are disloyal to the truth 8 and responsive only to what is wrong will experience anger and fury, crushing distress and anguish, every 9 human soul of them that actually does what is wrong— the Jew first, and the Greek also; but there will be glory, 10 honor, and peace for everyone who does right, the Jew first, and the Greek also, for God shows no partiality. 11

RELIGION A MATTER OF THE INNER LIFE, 2:17–29

Suppose you call yourself a Jew, and rely on law, and 2 boast about God, and can understand his will, and from 18

19 hearing the Law read can tell what is right, and you are
sure that you can guide the blind, enlighten people who
20 are in the dark, train the foolish, teach the young, since
you have knowledge and truth formulated in the Law—
21 why, then, will you teach others and refuse to teach
yourself? Will you preach against stealing, and yet steal
22 yourself? Will you warn men against adultery, and yet
practice it yourself? Will you pretend to detest idols,
23 and yet rob their temples? Will you boast of the Law and
24 yet dishonor God by breaking it? For, as the Scripture
says, the very name of God is abused among the heathen,
25 because of you! Circumcision will help you only if you
observe the Law; but if you are a lawbreaker, you might
26 as well be uncircumcised. So if people who are uncircumcised observe the requirements of the Law, will they not
27 be treated as though they were circumcised? And if, although they are physically uncircumcised, they obey the
Law, they will condemn you, who break the Law, al-
28 though you have it in writing, and are circumcised. For
the real Jew is not the man who is one outwardly, and
the real circumcision is not something physical and ex-
29 ternal. The real Jew is the man who is one inwardly,
and real circumcision is a matter of the heart, a spiritual,
not a literal, thing. Such a man receives his praise not
from men, but from God.

UPRIGHTNESS THE RESULT OF FAITH, 3:27-31

3 Then what becomes of our boasting? It is shut out.
On what principle? What a man does? No, but whether
28 a man has faith. For we hold that a man is made upright
by faith; the observance of the Law has nothing to do
29 with it. Does God belong to the Jews alone? Does he not
belong to the heathen too? Of course he belongs to the
30 heathen too; there is but one God, and he will make the
circumcised upright on the ground of their faith and the
31 uncircumcised upright because of theirs. Is this using
faith to overthrow law? Far from it. This confirms the
Law.

THE LOVE OF GOD AND THE WORK OF CHRIST, 5:1-21

So as we have been made upright by faith, let us live 5
in peace with God through our Lord Jesus Christ, by 2
whom we have been introduced through faith to the
favor of God that we now enjoy, and let us glory in our
hope of sharing the glory of God. More than that, we 3
ought to glory in our troubles, for we know that trouble
produces endurance, and endurance, character, and char- 4
acter, hope, and hope will not disappoint us. For, 5
through the holy Spirit that has been given us, God's
love has flooded our hearts. For when we were still help- 6
less, at the decisive moment Christ died for us godless
men. Why, a man will hardly give his life for an upright 7
person, though perhaps for a really good man some may
be brave enough to die. But God proves his love for us 8
by the fact that Christ died for us when we were still
sinners. So if we have already been made upright by his 9
death, it is far more certain that through him we shall be
saved from God's anger! If, when we were God's 10
enemies, we were reconciled to him through the death
of his Son, it is far more certain that now that we are
reconciled we shall be saved through sharing in his life!
More than that, we actually glory in God through our 11
Lord Jesus Christ, to whom we owe our reconciliation.

It is just like the way in which through one man sin 12
came into the world, and death followed sin, and so
death spread to all men, because all men sinned. It is true 13
sin was in the world before the Law was given, and men
are not charged with sin where there is no law. Still 14
death reigned from Adam to Moses, even over those who
had not sinned as Adam had, in the face of an express
command. So Adam foreshadowed the one who was to
come. But there is no comparison between God's gift 15
and that offense. For if one man's offense made the mass
of mankind die, God's mercy and his gift given through
the favor of the one man Jesus Christ have far more
powerfully affected mankind. Nor is there any compari- 16
son between the gift and the effects of that one man's sin.

That sentence arose from the act of one man, and was for condemnation; but God's gift arose out of many offenses
17 and results in acquittal. For if that one man's offense made death reign through that one man, all the more will those who receive God's overflowing mercy and his gift of uprightness live and reign through the one individual Jesus Christ.

18 So as one offense meant condemnation for all men, just so one righteous act means acquittal and life for all men.
19 For just as that one man's disobedience made the mass of mankind sinners, so this one's obedience will make the
20 mass of them upright. Then law slipped in, and multiplied the offense. But greatly as sin multiplied, God's mercy has far surpassed it, so that just as sin had reigned
21 through death, mercy might reign through uprightness and bring eternal life through Jesus Christ our Lord.

THE FREEDOM AND HAPPINESS OF THE BELIEVER,
8:1–11, 31–39

8 So there is no condemnation any more for those who
2 are in union with Christ Jesus. For the life-giving law of the Spirit through Christ Jesus has freed you from the
3 Law of sin and death. For though it was impossible for the Law to do it, hampered as it was by our physical limitations, God, by sending his own Son in our sinful physical form, as a sin-offering put his condemnation
4 upon sin through his physical nature, so that the requirement of the Law might be fully met in our case, since we live not on the physical but on the spiritual plane.
5 People who are controlled by the physical think of what is physical, and people who are controlled by the spiritual
6 think of what is spiritual. For to be physically minded means death, but to be spiritually minded means life and
7 peace. For to be physically minded means hostility to God, for it refuses to obey God's law, indeed it cannot
8 obey it. Those who are physical cannot please God. But
9 you are not physical but spiritual, if God's Spirit has really taken possession of you; for unless a man has Christ's spir-
10 it, he does not belong to Christ. But if Christ is in your

hearts, though your bodies are dead in consequence of sin, your spirits have life in consequence of uprightness. If the ¹¹ Spirit of him who raised Jesus from the dead has taken possession of you, he who raised Christ Jesus from the dead will also give your mortal bodies life through his Spirit that has taken possession of you.

Then what shall we conclude from this? If God is for ³¹ us, who can be against us? Will not he who did not spare ³² his own Son, but gave him up for us all, with that gift give us everything? Who can bring any accusation ³³ against those whom God has chosen? God pronounces them upright; who can condemn them? Christ Jesus who ³⁴ died, or rather who was raised from the dead, is at God's right hand, and actually pleads for us. Who can separate ³⁵ us from Christ's love? Can trouble or misfortune or persecution or hunger or destitution or danger or the sword? As the Scripture says,   ³⁶

"For your sake we are being put to death all day long,
We are treated like sheep to be slaughtered."

But in all these things we are more than victorious ³⁷ through him who loved us. For I am convinced that ³⁸ neither death nor life nor angels nor their hierarchies nor the present nor the future nor any supernatural forces either of height or depth will be able to separate us from ³⁹ the love God has shown in Christ Jesus our Lord!

THE DUTIES OF THE CHRISTIAN, IN THE WORLD, THE STATE, AND THE CHURCH, 12:1–21; 15:1–6

I appeal to you, therefore, brothers, by this mercy of 12 God, to offer your bodies in a living sacrifice that will be holy and acceptable to God; that is your rational worship. You must not adopt the customs of this world but ² by your new attitude of mind be transformed so that you can find out what God's will is—what is good, pleasing, and perfect.

By the favor that God has shown me, I would tell ³ every one of you not to think too highly of himself, but to think reasonably, judging himself by the degree of

4 faith God has allowed him. For just as there are many parts united in our human bodies, and the parts do not
5 all have the same function, so, many as we are, we form one body through union with Christ, and we are indi-
6 vidually parts of one another. We have gifts that differ with the favor that God has shown us, whether it is that
7 of preaching, differing with the measure of our faith, or of practical service, differing in the field of service, or the
8 teacher who exercises his gift in teaching, the speaker, in his exhortation, the giver of charity, with generosity, the office-holder, with devotion, the one who does acts
9 of mercy, with cheerfulness. Your love must be genuine. You must hate what is wrong, and hold to what is right.
10 Be affectionate in your love for the brotherhood, eager to show one another honor, not wanting in devotion, but
11
12 on fire with the Spirit. Serve the Lord. Be happy in your hope, steadfast in time of trouble, persistent in prayer.
13 Supply the needs of God's people, be unfailing in hospi-
14 tality. Bless your persecutors; bless them; do not curse
15 them. Rejoice with those who rejoice, weep with those
16 who weep. Live in harmony with one another. Do not be too ambitious, but accept humble tasks. Do not be
17 conceited. Do not pay anyone back with evil for evil. See that you are above reproach in the eyes of everyone.
18 If possible, for your part, live peacefully with everybody.
19 Do not take your revenge, dear friends, but leave room for God's anger, for the Scripture says, "Vengeance belongs
20 to me; I will pay them back, says the Lord." No! If your enemy is hungry, feed him! If he is thirsty, give him something to drink! For if you do, you will heap burning
21 coals upon his head! Do not be conquered by evil, but conquer evil with good.

15   It is the duty of us who are strong to put up with the weaknesses of those who are immature, and not just suit
2 ourselves. Everyone of us must try to please his neigh-
3 bor, to do him good, and help in his development. Christ
4 did not please himself, but as the Scripture says, "The reproaches of those who reproach you have fallen on me." For everything that was written in earlier times was

written for our instruction, so that by being steadfast and through the encouragement the Scriptures give, we might hold our hope fast. May God, from whom steadfastness 5 and encouragement come, give you such harmony with one another, in following the example of Christ Jesus, 6 that you may praise the God and Father of our Lord Jesus Christ with one accord and one voice.

THE DOXOLOGY, 16:25–27

To him who can make you strong by the good news 16 I bring and the preaching about Jesus Christ, through the disclosure of the secret kept back for long ages but now 26 revealed, and at the command of the eternal God made known through the writings of the prophets to all the heathen, to lead them to obedience and faith—to the one 27 wise God be glory forever through Jesus Christ. Amen.

THE LETTER TO THE PHILIPPIANS

· · ·

Paul's journey to Jerusalem with the collection had the most disastrous results, for as a result of it he was mobbed, arrested, and imprisoned, and after two years transferred to Rome for trial. To him at Rome his old friends the Philippians sent a man named Epaphroditus, with money for Paul's needs and instructions to look after his case.

But Epaphroditus fell sick in Rome, and for a time his life was despaired of. When he was out of danger and on the road to recovery, Paul decided that he must be sent back to Philippi. To prevent any possible unjust criticism of Epaphroditus for having failed to carry out the instructions of his Philippian principals, Paul puts in his hands a letter to the Philippians, telling how faithfully he has done his part, and charging them to give him a hearty welcome.

Our Philippians seems to consist of two letters: one warning them against the Judaizers and acknowledging the arrival of Epaphroditus with their gift, 3:2—4:23; the other urging them to be harmonious and unselfish, and explaining why he is sending Epaphroditus back to them after his illness, 1:1—3:1.

Paul's long and tedious imprisonment left the great task of the Greek mission to men less able to carry it forward, and must often have seemed to him doubly bitter on that account. Yet in the midst of heartbreaking discouragement Paul can tell the Philippians to let their minds dwell only on what is true, worthy, right, pure, amiable, kindly. This was the great lesson he had learned in his imprisonment, which had not made him morbid and sour but more than ever a source of cheer and hope to the Christian brotherhood.

. . .

THE PROGRESS OF THE GOSPEL, 1:12–26

Now I want to assure you, brothers, that what has 1 happened to me has actually resulted in furthering the preaching of the good news. Thus it is generally known 13 throughout the Imperial Guard and elsewhere that it is for the sake of Christ that I am in prison, and so most of 14 the Christian brothers have been exceedingly encouraged by my example to declare God's message without any fear of the consequences.

Some of them, it is true, are actually preaching the 15 Christ from jealousy and partisanship, but there are others who are doing it out of good-will. These latter do 16 it from love for me, for they know that God has put me where I am to defend our right to preach the good news. But the others are preaching the Christ not sincerely but 17 for their own ends, imagining that they are making my imprisonment harder to bear.

But what difference does it make? All that matters is 18 that, in one way or another, from false motives or honest ones, Christ is being made known; I am glad of that. Yes, and I expect to be glad, for I know that through your 19 prayers and the help of the Spirit of Jesus Christ, all this will turn out for my highest welfare, for I eagerly and 20 confidently hope that I shall never disgrace myself but that this time as always hitherto, living or dying, I shall do Christ credit by my unfailing courage.

For, as I see it, living means Christ and dying some- 21 thing even better. But if living on here means having my 22 labor bear fruit, I cannot tell which to choose. I am un- 23 decided between the two, for I long to depart and be with

24 Christ, for that is far, far better, and yet your needs
25 make it very necessary for me to stay on here. I am convinced of this, and so I know that I shall stay on and
serve you all, to help you to develop and to be glad in
26 your faith. So you will find in me fresh cause for Christian exultation, through having me with you again.

MEETING PERSECUTION IN THE SPIRIT OF CHRIST,
1:27—2:11

1   Whatever happens, show yourselves citizens worthy of
the good news of the Christ, so that whether I come and
see you or am kept away and only hear news of you, I
may know that you are standing firm with one spirit, one
purpose, fighting side by side for faith in the good news.
28 Never for a moment falter before your opponents, for your
fearlessness will be a sure sign for them of their coming
destruction, but to you it will be an omen, from God him-
29 self, of your deliverance. For you have been granted the
privilege not only of trusting in Christ but of suffering
30 for him. Take your part in the same struggle that you
have seen me engage in and that you hear I am still
keeping up.

2   So by whatever appeal there is in our relation to
Christ, by whatever incentive there is in love, by whatever participation there is in the Spirit, whatever affec-
2 tion and sympathy, make me perfectly happy by living
in harmony, with the same attitude of love, with the
3 same feeling and purpose. Do not act for selfish ends or
from vanity, but modestly treat one another as your
4 superiors. Do not take account of your own interests,
5 but of the interests of others as well. Have the same atti-
6 tude that Christ Jesus had. Though he possessed the
nature of God, he did not grasp at equality with God,
7 but laid it aside to take on the nature of a slave and be-
8 come like other men. When he had assumed human form,
he still further humbled himself and carried his obedience
9 so far as to die, and to die upon the cross. That is why
God has so greatly exalted him, and given him the name
10 above all others, so that in the name of Jesus everyone

should kneel, in heaven and on earth and in the underworld, and everyone should acknowledge Jesus Christ as 11
Lord, and thus glorify God the Father.

THE PURSUIT OF THE CHRISTIAN IDEAL, 3:4–16

If anyone thinks he can rely on his physical ad- 3
vantages, still more can I! I was circumcised when I was 5
eight days old. I am a descendant of Israel. I belong to
the tribe of Benjamin. I am a Hebrew, and the son of
Hebrews. As to the Law, I was a Pharisee; as to my zeal, 6
I was a persecutor of the church; and by the Law's standard of uprightness, no fault could be found with me. But 7
for the sake of Christ I have come to count my former
gains as loss. Why, I count everything as loss com- 8
pared with the supreme advantage of knowing Christ
Jesus my Lord. For his sake I have lost everything, and
think it rubbish, in order to gain Christ and be known to 9
be united to him, with any uprightness I may have not
based on law but coming through faith in Christ—the
uprightness that comes from God through faith. I want 10
to know him in the power of resurrection, and to share
his sufferings and even his death, in the hope of attaining 11
resurrection from the dead. Not that I have secured it 12
yet, or already reached perfection, but I am pressing on
to see if I can capture it, because I have been captured by
Jesus Christ. Brothers, I do not consider that I have cap- 13
tured it yet, only, forgetting what is behind me, and
straining toward what lies ahead, I am pressing toward 14
the goal, for the prize to which God through Christ
Jesus calls us upward. Let as many of us therefore as are 15
mature have this attitude. If you have any different attitude, God will make this clear to you. Only, we must 16
live up to what we have already attained.

THE PEACE OF GOD, 4:4–9

Goodbye, and the Lord be with you always. Again I 4
say, goodbye. Let all men see your forbearing spirit. The 5
Lord is coming soon. Have no anxiety about anything, 6
but make all your wants known to God in prayer and

7 entreaty, and with thanksgiving. Then, through your union with Christ Jesus, the peace of God, so far above any human thought, will guard your minds and thoughts.

8 Now, brothers, let your minds dwell on what is true, what is worthy, what is right, what is pure, what is amiable, what is kindly—on everything that is excellent

9 or praiseworthy. Do the things that you learned, received, and heard from me, and that you saw me do. Then God who gives peace will be with you.

THE LETTER TO THE COLOSSIANS

. . .

*Even while a prisoner at Rome, about 60–62 A.D.,
Paul was able to see his friends and to consult with them
about difficulties in their work. His prison thus became
almost an office to which various visitors came for counsel
and help. One of these was Epaphras, the minister of the
church at Colossae, in the Roman province of Asia, where
views were being advanced which threatened the place of
Christ and the democracy of Christian fellowship.*

*In the ancient world some thinkers found the gulf be-
tween the divine Being and their life in this material
world almost too great to pass. In a somewhat Platonic
fashion they came to bridge this gulf with range upon
range of ideal beings, the embodiments of virtues,
through communion with whom they felt that they could
gradually rise to higher and higher levels of existence
until they might finally enter upon the full experience of
God.*

*When such people came into the Christian church they
immediately recognized in Jesus one of these intermedi-
aries, but still clung to the others as promising to introduce them to even higher spiritual attainment. Their
communings with these beings were furthered by various
ascetic practices—fastings, vigils, and other forms of
abstinence, which denied the flesh and thus, as they
thought, exalted the spirit. And they came to look down
upon other Christians as people of inferior spiritual development.*

This was the situation at Colossae that was reported to Paul in his Roman prison by Epaphras, and to correct it Paul wrote Colossians. In it he declares that Jesus is the all-sufficient mediator, and that the others can have no place in the Christian way of life. The fullest and most divine spiritual attainment is to be reached through him alone. The ascetic practices so much in vogue at Colossae Paul declares religiously worthless, really exaggerating the significance of the body which they profess to discipline. To the great spiritual ideal which Paul has in view for the Christian believer they could contribute nothing. In Christ alone is to be found all that divine fulness that some of them have been seeking in fanciful speculations, and it is open to all Christians alike, no matter how humble or obscure.

. . .

THE SUPREME PLACE OF CHRIST, 1:16–20, 28

1   He is a likeness of the unseen God, born before any creature, for it was through him that everything was created in heaven and on earth, the seen and the unseen, angelic thrones, dominions, principalities, authorities—
17   all things were created through him and for him. He existed before all things and he sustains and embraces them
18   all. He is the head of the church, it is his body; for he is the beginning, the firstborn from among the dead—that
19   he might come to stand first in everything. For all the
20   divine fulness chose to dwell in him and through him to reconcile to God all things on earth or in heaven, making this peace through his blood shed on the cross.

28   And in spreading the news of him, we warn everyone and teach everyone all our wisdom, in order to bring everyone to Christian perfection.

UNION WITH CHRIST THE ONE RELIGIOUS NECESSITY,
2:1–23

For I want you to know what a fight I am putting up 2
for you and for our brothers in Laodicea, and for all who
do not know me personally, that your hearts may be
cheered. I want you to be united by love, and to have all 2
the benefit of assured knowledge in coming to know
Christ—that divine mystery in which all treasures of 3
wisdom and knowledge are to be found. What I mean is, 4
let nobody mislead you by specious arguments. For 5
though I am absent from you in person I am with you in
spirit, and I am glad to observe your harmony and the
solidity of your faith in Christ.

So just as you once accepted the Christ, Jesus, as your 6
Lord, you must live in vital union with him. You must 7
be rooted and built up in him and made strong in faith,
just as you were taught to be, overflowing with it in your
gratitude.

Take care that nobody exploits you through the pre- 8
tensions of philosophy, guided by human tradition, following material ways of looking at things, instead of following Christ. For it is in him that all the fulness of 9
God's nature lives embodied, and in union with him you 10
too are filled with it. He is the head of all your principalities and dominions. Through your relation to him 11
you have received, not a physical circumcision, but a circumcision effected by Christ, in stripping you of your
material nature, when in your baptism you were buried 12
with him and raised to life with him through your faith
in the power of God who raised him from the dead. Yes, 13
you who were dead through your misdeeds and physically uncircumcised, God raised to life with Christ. He 14
forgave us all our misdeeds, canceled the bond which
stood against us, with its requirements, and put it out of
our way when he nailed it to the cross. He disarmed the 15
principalities and dominions and displayed them openly,
triumphing over them through him.

So no one can call you to account for what you eat or 16
drink, or do about annual or monthly feasts or Sabbaths.

17 That was all only the shadow of something that was to
18 follow; the reality is found in Christ. No one can put you
in the wrong by persisting in studied humility and the
worship of angels, being absorbed in the visions he has
seen, and groundlessly conceited over his mere human
19 mind. Such people lose their connection with the head,
from which the whole body through its ligaments and
sinews must be governed and united if it is to grow in the
divine way.

20 If you have died with Christ to material ways of looking at things, why do you act as though you still be-
21 longed to the world, and submit to rules like "You must
not handle," "You must not taste," "You must not
22 touch"—referring to things that are all meant to be used
up and destroyed? This is to follow mere human rules
23 and regulations. Such practices pass for wisdom, with
their self-imposed devotions, their self-humiliation, and
their ascetic discipline, but they carry with them no real
distinction, they are really only a catering to the flesh.

THE NEW LIFE IN CHRIST, 3:1-17

3 If, then, you have been raised to life with Christ, set
your hearts on the things that are where Christ is, above,
2 seated at God's right hand. Fix your thoughts on the
things that are above, not on those that are on earth.
3 For you have died, and your life now lies hidden with
4 Christ in God. When Christ, who is our true life, shall
make his appearance, then you also will appear glorified
with him.

5 So treat as dead your physical nature, as far as immorality, impurity, passion, evil desire, and greed are con-
6 cerned; for it is really idolatry. It is on account of these
7 things that God's anger is coming. And you once practiced them as others do, when you lived that old earthly
8 life. But now you too must put them all aside—anger,
rage, spite, rough, abusive talk—these must be banished
9 from your lips. You must not lie to one another. For you
10 have stripped off your old self with its ways and have put
on that new self newly made in the likeness of its Crea-

tor, to know him fully. Here, what matters is not 11
"Greek" and "Jew," the circumcised and the uncircumcised, barbarian, Scythian, slave, freeborn, but Christ is
everything and in us all.

As persons chosen by God, then, consecrated and dear- 12
ly loved, you must clothe yourselves with tenderness of
heart, kindness, humility, gentleness, forbearance. You 13
must bear with one another and forgive one another, if
anyone has reason to be offended with anyone else. Just
as the Lord has forgiven you, so you must forgive. And 14
over all these put on love, which completes them and
fastens them all together. Let the ruling principle in 14
your hearts be Christ's peace, for in becoming members of
one body you have been called under its sway. And you
must be thankful. Let the message of Christ live in your 16
hearts in all its wealth of wisdom. Teach it to one another and train one another in it with thankfulness, with
psalms, hymns, and sacred songs, and sing to God with
all your hearts. And whatever you have to say or do, do 17
it all as followers of the Lord Jesus, and offer your thanksgiving to God the Father through him.

THE LETTER TO PHILEMON

. . .

Among Paul's visitors at Rome was a young man named Onesimus, who had been a slave in Laodicea, near Colossae, but had robbed his master and run away. Although the penalty for such an offense was very severe under Roman law, Paul thought Onesimus ought to return to his master and acknowledge his act, and Onesimus agreed to do so. It was arranged that he should accompany Tychicus, who was going to Asia to carry the letter to Colossae, which was only five or ten miles from Laodicea.

Paul took a terrible responsibility in sending Onesimus back to his master Philemon. It is true Philemon was a Christian, and as Onesimus had also become one, Paul could appeal to this new tie between them. But it must not be forgotten that in Roman times a master could do almost anything he pleased to a slave who had robbed him and run away, as Onesimus had done. Paul was sending Onesimus into the lion's mouth.

In these circumstances it is not strange that Paul did everything in his power to protect Onesimus. He wrote a letter commending him to Philemon, and offering to repay whatever Onesimus had taken from him. He addressed this letter not only to Philemon but to the church that met in his house, so that the whole brotherhood should be made aware of the situation, and the moral support of that church should be enlisted in Onesimus' behalf.

*But he did more than this. He included in his letter
to Colossae instructions that that letter should be sent
to Laodicea, and the letter from Laodicea read by them.
This published the whole matter to the Colossian church
as well, and the social pressure of both churches was
thus brought to bear upon the situation. If Philemon
was disposed to receive Onesimus kindly, he would be
widely applauded. But if he stood on his rights and
proposed to treat him with all the rigor the law allowed,
Paul had seen to it that he would have to justify himself before the whole local brotherhood.*

. . .

THE SALUTATION, 1–3

Paul, a prisoner for Jesus Christ, and brother Timothy, 1
to our dear fellow-worker Philemon, and our sister 2
Apphia, and our fellow-soldier Archippus, and the
church that meets in your house; God our Father and the 3
Lord Jesus Christ bless you and give you peace.

HE ASKS HIM TO PARDON ONESIMUS, 8–22

So although as a Christian I feel quite free to order 8
you to do what ought to be done, I prefer to appeal to 9
you in the name of love, simply as what I am—Paul, no
less an envoy of Christ Jesus, though now a prisoner for
him, I appeal to you for my child Onesimus, whose 10
father I have become here in prison. Once you found him 11
useless, but now he has become useful to you and to me,
and now that I send him back to you, it is like sending 12
my very heart. I would have liked to keep him with me, 13
to wait on me in your place while I am in prison for the
good news, but I do not wish to do anything without 14
your consent, so that your kindness might be voluntary,
and not have the appearance of compulsion. For perhaps 15
this is why you and he were parted for a while, that you
might have him back forever, not as a slave any longer 16

but more than a slave, a dear brother—dear especially to me, but how much dearer to you, both as a man and as
17 a Christian! So if you regard me as a comrade, welcome
18 him as you would me. And if he has caused you any loss
19 or owes you anything, charge it to my account. I, Paul, write this with my own hand: I will repay it—not to mention the fact that you owe me your very self besides.
20 Come, brother, let me make something out of you, in a Christian sense! Cheer my heart as a Christian.
21   I write you in full reliance upon your obedience; I
22 know that you will do even more than I ask. And get ready to entertain me too, for I hope that I shall be restored to you, in answer to your prayers.

THE GOSPEL ACCORDING TO MARK

· · ·

Peter was dead, and with his death those vivid memories of the words and deeds of Jesus which he had shared for so many years with Christians of the east and west perished as living voices forever from the earth.

But in Rome, where his last years had been spent, there was one man at least who had served as his interpreter and had so often put his Aramaic reminiscences into Greek for the Roman congregation that many of them had become fixed in his mind. Out of these memories grew the Gospel of Mark, and to this curious origin many of its strange features are due.

From the earliest times Christians had had an oral gospel—a memorized account of the acts and teachings of Jesus, such as Paul refers to in writing to the Corinthians, and this in general served their needs. It was to supplement this, not to embody it or replace it, that Mark was written, in Rome and not far from the year 70. It was written in the popular Graeco-Jewish vocabulary of demon and marvel, and was lightly esteemed in the ancient church in contrast with the later, richer works of Matthew and Luke, but no more dramatic and convincing account has ever been written of the heroic effort of Jesus to execute the greatest task ever conceived—to set up the Kingdom of God on earth.

JOHN THE FORERUNNER APPEARS, 1:1–8

1   The beginning of the good news of Jesus Christ.
2   As it is written in the prophet Isaiah,
     "Here I send my messenger on before you;
     He will prepare your way;
3   Hark! Someone is shouting in the desert,
     'Get the Lord's way ready,
     Make his paths straight,' "
4   John the baptizer appeared in the desert, and preached repentance and baptism in order to obtain the forgive-
5 ness of sins. And all Judea and everybody in Jerusalem went out to him there, and accepted baptism from him in
6 the Jordan River, acknowledging their sins. John's clothing was made of hair cloth, and the belt around his waist was leather, and he lived on dried locusts and wild
7 honey. And this was his message:
     "After me there is coming one stronger than I am, one
8 whose shoes I am not fit to stoop down and untie. I have baptized you in water, but he will baptize you in the holy Spirit."

JESUS' WORK IN GALILEE, 1:9–6:34, 45—9:50

1   It was in those days that Jesus came from Nazareth in
10 Galilee, and was baptized by John in the Jordan. And just as he was coming up out of the water he saw the heavens torn open and the Spirit coming down like a
11 dove to enter into him, and out of the heavens came a voice:
     "You are my Son, my Beloved! You are my Chosen!"
12   The spirit immediately drove him out into the desert.
13 And he remained in the desert for forty days, and Satan tried to tempt him there; and he was among the wild animals; but the angels waited on him.
14   After John was arrested, Jesus went into Galilee pro-
15 claiming the good news from God, saying,
     "The time has come and the reign of God is near; repent, and believe this good news."
16   As he was passing along the shore of the Sea of Galilee, he saw Simeon and his brother Andrew casting their nets

in the sea, for they were fishermen. Jesus said to them, 17
"Come, follow me, and I will make you fish for men."

They immediately abandoned their nets and followed 18
him. He went on a little farther and saw James, the son 19
of Zebedee, and his brother John; they too were in their
boat putting their nets in order. He immediately called
them. And they left their father Zebedee in the boat 20
with the hired men and went off after him.

They proceeded to Capernaum, and on the very first 21
Sabbath he went to the synagogue and taught. And they 22
were amazed at his teaching, for he taught them like one
who had authority, and not like the scribes. Just then 23
there was in their synagogue a man under the control of a
foul spirit, and he cried out,

"What do you want of us, Jesus, you Nazarene? Have 24
you come to destroy us? I know who you are, you are
God's holy One!"

Jesus reproved him, and said,   25
"Silence! Get out of him!"

The foul spirit convulsed the man and gave a loud cry 26
and went out of him. And they were all so amazed that 27
they discussed it with one another, and said,

"What does this mean? It is a new teaching! He gives
orders with authority even to the foul spirits, and they
obey him!"

And his fame immediately spread in all directions 28
through the whole neighborhood of Galilee.

As soon as they left the synagogue, they went with 29
James and John to the house of Simon and Andrew.
Simon's mother-in-law was in bed, sick with a fever, and 30
they immediately told him about her. And he went up 31
to her, and grasping her hand, he made her rise. And the
fever left her, and she waited on them.

In the evening, after sunset, they brought to him all 32
who were sick or possessed by demons, and the whole 33
town was gathered at the door. And he cured many who 34
were sick with various diseases, and drove out many
demons, and he would not let the demons speak, because they knew that he was Christ.

35 Early in the morning, long before daylight, he got up and left the house and went off to a lonely spot, and
36 prayed there. And Simon and his companions sought
37 him out and found him, and said to him,

"They are all looking for you!"

38 He said to them,

"Let us go somewhere else, to the neighboring country towns, so that I may preach in them, too, for that is why I came out here."

39 So he went all through Galilee, preaching in their synagogues and driving out the demons.

40 There came to him a leper appealing to him on his knees, saying to him,

"If you only choose, you can cure me."

41 And he pitied him and stretched out his hand and touched him, and said to him,

"I do choose! Be cured!"

42 And the leprosy immediately left him, and he was
43 cured. And Jesus immediately drove him away with
44 stern injunctions, saying to him,

"See that you say nothing about this to anybody, but begone! show yourself to the priest, and in proof of your cure make the offerings for your purification which Moses prescribed."

45 But he went off and began to talk so much about it, and to spread the story so widely, that Jesus could no longer go into a town openly, but stayed out in unfrequented places, and people came to him from every direction.

2 Some days later he came back to Capernaum, and peo-
2 ple heard that he was at home, and such a crowd gathered that after a while there was no room even around the
3 door, and he was telling them his message. And some people came bringing to him a man who was paralyzed,
4 four of them carrying him. As they could not get him near Jesus on account of the crowd, they broke open the roof just over his head, and through the opening they
5 lowered the mat with the paralytic lying on it. When Jesus saw their faith, he said to the paralytic,

"My son, your sins are forgiven."

There were some scribes sitting there pondering and 6
saying to themselves,

"Why does this man talk so? This is blasphemy. Who 7
can forgive sins but God alone?"

Jesus, at once perceiving by his spirit that they were 8
pondering over this, said to them,

"Why do you ponder over this in your minds? Which 9
is easier, to say to this paralytic, 'Your sins are forgiven,'
or to say to him, 'Get up and pick up your mat and walk'?
But to let you know that the Son of Man has authority 10
to forgive sins on earth," turning to the paralytic he said,
"I tell you, get up, pick up your mat, and go home!" 11

And he got up, and immediately picked up his mat 12
and went out before them all, so that they were all
astonished and acknowledged the power of God, saying,

"We never saw anything like this before."

He went out of the town again and along the shore, 13
and all the people came to him and he taught them. And 14
as he was passing along he saw Levi, the son of Alpheus,
sitting at the tollhouse, and he said to him,

"Follow me."

And he got up and followed him.

He was at table in his house, with many tax-collectors 15
and irreligious people who were at table with him and
his disciples, for there were many of them among his
followers. And when the scribes who were of the 16
Pharisees' party saw that he was eating with irreligious
people and tax-collectors, they said to his disciples,

"Why does he eat with tax-collectors and irreligious
people?"

Jesus heard it, and said to them, 17

"It is not well people but the sick who have to have
the doctor. I did not come to invite the pious but the
irreligious."

Now John's disciples and the Pharisees were keeping a 18
fast. And people came and asked him,

"Why is it that when John's disciples and the disciples

of the Pharisees are keeping the fast, yours are not keeping it?"

19 Jesus said to them,

"Can wedding guests fast while the bridegroom is with them? As long as they have the bridegroom with
20 them they cannot fast. But a time will come when the bridegroom will be taken from them, and when that day
21 comes, they will fast. No one sews a patch of unshrunken cloth on an old coat; or if he does, the patch tears away, the new from the old, and makes the hole worse than
22 ever. And no one pours new wine into old wine-skins; or if he does, the wine bursts the skins, and the wine is lost, and the skins too. New wine has to be put into fresh skins."

23 He happened to be passing through the wheat fields on the Sabbath, and his disciples began to pick the heads
24 of wheat as they made their way through. And the Pharisees said to him,

"Look! Why are they doing what it is against the law to do on the Sabbath?"

25 He said to them,

"Did you never read what David did, when he was in
26 need and hungry, he and his men? How is it that he went into the house of God when Abiathar was high priest, and ate the Presentation Loaves, which it is against the law for anyone but the priests to eat, and gave some to his companions too?"

27 And he said to them,
28 "The Sabbath was made for man, not man for the Sabbath, and so the Son of Man is master even of the Sabbath."

3 He went again to a synagogue, and there was a man
2 there with one hand withered. And they were watching him closely, to see whether he would cure him on the Sabbath, in order to get a charge to bring against him.
3 He said to the man with the withered hand,

"Get up and come forward."

4 And he said to them,

"Is it allowable to do people good on the Sabbath, or

to do them harm? To save life or kill?" But they made
no answer. And he looked around at them with anger, 5
hurt by their obstinacy, and he said to the man,
"Hold out your hand!"

And he held it out, and his hand was cured. Then the 6
Pharisees left the synagogue and immediately consulted
with the Herodians about Jesus, with a view to putting
him to death.

So Jesus retired with his disciples to the seashore, and 7
a great many people from Galilee followed him, and from 8
Judea and Jerusalem and Idumea and from the other side
of the Jordan and from the neighborhood of Tyre and
Sidon a great many who had heard of the things he was
doing came to him. He told his disciples to have a boat 9
always ready for his use, to prevent his being crushed by
the crowd. For he cured so many people that all who 10
had any ailments pressed up to him to touch him. And 11
whenever the foul spirits saw him, they fell down before
him and screamed out,

"You are the Son of God!" And he warned them re- 12
peatedly not to tell who he was.

And he went up the hillside and summoned to him 13
those whom he wanted, and they went to him. He 14
appointed twelve of them, whom he called apostles, to
be with him and to be sent out to preach, with power to
drive out the demons. These were the twelve he ap- 15 16
pointed: Peter, which was the name he gave to Simon, 17
James the son of Zebedee, and John, James's brother (he
named them Boanerges, that is, Sons of Thunder), An- 18
drew, Philip, Bartholomew, Matthew, Thomas, James
the son of Alpheus, Thaddeus, Simon the Zealot, and 19
Judas Iscariot, who betrayed him.

Then he went home. And again the crowd gathered in 20
such numbers that there was no chance for them even to
have their meals. His relatives heard of it and came over 21
to stop him, for they said that he was out of his mind.
And the scribes who had come down from Jerusalem 22
said that he was possessed by Beelzebub and drove out

23 demons by the help of the prince of demons. So he called them to him and spoke to them in figures, saying,

24 "How can Satan drive Satan out? If a kingdom is dis-
25 united, that kingdom cannot last. And if a household is
26 disunited, that household cannot last. And if Satan has rebelled against himself and become disunited, he cannot
27 last but is coming to his end. But no one can go into a strong man's house and carry off his property unless he first binds the strong man; after that he can plunder his
28 house. I tell you, men will be forgiven for everything,
29 for all their sins and all the abusive things they say. But whoever reviles the holy Spirit can never be forgiven, but is guilty of an unending sin."

30 This was because they said, "He is possessed by a foul spirit."

31 And his mother and his brothers came. And they stood outside the house and sent word in to him to come
32 outside to them. There was a crowd sitting around him when they told him,

"Your mother and your brothers are outside asking for you."

33 He answered,

"Who are my mother and my brothers?"

34 And looking around at the people sitting about him, he said,

35 "Here are my mother and my brothers! Whoever does the will of God is my brother and sister and mother."

4 Then he began again to teach by the seashore. And a crowd gathered around him so great that he got into a boat and sat in it, a little way from the shore, while all
2 the people were on the land close to the water. He taught them many lessons in figures, and said to them in the course of his teaching,

3
4 "Listen: A sower went out to sow, and as he was sow-ing, some of the seed chanced to fall by the path, and the
5 birds came and ate it up. Some of it fell on rocky ground, and where there was not much soil, and it sprang up at
6 once because the soil was not deep, but when the sun came up, it was scorched, and withered up, because it

had no root. Some of the seed fell among the thorns, and ₇
the thorns grew up and choked it out, and it yielded no
grain. And some fell on good soil, and came up and grew ₈
and yielded thirty, sixty, even a hundredfold."

And he said, ₉

"Let him who has ears be sure to listen!"

When he was by himself, those who stayed about him ₁₀
with the Twelve asked him about the figures he had used.
And he said to them, ₁₁

"To you has been intrusted the secret of the reign of
God, but to those outsiders everything is offered in ₁₂
figures, so that

" 'They may look and look and yet not see,
And listen and listen and yet not understand,
Lest possibly they should turn and be forgiven.' "

And Jesus said, ₁₃

"If you do not understand this figure, then how will you
understand my other figures? What the sower sows is the ₁₄
message. The ones by the path are those into whose ₁₅
hearts the message falls, and as soon as they hear it
Satan comes and carries off the message that has been
sown in their hearts. It is so too with the ones sown on ₁₆
the rocky ground; they gladly accept the message as soon
as they hear it, but it takes no real root in them and they ₁₇
last only a little while; then when trouble or persecution
comes because of the message they give it up at once. It
is different with those sown among the thorns. They are ₁₈
people who listen to the message, but the worries of the
time and the pleasure of being rich and passions for other ₁₉
things creep in and choke the message out and it yields
nothing. And the ones sown in good ground are the peo- ₂₀
ple who listen to the message and welcome it and yield
thirty, sixty, even a hundredfold.

"Do people get out the lamp," he said to them, "and ₂₁
then put it under the peck-measure, or under the bed,
instead of putting it up where it belongs? For no one ₂₂
hides anything except for the purpose of sometime
bringing it to light again, and people keep things secret

23 only to reveal them some day. If anyone has ears let him be sure to listen.

24   "Take care what you hear," he said to them. "The measure you give will be given to you, and even more
25 besides. For people who have will have more given them, and from people who have nothing, even what they have will be taken away.

26   "The reign of God," he said, "is like a man scattering
27 seed on the ground, and then sleeping at night and getting up by day, while the seed sprouts and comes up,
28 without his knowing it. The ground of itself is productive, putting forth first a blade, then a head, then fully
29 developed wheat in the head. But as soon as the crop will let him, the man goes in with his sickle, for the harvest time has come.

30   "How can we find any comparison," he said, "for the reign of God, or what figure can we use to describe it?
31 It is like a mustard seed, which, when sown in the ground, though it is the smallest of all the seeds in the
32 world, yet once sown, comes up and grows to be the largest of all the plants, and produces branches so large that the wild birds can roost under the shelter of it."

33   With many such figures he told them the message, as
34 far as they were able to receive it. He said nothing to them except in figures, but in private he explained everything to his own disciples.

35   That same day when it was evening he said to them, "Let us cross to the other side."

36   So they left the crowd and took him away in the boat in which he was sitting. There were other boats with
37 him. And a heavy squall of wind came on and the waves dashed into the boat, so that it was beginning to fill.
38 He was in the stern, asleep on the cushion. And they woke him up and said to him,

    "Master, does it make no difference to you that we are sinking?"

39   Then he awoke and reproved the wind, and said to the sea,

    "Hush! Silence!"

And the wind went down and there was a great calm. 40
And he said to them,

"Why are you afraid? Have you still no faith?"

And they were very much frightened, and said to one 41
another,

"Who can he be? For even the wind and the sea obey
him."

So they reached the other side of the sea, and landed 5
in the region of Gerasa. As soon as he got out of the 2
boat, a man possessed by a foul spirit came out of the
burial places near by to meet him. This man lived among 3
the tombs, and no one could any longer secure him even
with a chain, for he had often been fastened with fetters 4
and chains and had snapped the chains and broken the
fetters; and there was no one strong enough to master
him, and night and day he was always shrieking among 5
the tombs and on the hills and cutting himself with
stones. And catching sight of Jesus in the distance he ran 6
up and made obeisance to him and screamed out, 7

"What do you want of me, Jesus, son of the Most
High God? In God's name, I implore you, do not torture
me." For he was saying to him, 8

"You foul spirit, come out of this man."

He asked him, 9

"What is your name?"

He said,

"My name is Legion, for there are many of us."

And they begged him earnestly not to send them out of 10
that country.

Now there was a great drove of pigs feeding there on 11
the hillside. And they implored him, 12

"Send us among the pigs, let us go into them."

So he gave them permission. And the foul spirits came 13
out and went into the pigs, and the drove of about two
thousand rushed over the steep bank into the sea and
were drowned. And the men who tended them ran away 14
and spread the news in the town and in the country
around, and the people came to see what had happened.
When they came to Jesus and found the demoniac sitting 15

quietly with his clothes on and in his right mind—the same man who had been possessed by Legion—they were
16 frightened. And those who had seen it told them what had happened to the demoniac, and all about the pigs.
17 And they began to beg him to leave their district. As he
18 was getting into the boat, the man who had been
19 possessed begged to be allowed to go with him. And he would not permit it, but said to him,

"Go home to your own people, and tell them all the Lord has done for you and how he took pity on you."
20 And he went off and began to tell everybody in the Ten Towns all Jesus had done for him; and they were all astonished.

21 When Jesus had crossed again in the boat to the other side, a great crowd gathered about him as he stood on the
22 shore. And a man named Jairus, the leader of a synagogue, came up and seeing him threw himself at his feet
23 and appealed to him, saying,

"My little daughter is at the point of death. Come, lay your hands on her, so that she may get well and live!"
24 So he went with him. And a great crowd followed
25 him and pressed around him. And a woman who had had
26 a hemorrhage for twelve years and had had a great deal of treatment from various doctors and had spent all that she had and had not been benefited at all but had actually
27 grown worse, had heard about Jesus. And she came up in
28 the crowd behind him and touched his coat, for she said,

"If I can only touch his clothes, I shall get well."
29 The hemorrhage stopped at once, and she felt in her
30 body that she was cured. Jesus instantly perceived that healing power had passed from him, and he turned around in the crowd and said,

"Who touched my clothes?"
31 His disciples said to him,

"You see the crowd pressing around you, and yet you ask, 'Who touched me?' "
32 But he still looked around to see the person who had
33 done it. The woman, knowing what had happened to her, came forward frightened and trembling, and threw

herself down at his feet and told him the whole truth. And he said to her, 34

"My daughter, it is your faith that has cured you. Go in peace and be free from your disease."

Even as he spoke people came from the house of the 35 leader of the synagogue and said,

"Your daughter is dead. Why should you trouble the Master any further?"

But Jesus paid no attention to what they said, but said 36 to the leader of the synagogue,

"Do not be afraid, just have faith."

He let no one go with him but Peter, James, and 37 James's brother John. They came to the house of the 38 leader of the synagogue, and there he found everything in confusion, and people weeping and wailing. And he 39 went into the house and said to them,

"What is the meaning of all this confusion and crying? The child is not dead, she is asleep." And they laughed 40 at him. But he drove them all out, and took the child's father and mother and the men who were with him and went into the room where the child was lying. And he 41 grasped her hand and said to her,

"Taleitha, koum!"—that is to say, "Little girl, I tell you, get up!"

And the little girl immediately got up and walked 42 about, for she was twelve years old. The moment they saw it they were utterly amazed. And he strictly forbade 43 them to let anyone know of it, and told them to give her something to eat.

Leaving there he went, followed by his disciples, to 6 his own part of the country. When the Sabbath came he 2 began to teach in the synagogue. And the people were astonished when they heard him, and said,

"Where did he get all this? How does he come to have such wisdom? How are such marvelous things done 3 through him? Is he not the carpenter, Mary's son, and the brother of James, Joses, Judas, and Simon? And do not his sisters live here among us?"

And they took offense at him. Jesus said to them, 4

"A prophet is treated with honor everywhere except in his native place and among his relatives and at his home."

5 He could not do any wonder there, except that he put
6 his hands on a few sick people and cured them. And he wondered at their want of faith.

7 Then he went around among the villages teaching. And he called the Twelve to him and sent them off two
8 by two, giving them power over the foul spirits. He forbade them to take anything for the journey except a staff—no bread, no bag, no small change even in their
9 girdles; they were to go in sandals, and not to wear two
10 shirts. And he said to them,

"Whenever you go to stay at a house, remain in it till
11 you leave that place. If any place refuses to receive you or to listen to you, when you leave it shake off the very dust from the soles of your feet as a warning to them."

12 So they went out and preached that men should re-
13 pent, and drove out many demons, and cured many sick people by anointing them with oil.

14 King Herod heard of him, for his name was now well known, and people were saying that John the baptizer had risen from the dead, and that that was why he was
15 endowed with these extraordinary powers. But others said he was Elijah, and still others that he was a prophet
16 of the old prophetic kind. But when Herod heard of him he said,

"John, whom I beheaded, has risen from the dead."

17 For it was Herod who had sent and seized John and bound him and put him in prison, on account of Herodias, his brother Philip's wife, because Herod had married her.
18 John said to Herod,

"It is not right for you to be living with your brother's wife."

Herodias felt bitterly toward him and wanted him
19
20 killed. But she could not bring it about, for Herod stood in awe of John, knowing that he was an upright and holy man, and he protected him. And when he heard him talk he was very much disturbed, and yet he liked to hear

him. When a holiday came and Herod on his birthday 21 gave a banquet to his courtiers and officers and to the leading men of Galilee, Herodias' own daughter came in and danced for them. And Herod and his guests were de- 22 lighted, and the king said to the girl,

"Ask me for anything you like and I will give it to 23 you." And he made oath to her,

"I will give you whatever you ask me for, up to half my kingdom."

When she had left the room she said to her mother, 24 "What shall I ask him for?"

But she said,

"The head of John the baptizer."

And she hurried back at once to the king and asked 25 him for it, saying,

"I want you right away to give me John the Baptist's head on a platter."

The king was exceedingly sorry, but on account of his 26 oath and his guests he did not like to break his word to her, and he immediately sent one of his guard with orders 27 to get John's head. And he went off and beheaded him in the prison and brought back his head on a platter 28 and gave it to the girl, and the girl gave it to her mother. When his disciples heard of it they came and took his 29 body away and put it in a tomb.

The apostles rejoined Jesus and reported to him all 30 they had done and taught. And he said to them, 31

"Come away by yourselves to some quiet place, and rest a little while."

For people were coming and going in large numbers, and they had no time even for meals. So they set off by 32 themselves in their boat for a secluded place. And many 33 people saw them start and knew of it, and hurried around by land from all the neighboring towns, and got ahead of them. So when he got out of the boat, he found a great 34 crowd gathered, and his heart was touched at the sight of them, because they were like sheep that have no shepherd; and he proceeded to teach them a great deal.

He immediately had his disciples get into the boat and 45

cross before him to the other side toward Bethsaida,
46 while he was dismissing the crowd. When he had taken
47 leave of the people he went up the hill to pray. When
evening came on, the boat was in the middle of the sea,
48 and he was alone on shore. And he saw that they were
straining at the oars, for the wind was against them, and
toward morning he went out to them, walking on the
49 sea, and was going to join them. They saw him walking
on the sea, and thought it was a ghost and screamed
50 aloud, for they all saw him and were terrified. But he
immediately spoke to them and said,
"Take courage, it is I. Do not be afraid."
51 Then he went up to them and got into the boat. And
the wind fell. And they were perfectly beside themselves,
52 for they had not understood about the loaves, but their
minds were blinded.
53 They crossed over to the other side and came to
54 Gennesaret and moored the boat. As soon as they came
55 ashore, the people recognized Jesus, and they hurried all
over the countryside and began to bring the sick to him
56 on their mats, wherever they heard he was. And whatever village or town or farm he went to, they would lay
their sick in the market-place and beg him to let them
touch just the tassel of his cloak, and all who touched it
were cured.

7 The Pharisees gathered about him with some scribes
2 who had come from Jerusalem. They had noticed that
some of his disciples ate their food without first giving
3 their hands a ceremonial washing to purify them. For
the Pharisees and all the Jews observe the rules handed
down from their ancestors, and will not eat until they
4 have washed their hands in a particular way, and they
will not eat anything from the market without first
purifying it by sprinkling it, and they have a number of
other observances which have come down to them, in
5 the way of washing cups, pitchers, and basins. And the
Pharisees and the scribes asked him,
"Why do your disciples not observe the rules handed

down by our ancestors, but eat food without purifying
their hands?"

But he said to them,   6

"It was about you hypocrites that Isaiah prophesied
so finely, in the words,

" 'This people honor me with their lips,
   Yet their hearts are far away from me.
   But their worship of me is all in vain,   7
   For the lessons they teach are but human precepts.'

"You give up what God has commanded and hold fast   8
to what men have handed down.

"How skilful you are," he said to them, "in nullify-   9
ing what God has commanded in order to observe what
has been handed down to you. For Moses said, 'Honor   10
your father and your mother,' and again, 'Whoever
abuses his father or mother must be put to death.' But   11
you say, 'If a man says to his father or mother, "Anything of mine that might have been of use to you is Kor-
ban," ' that is, consecrated to God, you let him off from 12
doing anything more for his father or mother, and so you 13
nullify what God has said by what you have handed
down. You have many such practices."

He called the people to him again and said to   14
them,

"Listen to me, all of you, and understand this. Noth-   15
ing that goes into a man from outside can pollute him.
It is what comes out of a man that pollutes him."

When he had left the crowd and gone home, his dis-   17
ciples asked him what he meant by this figure. And he   18
said to them,

"Have not even you any understanding then? Do you
not see that nothing that goes into a man from outside
can pollute him, since it does not go into his heart but 19
into his stomach and then is disposed of?" So he declared
all food clean. He went on to say,   20

"It is what comes out of a man that pollutes him. For   21
it is from inside, from men's hearts, that designs of evil
come; immorality, stealing, murder, adultery, greed,   22
malice, deceit, indecency, envy, abusiveness, arrogance,

23 folly—all these evils come from inside, and they pollute a man."

24 He left that place and went to the neighborhood of Tyre and Sidon. And he went into a certain house, and wanted no one to know of it. And he could not keep it
25 secret, but a woman whose little daughter was possessed by a foul spirit immediately heard about him and came
26 and threw herself at his feet. Now the woman was a
27 Greek, of Syrophoenician birth. And she begged him to drive the demon out of her daughter. He said to her,

"Let the children first eat all they want, for it is not right to take the children's bread and throw it to the dogs."

28 But she answered,

"True, sir! and still the dogs under the table eat what the children leave!"

29 He said to her,

"If you can say that, go home; the demon has left your daughter."

30 And she went home and found the child lying on the bed, and the demon gone.

31 He left the neighborhood of Tyre again and went by way of Sidon to the Sea of Galilee, crossing the district
32 of the Ten Towns. And they brought to him a man who was deaf and hardly able to speak, and they begged him
33 to lay his hand on him. He took him off by himself away from the crowd, and put his fingers in the man's ears, and
34 touched his tongue with saliva. And he looked up to heaven and sighed, and said to him,

"Ephphatha!"—which means "Open."

35 And his ears were opened and his tongue was released
36 and he talked plainly. And Jesus forbade them to tell anyone about it, but the more he forbade them the more
37 they spread the news far and wide. And people were utterly amazed, and said,

"How well he has done everything! He even makes the deaf hear and the dumb speak!"

8 In those days when a great crowd had gathered again

and they had nothing to eat, he called his disciples to him and said to them,

"I pity these people, for they have been staying with me three days now, and they have nothing left to eat. And if I send them home hungry they will give out on the way, for some of them come from a distance."

His disciples replied,

"Where can anyone get bread enough, here in this solitude, to satisfy these people's hunger?"

"How many loaves have you?" he asked.

"Seven," they said.

Then he ordered the people to take their places on the ground. And he took the seven loaves and gave thanks and broke them in pieces and gave them to his disciples to pass, and they passed them to the people. They had a few small fish, and he blessed them and told the disciples to pass them also to the people. And they ate and satisfied their hunger. And the pieces that they left, that were picked up, filled seven baskets. There were about four thousand of the people. And he dismissed them. Then he immediately got into the boat with his disciples and went to the district of Dalmanutha.

The Pharisees came out and began a discussion with him, testing him by asking him how to show them a sign from heaven. And he sighed deeply and said,

"Why do the men of this day ask for a sign? I tell you, no sign will be given them."

And he left them and got into the boat again and crossed to the other side.

Now they had forgotten to bring any bread, and they had only one loaf with them in the boat. And he warned them, saying,

"Look out! Be on your guard against the yeast of the Pharisees and the yeast of Herod!"

They were discussing with one another their being without bread. And he noticed it and said to them,

"Why do you discuss your being without bread? Do you not yet see nor understand? Are your minds so dull? When you have eyes can you not see, and when you have

ears can you not hear? Do you not remember how many
19 baskets of pieces you picked up when I broke the five
loaves in pieces for those five thousand men?"
They said to him,
"Twelve."
20 "When I broke the seven loaves in pieces for the four
thousand, how many baskets of pieces did you pick up?"
They said to him,
"Seven"
21 He said to them,
"Do you not undertand yet?"
22 And they came to Bethsaida. And people brought a
23 blind man to him and begged him to touch him. He took
him by the hand and led him outside of the village, and
spitting in his eyes he laid his hands on him and asked
him,
"Do you see anything?"
24 He looked up and said,
"I can see people, for they look to me like trees, only
they are moving about."
25 Then he laid his hands on his eyes again, and he
looked steadily and was cured, and saw everything plain-
26 ly. And he sent him home and said to him,
"Do not even go into the village."
27 Then Jesus and his disciples went away to the villages
around Caesarea Philippi. On the way he questioned his
disciples and said to them,
"Who do people say that I am?"
28 They said to him,
"John the Baptist; others say Elijah, and others that
you are one of the prophets."
29 And he asked them,
"But who do you say that I am?"
Peter answered and said to him,
"You are the Christ."
30 And he warned them not to say this about him to
anyone.
31 Then he explained to them for the first time that the
Son of Man must go through much suffering, and be re-

[351]

fused by the elders and the high priests and the scribes, and be killed, and rise again three days after. He told 32 them this plainly. And Peter took him aside, and began to reprove him for it. But turning and seeing his disciples 33 he reproved Peter, and said,

"Get out of my sight, you Satan! for you do not side with God, but with men."

And he called the people and his disciples to him and 34 said to them,

"If anyone wants to go with me, he must disregard himself, and take his cross and follow me. For whoever 35 wants to preserve his own life will lose it, and whoever loses his life for me and for the good news will preserve it. For what good does it do a man to gain the whole 36 world and yet part with his life? For what can a man 37 give to buy back his life? For if anyone is ashamed of 38 me and my teaching in this unfaithful and sinful age, then the Son of Man will be ashamed of him, when he comes back in his Father's glory, with the holy angels." And he said to them, "I tell you, some of you who stand 9 here will certainly live to see the reign of God come in its might."

Six days after this Jesus took Peter, James, and John 2 with him, and led them up on a high mountain, off by themselves. And his appearance underwent a change in their presence, and his clothes shone whiter than any 3 earthly bleaching could make them. And Elijah appeared 4 to them, accompanied by Moses, and they talked with Jesus. Then Peter spoke, and said to Jesus, 5

"Master, how good it is that we are here! Let us put up three huts, one for you and one for Moses and one for Elijah." For he did not know what to say, they were so 6 frightened. And a cloud came and overshadowed them, 7 and from the cloud came a voice,

"This is my Son, my Beloved. Listen to him."

And suddenly, on looking around, they saw that there 8 was now no one with them but Jesus alone. As they were 9 going down the mountain, he cautioned them to let no one know what they had seen, until the Son of Man

10 should rise from the dead. And they did not forget what
he said, but discussed with one another what he meant
11 by the rising from the dead. And they asked him,

"Why do the scribes say that Elijah has to come first?"
12 He said to them,

"Elijah does come first, and reforms everything, and
does not the Scripture say of the Son of Man that he will
13 suffer much and be refused? Why, I tell you, not only has
Elijah come, but people have treated him just as they
pleased, as the Scripture says about him."
14 When they came to the disciples, they saw a great
crowd around them, and some scribes arguing with them.
15 And all the people were amazed when they saw him, and
16 they ran up to him and greeted him. And he asked them,

"What are you discussing with them?"
17 One of the crowd answered,

"Master, I brought my son to you, for he is possessed
18 by a dumb spirit, and wherever it seizes him it convulses
him, and he foams at the mouth and grinds his teeth; and
he is wasting away. I told your disciples to drive it out,
and they could not do it."
19 He answered them and said,

"O you unbelieving people, how long must I be with
you? How long must I put up with you? Bring him here
to me!"
20 And they brought the boy to him. As soon as the spirit
saw him, it convulsed the boy, and he fell down on the
21 ground and rolled about, foaming at the mouth. Jesus
asked the boy's father,

"How long has he been like this?"

And he said,
22 "From his childhood, and many a time it has thrown
him into the fire or into the water, to put an end to him.
But if there is anything you can do, take pity on us and
help us!"
23 Jesus said to him,

" 'If there is anything I can do!' Everything is possible for one who has faith!"
24 The boy's father immediately cried out,

[353]

"I have faith! Help my want of faith!"

Then Jesus, seeing that a crowd was rapidly gathering, 25
reproved the foul spirit and said to it,

"You deaf and dumb spirit, get out of him, I charge
you, and never enter him again!"

And it gave a cry and convulsed him terribly, and went 26
out of him.

And the boy was like a corpse, so that most of them
said that he was dead. But Jesus grasped his hand and 27
made him rise, and he stood up. When he had gone 28
home, and his disciples were alone with him, they asked
him,

"Why could not we drive it out?"

He said to them, 29

"This kind of thing can only be driven out by prayer."

And they left that place and made their way through 30
Galilee, and he did not wish anyone to know it; for he 31
was teaching his disciples, saying to them,

"The Son of Man is to be handed over to men, and
they will kill him, and three days after he is killed he
will rise again."

But they did not understand what he meant, and they 32
were afraid to ask him about it.

And they reached Capernaum. When he reached home, 33
he asked them,

"What was it that you were discussing on the way?"

But they made no answer, for on the way they had 34
been discussing with one another which of them was the
greatest. And he sat down and called the Twelve in, and 35
said to them,

"If anyone wishes to be first, he must be the last of all
and the servant of all."

And he took a child and made him stand among them, 36
and he put his arms around him, and said to them,

"Whoever welcomes one child like this on my ac- 37
count is welcoming me, and whoever welcomes me, welcomes not me but him who has sent me."

John said to him, 38

"Master, we saw a man driving out demons with your

name, and we told him not to do so, for he was not one
of our followers."

39   But Jesus said,

"Do not tell him not to do so, for there is no one who
40 will use my name to do a mighty act, and be able soon
after to abuse me. For the man who is not against us is
41 for us. For whoever gives you a cup of water to drink,
on the ground that you belong to Christ, I tell you, will
42 certainly not fail to be repaid. And whoever causes one
of these humble believers to fall might better have a
great millstone hung around his neck and be thrown into
43 the sea. If your hand makes you fall, cut it off. You
might better enter upon life maimed, than go with both
your hands to the pit, into the fire that cannot be put out.
45 And if your foot makes you fall, cut it off. You might
better enter upon life crippled, than be thrown with both
47 your feet into the pit. And if your eye makes you fall,
tear it out. You might better get into the Kingdom of
God with only one eye than be thrown with both your
48 eyes into the pit, where the worm that feeds upon them
49 never dies and the fire is never put out. Everyone must be
50 seasoned with fire. Salt is a good thing, but if salt loses
its strength, what will you use to season it? You must
have salt within you, and live in peace with one another."

JESUS CARRIES HIS MESSAGE TO JERUSALEM, 10:1—13:37

10   And he left that place and went into the district of
Judea and crossed the Jordan, and crowds of people again
gathered about him, and again he taught them as he was
2 accustomed to do. Some Pharisees came up, and in order
to test him asked him whether a man should be allowed
3 to divorce his wife. But he answered,

"What has Moses commanded you to do?"

4   They said,

"Moses permits a man to divorce his wife by drawing
up a written divorce-notice."

5   But Jesus said to them,

"It was on account of your perversity that he laid

down that law for you. But from the beginning of the 6
creation, 'God made them male and female. Therefore a 7
man must leave his father and mother, and he and his 8
wife must become one,' and so they are no longer two but
one. Therefore what God has joined together man must 9
not try to separate."

When they reached the house the disciples asked him 10
about this again. And he said to them, 11

"Anyone who divorces his wife and marries another
woman commits adultery against his former wife, and if 12
a woman divorces her husband and marries another
man, she is an adulteress."

And people brought children to him to have him touch 13
them, but the disciples reproved them for it. When Jesus 14
saw it, he was indignant, and said to them,

"Let the children come to me; do not try to stop them,
for the Kingdom of God belongs to such as they. I tell 15
you, whoever does not accept the Kingdom of God like a
child shall not enter it at all."

And he took the children in his arms and laid his hands 16
on them and blessed them.

As he was starting again on his journey, a man came 17
running up to him, and knelt at his feet and asked
him,

"Good master, what must I do to make sure of eternal
life?"

But Jesus said to him, 18

"Why do you call me good? No one is good but God 19
himself. You know the commandments—'Do not murder, Do not commit adultery, Do not steal, Do not bear
false witness, Do not defraud, Honor your father and
mother.'"

But he said to him, 20

"Master, I have obeyed all these commandments ever
since I was a child."

And Jesus looked at him and loved him, and he said to 21
him,

"There is one thing that you lack. Go, sell all you
have, and give the money to the poor, and then you will

have riches in heaven; and come back and be a follower
of mine."

22   But his face fell at Jesus' words, and he went away
much cast down, for he had a great deal of property.

23   And Jesus looked around and said to his disciples,
"How hard it will be for those who have money to
enter the Kingdom of God!"

24   But the disciples were amazed at what he said. And
Jesus said to them again,

25   "My children, how hard it is to enter the Kingdom of
God! It is easier for a camel to get through the eye of a
needle than for a rich man to get into the Kingdom of
God!"

26   They were perfectly astounded and said to him,
"Then who can be saved?"

27   Jesus looked at them and said,
"For men it is impossible, but not for God, for anything is possible for God."

28   Peter started to say to him,
"Well, we have left all we had, and have followed
you."

29   Jesus said,
"I tell you, there is no one who has given up home or
brothers or sisters or mother or father or children or land

30   for me and for the good news, but will receive now in this
life a hundred times as much in homes, brothers, sisters,
mothers, children, and lands, though not without per-

31   secution—and in the coming age eternal life. But many
who are first now will be last then, and the last will be
first."

32   As they went on their way up to Jerusalem, Jesus
walked ahead of them, and they were in dismay, and
those who still followed were afraid. And he took the
Twelve aside again and began to tell them what was
going to happen to him.

33   "See!" he said, "we are going up to Jerusalem, and the
Son of Man will be handed over to the high priests and
scribes, and they will condemn him to death and hand

34   him over to the heathen and they will ridicule him and

spit on him and flog him and kill him; and three days
after he will rise again."

And Zebedee's two sons, James and John, came up to 35
him and said,

"Master, we want you to do for us whatever we ask."
He said to them, 36

"What do you want me to do for you?"
They said to him, 37

"Let us sit one at your right hand and one at your left,
in your triumph."

Jesus said to them, 38

"You do not know what you are asking for. Can you
drink what I am drinking, or undergo the baptism that
I am undergoing?"

They said to him, 39

"Yes, we can."

Jesus said to them,

"Then you shall drink what I am drinking, and you
shall undergo the baptism that I am undergoing; but as 40
for sitting at my right or at my left, that is not mine to
give, but belongs to those for whom it is destined."

When the other ten heard of this they were at first very 41
indignant at James and John. And Jesus called them to 42
him, and said to them,

"You know that those who are supposed to rule the
heathen lord it over them, and their great men tyrannize
over them; but it is not to be so among you. Whoever 43
wants to be great among you must be your servant, and
whoever wants to hold the first place among you must be 44
everybody's slave. For the Son of Man himself has not 45
come to be waited on, but to wait on other people, and
to give his life to free many others."

And they came to Jericho. As he was leaving the town 46
with his disciples and a great crowd, Timaeus' son Barti-
maeus, a blind beggar, was sitting at the roadside.
When he heard that it was Jesus of Nazareth he began to 47
cry out,

"Jesus, you son of David, take pity on me!"

48 Many of the people rebuked him and told him to be still. But he cried out all the louder,
"You son of David, take pity on me!"
49 Jesus stopped and said,
"Call him here."
And they called the blind man and said to him,
"Courage now! Get up, he is calling you!"
50 And he threw off his coat and sprang to his feet and
51 went up to Jesus. Jesus spoke to him and said,
"What do you want me to do for you?"
The blind man said to him,
"Master, let me regain my sight!"
52 Jesus said to him,
"Go your way. Your faith has cured you."
And he immediately regained his sight and followed Jesus along the road.

11 When they were getting near Jerusalem, and had come to Bethphage and Bethany near the Mount of Olives,
2 Jesus sent two of his disciples on ahead, and said to them,
"Go to the village that lies in front of you, and as soon as you enter it you will find tied there a colt that has
3 never been ridden. Untie it and bring it here. And if anybody says to you, 'Why are you doing that?' say, 'The Master needs it, and will send it back here directly.' "
4 And they set off and found a colt tied in the street at
5 the door of a house, and they untied it. Some of the bystanders said to them,
"What are you doing, untying the colt?"
6 But they answered them as Jesus had told them to do,
7 and the men let them take it. So they brought the colt to Jesus, and they threw their coats over it and Jesus
8 mounted it. And many of the people spread their coats in the road, and others cut straw from the fields and
9 scattered it in his path. And those in front and those behind shouted,
"God bless him!
Blessed be he who comes in the Lord's name!
10 Blessed be the reign of our father David which is coming!

[359]

God bless him from on high!"

And he came into Jerusalem and into the Temple, and 11 looked it all over; then, as it was already late, he went out with the Twelve to Bethany.

On the next day, after they had left Bethany, he felt 12 hungry. And he saw in the distance a fig tree covered 13 with leaves, and he went up to it to see if he could find any figs on it. When he reached it he found nothing but leaves, for it was not the time for figs. And he spoke to 14 the tree and said to it,

"May no one ever eat fruit from you any more!"

And his disciples heard it.

When they reached Jerusalem, he went into the Tem- 15 ple, and began to drive out of it those who were buying or selling things in it, and he upset the money-changers' tables and the pigeon-dealers' seats, and he would not 16 allow anyone to carry anything through the Temple. And he taught them, and said, 17

"Does not the Scripture say, 'My house shall be called a house of prayer for all the nations'? But you have made it a robbers' cave."

The high priests and the scribes heard of this, and they 18 cast about for a way of destroying him, for they were afraid of him, for all the people were amazed at what he taught. So when evening came, he and his disciples 19 used to go out of the city.

In the morning as they were passing along, they saw 20 that the fig tree was withered, to its very roots. And 21 Peter remembered about it and said to him,

"Look, Master! The fig tree that you cursed is withered up!"

Jesus answered and said to them, 22

"Have faith in God! I tell you, whoever says to this 23 mountain, 'Get up and throw yourself into the sea!' and has no doubt in his mind, but has faith that what he says will happen, shall have it. Therefore I tell you, when- 24 ever you pray or ask for anything, have faith that it has been granted you, and you shall have it. And whenever 25 you stand up to pray, if you have a grievance against anyone, forgive him, so that your Father in heaven too may forgive you your offenses."

27 Then they went into Jerusalem again. And as Jesus was walking about in the Temple, the high priests, 28 scribes, and elders came up and said to him,

"What authority have you for doing as you do? And who gave you a right to do as you are doing?"

29 Jesus said to them,

"Let me ask you one question, and if you answer me, I will tell you what authority I have for doing as I do. 30 Was John's baptism from heaven or from men? Answer me."

31 And they argued with one another,

"If we say, 'It was from heaven,' he will say, 'Then 32 why did you not believe him?' Yet can we say, 'It was from men'?" For they were afraid of the people, because 33 all the people thought John was really a prophet. So they answered Jesus,

"We do not know."

Jesus said to them,

"Nor will I tell you what authority I have for doing as I do."

12 Then he began to speak to them in figures.

"A man once planted a vineyard and fenced it in and hewed out a wine-vat and built a watch tower, and he 2 leased it to tenants and left the neighborhood. At the proper time he sent a slave to the tenants to get from 3 them a share of the vintage. And they took him and 4 beat him and sent him back empty-handed. And again he sent another slave to them. And they beat him over the 5 head and treated him shamefully. And he sent another; and him they killed; and so with many others, some they 6 beat and some they killed. He still had one left to send, a dearly loved son. He sent him to them last of all, 7 thinking, 'They will respect my son.' But the tenants 8 said to one another, 'This is his heir! Come on, let us kill him, and the property will belong to us!' So they took him and killed him, and threw his body outside of the vineyard. What will the owner of the vineyard do?

He will come back and put the tenants to death and give 9
the vineyard to others. Did you never read this passage 10
of Scripture:

" 'That stone which the builders rejected
Has become the cornerstone;
This came from the Lord 11
And seems marvelous to us'?"

And they tried to have him arrested, but they were 12
afraid of the people, for they knew that the illustration
was aimed at them. And they left him and went away.

They sent some Pharisees and Herodians to him to 13
entrap him in argument. And they came up and said to 14
him,

"Master, we know that you tell the truth regardless
of the consequences, for you are not guided by personal
considerations, but teach the way of God with sincerity.
Is it right to pay the poll tax to the emperor or not?
Should we pay it, or refuse to pay it?" 15

But he saw through their pretense, and said to them,

"Why do you put me to such a test? Bring me a de-
narius to look at."

And they brought him one. He said to them, 16

"Whose head and title is this?"

And they told him,

"The emperor's."

And Jesus said, 17

"Pay the emperor what belongs to the emperor, and
pay God what belongs to God!"

And they were astonished at him.

Some of the Sadducees, who say there is no resurrec- 18
tion, came to him and asked him a question.

"Master," they said, "Moses made us a law that if a 19
man's brother died, leaving a wife but no child, the man
should marry the widow and raise up a family for his
brother. There were once seven brothers. And the eldest 20
married a wife and died, leaving no child. And the second 21
married her, and died without leaving any child, and so
did the third. And none of the seven left any child.
Finally, the woman died too. At the resurrection, which 22

23 one's wife will she be? For all seven of them married her."

24 Jesus said to them,

"Does not this show that you are wrong, and do not understand either the Scriptures or the power of God?
25 For when people rise from the dead, there is no marrying or being married, but they live as angels do in heaven.
26 But as to the dead being raised, have you never read in the Book of Moses, in the passage about the bush, how God said to him, 'I am the God of Abraham, the God of
27 Isaac, and the God of Jacob'? He is not God of dead men but of living! You are entirely wrong."

28 One of the scribes came up and heard them arguing. He saw that Jesus had answered them well, and he asked him,

"Which is the first of all the commands?"

29 Jesus answered,

30 "The first one is, 'Hear, Israel! The Lord our God is one lord, and you must love the Lord your God with your whole heart, your whole soul, your whole mind,
31 and your whole strength.' And this is the second: 'You must love your neighbor as you do yourself.' No other command is greater than these."

32 The scribe said to him,

"Really, Master, you have finely said that he stands
33 alone, and there is none but he, and to love him with one's whole heart, one's whole understanding, and one's whole strength, and to love one's neighbor as one's self is far more than all these burnt-offerings and sacrifices."

34 And Jesus saw that he answered thoughtfully, and he said to him,

"You are not far from the Kingdom of God!"

And no one ventured to ask him any more questions.

35 As Jesus was teaching in the Temple, he answered them and said,

36 "How can the scribes say that the Christ is a son of David? David himself, under the influence of the holy Spirit, said,

[363]

" 'The Lord has said to my lord, "Sit at my right hand
Until I put your enemies under your feet.' "

David himself calls him lord, and how can he be his son?" 37

The mass of the people liked to hear him. And in the 38
course of his teaching he said to them,

"Beware of the scribes who like to go about in long
robes and to be saluted with respect in public places, and 39
to have the front seats in the synagogues and the best
places at dinners—men that eat up widows' houses and 40
to cover it up make long prayers! They will get a far
heavier sentence!"

And he sat down facing the treasury and watched the 41
people dropping money into it; and many rich people
were putting in large sums. A poor widow came up and 42
dropped in two little copper coins which make a cent.
And he called his disciples to him and said, 43

"I tell you that this poor widow has put in more than
all these others who have been putting money into the
treasury. For they all gave of what they had to spare, 44
but she in her want has put in everything she possessed
—all she had to live on."

As he was leaving the Temple, one of his disciples said 13
to him,

"Look, Master! What wonderful stones and buildings?"

Jesus said to him, 2

"Do you see these great buildings? Not one stone shall
be left here upon another that shall not be torn down."

As he was sitting on the Mount of Olives opposite the 3
Temple, Peter, James, John, and Andrew asked him,
apart from the others,

"Tell us when this is to happen, and what the sign 4
will be when it is all just going to be carried out."

And Jesus said to them, 5

"Take care that no one misleads you about this. Many 6
will come under my name and say 'I am he,' and many
will be misled by them. But when you hear of wars and 7
rumors of war, you must not be alarmed. They have to 8
come, but it is not yet the end. For nation will rise in

arms against nation and kingdom against kingdom; there will be earthquakes here and there, there will be famines. This is only the beginning of the sufferings.

9 But you must be on your guard; they will hand you over to courts and you will be taken into synagogues and beaten, and you will be brought before governors and

10 kings on my account, to testify to them. For before the end the good news must be preached to all the heathen.

11 When they are taking you off to trial do not worry beforehand about what you ought to say, but say whatever is given you when the time comes, for it is not you that

12 will speak, but the holy Spirit. Brother will give up brother to be put to death, and the father his child, and children will turn against their parents and have them

13 put to death. You will be hated by everyone, because you bear my name. But he who holds out to the end will

14 be saved. But as soon as you see the dreadful desecration standing where he has no right to stand'' (the reader must take note of this), ''then those who are in Judea

15 must fly to the hills; a man on the roof of his house must not go down or go into the house to get anything out of

16 it, and a man in the field must not turn back to get his

17 coat. Alas for women who are with child at that time,

18 or who have babies! Pray that it may not be winter

19 when it comes, for there will be such misery in those days as there has never been since the beginning of God's

20 creation until now, and never will be again. If the Lord had not cut those days short, nobody would have escaped, but for the sake of his own chosen people he

21 has cut the days short. If anyone says to you at that time, 'Look! Here is the Christ!' or 'Look! There he

22 is!' do not believe it. For false Christs and false prophets will appear, and they will show signs and wonders to

23 mislead God's chosen people if they can. But you must be on your guard; I have told you all about it before-

24 hand. But in those days, when that misery is over, the sun will be darkened and the moon will not shed its light

25 and the stars will fall from the sky and the forces in the

26 sky will shake. Then they will see the Son of Man com-

ing on the clouds with great power and glory, and then 27
he will send out the angels and gather his chosen people
from the four winds, from one end of the world to the
other.

"Let the fig tree teach you the lesson. As soon as its 28
branches grow soft and put forth leaves you know that
summer is coming. So when you see these things hap- 29
pening, you must know that he is just at the door. I tell 30
you, these things will all happen before the present age
passes away. Earth and sky will pass away, but my 31
words will not. But about that day or hour no one 32
knows, not even the angels in heaven, nor the Son; only
the Father. You must look out and be on the alert, for 33
you do not know when it will be time; just as a man 34
when he leaves home to go on a journey, and puts his
slaves in charge, each with his duties, gives orders to
the watchman to keep watch. So you must be on the 35
watch, for you do not know when the master of the
house is coming—in the evening or at midnight or
toward daybreak or early in the morning—for fear he 36
should come unexpectedly and find you asleep. And 37
what I am telling you I mean for all—Be on the watch!"

HIS BETRAYAL, DEATH, AND RESURRECTION, 14:1—16:8

It was now two days before the festival of the Pass- 14
over and of Unleavened Bread. And the high priests and
scribes were casting about for a way to arrest him by
stealth and put him to death, for they said, 2

"It must not be during the festival, or there may be a
riot."

Jesus was in Bethany, at the house of Simon the leper, 3
and as he was at table, a woman came in, with an alabaster flask of pure nard perfume, very expensive; she
broke the flask and poured the perfume on his head. But 4
there were some who said indignantly to themselves,

"What was the use of wasting the perfume like that? 5
It might have been sold for more than sixty dollars, and
the money have been given to the poor."

And they grumbled at her. But Jesus said, 6

"Leave her alone. Why do you bother her? It is a fine
7 thing that she has done to me. For you always have the
poor among you, and whenever you please you can do
8 for them, but you will not always have me. She has done
all she could; she has perfumed my body in preparation
9 for my burial. I tell you, wherever the good news is
preached all over the world, what she has done will also
be told, in memory of her."

10 Then Judas Iscariot, one of the Twelve, went to the
11 high priests to betray Jesus to them. They were delighted to hear it and promised to pay him for it. So he
was watching for an opportunity to betray him to them.

12 On the first day of the festival of Unleavened Bread,
on which it was customary to kill the Passover lamb,
Jesus' disciples said to him,
"Where do you wish us to go and make the preparations for you to eat the Passover supper?"

13 So he sent away two of his disciples, saying to them,
"Go into the city, and you will meet a man carrying a
14 pitcher of water. Follow him, and whatever house he
goes into, say to the man of the house, 'The Master says,
"Where is my room where I can eat the Passover supper
15 with my disciples?" ' And he will show you a large room
upstairs, furnished and ready. Make your preparations
for us there."

16 So the disciples started and went into the city, and
found everything just as he had told them; and they
prepared the Passover supper.

17 When it was evening he came with the Twelve.
18 And when they were at the table eating, Jesus said,
"I tell you, one of you is going to betray me—one who
is eating with me."

19 And they were hurt, and said to him one after another,
"Can it be I?"

20 He said to them,
"It is one of the Twelve, who is dipping his bread in
21 the same dish with me. For the Son of Man is indeed to
go away as the Scriptures say of him, but alas for the man

by whom the Son of Man is betrayed! It would have been better for that man if he had never been born."

As they were eating, he took a loaf and blessed it, and 22 he broke it in pieces and gave it to them saying,

"Take this. It is my body."

And he took the wine cup and gave thanks and gave 23 it to them and they all drank from it. And he said to 24 them,

"This is my blood which ratifies the agreement, and is to be poured out for many people. I tell you, I will never 25 drink the product of the vine again till the day when I shall drink the new wine in the Kingdom of God."

After singing the hymn they went out of the city and 26 up the Mount of Olives. And Jesus said to them, 27

"You will all desert me, for the Scriptures say, 'I will strike the shepherd, and the sheep will be scattered.' But 28 after I am raised to life again I will go back to Galilee before you."

But Peter said to him, 29

"Even if they all desert you, I will not!"

Jesus said to him, 30

"I tell you, this very night before the cock crows twice you yourself will disown me three times!"

But he persisted vehemently, 31

"If I have to die with you, I will never disown you." And they all said the same thing.

They came to a place called Gethsemane, and he said 32 to his disciples,

"Sit down here while I pray."

And he took Peter, James, and John along with him, 33 and he began to feel distress and dread, and he said to 34 them,

"My heart is almost breaking. You must stay here and keep watch." And he went on a little way and threw 35 himself on the ground and prayed that if it were possible he might be spared the hour of trial; and he said, 36

"Abba!" that is, Father, "anything is possible for you! Take this cup away from me! Yet not what I please but what you do!"

37 When he went back he found them asleep and he said to Peter,
"Simon, are you asleep? Were you not able to watch
38 for one hour? You must all watch, and pray that you may not be subjected to trial. One's spirit is eager, but human nature is weak."

39 He went away again and prayed in the same words as before. When he came back he found them asleep again, for they could hardly keep their eyes open; and they did
41 not know what answer to make to him. When he came back for the third time, he said to them,
"Are you still sleeping and taking your rest? Enough of this! The time has come. See! the Son of Man is be-
42 trayed into the hands of wicked men. Get up, let us be going. Look! here comes my betrayer!"

43 Just at that moment, while he was still speaking, Judas, who was one of the Twelve, came up, and with him a crowd of men with swords and clubs, from the high
44 priests, scribes, and elders. Now the man who betrayed him had given them a signal, saying,
"The one I kiss is the man. Seize him and take him safely away."

45 So when he came he went straight up to Jesus and said, "Master!" and kissed him affectionately.
46 47 And they laid hands on him and seized him. But one of the bystanders drew his sword and struck at the high
48 priest's slave and cut his ear off. And Jesus spoke and said to them,
"Have you come out to arrest me with swords and
49 clubs, as though I were a robber? I have been among you day after day in the Temple teaching, and you never seized me. But let the Scriptures be fulfilled!"

50 Then all the disciples left him and made their escape.
51 And a young man followed him with nothing but a linen
52 cloth about his body; and they seized him, but he left the cloth behind and ran away naked.

53 They took Jesus away to the high priest, and all the
54 high priests, elders, and scribes came together. And Peter followed him at a distance, right into the court-

yard of the high priest and sat down with the attendants
and warmed himself at the fire. The high priests and the 55
whole council tried to get evidence against Jesus in order
to put him to death, and they could find none, for while 56
many gave false testimony against him their evidence
did not agree. Some got up and gave false testimony 57
against him to this effect:

"We ourselves have heard him say, 'I will tear down 58
this sanctuary built by men's hands, and in three days I
will build another, made without hands.' "

And even then their evidence did not agree. Then the 59
high priest got up and came forward into the center and 60
asked Jesus,

"Have you no answer to make? What about their evidence against you?"

But Jesus was silent and made no answer. The high 61
priest again questioned him and said to him,

"Are you the Christ, the son of the Blessed One?"

But Jesus said, 62

"I am! and you will all see the Son of Man seated at
the right hand of the Almighty and coming in the clouds
of the sky!"

Then the high priest tore his clothing, and said, 63

"What do we want of witnesses now? Did you hear 64
his blasphemy? What is your decision?"

And they all condemned him as deserving to be put to 65
death. And some started to spit at him and to blindfold
him and strike him, and say to him,

"Now show that you are a prophet!"

And the attendants slapped him as they took charge
of him.

While Peter was down in the courtyard, one of the 66
high priest's maids came up, and seeing Peter warming 67
himself, she looked at him and said,

"You were with this Jesus of Nazareth too!"

But he denied it, saying, 68

"I do not know or understand what you mean."

He went out into the gateway, And the maid saw him 69
there and began again to tell the bystanders,

"This fellow is one of them!"

70 But he denied it again. And again a little while after, the bystanders said to Peter,

"You certainly are one of them, for you are a Galilean!"

71 But he began to swear with the strongest oaths,

"I do not know this man that you are talking about!"

72 At that moment for the second time a cock crowed. And Peter remembered how Jesus had said to him, "Before the cock crows twice, you will disown me three times!" And at that, he wept aloud.

15 As soon as it was daylight, the high priests held a consultation with the elders and scribes, and they and the whole council bound Jesus and took him away and

2 handed him over to Pilate. Pilate asked him,

"Are you the king of the Jews?"

He answered,

"Yes."

3 And the high priests kept heaping accusations upon

4 him. But Pilate again asked him,

"Have you no answer to make? See what charges they are making against you."

5 But Jesus made no further answer at all, so that Pilate

6 wondered. Now at festival time he used to set free for

7 them one prisoner, whom they petitioned for. There was in prison a man called Barabbas, among some revolutionaries who in their outbreak had committed murder.

8 And a crowd of people came up and started to ask him for

9 the usual favor. Pilate asked them,

"Do you want me to set the king of the Jews free for you?"

10 For he knew that the high priests had handed him over

11 to him out of envy. But the high priests stirred up the crowd to get him to set Barabbas free for them instead.

12 And Pilate again said to them,

"Then what shall I do with the man you call the king of the Jews?"

13 They shouted back,

"Crucify him!"

And Pilate said to them, 14
"Why, what has he done that is wrong?"
But they shouted all the louder,
"Crucify him!"
And as Pilate wanted to satisfy the crowd, he set 15
Barabbas free for them, and after having Jesus flogged
handed him over to be crucified.

Then the soldiers took him inside the courtyard, that 16
is, of the governor's residence, and they called the whole
battalion together. And they dressed him up in a purple 17
cloak, and made a wreath of thorns and crowned him
with it, and they began to acclaim him, 18
"Long live the king of the Jews!"
And they struck him on the head with a stick and spat 19
at him, and they knelt down and did homage to him.
When they had finished making sport of him, they took 20
off the purple cloak and put his own clothes on him.

Then they took him out of the city to crucify him. 21
And they forced a passer-by, who was coming in from the
country, to carry his cross—one Simon, a Cyrenian, the
father of Alexander and Rufus. And they took him to the 22
place called Golgotha, which means the Place of the
Skull. They offered him drugged wine, but he would not 23
take it. Then they crucified him, and divided up his 24
clothes, drawing lots for them to see what each of them
should have. It was nine in the morning when they cruci- 25
fied him. And the notice of the charge against him read, 26
"The king of the Jews." They crucified two robbers 27
along with him, one at his right and one at his left. And 29
the passers-by jeered at him, shaking their heads and
saying,
"Aha! you who would tear down the sanctuary and
build one in three days! Come down from the cross and 30
save yourself!"
The high priests too made sport of him to one another 31
with the scribes and said,
"He saved others, but he cannot save himself! Let this 32
Christ, the king of Israel, come down from the cross now,

so that we may see it and believe!'' And the men who
were crucified with him abused him.

33   At noon darkness spread over the whole country, and
34 lasted until three in the afternoon. And at three o'clock
Jesus called out loudly,

"Eloi, Eloi, lama sabachthani?'' which means, "My
God, my God, why have you forsaken me?''

35   Some of the bystanders, when they heard it, said,
"See! He is calling for Elijah!''

36   One man ran off and soaked a sponge in common wine,
and put it on the end of a stick and held it up to him to
drink, saying,

"Let us see whether Elijah does come to take him
down!''

37
38   But Jesus gave a loud cry, and expired. And the curtain of the sanctuary was torn in two, from top to bot-
39 tom. And when the captain who stood facing him saw
how he expired he said,

"This man was certainly a son of God!''

40   There were some women also watching from a distance, among them Mary of Magdala, Mary the mother
41 of the younger James and of Joses, and Salome, who used
to accompany him and wait on him when he was in Galilee—besides many other women who had come up to
Jerusalem with him.

42   Although it was now evening, yet since it was the
Preparation Day, that is, the day before the Sabbath,
43 Joseph of Arimathea, a highly respected member of the
council, who was himself living in expectation of the
reign of God, made bold to go to Pilate and ask for Jesus'
44 body. Pilate wondered whether he was dead already, and
he sent for the captain and asked whether he was dead
45 yet, and when he learned from the captain that he was, he
46 gave Joseph permission to take the body. And he bought
a linen sheet and took him down from the cross and
wrapped him in the sheet, and laid him in a tomb that
had been hewn out of the rock, and rolled a stone against
47 the doorway of the tomb. And Mary of Magdala and

[373]

Mary, Joses' mother, were looking on and saw where he was put.

When the Sabbath was over, Mary of Magdala, Mary, 16 James' mother, and Salome bought spices, in order to go and anoint him. Then very early on the first day of 2 the week they went to the tomb, when the sun had just risen. And they said to one another, 3

"Who will roll the stone back from the doorway of the tomb for us?"

And they looked up and saw that the stone had been 4 rolled back, for it was very large. And when they went 5 into the tomb they saw a young man in a white robe sitting at the right, and they were utterly amazed. But he 6 said to them,

"You must not be amazed. You are looking for Jesus of Nazareth who was crucified. He has risen, he is not here. See! This is where they laid him. But go and say 7 to his disciples and to Peter, 'He is going before you to Galilee; you will see him there, just as he told you.' "

And they fled out of the tomb, for they were all trem- 8 bling and bewildered, and they said nothing about it to anyone, for they were afraid to do so.

THE GOSPEL ACCORDING TO MATTHEW

· · ·

A few years after the Gospel of Mark had made its appearance in Rome it was made the basis at the other end of the Christian world, in Antioch in Syria, of a much fuller account of Jesus' work which we know as the Gospel according to Matthew. Thoughtful Christians were perplexed by the failure of the Christian movement among the Jews. The prophets had said much about a messianic nation, yet the Messiah had come and the nation had refused him. There seemed to be a sharp contrast between the prophetic program and the actual march of events. On the other hand, the gospel was making great progress among the Greeks, and this enhanced the difficulty.

But an event had now occurred that threw a new light upon the problem. Jerusalem had fallen. This made a deep impression upon Jews and Christians alike, and to the Christians it seemed a just punishment of the nation for its rejection of its own Messiah. From this point of view the second evangelist, about A.D. 80, reviews the ministry and teaching of Jesus, adding to Mark's account a wealth of other material, especially of teaching, and shaping it all in and about six great discourses which form the framework of the gospel. Mark's picture of Jesus shows him as a doer, a man of action, but in Matthew Jesus is pre-eminently the teacher, and it is to his presentation of the teaching of Jesus that the world has turned ever since. The depth, beauty, and under-

[375]

standing of that teaching have caused Matthew's gospel to be called the " greatest book in the world."

. . .

THE BIRTH OF JESUS, 1:18—2:23

Now these were the circumstances of the birth of Jesus 1 Christ. Mary, his mother, was engaged to Joseph, but before they were married it was found that she was about to become a mother through the influence of the holy Spirit. But her husband, Joseph, was an upright man and 19 did not wish to disgrace her, and he decided to break off the engagement privately. But while he was thinking of 20 doing this, an angel of the Lord appeared to him in a dream, and said,

"Joseph, descendant of David, do not fear to take Mary, your wife, to your home, for it is through the influence of the holy Spirit that she is to become a mother. She will have a son, and you are to name him Jesus, for it 21 is he who is to save his people from their sins."

All this happened in fulfilment of what the Lord said 22 through the prophet,

"The maiden will be pregnant and will have a son, 23
And they will name him Immanuel"

—a word which means "God with us." So when Joseph 24 awoke from his sleep, he did as the angel of the Lord had directed him, and took his wife to his home. But he did 25 not live with her as a husband until she had had a son, and he named the child Jesus.

Now after the birth of Jesus at Bethlehem in Judea, in 2 the days of King Herod, astrologers from the east arrived at Jerusalem, and asked, 2

"Where is the newly born king of the Jews? For we have seen his star rise and we have come to do homage to him."

When King Herod heard of this he was troubled, and 3 all Jerusalem with him. So he called together all the 4 high priests and scribes of the people and asked them where the Christ was to be born. They said, 5

"At Bethlehem in Judea, for this is what the prophet wrote:

6　" 'And you, Bethlehem in Judah's land,
　　　You are by no means least important among the
　　　　leading places of Judah,
　　　For from you will come a leader
　　　Who will be the shepherd of my people Israel.' "

7　Then Herod secretly sent for the astrologers, and found out from them the exact time when the star ap-
8　peared. And he sent them to Bethlehem and said to them,

　　"Go and inquire particularly about the child, and when you have found him, bring me word, so that I may go and do homage to him too."

9　So they obeyed the king and went, and the star which they had seen rise led them on until it reached the place
10　where the child was, and stopped above it. When they
11　saw the star, they were very glad, and they went into the house and saw the child with his mother, Mary, and they threw themselves down and did homage to him. They opened their treasure boxes and presented the child
12　with gifts of gold, frankincense, and myrrh. Then, as they had been divinely warned in a dream not to go back to Herod, they returned to their own country by another way.

13　When they were gone an angel of the Lord appeared to Joseph in a dream, and said,

　　"Wake up! Take the child and his mother and make your escape to Egypt, and stay there until I tell you to leave. For Herod is going to look for the child in order to make away with him."

14　Then he awoke and took the child and his mother by night and took refuge in Egypt, to fulfil what the Lord
15　said by the prophet, "I called my son from Egypt."
16　Then Herod saw that he had been tricked by the as- trologers, and he was very angry, and he sent and made away with all the boys in Bethlehem and in all that neighborhood who were two years old or under, for that was the time he had learned from the astrologers by his

inquiries. Then the saying was fulfilled which was ut- 17
tered by the prophet Jeremiah,

"A cry was heard in Ramah!   18
    Weeping and great lamenting!
    Rachel weeping for her children,
    And inconsolable because they were gone."

But when Herod died, an angel of the Lord appeared 19
in a dream to Joseph in Egypt and said,   20

"Wake up! Take the child and his mother and go to
the land of Israel, for those who sought the child's life
are dead."

Then he awoke, and took the child and his mother and 21
went to the land of Israel. But hearing that Archelaus 22
was reigning over Judea in the place of his father, Herod,
he was afraid to return there; and being warned in a
dream, he took refuge in the region of Galilee, and he 23
went and settled in a town called Nazareth, in fulfilment
of the saying of the prophets,

"He shall be called a Nazarene."

THE TEMPTATION, 4:1–11

Then Jesus was guided by the Spirit into the desert, to **4**
be tempted by the devil. And he fasted forty days and 2
nights, and after it he was famished. And the tempter 3
came up and said to him,

"If you are God's son, tell these stones to turn into 4
bread!"

But he answered,

"The Scripture says, 'Not on bread alone is man to
live, but on every word that comes from the mouth of
God!'"

Then the devil took him to the holy city, and made 5
him stand on the summit of the Temple, and said to him, 6

"If you are God's son, throw yourself down, for the
Scripture says,

" 'He will give his angels orders about you,
    And they will lift you up with their hands
    So that you may never strike your foot against a
        stone!' "

7 Jesus said to him,
"The Scripture also says, 'You shall not try the Lord your God.' "

8 Again the devil took him to a very high mountain, and he showed him all the kingdoms of the world and
9 their splendor, and said to him,
"I will give all this to you, if you will fall on your knees and do homage to me."

10 Then Jesus said to him,
"Begone, Satan! For the Scripture says, 'You must do homage to the Lord your God, and worship him alone!' "

11 Then the devil left him, and angels came and waited on him.

JESUS BEGINS TO PREACH, 4:12–17

4 But when Jesus heard that John had been arrested, he
13 retreated to Galilee. And he left Nazareth and went and settled in Capernaum, by the sea, in the district of Zebu-
14 lon and Naphtali, in fulfilment of what was said by the prophet Isaiah,

15 "Zebulon's land, and Naphtali's land,
Along the road to the sea, across the Jordan,
Galilee of the nations!
16 The people that were living in darkness
Have seen a great light,
And on those who were living in the land of the shadow of death
A light has dawned!"

17 From that time Jesus began to preach and say,
"Repent! for the Kingdom of Heaven is coming!"

THE SERMON ON THE MOUNT, 5:1—7:29

5 When he saw the crowds of people he went up on the mountain. There he seated himself, and when his disciples had come up to him, he opened his lips to teach
2 them. And he said,

3 "Blessed are those who feel their spiritual need, for the Kingdom of Heaven belongs to them!

4 "Blessed are the mourners, for they will be consoled!

"Blessed are the humble-minded, for they will possess 5
the land!

"Blessed are those who are hungry and thirsty for 6
uprightness, for they will be satisfied!

"Blessed are the merciful, for they will be shown 7
mercy!

"Blessed are the pure in heart, for they will see God! 8

"Blessed are the peacemakers, for they will be called 9
God's sons!

"Blessed are those who have endured persecution for 10
their uprightness, for the Kingdom of Heaven belongs to
them!

"Blessed are you when people abuse you, and perse- 11
cute you, and falsely say everything bad of you, on my
account. Be glad and exult over it, for you will be richly 12
rewarded in heaven, for that is the way they persecuted
the prophets who went before you!

"You are the salt of the earth! But if salt loses its 13
strength, how can it be made salt again? It is good for
nothing but to be thrown away and trodden underfoot.
You are the light of the world! A city that is built upon 14
a hill cannot be hidden. People do not light a lamp and 15
put it under a peck-measure; they put it on its stand and
it gives light to everyone in the house. Your light must 16
burn that way among men so that they will see the
good you do, and praise your Father in heaven.

"Do not suppose that I have come to do away with 17
the Law or the Prophets. I have not come to do away
with them but to enforce them. For I tell you, as long as 18
heaven and earth endure, not one dotting of an *i* or crossing of a *t* will be dropped from the Law until it is all observed. Anyone, therefore, who weakens one of the 19
slightest of these commands, and teaches others to do so,
will be ranked lowest in the Kingdom of Heaven; but
anyone who observes them and teaches others to do so
will be ranked high in the Kingdom of Heaven. For I tell 20
you that unless your uprightness is far superior to that of
the scribes and Pharisees, you will never even enter the
Kingdom of Heaven!

21   "You have heard that the men of old were told 'You shall not murder,' and 'Whoever murders will have to
22 answer to the court.' But I tell you that anyone who gets angry with his brother will have to answer to the court, and anyone who speaks contemptuously to his brother will have to answer to the great council, and anyone who says to his brother 'You cursed fool!' will have to answer
23 for it in the fiery pit! So when you are presenting your gift at the altar, if you remember that your brother has
24 any grievance against you, leave your gift right there before the altar and go and make up with your brother;
25 then come back and present your gift. Be quick and come to terms with your opponent while you are on the way to court with him, or he may hand you over to the judge, and the judge may hand you over to the officer, and you
26 will be thrown into prison. I tell you, you will never get out again until you have paid the last penny!

27   "You have heard that men were told 'You shall
28 not commit adultery.' But I tell you that anyone who looks at a woman with desire has already committed
29 adultery with her in his heart. But if your right eye makes you fall, tear it out and throw it away, for you might better lose one part of your body than have it all thrown
30 into the pit! If your right hand makes you fall, cut if off and throw it away, for you might better lose one part of your body than have it all go down to the pit!

31   "They were told, 'Anyone who divorces his wife must
32 give her a certificate of divorce.' But I tell you that anyone who divorces his wife on any ground, except unfaithfulness, makes her commit adultery, and anyone who marries her after she is divorced commits adultery.

33   "Again, you have heard that the men of old were told, 'You shall not swear falsely, but you must fulfil
34 your oaths to the Lord.' But I tell you not to swear at
35 all, either by heaven, for it is God's throne, or by the earth, for it is his footstool, or by Jerusalem, for it is the
36 city of the great king. You must not swear by your own head, for you cannot make one single hair white or black.

But your way of speaking must be 'Yes' or 'No.' Any- 37
thing that goes beyond that comes from the evil one.

"You have heard that they were told, 'An eye for an 38
eye and a tooth for a tooth.' But I tell you not to resist 39
injury, but if anyone strikes you on your right cheek,
turn the other to him too; and if anyone wants to sue you 40
for your shirt, let him have your coat too. And if anyone 41
forces you to go one mile, go two miles with him. If any- 42
one begs from you, give to him, and when anyone wants
to borrow from you, do not turn away.

"You have heard that they were told, 'You must love 43
your neighbor and hate your enemy.' But I tell you, love 44
your enemies and pray for your persecutors, so that you 45
may show yourselves true sons of your Father in heaven,
for he makes his sun rise on bad and good alike, and
makes the rain fall on the upright and the wrongdoers.
For if you love only those who love you, what reward 46
can you expect? Do not the very tax-collectors do that?
And if you are polite to your brothers and no one else, 47
what is there remarkable in that? Do not the very heath-
en do that? So you are to be perfect, as your heavenly 48
Father is.

"But take care not to do your good deeds in public for 6
people to see, for, if you do, you will get no reward from
your Father in heaven. So when you are going to give to 2
charity, do not blow a trumpet before yourself, as the
hypocrites do, in the synagogues and the streets, to make
people praise them. I tell you, that is all the reward they
will get! But when you give to charity, your own left 3
hand must not know what your right hand is doing, so 4
that your charity may be secret, and your Father who sees
what is secret will reward you.

"When you pray, you must not be like the hypocrites, 5
for they like to pray standing in the synagogues and in
the corners of the squares, to let people see them. I tell
you, that is the only reward they will get! But when you 6
pray, go into your own room, and shut the door, and
pray to your Father who is unseen, and your Father who
sees what is secret will reward you. And when you pray, 7

do not repeat empty phrases as the heathen do, for they imagine that their prayers will be heard if they use words

8 enough. You must not be like them. For God, who is your Father, knows what you need before you ask him.

9 This, therefore, is the way you are to pray:
'Our Father in heaven,
Your name be revered!

10 Your kingdom come!
Your will be done on earth as it is done in heaven!

11 Give us today bread for the day,

12 And forgive us our debts, as we have forgiven our debtors.

13 And do not subject us to temptation,
But save us from the evil one.'

14 For if you forgive others when they offend you, your

15 heavenly Father will forgive you too. But if you do not forgive others when they offend you, your heavenly Father will not forgive you for your offenses.

16 "When you fast, do not put on a gloomy look, like the hypocrites, for they neglect their personal appearance to

17 let people see that they are fasting. I tell you, that is all

18 the reward they will get. But when you fast, perfume your hair and wash your face, so that no one may see that you are fasting, except your Father who is unseen, and your Father who sees what is secret, will reward you.

19 "Do not store up your riches on earth, where moths and rust destroy them, and where thieves break in and

20 steal them, but store up your riches in heaven, where moths and rust cannot destroy them, and where thieves

21 cannot break in and steal them. For wherever your treas-

22 ure is, your heart will be also. The eye is the lamp of the body. If then your eye is sound, your whole body will be

23 light, but if your eye is unsound, your whole body will be dark. If, therefore, your very light is darkness, how deep

24 the darkness will be! No slave can belong to two mas-ters, for he will either hate one and love the other, or stand by one and make light of the other. You cannot

25 serve God and money. Therefore, I tell you, do not worry about life, wondering what you will have to eat or drink,

or about your body, wondering what you will have to wear. Is not life more important than food, and the body than clothes? Look at the wild birds. They do not sow 26 or reap, or store their food in barns, and yet your heavenly Father feeds them. Are you not of more account than they? But which of you with all his worry can add a 27 single hour to his life? Why should you worry about 28 clothing? See how the wild flowers grow. They do not toil or spin, and yet I tell you, even Solomon in all his 29 splendor was never dressed like one of them. But if God 30 so beautifully dresses the wild grass, which is alive today and is thrown into the furnace tomorrow, will he not much more surely clothe you, you who have so little faith? So do not worry and say, 'What shall we have to 31 eat?' or 'What shall we have to drink?' or 'What shall we have to wear?' For these are all things the heathen are in 32 pursuit of, and your heavenly Father knows well that you need all this. But you must make his kingdom, and 33 uprightness before him, your greatest care, and you will have all these other things besides. So do not worry 34 about tomorrow, for tomorrow will have worries of his own. Let each day be content with its own ills.

"Pass no more judgments upon other people, so that 7 you may not have judgment passed upon you. For you 2 will be judged by the standard you judge by, and men will pay you back with the same measure you have used with them. Why do you keep looking at the speck 3 in your brother's eye, and pay no attention to the beam that is in your own? How can you say to your brother, 4 'Just let me get that speck out of your eye,' when all the time there is a beam in your own? You hypocrite! First 5 get the beam out of your own eye, and then you can see to get the speck out of your brother's eye.

"Do not give what is sacred to dogs, and do not throw 6 your pearls before pigs, or they will trample them under their feet and turn and tear you in pieces. Ask, and what 7 you ask will be given you. Search, and you will find what you search for. Knock, and the door will open to you. For it is always the one who asks who receives, and 8

the one who searches who finds, and the one who knocks
9 to whom the door opens. Which of you men when his
10 son asks him for some bread will give him a stone? Or if
11 he asks for a fish, will he give him a snake? So if you,
bad as you are, know enough to give your children what
is good, how much more surely will your Father in heav-
12 en give what is good to those who ask him for it! Therefore, you must always treat other people as you would
like to have them treat you, for this sums up the Law and
the Prophets.

13   "Go in at the narrow gate. For the road that leads to
destruction is broad and spacious, and there are many
14 who go in by it. But the gate is narrow and the road is
hard that leads to life, and there are few that find it.

15   "Beware of the false prophets, who come to you dis-
guised as sheep but are ravenous wolves underneath.
16 You can tell them by their fruit. Do people pick grapes
17 off thorns, or figs off thistles? Just so any sound tree bears
18 good fruit, but a poor tree bears bad fruit. No sound tree
can bear bad fruit, and no poor tree can bear good fruit.
19 Any tree that does not bear good fruit is cut down and
20
21 burned. So you can tell them by their fruit. It is not
everyone who says to me 'Lord! Lord!' who will get into
the Kingdom of Heaven, but only those who do the
22 will of my Father in heaven. Many will say to me on
that Day, 'Lord! Lord! Was it not in your name that we
prophesied, and by your name that we drove out demons,
23 and by your name that we did many mighty acts?' Then
I will say to them plainly, 'I never knew you! Go away
from me, you who do wrong!'

24   "Everyone, therefore, who listens to this teaching of
mine and acts upon it, will be like a sensible man who
25 built his house on rock. And the rain fell, and the rivers
rose, and the winds blew, and beat about that house, and
it did not go down, for its foundations were on rock.
26 And anyone who listens to this teaching of mine and does
not act upon it, will be like a foolish man who built his
27 house on sand. And the rain fell and the rivers rose, and

the winds blew and beat about that house, and it went down, and its downfall was complete."

When Jesus had finished this discourse, the crowds 28 were astounded at his teaching, for he taught them like 29 one who had authority and not like their scribes.

THE PREACHING OF THE KINGDOM, 10:1–42

Then he called his twelve disciples to him, and gave 10 them power over the foul spirits so that they could drive them out, and so that they could heal any disease or illness.

These are the names of the twelve apostles: first, Si- 2 mon, who was called Peter, and his brother Andrew, and James the son of Zebedee and his brother John, Philip 3 and Bartholomew, Thomas and Matthew the tax-collector, James the son of Alpheus and Thaddeus, Simon 4 the Zealot and Judas Iscariot who aftward betrayed him.

Jesus sent these twelve out, after giving them these 5 directions:

"Do not go among the heathen, or to any Samaritan 6 town, but proceed instead to the lost sheep of Israel's house. And as you go about, preach and say, 'The King- 7 dom of Heaven is at hand!' Cure the sick, raise the dead, 8 heal lepers, drive out demons. Give without payment, just as you received without payment. Do not accept 9 gold or silver or copper money to put in your pockets, and do not take a bag for your journey, nor two shirts, 10 nor shoes, nor a staff, for the workman deserves his food! Whatever town or village you come to, inquire for some 11 suitable person, and stay with him till you leave the place. And as you go into his house, wish it well. If the $^{12}_{13}$ house deserves it, the peace you wish it will come over it, but if it does not deserve it, your blessing will come back upon yourselves. And where no one will welcome you, 14 or listen to you, leave that house or town and shake off its very dust from your feet. I tell you, the land of Sodom 15 and Gomorrah will fare better on the Day of Judgment than that town.

"Here I am sending you out like sheep among wolves. 16

So you must be wise like serpents, and guileless like
17 doves. But be on your guard against men, for they will
give you up to their courts, and have you flogged in their
18 synagogues, and you will be brought before governors
and kings on my account, to bear your testimony before
19 them and the heathen. But when they give you up, you
must have no anxiety about how to speak or what to say,
for you will be told at the very moment what you ought
20 to say, for it is not you who will speak, it is the Spirit
21 of your Father that will speak through you. One brother
will give up another to death, and a father his child, and
children will turn against their parents, and have them
22 put to death. You will be hated by everybody on my account, but the man who holds out to the very end will be
23 saved. But when they persecute you in one town, make
your escape to another, for I tell you, you will not have
gone through all the towns of Israel before the Son of
24 Man arrives. A pupil is not better than his teacher, nor
25 a slave better than his master. A pupil should be satisfied to come to be like his teacher, or a slave to come to
be like his master. If men have called the head of the
house Beelzebub, how much worse names will they give
26 to the members of his household! So do not be afraid of
them. For there is nothing covered up that is not going
to be uncovered, nor secret that is not going to be known.
27 What I tell you in the dark you must say in the light, and
what you hear whispered in your ear, you must proclaim
28 from the housetops. Have no fear of those who kill the
body, but cannot kill the soul. You had better be afraid
of one who can destroy both soul and body in the pit.
29 Do not sparrows sell two for a cent? And yet not one of
them can fall to the ground against your Father's will.
30 But the very hairs on your heads are all counted. You
31 must not be afraid; you are worth more than a great many
32 sparrows! Therefore everyone who will acknowledge me
before men I will acknowledge before my Father in heav-
en, but anyone who disowns me before men, I will disown before my Father in heaven.
34   "Do not think that I have come to bring peace to the

earth. I have not come to bring peace but a sword. For I 35
have come to turn a man against his father and a daughter against her mother and a daughter-in-law against her
mother-in-law, and a man's enemies will be in his own 36
household. No one who loves father or mother more 37
than he loves me is worthy of me, and no one who loves
son or daughter more than he loves me is worthy of me,
and no one who will not take up his cross and follow me 38
is worthy of me. Whoever gains his life will lose it, and 39
whoever loses his life for my sake will gain it.

"Whoever welcomes you welcomes me, and whoever 40
welcomes me welcomes him who has sent me. Whoever 41
welcomes a prophet because he is a prophet will have the
same reward as a prophet, and whoever welcomes an upright man because he is upright will have the same reward as an upright man. And no one who will give the 42
humblest of my disciples even a cup of cold water because
he is my disciple, I tell you, can ever fail of his reward."

PARABLES OF THE KINGDOM, 13:1-54

That same day Jesus went out of his house and was 13
sitting on the seashore. And such great crowds gathered 2
about him that he got into a boat and sat down in it,
while all the people stood on the shore. And he told 3
them many things in figures, and said to them,

"A sower went out to sow, and as he was sowing, 4
some of the seed fell by the path and the birds came and
ate it up, and some fell on rocky ground where there was 5
not much soil and it sprang up at once, because the soil
was not deep, but when the sun came up it was scorched 6
and withered up, because it had no root. And some of it 7
fell among the thorns, and the thorns grew up and choked
it out. And some fell on good soil, and yielded some a 8
hundred, some sixty, and some thirty-fold. Let him who 9
has ears listen!"

His disciples came up and said to him, 10
"Why do you speak to them in figures?"
He answered, 11
"You are permitted to know the secrets of the King-

12 dom of Heaven, but they are not. For people who have will have more given to them, and will be plentifully supplied, and from people who have nothing even what

13 they have will be taken away. This is why I speak to them in figures, because though they look they do not see, and though they listen they do not hear or under-

14 stand. They are a fulfilment of Isaiah's prophecy,
" 'You will listen and listen, and never understand,
And you will look and look, and never see!

15 For this nation's mind has grown dull,
And they hear faintly with their ears,
And they have shut their eyes,
So as never to see with their eyes,
And hear with their ears,
And understand with their minds, and turn back,
And let me cure them!'

16 "But blessed are your eyes, for they do see, and your

17 *ears, for they do hear. For I tell you, many prophets and upright men have longed to see what you see, and could not see it, and to hear what you hear, and could not hear it.

18 "You must listen closely then to the figure of the sow-

19 er. When anyone hears the teaching of the kingdom and does not understand it, the evil one comes and robs him

20 of the seed that has been sown in his mind. That is what was sown along the path. And what was sown upon the rocky soil means the man who hears the message and at

21 once accepts it joyfully, but it takes not real root in him, and lasts only a little while, and when trouble or persecu- tion comes because of the message, he gives it up at once.

22 And what was sown among the thorns means the man who listens to the message, and then the worries of the time and the pleasure of being rich choke the message

23 out, and it yields nothing. And what was sown in good ground means the man who listens to the message and understands it, and yields one a hundred, and another sixty, and another thirty-fold."

24 Another figure which he used in speaking to them was this:

"The Kingdom of Heaven is like a man who sowed good seed in his field, but while people were asleep his 25 enemy came and sowed weeds among the wheat, and went away. And when the wheat came up and ripened, 26 the weeds appeared too. And the owner's slaves came to 27 him and said, 'Was not the seed good that you sowed in your field, sir? So where did these weeds come from?' He 28 said to them, 'This is some enemy's doing.' And they said to him, 'Do you want us to go and gather them up?' But he said, 'No, for in gathering up the weeds you may 29 uproot the wheat. Let them both grow together until 30 harvest time, and when we harvest I will direct the reapers to gather up the weeds first and tie them up in bundles to burn, but get the wheat into my barn.' "

Another figure which he used in speaking to them was 31 this:

"The Kingdom of Heaven is like a mustard seed which a man took and sowed in his field. It is the smallest of all •32 seeds, but when it is grown it is the largest of plants and grows into a tree, so that the wild birds come and roost in its branches."

Another figure which he used with them was this: 33

"The Kingdom of Heaven is like yeast, which a woman took and buried in a bushel of flour until it had all risen."

Jesus said all this to the crowds in figures, and told 34 them nothing except in figures, to fulfil what was said 35 by the prophet,

"I will open my mouth in figures,
I will utter things that have been hidden since the
 creation."

Then he left the crowds and went into his house. And 36 his disciples came up to him and said,

"Explain to us the figure of the weeds in the field."

He answered, 37

"The sower who sows the good seed is the Son of Man. 38 The field is the world. The good seed is the people of the kingdom. The weeds are the wicked. The enemy who 39 sowed them is the devil. The harvest is the close of the

40 age, and the reapers are angels. So just as the weeds are gathered up and burned, this is what will happen at the
41 close of the age; the Son of Man will send out his angels, and they will gather up out of his kingdom all the causes
42 of sin and the wrongdoers and throw them into the blazing furnace; there they will wail and grind their teeth.
43 Then the upright will shine out like the sun, in their Father's kingdom. Let him who has ears listen!
44 "The Kingdom of Heaven is like a hoard of money, buried in a field, which a man found, and buried again. And he was overjoyed, and went and sold everything he had and bought the field.
45 "Again, the Kingdom of Heaven is like a dealer in
46 search of fine pearls. He found one costly pearl, and went and sold everything he had, and bought it.
47 "Again, the Kingdom of Heaven is like a net that was let down into the sea, and inclosed fish of all kinds.
48 When it was full, they dragged it up on the beach, and sat down and sorted the good fish into baskets and threw
49 the bad away. That is what will happen at the close of the age. The angels will go out and remove the wicked from among the upright, and throw them into the blaz-
50 ing furnace. There they will wail and grind their teeth.
51 "Do you understand all this?"
They said to him,
"Yes."
52 He said to them,
"Then remember that every scribe who has become a disciple of the Kingdom of Heaven must be like a householder who can supply from his storeroom new things as well as old."
53 When Jesus had finished these figures, he left that
54 place, and went to his own part of the country.

HUMILITY AND FORGIVENESS, 18:1–35

18 Just at that time the disciples came up and asked Jesus, "Who is really greatest in the Kingdom of Heaven?"
2 He called a child to him and had him stand among
3 them, and he said,

[391]

"I tell you, unless you change and become like children, you will never get into the Kingdom of Heaven at all. Anyone, therefore, who is as unassuming as this 4 child is the greatest in the Kingdom of Heaven, and any- 5 one who welcomes one child like this on my account welcomes me. But whoever hinders one of these children 6 who believe in me might better have a great millstone hung around his neck and be sunk in the open sea. Alas 7 for the world for such hindrances! They have to come, but alas for the man who causes them!

"But if your own hand or your own foot makes you 8 fall, cut it off and throw it away. You might better enter upon life maimed or crippled than keep both hands and feet but be thrown into the everlasting fire. And if your 9 own eye makes you fall, dig it out and throw it away. You might better enter upon life with only one eye than be thrown with both eyes into the fiery pit.

"Beware of feeling scornful of one single little child, for 10 I tell you that in heaven their angels have continual access to my Father in heaven. What do you think? If a 12 man has a hundred sheep and one of them strays away, will he not leave the ninety-nine on the hills, and go in search of the one that is astray? And if he happens to find 13 it, I tell you he rejoices more over it than he does over the ninety-nine that did not stray. In just that way, it is 14 the will of my Father in heaven that not a single one of these children be lost.

"But if your brother wrongs you, go to him and show 15 him his fault while you are alone with him. If he listens to you, you have won back your brother. But if he will 16 not listen, take one or two others with you, so that everything may be supported by the testimony of two or three witnesses. If he refuses to listen to them, tell the 17 congregation. And if he refuses to listen to it, treat him as a heathen or a tax-collector.

"I tell you, whatever you forbid on earth will be held 18 in heaven to be forbidden, and whatever you permit on earth will be held in heaven to be permitted. Again, 19 I tell you, if even two of you here on earth agree about

[392]

what they shall pray for, it will be given them by my
20 Father in heaven. For wherever two or three are gathered as my followers, I am there amongst them."
21   Then Peter came to him and said,
"Master, how many times am I to forgive my brother
when he wrongs me? Seven times over?"
22   Jesus said to him,
"Not seven times over, I tell you, but seventy-seven
23 times over! For this reason the Kingdom of Heaven may
be compared to a king, who resolved to settle accounts
24 with his slaves. And when he set about doing so, a man
25 was brought in who owed him ten million dollars. And
as he could not pay, his master ordered him to be sold,
with his wife and children and all he had, in payment of
26 the debt. So the slave threw himself down before him
and implored him, 'Give me time, and I will pay you all
27 of it.' And his master's heart was touched, and he let the
28 slave go and cancelled the debt. But when the slave went
out he met a fellow-slave of his who owed him twenty
dollars, and he caught him by the throat and began to
29 choke him, saying, 'Pay me what you owe!' So his fellow-slave threw himself down before him, and begged
30 him, 'Give me time, and I will pay you.' But he refused
and went and had him put in prison until he should pay
31 the debt. When his fellow-slaves saw what had happened,
they were greatly distressed, and they went to their mas-
32 ter and reported the whole matter to him. Then his master called him in and said to him, 'You wicked slave! I
cancelled all that debt of yours when you entreated me.
33 Ought you not to have taken pity on your fellow-slave,
34 as I did on you?' So his master in his anger handed him
over to the jailers, until he should pay all he owed him.
35 That is what my heavenly Father will do to you, if you
do not each forgive your brothers from your hearts!"

THE FAULTS OF THE PHARISEES, 23:1–39

23   Then Jesus said to the crowds and to his disciples,
2   "The scribes and Pharisees have taken Moses' seat.
3   So do everything they tell you, and observe it all, but do

[393]

not do as they do, for they talk but do not act. They tie 4
up heavy loads and have them put on men's shoulders,
but they will not lift a finger to move them. They do 5
everything they do to have men see it. They wear wide
Scripture texts as charms, and they wear large tassels,
and they like the best places at dinners and the front seats 6
in the synagogues, and to be saluted with respect in pub- 7
lic places, and to have men call them 'Rabbi.' But you 8
must not let people call you 'Rabbi,' for you have only
one teacher, and you are all brothers. And you must not 9
call anyone on earth your father, for you have only one
father, your heavenly Father. And you must not let men 10
call you master, for you have only one master, the Christ.
But he who is greatest among you must be your servant. 11
Whoever exalts himself will be humbled and whoever 12
humbles himself will be exalted.

"But alas for you, you hypocritical scribes and Phari- 14
sees, for you lock the doors of the Kingdom of Heaven in
men's faces, for you will neither go in yourselves nor let
those enter who are trying to do so. Alas for you, you 15
hypocritical scribes and Pharisees, for you scour land and
sea to make one convert, and when he is converted you
make him twice as fit for the pit as you are. Alas for you, 16
you blind guides, who say, 'If anyone swears by the sanctuary, it does not matter, but if anyone swears by the
gold of the sanctuary, it is binding.' Blind fools! which is 17
greater, the gold, or the sanctuary that makes the gold
sacred? You say, 'If anyone swears by the altar, it does 18
not matter, but if anyone swears by the offering that is on
it, it is binding.' You blind men! Which is greater, the 19
offering, or the altar that makes the offering sacred?
Anyone who swears by the altar is swearing by it and by 20
everything that is on it, and anyone who swears by the 21
sanctuary is swearing by it and by him who dwells in it;
and anyone who swears by heaven is swearing by the 22
throne of God and by him who sits upon it.

"Alas for you, you hypocritical scribes and Pharisees, 23
for you pay tithes on mint, dill, and cummin, and you
have let the weightier matters of the Law go—justice,

mercy, and integrity. But you should have observed
24 these, without overlooking the others. You blind guides!
straining out the gnat, and yet swallowing the camel!
25 Alas for you, you hypocritical scribes and Pharisees, for
you clean the outside of the cup and the dish, but inside
26 they are full of greed and self-indulgence. You blind
Pharisee! You must first clean the inside of the cup and
27 dish, so that the outside may be clean too. Alas for you,
you hypocritical scribes and Pharisees, for you are like
white-washed tombs! They look well on the outside, but
inside they are full of the bones of the dead, and all that
28 is unclean. So you outwardly appear to men to be upright, but within you are full of hypocrisy and wickedness.
29   "Alas for you, you hypocritical scribes and Pharisees,
for you build tombs for the prophets, and decorate the
30 monuments of the upright, and say, 'If we had been living
in the times of our fathers, we would not have joined in
31 the murder of the prophets.' So you bear witness against
yourselves that you are descended from the murderers of
32 the prophets. Go on and fill up the measure of your fore-
33 fathers' guilt. You serpents! You brood of snakes! How
34 can you escape being sentenced to the pit? This is why I
am going to send you prophets, wise men and scribes,
some of whom you will kill and crucify, and some you
will flog in your synagogues and hunt from one town to
35 another; it is that on your heads may come all the righteous blood shed on the earth from the blood of Abel the
upright to the blood of Zechariah, Barachiah's son,
whom you murdered between the sanctuary and the al-
36 tar! I tell you, all this will come upon this age!
37   "O Jerusalem, Jerusalem! murdering the prophets, and
stoning those who are sent to her, how often I have
longed to gather your children around me, as a hen gath-
38 ers her brood under her wings, but you refused! Now I
39 leave you to yourselves. For I tell you, you will never see
me again until you say, 'Blessed be he who comes in the
Lord's name!'"

THE DOOM OF THE CITY, AND THE END OF THE AGE, 24:1-51

And Jesus left the Temple and was going away, when 24 his disciples came up to him to call his attention to the Temple buildings. But he answered, 2

"Do you see all this? I tell you, not one stone will be left here upon another but shall be torn down."

As he was sitting on the Mount of Olives, the disciples 3 came up to him by themselves, and said to him,

"Tell us when this is to happen, and what will be the sign of your coming, and of the close of the age."

Jesus answered, 4

"Take care that no one misleads you about this. For 5 many will come under my name, and say, 'I am the Christ,' and many will be misled by them. You will hear 6 of wars and rumors of war; do not let yourselves be alarmed. They have to come, but that is not the end. 7 For nation will rise in arms against nation, and kingdom against kingdom, and there will be famines and earthquakes here and there. All this is only the beginning of 8 the sufferings. Then they will hand you over to persecu- 9 tion and they will put you to death, and you will be hated by all the heathen because you bear my name. Then many will fall away and betray one another and 10 hate one another. Many false prophets will appear, and 11 many will be misled by them, and because of the increase 12 of wickedness, most men's love will grow cold. But he 13 who holds out to the end will be saved. And this good 14 news of the kingdom will be preached all over the world, to testify to all the heathen, and then the end will come.

"So when you see the dreadful desecration, of which 15 the prophet Daniel spoke, set up in the Holy Place"— the reader must take note of this—"then those who are 16 in Judea must fly to the hills; a man on the roof of his 17 house must not go down to get things out of it, and a 18 man in the field must not turn back to get his coat. But 19 alas for women who are with child at that time or who have babies! And pray that you may not have to fly in 20

[396]

21 winter or on the Sabbath, for there will be greater misery then than there has ever been from the beginning of crea-
22 tion until now, or ever will be again. If those days had not been cut short, nobody would have escaped, but for the sake of God's people those days will be cut short.

23 "If anyone says to you at that time, 'Look! here is the
24 Christ!' or 'There he is!' do not believe it, for false Christs and false prophets will appear, and they will show great signs and wonders to mislead God's chosen people if they
25 can. Here I have told you beforehand. So if they say to
26 you, 'There he is, in the desert!' do not go out there;
27 'Here he is, in a room in here!' do not believe it. For just
28 as the lightning starts in the east and flashes to the west, so the coming of the Son of Man will be. Wherever there is a dead body, the vultures will flock.

29 "But immediately after the misery of those days, the sun will be darkened, and the moon will not shed its light, and the stars will fall from the sky, and the forces
30 of the sky will shake. Then the sign of the Son of Man will appear in the sky, and all the nations of the earth will lament when they see the Son of Man coming on the
31 clouds of the sky, in all his power and splendor. And he will send out his angels with a loud trumpet-call, and they will gather his chosen people from the four winds, from one end of the sky to the other.

32 "Let the fig tree teach you the lesson. As soon as its branches grow soft and put forth leaves, you know that
33 summer is coming. So when you see all these things, you
34 must know that he is just at the door. I tell you, these things will all happen before the present age passes away.
35 Earth and sky will pass away but my words will never
36 pass away. But about that day or hour no one knows, not even the angels in heaven nor the Son, but only the
37 Father. For just as it was in the time of Noah, it will be
38 at the coming of the Son of Man. For just as in those days before the flood people were eating and drinking, marry-ing and being married, until the very day Noah entered
39 the ark, and knew nothing about it until the flood came and destroyed them all, so it will be at the coming of the

Son of Man. Two men will be in the field; one will be 40
taken and one left. Two women will be grinding with 41
the handmill; one will be taken and one left. So you 42
must be on the watch, for you do not know on what day
your Master is coming. But you may be sure of this, that 43
if the master of the house had known in what part of the
night the thief was coming, he would have been on the
watch, and would not have let his house be broken into.
Therefore you must be ready too, for the Son of Man is 44
coming at a time when you do not expect him.

"Who then will be the faithful, thoughtful slave 45
whom his master put in charge of his household, to give
the members of it their supplies at the proper time?
Blessed is that slave if his master when he returns finds 46
him doing it. I tell you, he will put him in charge of all 47
his property. But if he is a bad slave and says to himself, 48
'My master is going to stay a long time,' and begins to
beat the other slaves, and eats and drinks with drunk- 49
ards, that slave's master will come back some day when 50
he does not expect him, and at some time of which he
does not know and will cut him in two, and put him 51
with the hypocrites, to weep and gnash his teeth.

FINAL PARABLES: THE BRIDESMAIDS, THE TALENTS,
AND THE JUDGMENT, 25:1–46

"Then the Kingdom of Heaven will be like ten brides- 25
maids who took their lamps and went out to meet the
bridegroom. Now five of them were foolish and five were 2
sensible. For the foolish ones brought their lamps but 3
brought no oil with them, but the sensible ones with 4
their lamps brought oil in their flasks. As the bride- 5
groom was slow in coming, they all grew drowsy and fell
asleep. But in the middle of the night there was a shout 6
'Here is the bridegroom! Come out and meet him!' Then 7
all the bridesmaids awoke, and trimmed their lamps.
And the foolish ones said to the sensible ones, 'Give us 8
some of your oil, for our lamps are going out.' But the 9
sensible ones answered, 'There may not be enough for us
and you. You had better go to the dealers and buy your-

10 selves some.' But while they were gone to buy it, the bridegroom arrived, and the ones that were ready went in with him to the wedding banquet, and the door was
11 closed. Afterward the other bridesmaids came and said,
12 'Sir! Sir! Open the door for us!' But he answered, 'I tell
13 you, I do not know you!' So you must be on the watch, for you do not know either the day or the hour.
14   "For it is just like a man who was going on a journey, and called in his slaves, and put his property in their
15 hands. He gave one five thousand dollars, and another two thousand, and another one thousand; to each accord-
16 ing to his ability. Then he went away. The man who had received the five thousand dollars immediately went into business with the money, and made five thousand more.
17 In the same way the man who had received the two thou-
18 sand made two thousand more. But the man who had received the one thousand went away and dug a hole in the
19 ground and hid his master's money. Long afterward, their master came back and settled accounts with them.
20 And the man who had received the five thousand dollars came up bringing him five thousand more, and said, 'Sir, you put five thousand dollars in my hands; here I have
21 made five thousand more.' His master said to him, 'Well done, my excellent, faithful slave! you have been faithful about a small amount; I will put a large one into your
22 hands. Come, share your master's enjoyment!' And the man who had received the two thousand came up and said 'Sir, you put two thousand dollars into my hands;
23 here I have made two thousand more.' His master said to him, 'Well done, my excellent, faithful slave! you have been faithful about a small amount; I will put a large one into your hands. Come! share your master's en-
24 joyment.' And the man who had received the one thousand came up and said, 'Sir, I knew you were a hard man, who reaped where you had not sown, and gathered where
25 you had not threshed, and I was frightened, and I went and hid your thousand dollars in the ground. Here is
26 your money!' His master answered, 'You wicked, idle slave! You knew that I reaped where I had not sown and

gathered where I had not threshed? Then you ought to 27
have put my money in the bank, and then when I came
back I would have gotten my property with interest. So 28
take the thousand dollars away from him, and give it to
the man who has the ten thousand, for the man who has 29
will have more given him, and will be plentifully supplied, and from the man who has nothing even what he
has will be taken away. And put the good-for-nothing 30
slave out into the darkness outside, to weep and grind his
teeth there.'

"When the Son of Man comes in his splendor, with all 31
his angels with him, he will take his seat on his glorious
throne, and all the nations will be gathered before him, 32
and he will separate them from one another, just as
a shepherd separates his sheep from his goats, and he will 33
put the sheep at his right hand and the goats at his left.
Then the king will say to those at his right, 'Come, you 34
whom my Father has blessed, take possession of the
kingdom which has been destined for you from the creation of the world. For when I was hungry, you gave me 35
food, when I was thirsty you gave me something to
drink, when I was a stranger, you invited me to your
homes, when I had no clothes, you gave me clothes, 36
when I was sick, you looked after me, when I was in prison, you came to see me.' Then the upright will answer, 37
'Lord, when did we see you hungry and give you food, or
thirsty, and give you something to drink? When did we 38
see you a stranger, and invite you home, or without
clothing, and supply you with it? When did we see you 39
sick or in prison, and go to see you?' The king will an- 40
swer, 'I tell you, in so far as you did it to one of the
humblest of these brothers of mine, you did it to me.'
Then he will say to those at his left, 'Begone, you ac- 41
cursed people, to the everlasting fire destined for the devil
and his angels! For when I was hungry, you gave me 42
nothing to eat, and when I was thirsty you gave me nothing to drink, when I was a stranger, you did not invite 43
me home, when I had no clothes, you did not supply me,
when I was sick and in prison, you did not look after me.'

44 Then they in turn will answer, 'Lord, when did we see you hungry, or thirsty, or a stranger, or in need of clothes, or sick, or in prison, and did not wait upon you?'
45 Then he will answer, 'I tell you, in so far as you failed to do it for one of these people who are humblest, you failed
46 to do it for me.' Then they will go away to everlasting punishment, and the upright to everlasting life.''

THE RESURRECTION AND THE GREAT COMMISSION,
28:1-20

28 After the Sabbath, as the first day of the week was dawning, Mary of Magdala and the other Mary went to
2 look at the tomb. And there was a great earthquake. For an angel of the Lord came down from heaven and
3 went and rolled the stone back and sat upon it. His appearance was like lightning and his clothing was as
4 white as snow. The men on guard trembled with fear of
5 him, and became like dead men. And the angel said to the women,
"You need not be afraid. I know that you are looking
6 for Jesus who was crucified. He is not here, he has risen, as he said he would do. Come and see the place where he
7 was lying. Now go quickly and tell his disciples, 'He has risen from the dead, and is going back to Galilee before you. You will see him there.' Now I have given you my message.''
8 And they hurried away from the tomb frightened and yet overjoyed, and ran to tell the news to his disciples.
9 And Jesus himself met them, and said,
"Good morning!''
And they went up to him and clasped his feet, and
10 bowed to the ground before him. Jesus said to them,
"You need not be afraid. Go and tell my brothers to go to Galilee and they will see me there.''
11 While they were on their way, some of the guard went into the city and reported to the high priests all that had
12 happened. And they got together and consulted with the
13 elders, and gave the soldiers a large sum of money, and said to them,

"Tell people that his disciples came in the night and stole him away while you were asleep. And if news of it 14 reaches the governor, we will satisfy him, and see that you do not get into trouble."

So they took the money and did as they were told. And 15 this story has been current among the Jews ever since.

And the eleven disciples went to Galilee to the moun- 16 tain to which Jesus had directed them. There they saw 17 him and bowed down before him, though some were in doubt about it.

And Jesus came up to them and said,   18

"Full authority in heaven and on the earth has been given to me. Therefore go and make disciples of all the 19 heathen, baptize them in the name of the Father, the Son, and the holy Spirit, and teach them to observe all 20 the commands that I have given you. I will always be with you, to the very close of the age."

THE GOSPEL ACCORDING TO LUKE
AND THE ACTS OF THE APOSTLES
· · ·

By A.D. 90 there had come to exist a number of accounts of Jesus' work and teaching which, taken together with the oral gospel still in use, might well confuse the ordinary believer by their variety and dissimilarity. Meantime the Christian movement had spread over the Greek world with remarkable quickness, and the new faith was already bidding fair to challenge the old national cults and the new mystery religions for supremacy. It was time to write the story of its beginnings.

It was to meet this twofold need, to unify the written accounts of Jesus' life and teaching, and to chronicle the rise and spread of Christianity from its beginnings in Judea to its establishment in Rome, the center of the ancient world, that Luke wrote what we know as his gospel and the Book of Acts. But he produced them as one work, in two volumes, basing them expressly upon sources, and introducing them with a Preface and Dedication.

For the gospel he had the principal sources Matthew had used, with some additions, but he followed Mark's order much more closely. For his second volume he had his own memories of Paul and his journeys, some of which he shared, while his long stay in Judea when Paul was in prison at Caesarea had given him great opportunities to hear just such stories of the early days of the movement as the first part of Acts contains. In fact, it was precisely to a Greek from the outer world that they would be most interesting and appealing, and here Luke is quite in line with those ancient Greek visitors to the east—Mesopotamia and Egypt—who traveled widely and inquiringly and then returned to relate their strange discoveries to their countrymen at home. Such was the work of the logographers Hecataeus and Herodotus, and such for his day was the work of Luke. Things he heard while in Palestine he would remember and often repeat, and then when the great idea of sketching the history of the Christian movement at last came to him, in the hour of its success, he found himself already possessed of what he most needed for his work.

Luke's two volumes are especially marked by social, humanitarian, and historical interests; for what little we know of dates, ages, and early Christian chronology we owe altogether to him. They have also an apologetic tone; they would defend Christians from the suspicion of disloyalty and agitation. Luke's fondness for poetry has preserved a whole cycle of canticles for us. The swift, flowing narrative of the Acts carries us from one dramatic scene to another in the splendid centers of the Graeco-Roman world—Jerusalem, Antioch, Ephesus, Athens, Rome—as the Christian movement first gropes its way out from Jewish circles successively to proselytes, Samaritans, and Greeks; then is carried out into the Greek cities of the west, then crosses from Asia into Europe, and at last is seen planted in Rome itself. And in it all Luke sees the providential hand of God shaping the decisions and movements of his people to his own great purposes.

THE GOSPEL ACCORDING TO LUKE

THE PREFACE, 1:1–4

1 Many writers have undertaken to compose accounts of
2 the movement which has developed among us, just as the
original eye-witnesses who became teachers of the mes-
3 sage have handed it down to us. For that reason, Theophilus, and because I have investigated it all carefully
from the beginning, I have determined to write a con-
4 nected account of it for Your Excellency, so that you may
be reliably informed about the things you have been
taught.

THE BIRTH OF JOHN, 1:5–80

1 In the days when Herod was king of Judea, there was
a priest named Zechariah who belonged to the division
of Abijah. His wife was also a descendant of Aaron, and
6 her name was Elizabeth. They were both upright in the
sight of God, blamelessly observing all the Lord's com-
7 mands and requirements. They had no children, for Elizabeth was barren; and they were both advanced in life.
8 Once when he was acting as priest before God, when
9 his division was on duty, it fell to his lot, according to
the priests' practice, to go into the sanctuary of the Lord
10 and burn the incense, while all the throng of people was
11 outside, praying at the hour of the incense offering. And
an angel of the Lord appeared to him, standing at the
12 right of the altar of incense. When Zechariah saw him
13 he was startled and overcome with fear. And the angel
said to him,
"Do not be afraid, Zechariah, for your prayer has been
heard. Your wife Elizabeth will bear you a son, and you
14 are to name him John. This will bring gladness and de-
15 light to you, and many will rejoice over his birth. For he
will be great in the sight of the Lord. He will drink no
wine or strong drink, but he will be filled with the holy
16 Spirit from his very birth, and he will turn many of Is-
17 rael's descendants to the Lord their God. He will go before him with the spirit and the power of Elijah, to recon-

[405]

cile fathers to their children, and to bring the disobedient back to the wisdom of upright men, to make a people perfectly ready for the Lord.''

Zechariah said to the angel,   18

"How am I to know that this is so? For I am an old man, and my wife is advanced in life.''

The angel answered,   19

"I am Gabriel. I stand in the very presence of God. I have been sent to speak to you and to tell you this good news. Now you will keep silent and be unable to speak 20 until the day when this happens, because you have not believed what I have said, for it will all be fulfilled in due time.''

The people were waiting for Zechariah, and wonder- 21 ing that he stayed so long in the sanctuary. But when he 22 came out he could not speak to them, and they knew that he had seen a vision in the sanctuary. For his part, he kept making signs to them, and remained dumb. And 23 when his period of service was over, he went back to his home.

Soon afterward his wife Elizabeth began to expect a 24 child, and she kept herself in seclusion for five months.

"This is what the Lord has done for me,'' she said, 25 "now that he has deigned to remove the disgrace I have endured.''

In the sixth month the angel Gabriel was sent by God 26 to a town in Galilee called Nazareth, to a maiden there 27 who was engaged to be married to a man named Joseph, a descendant of David. The maiden's name was Mary. And the angel went into the town and said to her, 28

"Good morning, favored woman! The Lord be with you!''

But she was startled at what he said, and wondered 29 what this greeting meant. And the angel said to her, 30

"Do not be afraid, Mary, for you have gained God's approval. You are to become a mother and you will give 31 birth to a son, and you are to name him Jesus. He will be 32 great and will be called the Son of the Most High. The Lord God will give him the throne of his forefather Da-

³³ vid, and he will reign over Jacob's house forever; his reign will have no end.''

³⁴ Mary said to the angel,
"How can this be, when I have no husband?"

³⁵ The angel answered,
"The holy Spirit will come over you, and the power of the Most High will overshadow you. For that reason
³⁶ your child will be called holy, and the Son of God. And your relative, Elizabeth, although she is old, is going to give birth to a son, and this is the sixth month with her
³⁷ who was said to be barren. For nothing is ever impossible for God.''

³⁸ And Mary said,
"I am the Lord's slave. Let it be as you say."
Then the angel left her.

³⁹ In those days Mary set out and hurried to the hill-
⁴⁰ country, to a town in Judah, and she went to Zechariah's
⁴¹ house and greeted Elizabeth. When Elizabeth heard
⁴² Mary's greeting, the babe stirred within her. And Elizabeth was filled with the holy Spirit and she gave a great cry, and said,

"You are the most favored of women,
And blessed is your child!
⁴³ Who am I,
To have the mother of my Lord come to me?

⁴⁴ "For the moment your greeting reached my ears,
The child stirred with joy within me!
⁴⁵ Blessed is she who has believed,
For what the Lord has promised her will be fulfilled!''

⁴⁶ And Mary said,

"My heart extols the Lord,
⁴⁷ My spirit exults in God my Savior.
⁴⁸ For he has noticed his slave in her humble station,
For from this time all the ages will think me favored!

[407]

"For the Almighty has done wonders for me, 49
How holy his name is!
He shows his mercy age after age 50
To those who fear him.

"He has done mighty deeds with his arm, 51
He has routed the proud-minded,
He has dethroned monarchs and exalted the poor, 52
He has satisfied the hungry with good things, and 53
sent the rich away empty-handed.

"He has helped his servant Israel, 54
Remembering his mercy,
As he promised our forefathers 55
To have mercy on Abraham and his descendants
forever!"

So Mary stayed with her about three months, and then 56
returned home.

Now the time came for Elizabeth's child to be born, 57
and she gave birth to a son. Her neighbors and relatives 58
heard of the great mercy the Lord had shown her, and
they came and congratulated her. On the eighth day they 59
came to circumcise the child, and they were going to
name him Zechariah, after his father. But his mother 60
said,

"No! He is to be named John."

They said to her, 61

"There is no one among your relatives who bears that
name."

But they made signs to the child's father and asked 62
him what he wished to have the child named. He asked 63
for a writing tablet, and wrote,

"His name is John."

And they were all amazed. Then his voice and the use 64
of his tongue were immediately restored, and he blessed
God aloud. And all their neighbors were overcome with 65
fear, and all over the hill-country of Judea all these
stories were told, and everyone who heard them kept 66
them in mind, and said,

"What is this child going to be?" For the Lord's hand was with him.

67 And his father Zechariah was filled with the holy Spirit and he uttered a divine message, saying,

68 "Blessings on the Lord, the God of Israel,
Because he has turned his attention to his people,
and brought about their deliverance,
69 And he has produced a mighty Savior for us
In the house of his servant David.

70 "By the lips of his holy prophets he promised of old to do this—
71 To save us from our enemies and from the hands of all who hate us,
72 Thus showing mercy to our forefathers,
And keeping his sacred agreement,

73 "And the oath that he swore to our forefather Abraham,
74 That we should be delivered from the hands of our enemies,
75 And should serve him in holiness and uprightness, unafraid,
In his own presence all our lives.

76 "And you, my child, will be called a prophet of the Most High,
For you will go before the Lord to make his way ready,
77 Bringing his people the knowledge of salvation
Through the forgiveness of their sins.

78 "Because the heart of our God is merciful,
And so the day will dawn upon us from on high,
79 To shine on men who sit in darkness and the shadow of death,
And guide our feet into the way of peace."

80 And the child grew up and became strong in the Spirit, and he lived in the desert until the day when he proclaimed himself to Israel.

THE BIRTH OF JESUS, 2:1–52

In those days an edict was issued by the Emperor Au- 2
gustus that a census of the whole world should be taken.
It was the first census, taken when Quirinius was gov- 2
ernor of Syria. So everyone went to his own town to reg- 3
ister. And Joseph went up from Galilee from the town of 4
Nazareth to Judea to the city of David called Bethlehem,
because he belonged to the house and family of David, to 5
register with Mary, who was engaged to him and who
was soon to become a mother. While they were there, 6
the time came for her child to be born, and she gave birth 7
to her first-born son; and she wrapped him up, and laid
him in a manger, for there was no room for them at the
inn.

There were some shepherds in that neighborhood 8
keeping watch through the night over their flock in the
open fields. And an angel of the Lord stood by them, and 9
the glory of the Lord shone around them, and they were
terribly frightened. The angel said to them, 10
"Do not be frightened, for I bring you good news of a
great joy that is to be felt by all the people, for today, in
the town of David, a Savior for you has been born who is 11
your Messiah and Lord. And this will prove it to you: 12
You will find a baby wrapped up and lying in a manger."

Suddenly there appeared with the angel a throng of 13
the heavenly army, praising God, saying,
"Glory to God in heaven and on earth! 14
Peace to the men he favors!"

When the angels left them and returned to heaven, the 15
shepherds said to one another,
"Come! Let us go over to Bethlehem, and see this
thing that has happened, that the Lord has told us of!"

And they hurried there, and found Mary and Joseph, 16
with the baby lying in the manger. When they saw this, 17
they told what had been said to them about this child.
And all who heard it were amazed at what the shepherds 18
told them, but Mary treasured up all they had said, and 19
pondered over it. And the shepherds went back glorify- 20

ing God and praising him for all that they had heard and seen in fulfilment of what they had been told.

21 When he was eight days old and it was time to circumcise him, he was named Jesus, as the angel had named him, before his birth was first expected.

22 When their purification period under the Law of Moses was over, they took him up to Jerusalem to present him 23 to the Lord, in fulfilment of the requirement of the Law of the Lord, "Every first-born male shall be considered 24 consecrated to the Lord," and to offer the sacrifice prescribed in the Law of the Lord, "A pair of turtle-doves or two young pigeons."

25 Now there was a man in Jerusalem named Symeon, an upright, devout man, who was living in expectation of the comforting of Israel, and under the influence of the 26 holy Spirit. It had been revealed to him by the holy Spirit that he should not die without seeing the Lord's Mes- 27 siah. And under the Spirit's influence he went into the Temple, and when Jesus' parents brought him there to do 28 for him what the Law required, Symeon also took him in his arms and blessed God, and said,

29 "Now, Master, you will let your slave go free
In peace, as you promised,
30 For my eyes have seen your salvation
31 Which you have set before all the nations,
32 A light of revelation for the heathen,
And a glory to your people Israel!"

33 The child's father and mother were astonished at what 34 Symeon said. And he gave them his blessing, and said to Mary, the child's mother,
"This child is destined to cause the fall and rise of many in Israel, and to be a portent that will be much de- 35 bated—you yourself will be pierced to the heart—and so the thoughts of many minds will be revealed."

36 There was also a prophetess there named Hannah, the daughter of Phanuel, who belonged to the tribe of Asher. She was very old, for after her girlhood she had been 37 married for seven years, and she had been a widow until she was now eighty-four. She never left the Temple, but

worshiped night and day with fasting and prayer. She 38
came up just at that time and gave thanks to God and
spoke about the child to all who were living in expectation of the liberation of Jerusalem.

When they had done everything that the Law of the 39
Lord required, they returned to Galilee, to their own
town of Nazareth.

And the child grew up and became strong and thought- 40
ful, with God's blessing resting on him.

His parents used to go to Jerusalem every year at the 41
Passover Festival. And when he was twelve years old, 42
they went up as usual to the festival and made their customary stay. When they started back the boy Jesus 43
stayed behind in Jerusalem without his parents' knowledge. They supposed that he was somewhere in the par- 44
ty, and traveled until the end of the first day's journey,
and then they looked everywhere for him among their relatives and acquaintances. As they could not find him, 45
they went back to Jerusalem in search of him. And on 46
the third day they found him in the Temple, sitting
among the teachers, listening to them and asking them
questions, and everyone who heard him was astonished 47
at his intelligence and at the answers he made. When his 48
parents saw him they were amazed, and his mother said
to him,

"My child, why did you treat us like this? Here your
father and I have been looking for you, and have been
very anxious."

He said to them,   49

"How did you come to look for me? Did you not know
that I must be at my Father's house?"

But they did not understand what he told them. And 50 51
he went back with them to Nazareth and obeyed them.
And his mother treasured all these things up in her
mind.

As Jesus grew older he gained in wisdom and won the 52
approval of God and men.

JOHN'S PREACHING, 3:1–6, 18–20

3   In the fifteenth year of the reign of the Emperor Tiberius, when Pontius Pilate was governor of Judea, and Herod governor of Galilee, while his brother Philip was governor of the territory of Iturea and Trachonitis, and
2   Lysanias was governor of Abilene, in the high priesthood of Annas and Caiaphas, a message from God came to
3   Zechariah's son John in the desert. And he went all through the Jordan Valley preaching repentance and bap-
4   tism in order to obtain the forgiveness of sins, as the book of the sermons of the prophet Isaiah says,

"Hark! Someone is shouting in the desert,
Get the Lord's way ready!
Make his paths straight.
5   Every hollow must be filled up,
And every mountain and hill leveled.
What is crooked is to be made straight,
And the rough roads are to be made smooth,
6   And all mankind is to see how God can save!"

18   So with many varied exhortations he would preach the
19   good news to the people, but Herod the governor, whom he condemned because of Herodias, his brother's wife,
20   and all the wicked things Herod had done, crowned them all by putting John in prison.

JESUS BEGINS HIS PREACHING, 4:14–30

4   Under the power of the Spirit Jesus returned to Galilee,
15   and news of him went all over that region. And he taught in their synagogues, and was honored by them all.
16   And he came to Nazareth, where he had been brought up, and on the Sabbath he went to the synagogue, as he was accustomed to do, and stood up to read the Scrip-
17   tures. And the roll of the prophet Isaiah was handed to him, and he unrolled it and found the place where it says,
18   "The spirit of the Lord is upon me,
For he has consecrated me to preach the good news to the poor,
He has sent me to announce to the prisoners their release and to the blind the recovery of their sight,

[413]

To set the down-trodden at liberty,
To proclaim the year of the Lord's favor!" 19
And he rolled up the roll and gave it back to the at- 20
tendant and sat down. The eyes of everyone in the synagogue were fixed upon him. And he began by saying to 21
them,
"This passage of Scripture has been fulfilled here in
your hearing today!"
And they all spoke well of him and were astonished at 22
the winning words that fell from his lips, and they said,
"Is he not Joseph's son?"
He said to them, 23
"No doubt you will quote this proverb to me: 'Doctor, cure yourself! Do the things here in your own country that we hear you did at Capernaum.' I tell you," said 24
he, "no prophet is welcome in his own country. But, I 25
tell you, there were plenty of widows in Israel in Elijah's
time, when the sky was closed for three years and a half,
and there was a great famine all over the land, and Elijah 26
was not sent to one of them, but to a widow at Zarephath
in Sidon. And there were plenty of lepers in Israel in the 27
time of the prophet Elisha, and none of them was cured,
but Naaman the Syrian."
And when the people in the synagogue heard this, 28
they were all very angry, and they got up and drove him 29
out of the town and took him to the brow of the hill on
which their town was built, intending to throw him
down from it. But he made his way through the midst of 30
them and went on.

THE FOUR FISHERMEN, 5:1-11

Once as the crowd was pressing about him to hear 5
God's message, he happened to be standing by the Lake
of Gennesaret, and he saw two boats on the shore of the 2
lake, for the fishermen had gotten out of them and were
washing their nets. And he got into one of the boats, 3
which belonged to Simon, and asked him to push out a
little from the shore. Then he sat down and taught the

4 crowds of people from the boat. When he stopped speaking, he said to Simon,

"Push out into deep water, and then put down your
5 nets for a haul." Simon answered,

"Master, we worked all night and caught nothing, but as you tell me to do it, I will put down the nets."

6 So they did so, and inclosed such a shoal of fish that
7 their nets began to break. And they signaled to their comrades in the other boat to come and help them. And they came, and they filled both boats so full that they
8 began to sink. When Simon Peter saw it, he fell down at Jesus' feet and said,

"Leave me, Master, for I am a sinful man."

9 For he and all the men with him were perfectly amazed
10 at the haul of fish they had made, and so were Zebedee's sons, James and John, who were Simon's partners. Jesus said to Simon,

"Do not be afraid. From now on you are to catch men!"

11 And they brought the boats to land and left everything and followed him.

THE PHARISEE'S DINNER, 7:36–50

7 One of the Pharisees asked him to have dinner with him, and he went to the Pharisee's house and took his
37 place at the table. Now there was a woman in the town who was leading a sinful life, and when she learned that he was having dinner at the Pharisee's house, she got an
38 alabaster flask of perfume, and came and stood behind him at his feet, weeping, and began to wet his feet with her tears, and she wiped them with her hair, and kissed
39 them, and put the perfume on them. When the Pharisee who had invited him saw this, he said to himself,

"If this man were really a prophet, he would know who and what the woman is who is touching him, for she leads a wicked life."

40 Jesus answered him, and said to him,

"Simon, there is something I want to say to you."
He said,

"Proceed, Master."

"Two men were in debt to a money-lender. One owed 41
him a hundred dollars and the other ten. As they could 42
not pay him, he canceled what they owed him. Now
which of them will be more attached to him?"

Simon answered, 43

"The one, I suppose, for whom he canceled most."

"You are right," he said. And turning to the woman, 44
he said to Simon,

"Do you see this woman? I came to your house; you did
not give me any water for my feet, but she has wet my
feet with tears and wiped them with her hair. You did 45
not give me a kiss, but from the moment I came in she has
not stopped kissing my feet. You did not put any oil 46
upon my head, but she has put perfume upon my feet.
Therefore, I tell you, her sins, many as they are, are for- 47
given, for she has loved me so much. But the man with
little to be forgiven loves me but little."

And he said to her, 48

"Your sins are forgiven!"

The men at table with him began to say to themselves, 49

"Who is this man, who even forgives sins?"

But he said to the woman, 50

"It is your faith that has saved you. Go in peace."

STRIKING TALKS WITH DISCIPLES, 9:46—10:1, 17–24

A discussion arose among them as to which of them 9
would be the greatest. But Jesus knew the question that 47
was in their minds and he took a child and made him
stand by his side, and said to them, 48

"Whoever welcomes this child on my account is welcoming me, and whoever welcomes me, welcomes him
who has sent me. For it is the lowliest among you all
who is really great."

John answered, 49

"Master, we saw a man driving out demons with your
name, and we told him not to do so, for he does not go
with us."

Jesus said to him, 50

"Do not try to stop him, for the man who is not against you is for you."

51 As the time approached when he was to be taken up to heaven, he set his face toward Jerusalem, and sent mes-
52 sengers before him. They started out and went into a
53 Samaritan village, to make preparations for him. And the people there would not receive him, because he was
54 going to Jerusalem. When the disciples, James and John, saw this, they said,

"Master, will you have us order fire to come down from heaven and consume them?"

55
56 But he turned and reproved them. And they went on to another village.

57 As they were going along the road, a man said to him,
"I will follow you wherever you go."

58 Jesus said to him,
"Foxes have holes, and wild birds have nests, but the Son of Man has nowhere to lay his head!"

59 He said to another,
"Follow me."
But he said,
"Let me first go and bury my father."

60 Jesus said to him,
"Leave the dead to bury their own dead; you must go and spread the news of the Kingdom of God!"

61 Yet another man said to him,
"Master, I am going to follow you, but let me first say goodbye to my people at home."

62 Jesus said to him,
"No one who puts his hand to the plough, and then looks back, is fitted for the Kingdom of God."

10 After this the Master appointed seventy-two others, and sent them on before him, two and two, to every town or place to which he intended to come.

17 The seventy-two came back delighted, and said,
"Master, when we use your name the very demons submit to us!"

18 He said to them,
"I saw Satan fall from heaven like a flash of lightning!

[417]

Here I have given you the power to tread on snakes and ₁₉
scorpions, and to trample on all the power of the enemy.
Nothing will hurt you at all. But do not be glad that the ₂₀
spirits submit to you, but be glad that your names are
enrolled in heaven."

At that moment he was inspired with joy, and said, ₂₁
"I thank you, Father, Lord of heaven and earth, for
hiding all this from the learned and intelligent, and re-
vealing it to children! Yes, I thank you, Father, for
choosing to have it so! Everything has been handed over ₂₂
to my by my Father, and no one knows who the Son is
but the Father, nor who the Father is but the Son, and
anyone to whom the Son chooses to reveal him."

And he turned to his disciples when they were alone, ₂₃
and said,

"Blessed are the eyes that see what you see! For I tell ₂₄
you, many prophets and kings have wished to see what
you see, and could not see it, and to hear what you hear,
and could not hear it!"

THE GOOD SAMARITAN, 10:25-37

Then an expert in the Law got up to test him and said, **10**
"Master, what must I do to make sure of eternal life?"
Jesus said to him, ₂₆
"What does the Law say? How does it read?"
He answered, ₂₇
" 'You must love the Lord your God with your whole
heart, your whole soul, your whole strength, and your
whole mind' and 'your neigbor as you do yourself.' "
Jesus said to him, ₂₈
"You are right. Do that, and you will live."
But he, wishing to justify his question, said, ₂₉
"And who is my neighbor?"
Jesus replied, ₃₀
"A man was on his way down from Jerusalem to Jeri-
cho, when he fell into the hands of robbers, and they
stipped him and beat him and went off leaving him half
dead. Now a priest happened to be going that way, and ₃₁
when he saw him, he went by on the other side of the

32 road. And a Levite also came to the place, and when he
33 saw him, he went by on the other side. But a Samaritan
who was traveling that way came upon him, and when
34 he saw him he pitied him, and he went up to him and
dressed his wounds with oil and wine and bound them
up. And he put him on his own mule and brought him to
35 an inn and took care of him. The next day he took out a
dollar and gave it to the innkeeper and said, 'Take care of
him, and whatever more you spend I will refund to you
36 on my way back.' Which of these three do you think
proved himself a neighbor to the man who fell into the
robbers' hands?"
37 He said,
"The man who took pity on him."
Jesus said to him,
"Go and do so yourself!"

RIGHT AND WRONG CHOICES, 10:38-42; 12:13-21

10   As they continued their journey, he came to a certain
village, and a woman named Martha welcomed him to
39 her house. She had a sister named Mary, who seated herself at the Master's feet, and listened to what he was say-
40 ing. But Martha was worried with all she had to do for
them, and she came up and said,
"Master, does it make no difference to you that my
sister has left me to do all the work alone? Tell her to
help me."
41 The Master answered,
"Martha, Martha, you are worried and anxious about
many things, but our wants are few, indeed there is only
42 one thing we need. For Mary has chosen the right thing,
and it must not be taken away from her."
Someone in the crowd said to him,
12   "Master, tell my brother to give me my share of our
inheritance."
14   But he said to him,
"Who made me a judge or arbitrator of your affairs?"
15 And he said to them,
"Take care! You must be on your guard against any

form of greed, for a man's life does not belong to him, no matter how rich he is."

And he told them this story: 16

"A certain rich man's lands yielded heavily. And he 17 said to himself, 'What am I going to do, for I have nowhere to store my crops?' Then he said, 'This is what I 18 will do; I will tear down my barns and build larger ones, and in them I will store all my grain and my goods. And 19 I will say to my soul, "Soul, you have great wealth stored up for years to come. Now take your ease; eat, drink, and enjoy yourself." ' But God said to him, 'You 20 fool! This very night your soul will be demanded of you. Then who will have all you have prepared?' That is the 21 way with the man who lays up money for himself, and is not rich with God."

SAYINGS AT A PHARISEE'S TABLE, 14:1–24

One Sabbath, when he went to take a meal at the house **14** of a member of the council who was a Pharisee, they were watching him closely. There was a man in front of him 2 who had dropsy. And Jesus said to the Pharisees and the 3 experts in the Law,

"Is it right to cure people on the Sabbath or not?"

But they made no answer. And he took hold of the 4 man and cured him and sent him away. Then he said to 5 them,

"Who among you, if his child or his ox falls into a well, will not pull him out at once on the Sabbath?" 6 And they could make no reply to this.

He noticed that the guests picked out the best places, 7 and he gave them this illustration:

"When someone invites you to a wedding supper, do 8 not take the best place, for someone more distinguished than you are may have been invited, and your host will 9 come and say to you 'Make room for this man,' and then you will proceed in confusion to take the poorest place. But when you are invited anywhere, go and take the 10 poorest place, so that when your host comes in, he will say to you, 'My friend, come to a better place.' So you

will be shown consideration before all the other guests.
11 For everyone who exalts himself will be humbled, but the man who humbles himself will be exalted.''

12 And he said to the man who had invited him,
"When you give a luncheon or a dinner, do not invite your friends or your brothers or your relatives or your rich neighbors, for then they will invite you in return
13 and you will be repaid. But when you give an entertainment, invite people who are poor, maimed, lame, or
14 blind. Then you will be blessed, because they cannot repay you; for you will be repaid at the resurrection of the upright.''

15 One of the other guests heard this, and said to him,
"Blessed is the man who shall be at the banquet in the Kingdom of God!''

16 He said to him,
"A man once gave a great dinner, and invited a large
17 number to it, and when the dinner hour came, he sent around his slave, to say to those who were invited,
18 'Come! for it is now ready!' And they all immediately began to excuse themselves. The first one said to him, 'I have bought a piece of land, and I must go and look at it.
19 Please have me excused.' Another said, 'I have bought five yoke of oxen, and I am going to examine them.
20 Please have me excused.' Another said, 'I have married,
21 and so I cannot come.' So the slave went back, and reported this to his master. Then the master of the house was angry and said to his slave, 'Hurry out into the streets and squares of the city, and bring the poor, the
22 maimed, the blind, and the lame in here!' And the slave said, 'What you ordered, sir, has been done, and there is
23 still room.' And the master said to the slave, 'Go out on the roads, and among the hedges, and make them come
24 in, so that my house may be full. For I tell you that none of those men who were invited shall have any of my dinner!' ''

THE COST OF DISCIPLESHIP, 14:25–35

14 There were great crowds accompanying him, and once he turned and said to them,

[421]

"If anyone comes to me without hating his own father 26
and mother and wife and children and brothers and sisters, and his very life too, he cannot be a disciple of mine.
For no one who does not take up his own cross and come 27
after me can be a disciple of mine. What man among you 28
if he wishes to build a tower does not first sit down and
estimate the cost of it, to see whether he has enough to
complete it? Or else when he has laid his foundation 29
and cannot finish the building, everyone who sees it will
begin to ridicule him, and say, 'This man started to erect 30
a building, and could not finish it!' Or what king, if he 31
is going to meet another king in battle, does not sit down
first and consider whether he is able with ten thousand
men to meet the other who is coming against him with
twenty thousand? And if he cannot, while the other is 32
still far away, he sends envoys to him and asks on what
terms he will make peace. In just that way, no one of 33
you who does not say goodbye to all he has can be a disciple of mine. Salt is good; but if salt loses its strength, 34
what can it be seasoned with? It is fit neither for the 35
ground nor the manure heap; people throw it away. Let
him who has ears to hear with, listen!"

THE LOST SHEEP, 15:1–10

All the tax-collectors and irreligious people were 15
crowding up to hear him. And the Pharisees and scribes 2
grumbled, and said,

"This man welcomes irreligious people, and even eats
with them!"

So in speaking to them he used this figure: 3

"What man among you, if he has a hundred sheep, and 4
loses one of them, does not leave the ninety-nine in the
wilderness, and go in search of the one that is lost, until
he finds it? And when he finds it, he puts it on his shoul- 5
ders with joy, and when he reaches home, he calls in his 6
friends and neighbors, and says to them, 'Congratulate
me, for I have found my lost sheep!' I tell you, in just 7
that way there will be more joy in heaven over one sinful
person who repents, than over ninety-nine upright people

8 who do not need any repentance. Or what woman who has ten silver coins and loses one, does not light the lamp and sweep the house and look carefully until she finds it?
9 And when she finds it, she calls in her friends and neighbors, and says to them, 'Congratulate me, for I have
10 found the coin that I lost!' In just that way, I tell you, there is joy among the angels of God over one sinful person who repents!"

THE PRODIGAL SON, 15:11–32

15 And he said,
12 "A man had two sons. The younger of them said to his father, 'Father, give me my share of the property.'
13 So he divided his property between them. Not many days later, the younger son gathered up all he had, and went away to a distant country, and there he squandered
14 his property by fast living. After he had spent it all, a severe famine arose in that country, and he began to be in
15 want. And he went and hired himself out to a resident of the country, and he sent him into his fields to tend pigs.
16 And he was ready to fill himself with the pods the pigs were eating, and no one would give him anything.
17 When he came to himself he said, 'How many hired men my father has, who have more than enough to eat, and
18 here I am, dying of hunger! I will get up, and go to my father, and say to him, "Father, I have sinned against
19 heaven and in your eyes; I no longer deserve to be called
20 your son; treat me like one of your hired men!" ' And he got up and went to his father. But while he was still a long way off, his father saw him, and pitied him, and ran
21 and fell on his neck, and kissed him. His son said to him, 'Father, I have sinned against heaven, and in your eyes; I no longer deserve to be called your son; treat me like
22 one of your hired men!' But his father said to his slave, 'Make haste and get out the best robe, and put it on him,
23 and put a ring on his hand, and shoes on his feet; and get the calf we are fattening, and kill it, and let us feast and
24 celebrate, for my son here was dead, and he has come to life; he was lost, and he is found!' So they began to cele-

brate. But his elder son was in the field. When he came 25
in and approached the house, he heard music and dancing, and he called one of the servants to him and asked 26
him what it meant. He said to him, 'Your brother has 27
come, and your father has killed the calf he has been fattening, because he has gotten him back alive and well.'
But he was angry, and would not go into the house. And 28
his father came out and urged him. And he said to his 29
father, 'Here I have served you all these years, and have
never disobeyed an order of yours, and you have never
given me a kid, so that I could entertain my friends. But 30
when your son here came, who has eaten up your property
with women of the street, for him you killed the calf
you have been fattening!' But he said to him, 'My child, 31
you have been with me all the time, and everything I
have is yours. But we had to celebrate and be glad, be- 32
cause your brother was dead, and has come to life, and
was lost and is found!' ''

THE RICH MAN AND LAZARUS, 16:19–31

''There was once a rich man, who used to dress in pur- 16
ple and fine linen, and to live in luxury every day. And a 20
beggar named Lazarus was put down at his gate covered
with sores and eager to satisfy his hunger with what 21
was thrown away from the rich man's table. Why, the
very dogs came and licked his sores. And it came about 22
that the beggar died and was carried away by the angels
to the companionship of Abraham, and the rich man too
died and was buried. And in Hades he looked up, tor- 23
mented as he was, and saw Abraham far away, with
Lazarus beside him. And he called to him and said, 'Fa- 24
ther Abraham! take pity on me, and send Lazarus to dip
the tip of his finger in water and cool my tongue, for I am
in torment, here in the flames!' And Abraham said, 'My 25
child, remember that you received your blessings in your
lifetime, and Lazarus had his misfortunes in his; and now
he is being comforted here, while you are in anguish. Be- 26
sides there is a great chasm set between you and us, so
that those who want to go over from this side to you

cannot, and they cannot cross from your side to us.'
27 And he said, 'Then I beg you, father, to send him to my
28 father's house, for I have five brothers; let him warn
them so that they will not also come to this place of
29 torture.' Abraham answered, 'They have Moses and the
30 prophets; let them listen to them.' But he said, 'No!
Father Abraham, but if someone will go to them from
31 the dead, they will repent!' He answered, 'If they will
not listen to Moses and the prophets, they will not be
convinced even if someone rises from the dead!' "

GRATITUDE AND PRAYER, 17:11–21; 18:1–14

17 It happened that, on his way to Jerusalem, he passed
12 through Samaria and Galilee. And as he was going into
one village he met ten lepers, and they stood at some dis-
13 tance from him, and raising their voices, said,
"Jesus, Master, take pity on us!"
14 And when he saw them, he said to them,
"Go and show yourselves to the priests."
15 And as they went they were cured. But one of them,
when he saw that he was cured, came back, loudly prais-
16 ing God, and fell on his face at Jesus' feet, and thanked
17 him. He was a Samaritan. And Jesus said,
18 "Were not all ten cured? Where are the other nine?
Was no one found to return and give thanks to God except this foreigner?"
19 And he said to him,
"Stand up and go! Your faith has cured you."
20 He was once asked by the Pharisees when the Kingdom of God would come, and he answered,
21 "The Kingdom of God is not coming visibly, and people will not say, 'Look! Here it is!' or 'There it is!' for
the Kingdom of God is within you."
18 He gave them an illustration to show that they must
2 always pray and not give up, and he said,
"There was once in a city a judge who had no fear of
3 God and no respect for men. There was a widow in the
city and she came to him and said, 'Protect me from my
4 opponent.' And he would not for a time, but afterward

[425]

he said to himself, 'Though I have no fear of God nor respect for men, yet because this widow bothers 5 me, I will protect her, so that she may not finally wear me out with her coming.' "

And the Master said, 6

"Listen to what this dishonest judge said! Then will 7 not God provide protection for his chosen people, who cry out to him day and night? I tell you, he will make haste to provide it! But when the Son of Man comes, will 8 he find faith on earth?"

To some who were confident of their own uprightness, 9 and thought nothing of others, he used this illustration:

"Two men went up to the Temple to pray; one was a 10 Pharisee and the other a tax-collector. The Pharisee 11 stood up and uttered this prayer to himself: 'O God, I thank you that I am not like other men, greedy, dishonest, or adulterous, like that tax-collector. I fast two days 12 in the week; I pay tithes on everything I get.' But the 13 tax-collector stood at a distance and would not even raise his eyes to heaven, but struck his breast, and said, 'O God, have mercy on a sinner like me!' I tell you, it was 14 he who went back to his house with God's approval, and not the other. For everyone who exalts himself will be humbled, but the man who humbles himself will be exalted."

ZACCHEUS, 19:1–10

And he went into Jericho and was passing through it. **19** Now there was a man named Zaccheus, the principal tax- 2 collector, a rich man, who wanted to see who Jesus was, 3 and he could not because of the crowd, for he was a small man. So he ran on ahead and climbed up into a sycamore 4 tree, to see him, for Jesus was coming that way. When 5 Jesus reached the place, he looked up and said to him,

"Zaccheus, come down quickly! for I must stay at your house today."

And he came down quickly and welcomed him gladly. 6 And when they saw this, everyone complained, and said, 7

"He has gone to stay with an irreligious man!"

8 But Zaccheus stopped and said to the Master,
"See, Master! I will give half my property to the poor, and if I have defrauded anyone of anything, I will pay him four times as much."

9 Jesus said to him,
"Salvation has come to this house today, for he too is
10 a descendant of Abraham. For the Son of Man has come to search for what was lost and to save it."

PILATE AND HEROD, 23:1–12

23 Then they arose in a body and took him to Pilate, and they made this charge against him:

2 "Here is a man whom we have found misleading our nation, and forbidding the payment of taxes to the emperor, and claiming to be an anointed king himself."

3 And Pilate asked him,
"Are you the king of the Jews?"
He answered,
"Yes."

4 And Pilate said to the high priests and the crowd,
"I cannot find anything criminal about this man."

5 But they persisted and said,
"He is stirring up the people all over Judea by his teaching. He began in Galilee and he has come here."

6 When Pilate heard this, he asked if the man were a
7 Galilean and learning that he belonged to Herod's jurisdiction, he turned him over to Herod, for Herod was in
8 Jerusalem at that time. When Herod saw Jesus he was delighted, for he had wanted for a long time to see him, because he had heard about him and he hoped to see some
9 wonder done by him. And he questioned him at some
10 length, but he made him no answer. Meanwhile the high priests and the scribes stood by and vehemently accused
11 him. And Herod and his guards made light of him and ridiculed him, and they put a gorgeous robe on him and
12 sent him back to Pilate. And Herod and Pilate became friends that day, for they had been at enmity before.

ON THE WAY TO CRUCIFIXION, 23:26–31

As they led Jesus away, they seized a man named Si- 23
mon, from Cyrene, who was coming in from the country,
and put the cross on his back, for him to carry behind
Jesus. He was followed by a great crowd of people and of 27
women who were beating their breasts and lamenting
him. But Jesus turned to them and said, 28
"Women of Jerusalem, do not weep for me but weep for
yourselves and for your children, for a time is coming 29
when they will say, 'Happy are the childless women, and
those who have never borne or nursed children!' Then 30
people will begin to say to the mountains, 'Fall on us!'
and to the hills, 'Cover us up!' For if this is what they do 31
when the wood is green, what will happen when it is
dry?"

THE PENITENT THIEF, 23:39–43

One of the criminals who were hanging there, abused 23
him, saying,
"Are you not the Christ? Save yourself and us too!"
But the other reproved him and said, 40
"Have you no fear even of God when you are suffering
the same penalty? And we are suffering it justly, for we 41
are only getting our deserts, but this man has done noth-
ing wrong."
And he said, 42
"Jesus, remember me when you come into your king-
dom!"
And he said to him, 43
"I tell you, you will be in Paradise with me today!"

AFTER THE RESURRECTION, 24:13–53

That same day two of them were going to a village 24
called Emmaus, about seven miles from Jerusalem, and 14
they were talking together about all these things that
had happened. And as they were talking and discussing 15
them, Jesus himself came up and went with them, but 16
they were prevented from recognizing him. And he said 17
to them,

"What is all this that you are discussing with each other on your way?"

18 They stopped sadly, and one of them named Cleopas said to him,

"Are you the only visitor to Jerusalem who does not know what has happened there lately?"

19 And he said,

"What is it?"

They said to him,

"About Jesus of Nazareth, who in the eyes of God and of all the people was a prophet mighty in deed and word,

20 and how the high priests and our leading men gave him

21 up to be sentenced to death, and had him crucified. But we were hoping that he was to be the deliverer of Israel. Why, besides all this, it is three days since it happened.

22 But some women of our number have astounded us. They went to the tomb early this morning and could not find

23 his body, but came back and said that they had actually

24 seen a vision of angels who said that he was alive. Then some of our party went to the tomb and found things just as the women had said, but they did not see him."

25 Then he said to them,

"How foolish you are and how slow to believe all

26 that the prophets have said! Did not the Christ have to suffer thus before entering upon his glory?"

27 And he began with Moses and all the prophets and explained to them the passages all through the Scriptures

28 that referred to himself. When they reached the village to which they were going, he acted as though he were

29 going on, but they urged him not to, and said,

"Stay with us, for it is getting toward evening, and the day is nearly over."

30 So he went in to stay with them. And when he took his place with them at table, he took the bread and blessed it and broke it in pieces and handed it to them.

31 Then their eyes were opened and they knew him, and he

32 vanished from them. And they said to each other,

"Did not our hearts glow when he was talking to us on the road, and was explaining the Scriptures to us?"

And they got up immediately and went back to Jerusalem, and found the eleven and their party all together, and learned from them that the Master had really risen and had been seen by Simon. And they told what had happened on the road, and how they had known him when he broke the bread in pieces. 33 34 35

While they were still talking of these things, he himself stood among them. They were startled and panic stricken, and thought they saw a ghost. But he said to them, 36 37 38

"Why are you so disturbed, and why do doubts arise in your minds? Look at my hands and feet, for it is I myself! Feel of me and see, for a ghost has not flesh and bones, as you see I have." 39

But they could not yet believe it for sheer joy and they were amazed. And he said to them, 41

"Have you anything here to eat?"

And they gave him a piece of broiled fish, and he took it and ate it before their eyes. 42 43

Then he said to them, 44

"This is what I told you when I was still with you—that everything that is written about me in the Law of Moses and the Prophets and the Psalms must come true."

Then he opened their minds to the understanding of the Scriptures, and said to them, 45 46

"The Scriptures said that Christ should suffer as he has done, and rise from the dead on the third day, and that repentance leading to the forgiveness of sins should be preached to all the heathen in his name. You are to be witnesses to all this, beginning at Jerusalem. And I will send down upon you what my Father has promised. Wait here in the city until you are clothed with power from on high." 47 48 49

And he led them out as far as Bethany. Then he lifted up his hands and blessed them. And as he was blessing them, he parted from them. And they went back with great joy to Jerusalem, and were constantly in the Temple, blessing God. 50 51 52 53

THE ACTS OF THE APOSTLES

THE ASCENSION, 1:1–14

1 In my first volume, Theophilus, I dealt with all that
2 Jesus did and taught from the beginning until the day
when through the holy Spirit he gave the apostles he had
chosen their instructions, and was taken up to heaven.
3 He had shown himself alive to them after he had suffered,
in many convincing ways, appearing to them through
forty days, and telling them about the Kingdom of God.
4 And once when he ate with them, he instructed them not
to leave Jerusalem, but to wait for what the Father had
promised.
5 "You have heard me speak of it," he said, "for John
baptized people in water, but in a few days you will be
baptized in the holy Spirit."
6 So those who were present asked him,
"Master, is this the time when you are going to re-
establish the kingdom for Israel?"
7 He said to them,
"It is not for you to know times and dates which the
8 Father has fixed by his own authority, but you will be
given power when the holy Spirit comes upon you, and
you will be witnesses for me in Jerusalem and all over
Judea and Samaria and to the very ends of the earth."
9 As he said this, he was caught up before their eyes and
10 a cloud took him up from their sight. And while they
were gazing after him into the sky, two men dressed in
11 white suddenly stood beside them, and said to them,
"Men of Galilee, why do you stand looking up into
the sky? This very Jesus who has been caught up from
you into heaven will come in just the way that you have
seen him go up to heaven."
12 Then they went back to Jerusalem from the hill called
the Olive-orchard, which is near Jerusalem, half a mile
away.

When they entered the city they went to the upstairs 13 room where they were staying. There were Peter, John, James and Andrew, Philip and Thomas, Bartholomew and Matthew, James, the son of Alpheus, Simon the Zealot, and Judas, the son of James. They were all de- 14 voting themselves with one mind to prayer, with the women and Mary, Jesus' mother, and his brothers.

THE COMING OF THE SPIRIT AT PENTECOST, 2:1-4

On the day of the Harvest Festival, they were all 2 meeting together, when suddenly there came from the 2 sky a sound like a violent blast of wind, and it filled the whole house where they were sitting. And they saw 3 tongues like flames separating and settling one on the head of each of them, and they were all filled with the 4 holy Spirit and began to say in foreign languages whatever the Spirit prompted them to utter.

Now there were devout Jews from every part of the 5 world living in Jerusalem. And when this sound was 6 heard, the crowd gathered in great excitement, because each one heard them speaking in his own language. They were perfectly amazed and said in their astonish- 7 ment,

"Are not all these men who are speaking Galileans? Then how is it that each of us hears his own native 8 tongue? Parthians, Medes, Elamites, residents of Meso- 9 potamia, of Judea and Cappadocia, of Pontus and Asia, of Phrygia and Pamphylia, of Egypt and the district of 10 Africa about Cyrene, visitors from Rome, Jews and proselytes, Cretans and Arabs—we all hear them tell in our 11 native tongues the mighty deeds of God."

And they were all amazed and bewildered and said to 12 one another,

"What can this mean?"

But others said derisively, 13

"They have had too much new wine!"

Then Peter stood up with the eleven around him, and 14 raising his voice addressed them.

"Men of Judea," he said, "and all you residents of

Jerusalem, let me explain this to you, and pay attention
15 to what I say. These men are not drunk as you suppose,
16 for it is only nine in the morning. But this is what was
predicted by the prophet Joel,
17   " 'It will come about in the last days, God says,
         That I will pour out my Spirit upon all mankind;
         Your sons and daughters will become prophets,
         Your young men will have visions,
         And your old men will have dreams.
18   Even on my slaves, both men and women,
         I will pour out my Spirit in those days,
         And they will become prophets.
19   I will show wonders in the sky above,
         And signs on the earth below,
         Blood and fire and thick smoke.
20   The sun will turn to darkness,
         And the moon to blood,
         Before the coming of the great, splendid Day of the
            Lord.
21   Then everyone who calls on the name of the Lord
            will be saved.'
22   "Men of Israel, listen to what I say. Jesus of Nazareth,
as you know, was a man whom God commended to you
by the wonders, portents, and signs that God did right
23 among you through him. But you, by the fixed purpose
and intention of God, handed him over to wicked men,
24 and had him crucified. But God set aside the pain of
death and raised him up, for death could not control him.
25 For David says of him,
      " 'I constantly regarded the Lord before me,
         For he is at my right hand, so that I may not be
            displaced.
26   Therefore my heart is glad, and my tongue rejoices,
         And my body will still live in hope.
27   For you will not desert my soul in death,
         You will not let your Holy One be destroyed.
28   You have made the ways of life known to me,
         And you will fill me with joy in your presence.'
29   "Brothers, one may say to you confidently of the pa-

triarch David that he died and was buried, and his grave
is here among us to this very day. But as he was a proph- 30
et, and knew that God had promised him with an oath
that he would put one of his descendants upon his throne,
he foresaw the resurrection of the Christ and told of it, 31
for he was not deserted in death and his body was not destroyed. He is Jesus, whom God raised from the dead, 32
and to whose resurrection we are all witnesses. So he has 33
been exalted to God's right hand, and has received from
his Father and poured over us the holy Spirit that had
been promised, as you see and hear.

"For David did not go up to heaven, but he said, 34
" 'The Lord said to my lord, Sit at my right hand,
Until I make your enemies your footstool.' 35
"Therefore the whole nation of Israel must under- 36
stand that God has declared this Jesus whom you cruci-
fied both Lord and Christ."

When they heard this, they were stung to the heart, 37
and they said to Peter and the rest of the apostles,

"Brothers, what shall we do?"

Peter said to them, 38

"You must repent, and every one of you be baptized in
the name of Jesus Christ, in order to have your sins forgiven; then you will receive the gift of the holy Spirit,
for the promise of it belongs to you and your children, as 39
well as to all those far away whom the Lord our God
calls to him."

He said much besides in giving his testimony, and 40
urged them to save themselves from that crooked age.
So they welcomed his message and were baptized, and 41
about three thousand people joined them that day.

PETER AND JOHN IN JERUSALEM, 3:1–10; 4:1–22

Peter and John were on their way up to the Temple for 3
the three o'clock hour of prayer, when a man who had 2
been lame from his birth was carried by. He used to be
placed every day at what was known as the Beautiful
Gate of the Temple, to beg from the people on their way
into the Temple, and when he saw Peter and John on the 3

point of going into the Temple he asked them to give
4 him something. Peter fixed his eyes on him, as John did
also, and said to him,
"Look at us!"
5 He looked at them, supposing that they were going to
6 give him something. But Peter said,
"I have no silver or gold, but I will give you what I
have. In the name of Jesus Christ of Nazareth, walk!"
7 And he took him by the right hand and raised him up,
8 and his feet and ankles immediately became strong, and
he sprang to his feet and began to walk, and he went into
the Temple with them, walking, leaping, and praising
9 God. When all the people saw him walking about,
10 praising God, and recognized him as the man who used to
sit and beg at the Beautiful Gate of the Temple, they were
perfectly astonished and amazed at what had happened
to him.

4 As they were talking in this way to the people, the high
priests, the commander of the Temple, and the Sadducees
2 came up to them, greatly disturbed because they were
teaching the people and declaring that in the case of Jesus
3 there had been a resurrection from the dead. They arrested them, and as it was already evening, they shut them
4 up until morning. But many of those who had heard
what they said believed it, and their number grew to be
about five thousand.
5 On the next day the leading members of the council,
6 the elders, and the scribes met in Jerusalem, with Annas
the high priest, Caiaphas, John, Alexander, and all who
7 belonged to the high priest's family. They had the apostles brought before them and demanded of them,
"By what power or authority have men like you done
this?"
8 Then Peter, filled with the holy Spirit, said to them,
9 "Leaders of the people and members of the council, if
it is for a benefit conferred upon a helpless man, and as to
how he was cured, that we are called to account here to-
10 day, you and the people of Israel must all know that it is
through the power of Jesus Christ of Nazareth whom you

crucified but whom God raised from the dead, that he stands here before you well. He is the stone that you 11 builders rejected, which has become the cornerstone. There is no salvation through anyone else, for there is no 12 one else in the world who has been named to men as their only means of being saved."

They were amazed to see how outspoken Peter and 13 John were, and to find that they were uneducated men with no advantages. They recognized them as companions of Jesus, and seeing the man who had been cured 14 standing beside them, they had nothing to say. But they 15 ordered them out of the presence of the council and conferred together. They said, 16

"What are we to do with these men? For it is plain to everyone in Jerusalem that an extraordinary wonder has been done by them. We cannot deny that. But to keep it 17 from spreading farther among the people, let us warn them to say nothing to anyone else at all about this person."

So they called them in and ordered them not to speak 18 or teach at all about the name of Jesus. But Peter and 19 John answered them,

"You must decide whether it is right in the sight of God to obey you instead of him, for we cannot help tell- 20 ing of what we have seen and heard."

But after further threats they let them go, as they 21 could find no way to punish them, on account of the people, who were all giving honor to God for what had happened, for the man on whom this wonder of healing had 22 been done was more than forty years old.

ANANIAS AND SAPPHIRA, 4:32—5:14

There was but one heart and soul in the multitude 4 who had become believers, and not one of them claimed anything that belonged to him as his own, but they shared everything they had with one another. The apos- 33 tles gave their testimony to the resurrection of the Lord Jesus with great power, and God's favor rested richly upon them. No one among them was in any want, for 34

any who owned lands or houses would sell them and bring the proceeds of the sale and put them at the dis-
35 posal of the apostles; then they were shared with every-
36 one in proportion to his need. Joseph, a Levite, and a native of Cyprus, whom the apostles had named Barnabas,
37 which means Son of Encouragement, sold a piece of land that belonged to him, and brought the proceeds and put them at the disposal of the apostles.

5 But a man named Ananias, who, with his wife Sap-
2 phira, had sold a piece of property, with his wife's con-
nivance appropriated some of the price received, and brought only a part of it to put at the disposal of the
3 apostles. And Peter said,

"Ananias, why has Satan taken such possession of your heart that you should lie to the holy Spirit, by ap-
4 propriating part of the price of your land? As long as it was unsold was it not yours, and after it was sold was not the money under your control? How could you think of doing such a thing? You did not lie to men but to God!"

5 When Ananias heard these words he fell down and expired, and everyone who heard them spoken was ap-
6 palled. The younger men got up and wrapping his body
7 up carried it out and buried it. About three hours later, his wife came in, without having learned what had hap-
8 pened. Peter said to her,

"Tell me, did you sell the land for such and such a sum?"

"Yes," she said, "that was it."
9 Peter said to her,

"How could you two agree to test the Spirit of the Lord? There at the door are the footsteps of the men who buried your husband, and they will carry you out also."
10 She instantly fell down at his feet and expired. When the young men came in they found her dead, and they
11 carried her out and buried her beside her husband. And the whole church and all who heard this were appalled.
12 They would all meet together in Solomon's Colonnade.
13 None of the others dared to associate with them, but the

people made much of them, and men and women in in- 14
creasing numbers believed in the Lord and joined them.

THE WORK AND DEATH OF STEPHEN, 6:1—7:40, 51—8:8

In those days, as the number of the disciples was in- 6
creasing, complaints were made by the Greek-speaking
Jews against the native Jews that their widows were being neglected in the daily distribution of food. So the 2
Twelve called in the whole body of disciples and said to
them,

"It is not desirable that we should give up preaching
the word of God to keep accounts. You, brothers, must 3
pick out from your number seven men of good standing,
who are wise and full of the Spirit, and we will put them 4
in charge of this matter, while we devote ourselves to
prayer and to delivering the message."

This plan met the approval of the whole body, and 5
they selected Stephen, a man full of faith and of the holy
Spirit, with Philip, Prochorus, Nicanor, Timon, Par-
menas, and Nicholas of Antioch, who had been a convert
to Judaism. They brought these men before the apostles, 6
and they prayed and laid their hands upon them.

So God's message continued to spread; the number of 7
the disciples in Jerusalem increased rapidly, and a great
many priests accepted the faith.

Stephen, greatly strengthened by God's favor, did re- 8
markable signs and wonders among the people. But 9
members of the synagogue known as that of the Libyans,
Cyreneans, and Alexandrians, and men from Cilicia and
Asia undertook to debate with Stephen, but they could 10
not meet his wisdom and the inspiration with which he
spoke. So they instigated people to say, 11

"We have heard him use abusive language about
Moses and about God."

They aroused the people, the elders, and the scribes, 12
and they set upon him and seized him, and brought him
before the council. Then they brought forward false wit- 13
nesses, who said,

"This man is constantly saying things against this

14 holy place and against the Law, for we have heard him say that Jesus of Nazareth will tear this place down and change the customs that have been handed down to us by Moses."

15 Everyone who sat in the council fixed his eyes on him,
7 and they saw that his face was like that of an angel. The high priest said,

"Is this statement true?"

2 He answered,

"Brothers and fathers, listen. The glorious God appeared to our forefather Abraham when he was in Meso-
3 potamia, before he settled in Haran, and he said to him, 'Leave your country and your relatives and come to the
4 country that I will show you.' So he left the country of the Chaldeans and went to live in Haran, and from there after the death of his father, God caused him to move
5 into this country where you now live. He gave him no property in it, not a single foot, but he promised to give it to him and his posterity after him permanently, though
6 he had no children at that time. This was what God said: 'His descendants will be strangers, living in a foreign land, and they will be enslaved and misused for four
7 hundred years, and I will sentence the nation that has enslaved them,' God said, 'and afterward they will leave
8 that country and worship me on this spot.' And he made the agreement of circumcision with him, and so Abraham became the father of Isaac and circumcised him on the eighth day, and Isaac became the father of Jacob, and
9 Jacob of the twelve patriarchs. The patriarchs became jealous of Joseph and sold him into slavery in Egypt.
10 But God was with him, and rescued him from all his troubles, and enabled him to win favor and to show wisdom when he stood before Pharaoh, king of Egypt, and he appointed him governor of Egypt and of his whole house-
11 hold. Then a famine spread all over Egypt and Canaan, and there was great suffering, and our forefathers could
12 not find any food. But Jacob heard that there was food in Egypt, and he sent our forefathers on their first visit
13 there. On their second visit, Joseph made himself known

to his brothers, and Pharaoh learned of Joseph's parentage. Then Joseph sent and invited his father Jacob and all his relatives, seventy-five in all, and Jacob came down to Egypt. There he and our forefathers died, and they were carried back to Shechem, and laid in the tomb that Abraham had bought for a sum of money from the sons of Hamor in Shechem. As the time drew near for the fulfilment of the promise God had made to Abraham, the people became more and more numerous in Egypt, until another king, who knew nothing about Joseph, became ruler of Egypt. He took advantage of our people and oppressed our forefathers, making them abandon their infant children, so that they should not live. It was at this time that Moses was born. He was a wonderfully beautiful child, and for three months he was taken care of in his father's house. When he was abandoned, the daughter of Pharaoh adopted him and brought him up as her own son. So Moses was educated in all the Egyptian culture; he was strong in speech and action. When he was forty years old, it occurred to him to visit his brothers, the descendants of Israel. Seeing one of them being imposed upon, he interfered and defended the man who was being ill treated, striking down the Egyptian. He supposed that his brothers would understand that God was using him as the means of delivering them, but they did not. The next day, he came across two of them fighting and tried to pacify them. He said to them, 'You are brothers. Why should you injure each other?' But the aggressor thrust him off, saying, 'Who made you our ruler and judge? Do you mean to kill me as you did that Egyptian yesterday?' At those words Moses fled, and went and lived for a time in Midian, and two sons were born to him there. When forty years had passed, an angel appeared to him in the desert of Mount Sinai, in the flame of a burning bush. When Moses saw it he wondered at the sight, and when he went up to see what it was, the voice of the Lord said, 'I am the God of your forefathers, the God of Abraham, Isaac, and Jacob.' Moses was terrified and did not dare to look at it. Then the Lord said

to him, 'Take off your shoes, for the place where you are
34 standing is holy ground. I have seen all the oppression of
my people in Egypt, and I have heard their groans, and I
have come down to save them. So come! I will make you
35 my messenger to Egypt!' The Moses whom they had refused, saying to him, 'Who made you our ruler and
judge?' God sent both to rule and to deliver them, with
the help of the angel who had appeared to him in the
36 bush. It was he who brought them out of Egypt, and did
wonders and signs there, and at the Red Sea, and for forty
37 years in the desert. This was the Moses who said to the
descendants of Israel, 'God will make a prophet rise from
among your brothers to teach you, just as he made me
38 rise.' It was he who with the congregation in the desert
went between the angel who spoke to him on Mount
Sinai and our forefathers, and received and communi-
39 cated to you utterances that still live. Yet our forefathers
would not listen to him, but thrust him off, and their
40 hearts turned back to Egypt, for they said to Aaron,
'Make us gods to march in front of us, for as for this
Moses, who brought us out of Egypt, we do not know
51 what has become of him!' You stubborn people, with
heathen hearts and ears, you are always opposing the
52 holy Spirit, just as your forefathers did! Which of the
prophets did your forefathers not persecute? They killed
the men who foretold the coming of the Righteous One,
53 whom you have now betrayed and killed—you who had
the Law given to you by angels, and did not obey it!''
54   When they heard that, they were enraged and ground
55 their teeth at him. But he, full of the holy Spirit, looked
up to heaven and saw God's glory and Jesus standing at
56 God's right hand. And he said,
   "Look! I can see heaven open, and the Son of Man
standing at God's right hand!''
57   But they uttered a great shout and stopped their ears,
58 and they rushed upon him all together, and dragged him
out of the city and stoned him, the witnesses throwing
down their clothes at the feet of a young man named Saul.
59 As they stoned Stephen, he prayed,

[441]

"Lord Jesus, receive my spirit!"
Then falling on his knees, he cried out,   60
"Lord, do not lay this sin up against them!"
With these words he fell asleep. And Saul entirely ap-   8
proved of his being put to death.

A great persecution of the church in Jerusalem broke
out that day, and they were all scattered over Judea and
Samaria except the apostles. Some pious men buried Ste-   2
phen and loudly lamented him. But Saul harassed the   3
church. He went into one house after another, and drag-
ging out men and women, put them in prison.

Those who were scattered went from place to place   4
preaching the good news of the message. Philip reached   5
the city of Samaria, and proclaimed the Christ to them.
When the people heard Philip and saw the signs that he   6
showed they were all interested in what he had to say,
for with loud cries foul spirits came out of many who had   7
been possessed by them, and many paralytics and lame
people were cured. So there was great rejoicing in that   8
city.

THE CONVERSION OF AN ETHIOPIAN, 8:26-40

But an angel of the Lord said to Philip,   8
"Get up and go south, by the road that runs from Jerusalem to Gaza." (The town is now deserted.)
So he got up and went. Now there was an Ethiopian   27
eunuch, a member of the court of Candace, queen of Ethiopia, her chief treasurer, who had come up to Jerusalem
to worship, and was on his way home. He was sitting in   28
his car, reading the prophet Isaiah. Then the Spirit said   29
to Philip,
"Go up and stay by that car."
Philip ran up and heard him reading the prophet   30
Isaiah, and he said to him,
"Do you understand what you are reading?"
"Why, how can I," he answered, "unless someone ex-   31
plains it to me?" And he invited Philip to get in and sit
beside him. This was the passage of Scripture that he   32
was reading:

"Like a sheep he was led away to be slaughtered,
And just as a lamb is dumb before its shearer,
He does not open his mouth.

33   His sentence ended in his humiliation.
Who will tell the story of his posterity?
For his life is perished from the earth."

34   "Tell me, of whom is the prophet speaking?" said the eunuch to Philip, "Of himself, or of someone else?"
35   Then Philip began, and starting from this passage, he
36 told him the good news about Jesus. As they went on along the road, they came to some water, and the eunuch said,
"Here is some water! What is there to prevent my being baptized"
38   So he ordered the car to stop, and Philip and the eunuch went down into the water, and Philip baptized
39 him. When they came out of the water, the Spirit of the Lord hurried Philip away, and the eunuch saw nothing more of him. Full of joy, he went on with his journey,
40 while Philip found himself at Ashdod and went on telling the good news in all the towns all the way to Caesarea.

THE CONVERSION OF SAUL THE PERSECUTOR, 9:1–31

9   Now Saul, still breathing murderous threats against
2 the Lord's disciples, went to the high priest and asked him for letters to the synagogues in Damascus, so that if he found any men or women there who belonged to the
3 Way, he might bring them in chains to Jerusalem. But on his journey, as he was approaching Damascus, a sud-
4 den light flashed around him from heaven, and he fell to the ground. Then he heard a voice saying to him,
"Saul! Saul! Why do you persecute me?"
5   "Who are you, sir?" he asked.
6   "I am Jesus, whom you are persecuting," said the voice. "But get up and go into the city, and there you will be told what you ought to do."
7   Saul's fellow-travelers stood speechless, for they heard

the voice but could not see anyone. When he got up from 8
the ground and opened his eyes he could see nothing.
They had to take him by the hand and lead him into
Damascus, and for three days he could not see, and nei- 9
ther ate nor drank.

There was at Damascus a disciple named Ananias, and 10
the Lord said to him in a vision,

"Ananias!"

And he answered,

"Yes, Lord!"

The Lord said to him, 11

"Get up and go to the street called the Straight Street,
and ask at the house of Judas for a man named Saul, from
Tarsus, for he is there praying. He has had a vision and 12
seen a man named Ananias come in and lay his hands on
him, to restore his sight."

But Ananias answered, 13

"Lord, I have heard many people tell of this man, and
the harm he has done to your people in Jerusalem. He is 14
here with authority to arrest everyone who calls upon
your name."

The Lord said to him, 15

"Go! This man is the means I have chosen for carrying my name among the heathen and their kings, and
among the descendants of Israel. For I am going to show 16
him what he will have to endure for my sake."

Ananias set out and went to the house, and there he 17
laid his hands upon Saul, and said to him,

"Saul, my brother, I have been sent by the Lord Jesus,
who appeared to you on your journey, so that you may
regain your sight and be filled with the holy Spirit."

Something like scales immediately dropped from his 18
eyes, and his sight was restored, and he got up and was 19
baptized, and, after taking some food, regained his
strength.

Saul stayed for some time with the disciples at Damas- 20
cus, and began at once to declare in the synagogues that
Jesus was the Son of God. Everyone was astonished, 21
and said,

"Is not he the man who made such havoc of the people in Jerusalem who call upon that name, and who came here especially for the purpose of arresting such persons and taking them before the high priests?"

22 But Saul grew more and more powerful, and bewildered the Jews who lived in Damascus by his proofs that Jesus was the Christ.

23 After some time had passed, the Jews made a plot to
24 kill him, but Saul found out about the plot. They watched the city gates day and night, in order to kill
25 him, but his disciples took him one night and let him down over the wall, lowering him in a basket.

26 When he reached Jerusalem he tried to join the disciples, and they were all afraid of him, for they could not
27 believe that he was really a disciple. But Barnabas got hold of him and introduced him to the apostles, and he told them how on his journey he had seen the Lord, and that he had spoken to him, and how boldly he had spo-
28 ken for the cause of Jesus at Damascus. After that, he as-
29 sociated with them freely in Jerusalem, and spoke boldly for the Lord's cause, talking and debating with the
30 Greek-speaking Jews. But they tried to kill him. When the brothers found this out, they took him down to Caesarea, and sent him away to Tarsus.

31 So the church all over Judea, Galilee, and Samaria was at peace and became established. It lived in reverence for the Lord, and stimulated by the holy Spirit, it grew steadily in numbers.

PETER'S REPORT AT JERUSALEM; THE CONVERSION OF A ROMAN, 11:1–18

11 The apostles and brothers all over Judea heard that the
2 heathen had also accepted God's message, and when Peter returned to Jerusalem, the advocates of circumcision
3 took him to task, charging him with having visited and
4 eaten with men who were not Jews. Then Peter explained the matter to them from beginning to end. He said,
5 "I was praying in the town of Joppa, and while in a trance I had a vision. Something like a great sheet came

down out of the sky, lowered by its four corners. It came 6
right down to me, and when I looked at it, I saw in it
quadrupeds, wild animals, reptiles, and wild birds. And 7
I heard a voice say to me, 'Get up, Peter! Kill something
and eat it!' But I said, 'Never, sir! For nothing that was 8
not ceremonially cleansed has ever passed my lips.' Then 9
the voice from heaven answered again, 'Do not call what
God has cleansed unclean!' This happened three times; 10
then it was all drawn back again into the sky. Just at 11
that moment three men, who had been sent from Caesarea
to find me, reached the house where we were staying,
and the Spirit told me not to hesitate to go with them. 12
These six brothers here also went with me, and we went
to the man's house. Then he told us how he had seen the 13
angel stand in his house and say, 'Send to Joppa for a man
named Simon who is also called Peter, and he will tell 14
you things that will save you and your whole household.'
When I began to speak to them, the holy Spirit fell upon 15
them just as it did upon us at the beginning, and I re- 16
membered the saying of the Lord, 'John baptized in
water, but you will be baptized in the holy Spirit.' So if 17
God had given them the same gift that we received when
we believed in the Lord Jesus Christ, who was I, to be
able to interfere with God?''

When they heard this, they made no further objection, 18
but they gave honor to God, and said,

"Then God has given even the heathen repentance and
the hope of life!"

THE GOSPEL REACHES GREEKS AT ANTIOCH, 11:19-26

The fugitives from the persecution that had broken 11
out over Stephen went all the way to Phoenicia, Cyprus,
and Antioch, but they told the message to none but
Jews. There were some men from Cyprus and Cyrene 20
among them, however, who when they reached Antioch
spoke to the Greeks also, and told them the good news
about the Lord Jesus. The Lord's hand was with them, 21
and there were a great many who believed and turned to
the Lord. The news about them came to the ears of the 22

church in Jerusalem, and they sent Barnabas all the way
23 to Antioch. When he reached there and saw the favor
God had shown them, he was delighted, and encouraged
them all to be resolute and steadfast in their devotion to
24 the Lord, for he was an excellent man, full of the holy
Spirit and faith. So a considerable number of people
25 came over to the Lord. Then Barnabas went over to Tar-
26 sus to seek out Saul, and found him and brought him to
Antioch. The result was that for a whole year they met
with the church, and taught large numbers of people, and
it was at Antioch that the disciples first came to be
known as Christians.

THE GOSPEL IS CARRIED WESTWARD, 13:1–14, 44—14:28

13 There were at Antioch in the church there a number
of prophets and teachers—Barnabas, Symeon who was
called Niger, Lucius the Cyrenian, Manaen, who had
2 been brought up with Herod the governor, and Saul. As
they were engaged in worshiping the Lord and in fasting,
the holy Spirit said,
"Set Barnabas and Saul apart for me, for the work to
which I have called them."
3 So after fasting and prayer, they laid their hands upon
them and let them go.
4 Being sent out in this way by the holy Spirit, they
went down to Seleucia and sailed from there to Cyprus.
5 When they reached Salamis, they proclaimed God's message in the Jewish synagogues. They had John with them
as their assistant.
6 They went through the whole island as far as Paphos,
and there they came across a Jewish magician and false
7 prophet named Barjesus. He was attached to the governor, Sergius Paulus, who was an intelligent man. He sent
for Barnabas and Saul and asked them to let him hear
8 God's message. But Elymas the magician—for that is
the meaning of his name—opposed them, and tried to
9 keep the governor from accepting the faith. But Saul,
10 who was also called Paul, was filled with the holy Spirit,
and looked at him and said,

[447]

"You monster of underhandedness and cunning! You son of the devil! You enemy of all that is right! Will you never stop trying to make the Lord's straight paths crooked? The Lord's hand is right upon you, and you 11 will be blind and unable even to see the sun for a time."

Instantly a mist of darkness fell upon him, and he groped about for someone to lead him by the hand. Then 12 the governor, seeing what had happened, believed, and was thunderstruck at the Lord's teaching.

Paul and his companions sailed from Paphos and went 13 to Perga in Pamphylia. There John left them and returned to Jerusalem, but they went on from Perga and reached Antioch in Pisidia. On the Sabbath they went to 14 the synagogue there and took seats.

The next Sabbath almost all the town gathered to hear 44 God's message. But when the Jews saw the crowd, they 45 were very jealous, and they contradicted what Paul said and abused him. Then Paul and Barnabas spoke out 46 plainly, and said,

"God's message had to be told to you first, but since you thrust it off and judge yourselves unworthy of eternal life, we now turn to the heathen. For these are the 47 orders the Lord has given us:

" 'I have made you a light for the heathen,
    To be the means of salvation to the very ends of the
        earth!' "

When the heathen heard this they were delighted, and 48 praised God's message, and all who were destined for eternal life believed, and the Lord's message spread all 49 over the country. But the Jews stirred up the well-to-do 50 religious women and the leading men of the town, and they started a persecution against Paul and Barnabas, and drove them out of their district. They shook off the dust 51 from their feet in protest, and went to Iconium. But the 52 disciples continued to be full of joy and of the holy Spirit.

At Iconium in the same way, they went to the Jewish 14 synagogue and spoke with such power that a great num-

2 ber of both Jews and Greeks believed. But the Jews who
refused their message stirred up the heathen and poisoned
3 their minds against the brothers. They spent some time
there, speaking fearlessly and relying upon the Lord,
who bore witness to his gracious message by letting signs
4 and wonders be done by them. But the people of the
town were divided, some siding with the Jews and some
5 with the apostles. And when there was a movement on
the part of both the heathen and the Jews with the au-
6 thorities to insult and stone them, and they became aware
of it, they made their escape to the Lycaonian towns of
7 Lystra and Derbe and the country around, and there they
went on preaching the good news.

8   In the streets of Lystra a man used to sit who had not
the use of his feet. He had been lame from his birth, and
9 had never been able to walk. He was listening to Paul as
he talked, when Paul looked at him and, seeing that he
10 had faith that he would be cured, said to him loudly,
  "Stand on your feet!"

11   And he sprang up and began to walk. The crowds, seeing what Paul had done, shouted in the Lycaonian language,
  "The gods have come down to us in human form!"
12   They called Barnabas Zeus, and Paul, because he was
13 the principal speaker, Hermes. The priest of the temple
of Zeus that stood at the entrance to the town came with
crowds of people to the gates, bringing bulls and gar-
14 lands, meaning to offer sacrifice to them. But when the
apostles, Barnabas and Paul, heard of it, they rushed into
15 the crowd, tearing their clothes and shouting,
  "Friends, why are you doing this? We are only human
beings like you, and we bring you the good news that you
should turn from these follies to a living God, who made
16 heaven and earth and sea and all that they contain. In
ages past he let all the heathen follow their own ways;
17 though he did not fail to give some evidence about himself, through his kindnesses to you, in sending you rain
from heaven and fruitful seasons, giving you food and
happiness to your heart's content."

[449]

Even with these words they could hardly restrain the 18
people from offering sacrifice to them.

But some Jews came from Antioch and Iconium, and 19
won the people over, and they stoned Paul and dragged
him out of the town, thinking that he was dead. But the 20
brothers gathered about him, and he got up and re-en-
tered the town. The next day he went on with Barnabas
to Derbe. They proclaimed the good news in that town 21
and made a number of disciples. Then they returned to
Lystra, Iconium, and Antioch, reassuring the disciples 22
and encouraging them to stand by the faith and remind-
ing them that we have to undergo many hardships to get
into the Kingdom of God. They appointed elders for 23
them in each church, and with prayer and fasting they
committed them to the Lord in whom they had believed.
Then they crossed Pisidia and entered Pamphylia. They 24 25
told their message in Perga, then went on to Attalia, and 26
from there they sailed back to Antioch, where they had
first been commended to God's favor for the work which
they had now finished. When they arrived there, they 27
called the church together, and reported how God had
worked with them, and how he had opened the way to
faith for the heathen. There they stayed for a long time 28
with the disciples.

GREEK CHRISTIANITY RECOGNIZED, 15:1-35

Some people came down from Judea and began to teach 15
the brothers that unless they were circumcised as Moses
prescribed, they could not be saved. This created a dis- 2
turbance and a serious discussion between Paul and Barnabas and them, and it was agreed that Paul and Barnabas and some others of their number should go up to Jerusalem to confer with the apostles and elders about this
question.

The church saw them off upon their journey, and as 3
they traveled through Phoenicia and Samaria they told of
the conversion of the heathen, and caused great rejoicing
among all the brothers. When they reached Jerusalem, 4
they were welcomed by the church, the apostles, and the

elders, and they reported how God had worked with
5 them. But some members of the Pharisee's party who had
become believers got up and said that such converts ought
to be circumcised and told to obey the Law of Moses.

6   The apostles and elders had a meeting to look into this
7 matter. After a long discussion, Peter got up and said to
them,

     "Brothers, you know that in the early days God chose
that of you all I should be the one from whose lips the
heathen should hear the message of the good news and
8 believe it. And God who knows men's hearts testified
for them by giving them the holy Spirit just as he had
9 done to us, making no difference between us and them,
10 but cleansing their hearts by faith. Then why do you
now try to test God, by putting on the necks of these disciples a yoke that neither our forefathers nor we have
11 been able to bear? Why, we believe that it is by the mercy of the Lord Jesus that we are saved just as they are."

12   This quieted the whole meeting, and they listened
while Barnabas and Paul told of the signs and wonders
which God had done among the heathen through them.
13 When they finished James made this response:
14   "Brothers, listen to me. Symeon has told how God
first showed an interest in taking from among the heath-
15 en a people to bear his name. And this agrees with the
predictions of the prophets which say,
16   " 'Afterward I will return, and rebuild David's fallen
         dwelling.

     I will rebuild its very ruins, and set it up again,
17   So that the rest of mankind may seek the Lord,
     And all the heathen who are called by my name,
18   Says the Lord, who has been making this known
         from of old.'
19 In my opinion, therefore, we ought not to put obstacles
in the way of those of the heathen who are turning to
20 God, but we should write to them to avoid anything
that has been contaminated by idols, immorality, the
21 meat of strangled animals, and the tasting of blood. For
Moses for generations past has had his preachers in every

[451]

town, and has been read aloud in the synagogues every Sabbath.''

Then the apostles and elders with the whole church 22 resolved to select representatives and send them with Paul and Barnabas to Antioch. They were Judas who was called Barsabbas, and Silas, both leading men among the brothers. They were the bearers of this letter: ''The 23 apostles and the brothers who are elders send greeting to the brothers of heathen birth in Antioch, Syria, and Cilicia. As we have heard that some of our number, with- 24 out any instructions from us, have disturbed you by their teaching and unsettled your minds, we have unanimously 25 resolved to select representatives and send them to you with our dear brothers Barnabas and Paul, who have 26 risked their lives for the sake of our Lord Jesus Christ. So we send Judas and Silas to you, to give you this same 27 message by word of mouth. For the holy Spirit and we 28 have decided not to lay upon you any burden but this indispensable one, that you avoid whatever has been sacri- 29 ficed to idols, the tasting of blood and of the meat of animals that have been strangled, and immorality. Keep yourselves free from these things and you will get on well. Goodbye.''

So the delegates went down to Antioch and gathered 30 the congregation together and delivered the letter; and 31 when they read it they were delighted with the encouragement it gave them. Judas and Silas were themselves 32 prophets, and gave the brothers much encouragement and strength by their words. After they had stayed some 33 time, the brothers let them go, with a greeting to those who had sent them.

But Paul and Barnabas stayed on in Antioch and 35 taught, and with many others preached the good news of the Lord's message.

THE GOSPEL ENTERS EUROPE AND IS PLANTED IN MACEDONIA AND GREECE, 15:36—18:28

Some time after, Paul said to Barnabas, 15 ''Come, let us go back and revisit the brothers in each of the towns where we made the Lord's message known, to see how they are doing."

37 Now Barnabas wanted to take John who was called 38 Mark with them. But Paul did not approve of taking with them a man who had deserted them in Pamphylia 39 instead of going on with them to their work. They differed so sharply about it that they separated, and Barna- 40 bas took Mark and sailed for Cyprus. But Paul selected Silas and set out, the brothers commending him to the 41 Lord's favor. He traveled through Syria and Cilicia and strengthened the churches.

16 He went to Derbe and Lystra also. At Lystra there was a disciple named Timothy whose mother was a Jewish 2 Christian while his father was a Greek, and who was highly thought of by the brothers in Lystra and Iconium. 3 Paul wished to take this man on with him, and so on account of the Jews in that district he had him circumcised, 4 for they all knew that his father was a Greek. As they traveled on from one town to another, they passed on to the brothers for their observance the decisions that had 5 been reached by the apostles and elders at Jerusalem. So the churches became stronger and stronger in the faith, and their numbers increased from day to day.

6 Thus they crossed Phrygia and Galatia. The holy Spirit prevented them from delivering the message in Asia, 7 and when they reached Mysia they tried to get into 8 Bithynia, but the Spirit of Jesus would not permit it, and 9 they passed Mysia and came down to Troas. There Paul had a vision one night; a Macedonian was standing appealing to him and saying,

"Come over to Macedonia and help us."

10 As soon as he had this vision, we made efforts to get on to Macedonia, concluding that God had called us to tell them the good news.

11 So we sailed from Troas, and ran a straight course to 12 Samothrace, and next day to Neapolis. From there we went to Philippi, a Roman garrison town, and the principal place in that part of Macedonia.

13 In this town we stayed for some days. On the Sabbath

we went outside the gates, to the bank of the river where we supposed there was a praying place, and we sat down and talked with the women who gathered there. One of 14 our hearers was a woman named Lydia, a dealer in purple goods, from the town of Thyatira. She was a believer in God, and the Lord touched her heart, and led her to accept Paul's teaching. When she and her household were 15 baptized, she appealed to us, and said,

"If you are really convinced that I am a believer in the Lord, come and stay at my house." And she insisted upon our coming.

Once as we were on our way to the praying place a 16 slave-girl met us who had the gift of ventriloquism and made her masters a great deal of money by her fortune-telling. This girl would follow Paul and the rest of us, 17 crying out,

"These men are slaves of the Most High God, and they are making known to you a way of salvation."

She did this for a number of days, until Paul, very 18 much annoyed, turned and said to the spirit in her,

"In the name of Jesus Christ I order you to come out of her!" And it came out instantly.

But when her masters saw that their hopes of profits 19 were gone, they seized Paul and Silas, dragged them to the public square, to the authorities, and brought them 20 before the chief magistrates.

"These men," they said, "are Jews, and they are making a great disturbance in our town. They are advocat- 21 ing practices which it is against the law for us as Romans to adopt or observe."

The crowd also joined in the attack on them, and the 22 magistrates had them stripped and beaten. After beating 23 them severely, they put them in jail, and gave the jailer orders to keep close watch of them. He, having had such 24 strict orders, put them into the inner cell, and fastened their feet in the stocks. But about midnight, as Paul and 25 Silas were praying and singing hymns of praise to God, and the prisoners were listening to them, suddenly there 26 was such an earthquake that the jail shook to its founda-

tions; all the doors flew open, and everybody's chains
27 were unfastened. It woke up the jailer, and when he saw
that the doors of jail were open, he drew his sword and
was just going to kill himself, supposing that the prison-
28 ers had escaped. But Paul shouted out,

"Do not do yourself any harm! We are all here!"

29 Then he called for lights and rushed in, and fell trem-
30 bling at the feet of Paul and Silas. He led them out of the
jail and said to them,

"Gentlemen, what must I do to be saved?"

31 "Believe in the Lord Jesus," they said, "and you and
your household will be saved!"

32 Then they told God's message to him and to all the
33 members of his household. And right then in the night,
he took them and washed their wounds, and he and all
34 his household were baptized immediately. Then he took
them up to his house and offered them food, and he and
all his household were very happy over their new faith in
35 God. In the morning the magistrates sent policemen
36 with instructions to let the men go. The jailer reported
this message to Paul, saying,

"The magistrates have sent orders that you are to be
released. So you can take your leave and go unmolested."

37 But Paul said to them,

"They had us beaten in public without giving us a
trial, and put us in jail, although we are Roman citizens!
And now are they going to dismiss us secretly? By no
means! Have them come here themselves and take us
out!"

38 The policemen delivered this message to the magis-
39 trates, and they were alarmed when they heard that they
were Roman citizens, and came and conciliated them,
and took them out of the jail, and begged them to leave
40 the town. After leaving the jail they went to Lydia's
house, and saw the brothers and encouraged them. Then
they left the town.

17 After passing through Amphipolis and Apollonia,
they reached Thessalonica, where the Jews had a syna-
2 gogue. Paul went to it as he was accustomed to do, and

for three Sabbaths he discussed the Scriptures with them, explaining them and showing that the Christ had to suffer and rise from the dead. 3

"Jesus," he said, "of whom I am telling you, is the Christ!"

He convinced some of them, and they joined Paul and Silas, along with a great many devout Greeks and a number of the principal women. This offended the Jews and they gathered some unprincipled loafers, formed a mob and started a riot in the town. They attacked Jason's house, to find them and bring them out among the people. As they could not find them, they dragged Jason and some of the brothers before the town magistrates, shouting, 4 5 6

"The men who have made trouble all over the world have come here too, and Jason has taken them in. They all disobey the emperor's decrees, and claim that someone else called Jesus is king." 7

The crowd and the magistrates were very much excited at hearing this, and they put Jason and the others under bonds before they let them go. 8 9

The brothers sent Paul and Silas away immediately, in the course of the following night, to Berea. On arriving there they went to the Jewish synagogue. The Jews there were more high-minded than those at Thessalonica, and received the message with great eagerness and studied the Scriptures every day, to find out whether it was true. Many of them became believers and so did no small number of Greek women of position, and men too. But when the Jews at Thessalonica found out that God's message had been delivered at Berea by Paul, they came there too, to excite and stir up the populace. Then the brothers immediately sent Paul off to the coast, while Silas and Timothy stayed behind. The men who went with Paul took him all the way to Athens, and came back with instructions for Silas and Timothy to rejoin them as soon as possible. 10 11 12 13 14 15

While Paul waited for them at Athens, he was exasperated to see how idolatrous the city was. He had dis- 16 17

cussions at the synagogue with the Jews and those who worshiped with them, and every day in the public square
18 with any whom he happened to find. Some of the Epicurean and Stoic philosophers debated with him. Some of them said,

"What is this rag-picker trying to make out?"
Others said,
"He seems to be preaching some foreign deities."
This was because he was telling the good news of Jesus
19 and the resurrection. So they took him and brought him to the council of the Areopagus and said,
20 "May we know just what this new teaching of yours is? Some of the things you tell us sound strange to us, and we want to know just what they mean."
21 For all Athenians and all visitors there from abroad used to spend all their time telling or listening to something new.
22 Then Paul stood up in the middle of the council and said,

"Men of Athens, from every point of view I see that
23 you are extremely religious. For as I was going about and looking at the things you worship, I even found an altar with this inscription: 'To an Unknown God.' So it is what you already worship in ignorance that I am now
24 telling you of. God who created the world and all that is in it, since he is Lord of heaven and earth, does not live
25 in temples built by human hands, nor is he waited on by human hands as though he were in need of anything, for he himself gives all men life and breath and everything.
26 From one forefather he has created every nation of mankind, and made them live all over the face of the earth, fixing their appointed times and the limits of their lands,
27 so that they might search for God, and perhaps grope for him and find him, though he is never far from any of us.
28 For it is through union with him that we live and move and exist, as some of your poets have said,
" 'For we are also his offspring.'
29 So if we are God's children we ought not to imagine that the divine nature is like gold or silver or stone, wrought

by human art and thought. While God overlooked those 30 times of ignorance, he now calls upon all men everywhere to repent, since he has fixed a day on which he will justly 31 judge the world through a man whom he has appointed, and whom he has guaranteed to all men by raising him from the dead.''

When they heard of the resurrection of the dead, some 32 of them sneered, but others said,

"We should like to hear you again on this subject."

So Paul left the council. Some persons joined him, 33 however, and became believers, among them Dionysius, 34 a member of the council, and a woman named Damaris, and some others.

After this he left Athens and went to Corinth. There 18 he found a Jew named Aquila, a native of Pontus, who had recently come from Italy with his wife Priscilla, because Claudius had ordered all Jews to leave Rome. Paul 3 went to see them, and as they practiced the same trade, he stayed with them, and they worked together, for they were tent-makers. Every Sabbath he would preach in the 4 synagogue, and try to convince both Jews and Greeks.

By the time Silas and Timothy arrived from Mace- 5 donia, Paul was absorbed in preaching the message, emphatically assuring the Jews that Jesus was the Christ. But as they contradicted and abused him, he shook his 6 clothes in protest, and said to them,

"Your blood be on your own heads! I am not to blame for it! After this I will go to the heathen."

So he moved to the house of a devout proselyte named 7 Titius Justus, which was next door to the synagogue. But Crispus, the leader of the synagogue, believed in the 8 Lord, and so did all his household, and many of the people of Corinth heard Paul and believed and were baptized. One night the Lord said to Paul in a vision, 9

"Do not be afraid! Go on speaking and do not give up, 10 for I am with you, and no one shall attack you or injure you, for I have many people in this city."

So he settled there for a year and a half, and taught 11 them God's message.

12   While Gallio was governor of Greece the Jews made a concerted attack upon Paul, and brought him before the governor.

13   "This fellow," they said, "is trying to induce people to worship God in ways that are against the law."

14   Before Paul could open his lips, Gallio said to the Jews,
"If some misdemeanor or rascality were involved, Jews, you might reasonably expect me to listen to you.

15   But as it is only a question of words and titles and your own law, you must look after it yourselves. I refuse to decide such matters."

16   And he drove them away from the court. Then they all
17   seized Sosthenes, the leader of the synagogue, and beat him in front of the court. But Gallio paid no attention to it.

18   Paul stayed some time longer, and then bade the brothers goodbye and sailed for Syria, with Priscilla and Aquila. At Cenchreae he had his hair cut, because of a
19   vow he had been under. When they reached Ephesus he left them there. He went to the synagogue there and had
20   a discussion with the Jews. They asked him to stay long-
21   er, but he would not consent. He bade them goodbye, saying,
"I will come back to you again if it is God's will."

22   Then he sailed from Ephesus. When he reached Caesarea, he went up to Jerusalem and paid his respects to the
23   church, and then went on to Antioch. After spending some time there, he started out again, and traveled systematically through Galatia and Phrygia, reassuring all the disciples.

24   A Jew named Apollos, a native of Alexandria, came to Ephesus. He was an eloquent man, skilful in the use of
25   the Scriptures. He had had some instruction about the Way of the Lord, and he talked with burning zeal and taught painstakingly about Jesus, though he knew of no
26   baptism but John's. He spoke very confidently in the synagogue at first, but when Priscilla and Aquila heard him, they took him home and explained the Way of God to

him more correctly. As he wanted to cross Greece, the 27
brothers wrote to the disciples there, urging them to welcome him. On his arrival there he was of great service to
those who through God's favor had become believers, for 28
he vigorously refuted the Jews in public, and showed from
the scriptures that Jesus was the Christ.

THE GOSPEL IN EPHESUS, 19:1, 23—20:38

It was while Apollos was in Corinth that Paul, after 19
passing through the interior, reached Ephesus.

Just at that time a great commotion arose about the 23
Way. A silversmith named Demetrius was making large 24
profits for his workmen by the manufacture of silver
shrines of Artemis. He got the workmen in that and sim- 25
ilar trades together, and said to them,

"Men, you know that this business is the source of our
prosperity, and you see and hear that not only in Ephesus 26
but almost all over Asia, this man Paul has persuaded and
drawn away numbers of people, telling them that gods
made by human hands are not gods at all. There is dan- 27
ger, therefore, not only that this business of ours will be
discredited, but also that the temple of the great goddess
Artemis will be neglected and the magnificence of her
whom all Asia and the world worship will be a thing of
the past!"

When they heard this, they became very angry, and 28
cried,

"Great Artemis of Ephesus!"

So the commotion spread all over the city, and by a 29
common impulse the people rushed to the theater, drag-
ging with them two Macedonians, Gaius and Aristarchus, Paul's traveling companions. Paul wanted to go be- 30
fore the people himself, but the disciples would not allow
it. Some of the religious authorities also, who were 31
friends of his, sent to him and begged him not to venture
into the theater. Meanwhile the people were shouting, 32
some one thing and some another, for the meeting was in
confusion, and most of them had no idea why they had
come together. Some of the crowd called upon Alexan- 33

der, as the Jews had pushed him to the front, and he made a gesture with his hand and was going to speak in de-
34 fense of them to the people. But when they saw that he was a Jew, a great shout went up from them all, and they cried for two hours,

"Great Artemis of Ephesus!"

35 At last the recorder quieted the mob and said,

"Men of Ephesus, who in the world does not know that the city of Ephesus is the guardian of the temple of the great Artemis, and of the image that fell down from
36 the sky? So as these facts are undeniable, you must be
37 calm, and not do anything reckless. For you have brought these men here, though they have not been guilty of disloyalty nor uttered any blasphemy against our
38 goddess. If Demetrius and his fellow-craftsmen have a charge to bring against anyone, there are the courts and
39 the governors; let them take legal action. But if you require anything beyond that, it must be settled before the
40 regular assembly. For we are in danger of being charged with rioting in connection with today's events, though there is really nothing about this commotion that we will not be able to explain."

41 With these words he dismissed the assembly.

20 When the confusion was over, Paul sent for the disciples and encouraged them. Then he bade them goodbye
2 and started for Macedonia. After traveling through those districts and giving the people a great deal of encourage-
3 ment, he went on to Greece where he stayed for three months. Just as he was going to sail for Syria, the Jews made a plot against him, and he made up his mind to
4 return by way of Macedonia. He was accompanied by Sopater of Berea, the son of Pyrrhus, Aristarchus and Secundus, from Thessalonica, Gaius of Derbe, Timothy, and
5 Tychicus and Trophimus, from Asia. They went on to
6 Troas and waited for us there, while we sailed from Philippi after the festival of Unleavened Bread, and joined them at Troas five days later. There we stayed a week.

7 On the first day of the week, when we had met for the breaking of bread, Paul addressed them, as he was going

[461]

away the next morning, and he prolonged his address until midnight. There were a great many lamps in the 8 upstairs room where we met and a young man named 9 Eutychus, who was sitting at the window, became very drowsy as Paul's address grew longer and longer, and finally went fast asleep and fell from the third story to the ground, and was picked up for dead. But Paul went 10 downstairs, and threw himself upon him, and put his arms around him.

"Do not be alarmed," he said, "he is still alive."

Then he went upstairs again, and broke the bread, and 11 ate, and after a long talk with them that lasted until daylight, he went away. They took the boy home alive, and 12 were greatly comforted.

We had already gone on board the ship and sailed for 13 Assos, intending to take Paul on board there, for that was the arrangement he had made, as he intended to travel there by land. So when he met us at Assos, we took him 14 on board and went on to Mitylene. Sailing from there, 15 we arrived off Chios on the following day. On the next we crossed to Samos, and on the next we reached Miletus. For Paul had decided to sail past Ephesus, so that he 16 would not have to lose any time in Asia, for he was hurrying to reach Jerusalem, if possible, by the day of the Harvest Festival.

From Miletus he sent to Ephesus for the elders of the 17 church. When they came, he said to them, 18

"You know well enough how I lived among you all the time from the first day I set foot in Asia, and how I 19 served the Lord most humbly and with tears, through all the trials that I encountered because of the plots of the Jews. I never shrank from telling you anything that was 20 for your good, nor from teaching you in public or at your houses, but earnestly urged Greeks as well as Jews to 21 turn to God in repentance and to believe in our Lord Jesus. I am here now on my way to Jerusalem, for the 22 Spirit compels me to go there, though I do not know what will happen to me there, except that in every town 23 I visit, the holy Spirit warns me that imprisonment and

[462]

24 persecution are awaiting me. But my life does not matter, if I can only finish my race and do the service intrusted to me by the Lord Jesus, of declaring the good
25 news of God's favor. Now I know perfectly well that none of you among whom I went about preaching the
26 Kingdom of God will ever see my face again. Therefore I declare to you today that I am not responsible for the
27 blood of any of you, for I have not shrunk from letting
28 you know God's purpose without reserve. Take care of yourselves and of the whole flock, of which the holy Spirit has made you guardians, and be shepherds of the church of God, which he got at the cost of his own life.
29 I know that after I am gone savage wolves will get in
30 among you and will not spare the flock, and from your own number men will appear and teach perversions of the
31 truth in order to draw the disciples away after them. So you must be on your guard and remember that for three years, night and day, I never stopped warning any one of
32 you, even with tears. Now I commit you to the Lord, and to the message of his favor, which will build you up and give you a place among those whom God has conse-
33 crated. I have never coveted anyone's gold or silver or
34 clothes. You know well enough that these hands of mine
35 provided for my needs and my companions. I showed you in every way that by hard work like that we must help those who are weak and remember the words of the Lord Jesus, for he said, 'It makes one happier to give than to be given to.' "
36 With these words, he knelt down with them all and
37 prayed. They all wept aloud, and throwing their arms
38 about Paul's neck they kissed him affectionately, for they were especially saddened at his saying that they would never see his face again. Then they accompanied him to the ship.

PAUL IS MOBBED IN JERUSALEM, 21:15–40

21 After this we made our preparations and started for
16 Jerusalem. Some of the disciples from Caesarea went with us and took us to the house of Mnason, a man from Cy-

prus, one of the early disciples, to spend the night. When 17
we reached Jerusalem, the brothers there gave us a hearty
welcome. On the next day we went with Paul to see 18
James, and all the elders came in. Paul greeted them 19
warmly and gave a detailed account of what God had
done among the heathen through his efforts. They 20
praised God when they heard it, and they said to him,

"You see, brother, how many thousand believers there
are among the Jews, all of them zealous upholders of the
Law. They have been told that you teach all Jews who 21
live among the heathen to turn away from Moses, and
that you tell them not to circumcise their children nor to
observe the old customs. What then? They will be sure 22
to hear that you have come. So do what we tell you. We 23
have four men here who are under a vow. Join them, un- 24
dergo the rites of purification with them, and pay their
expenses so that they can have their heads shaved. Then
everybody will understand that there is no truth in the
stories about you, but that you yourself observe the Law.
As for the heathen who have become believers, we have 25
written them our decision that they must avoid anything
that has been contaminated by idols, the tasting of blood,
the meat of strangled animals, and immorality."

Then Paul joined the men and went through the rites of 26
purification with them and the next day went to the
Temple to give notice of the time when, upon the offering
of the sacrifice for each one of them, their days of purification would be over.

The seven days were almost over when the Jews from 27
Asia caught sight of him in the Temple, and stirred up all
the crowd and seized him, shouting, 28

"Men of Israel, help! This is the man who teaches
everybody everywhere against our people and the Law
and this place, and besides he has actually brought
Greeks into the Temple and desecrated this sacred place."

For they had previously seen Trophimus of Ephesus 29
with him in the city, and they supposed that Paul had
brought him into the Temple. The whole city was 30
thrown into confusion, and the people hurried together,

[464]

and seized Paul and dragged him outside of the Temple,
31 the gates of which were immediately shut. They were
trying to kill him when the news reached the colonel of
32 the regiment that all Jerusalem was in a tumult. He immediately got some officers and men and hurried down
among them, and when they saw the colonel and the sol-
33 diers they stopped beating Paul. Then the colonel came
up and seized him, and ordered him to be bound with two
chains, and then inquired who he was and what he had
34 been doing. Some of the crowd shouted one thing and
some another, and as he could not find out the facts on account of the confusion, he ordered him to be taken into
35 the barracks. When Paul got to the steps, he was actu-
36 ally carried by the soldiers, on account of the violence of
the mob, for the mass of people followed them shouting,
"Kill him!"

37   Just as they were going to take him into the barracks,
Paul said to the colonel,
"May I say something to you?"

38   "Do you know Greek?" the colonel asked. "Are you
not the Egyptian who some time ago raised the four thousand cut-throats and led them out into the desert?"

39   "I am a Jew," Paul answered, "from Tarsus, in Cilicia,
a citizen of no insignificant city. I beg you to let me speak
to the people."

40   He gave him permission, and Paul standing on the
steps made a gesture to the people, and when they had become quiet he spoke to them in Hebrew.

PAUL ADDRESSES THE MOB, 22:1-22

22   "Brothers and fathers," he said, "listen to what I have
to say in my defense."

2   When they heard him speak to them in Hebrew, they
became even more quiet, and he said,

3   "I am a Jew, and I was born in Tarsus in Cilicia, but
was brought up here in this city, and thoroughly educated under the teaching of Gamaliel in the Law of our
forefathers. I was zealous for God, just as all of you are
4 today. I persecuted this Way even to the death, and

[465]

bound both men and women and put them in prison, as 5
the high priest and the whole council will bear me witness. In fact, they gave me letters to the brothers in Damascus and I went there to bind those who were there
and bring them back to Jerusalem to be punished. But on 6
my way, as I was approaching Damascus, suddenly about
noon, a blaze of light flashed around me from heaven, and 7
I fell upon the ground and heard a voice say to me, 'Saul!
Saul! Why do you persecute me?' I answered, 'Who are 8
you, sir?' 'I am Jesus of Nazareth,' he said, 'whom you
are persecuting.' The men who were with me saw the 9
light, but they did not hear the voice of the one who was
speaking to me. Then I said, 'What am I to do, sir?' 10
The Lord said to me, 'Get up and go into Damascus.
There you will be told of all you are destined to do.' As I 11
could not see, because of the dazzling light, my companions had to lead me by the hand, and so I reached Damascus. There a man named Ananias, a devout observer of 12
the Law, highly respected by all the Jews who lived
there, came to see me, and standing by my side, said to 13
me, 'Saul, my brother, regain your sight!' Then instantly
I regained my sight and looked at him, and he said, 'The 14
God of our forefathers has appointed you to learn his will
and to see his Righteous One and hear him speak, for you 15
shall be his witness before all men of what you have seen
and heard. And now, why do you delay? Get up and be 16
baptized, and wash out your sins, calling on his name.' 17
After I had returned to Jerusalem, one day when I was
praying in the Temple, I fell into a trance, and saw him 18
saying to me, 'Make haste and leave Jerusalem at once, for
they will not accept your evidence about me.' And I said, 19
'Lord, they know that I used to go through one synagogue after another, and to imprison and flog those who
believed in you, and when the blood of your witness Ste- 20
phen was being shed, I stood by and approved it, and
took charge of the clothes of the men who killed him.'
But he said to me, 'Go! I will send you far away to the 21
heathen.' "

22 They had listened to him until he said that, but then they shouted,
"Kill him and get him out of the world! A creature like that ought not to be allowed to live!"

PAUL'S ARREST AND IMPRISONMENT, 22:23–30; 23:6–35, 24:27

22
24 As they were shouting and throwing their clothes about and flinging dust into the air, the colonel ordered Paul brought into the barracks, and gave directions that he should be examined under the lash, so that he might
25 find out why they made such an outcry against him. But when they had strapped him up, Paul said to the officer who was standing near,
"Is it legal for you to flog a Roman citizen, and without giving him a trial?"
26 Upon hearing this, the officer went to the colonel and reported it.
"What do you propose to do?" he said. "This man is a Roman citizen."
27 Then the colonel came to Paul and said,
"Tell me, are you a Roman citizen?"
"Yes," he said.
28 "I had to pay a large sum for my citizenship," said the colonel.
"But I am a citizen by birth," said Paul.
29 Then the men who had been going to examine him immediately left him, and the colonel himself was alarmed to find that Paul was a Roman citizen and that he had had him bound.
30 The next day, as he wished to find out the real reason why the Jews denounced him, he had him unbound and ordered the high priests and the whole council to assemble, and took Paul down and brought him before them.
23 Knowing that part of them were Sadducees and part of them Pharisees, Paul called out in the council,
"Brothers, I am a Pharisee, and the son of Pharisees! It is for my hope for the resurrection of the dead that I am on trial!"

When he said that, a dispute arose between the Phari- 7
sees and the Sadducees, and the meeting was divided. For 8
the Sadducees hold that there is no resurrection and that
there are no angels or spirits, while the Pharisees believe
in all three. So there was a great uproar, and some scribes 9
of the Pharisees' party got up and insisted,

"We find nothing wrong with this man. Suppose some
spirit or angel really spoke to him!"

As the dispute was becoming violent, the colonel be- 10
gan to be afraid that they would tear Paul in pieces, and
ordered the soldiers to go down and get him away from
them and bring him into the barracks.

On the following night the Lord stood beside him and 11
said,

"Courage! For just as you have testified for me in Jerusalem, you must testify in Rome also."

In the morning, the Jews made a conspiracy and took 12
an oath not to eat or drink till they had killed Paul.
There were more than forty of them involved in this plot, 13
and they went to the high priests and elders and said to 14
them,

"We have taken a solemn oath not to touch anything
to eat till we have killed Paul. Now you and the council 15
must suggest to the colonel that he should have Paul
brought down to you, as you mean to look into his case
more carefully, and we will be ready to kill him before he
gets down."

But Paul's nephew heard of the plot, and he came and 16
got into the barracks, and told Paul. Paul called one of 17
the officers and said to him,

"Take this young man to the colonel, for he has something to tell him."

So he took him to the colonel, and said, 18

"The prisoner Paul called me to him and asked me to
bring this young man to you, as he has something to say
to you."

So the colonel took him by the arm and stepping aside 19
where they could be alone, asked,

"What is it that you have to tell me?"

20 "The Jews," he answered, "have agreed to ask you to bring Paul down to the council tomorrow, on the ground that you mean to have a fuller inquiry made into his case.

21 But do not let them persuade you, for more than forty of them are lying in wait for him, and they have taken an oath not to eat or drink till they have killed him. They are all ready now, and are only waiting to get your promise."

22 So the colonel sent the youth away, directing him not to tell anyone that he had given him this information.

23 Then he called in two of his officers and said to them,

"Get two hundred men ready to march to Caesarea, with seventy mounted men and two hundred spearmen,

24 by nine o'clock tonight." They were also to provide horses for Paul to ride, so that they might take him in

25 safety to Felix, the governor, to whom he wrote a letter to this effect:

26 "Claudius Lysias sends greetings to his Excellency

27 Felix, the governor. This man had been seized by the Jews and they were just going to kill him when I came upon them with my men and rescued him, as I had

28 learned that he was a Roman citizen. As I wanted to learn what charge they made against him, I had him

29 brought before their council, and found that their accusations had to do with questions about their Law, but that he was not charged with anything that would call

30 for his death or imprisonment. As I have been informed that a plot against him is brewing, I am sending him on to you at once, and directing his accusers to present their charges against him before you."

31 Then the soldiers took Paul, as they had been ordered to do, and escorted him as far as Antipatris that night.

32 The next day, they returned to the barracks, leaving the

33 mounted men to go on with him, and they on reaching Caesarea delivered the letter to the governor and handed

34 Paul over to him. After reading the letter, he asked Paul what province he belonged to, and when he learned that

35 he was from Cilicia, he said,

"I will hear your case as soon as your accusers arrive."

And he gave orders that he should be kept in Herod's palace.

But when two whole years had passed, Felix was suc- 24 ceeded by Porcius Festus, and as he wanted to gratify the Jews, Felix left Paul in prison.

PAUL'S DEFENSE BEFORE AGRIPPA, 25:1—26:32

Three days after his arrival in the province, Festus 25 went up from Caesarea to Jerusalem, and the high priests 2 and Jewish leaders presented their charges against Paul, and begged him as a favor to order Paul to come to Jeru- 3 salem, plotting to kill him on the way. Festus answered 4 that Paul was being kept in custody at Caesarea, and that he himself was going there soon.

"So have your principal men go down with me," he 5 said, "and present charges against the man, if there is anything wrong with him."

After staying only eight or ten days there, he went 6 down to Caesarea, and the next day took his place in the judge's chair, and ordered Paul brought in. When he 7 came, the Jews who had come down from Jerusalem surrounded him, and made a number of serious charges against him, which they could not substantiate. Paul 8 said in his own defense,

"I have committed no offense against the Jewish Law or the Temple or the emperor."

Then Festus, wishing to gratify the Jews, said to Paul, 9 "Will you go up to Jerusalem and be tried there before me on these charges?"

But Paul said, 10

"I am standing before the emperor's court, where I ought to be tried. I have done the Jews no wrong, as you can easily see. If I am guilty and have done anything 11 that deserves death, I do not refuse to die; but if there is no truth in the charges that these men make against me, no one can give me up to them; I appeal to the emperor."

Then Festus after conferring with the council an- 12 swered,

"You have appealed to the emperor, and to the emperor you shall go!"

13 Some time after, King Agrippa and Bernice came to
14 Caesarea on a state visit to Festus, and as they stayed there several days, Festus laid Paul's case before the king. "There is a man here," he said, "who was left in pri-
15 son by Felix, and when I was at Jerusalem the Jewish high priests and elders presented their case against him,
16 and asked for his conviction. I told them that it was not the Roman custom to give anybody up until the accused met his accusers face to face and had a chance to defend
17 himself against their accusations. So they came back here with me and the next day without losing any time I took my place in the judge's chair and ordered the man
18 brought in. But when his accusers got up, they did not charge him with any such crimes as I had expected.
19 Their differences with him were about their own religion and about a certain Jesus who had died but who Paul said
20 was alive. I was at a loss as to how to investigate such matters, and I asked him if he would like to go to Jeru-
21 salem and be tried on these charges there. But Paul appealed to have his case reserved for his Majesty's decision and I have ordered him kept in custody until I can send him to the emperor."

22 "I should like to hear the man myself," Agrippa said to Festus.

"You shall hear him tomorrow," Festus answered.

23 So the next day, Agrippa and Bernice came with great pomp and went into the audience-room attended by officers and the leading citizens of the town, and at
24 the command of Festus Paul was brought in. Then Festus said,

"King Agrippa and all who are present, you see here the man about whom the whole Jewish people have applied to me both at Jerusalem and here, clamoring that he
25 ought not to live any longer. I could not find that he had done anything for which he deserved death, but as he ap-
26 pealed to his Majesty I decided to send him to him. Yet I have nothing definite to write to our sovereign about

him. So I have brought him before you all, and especially before you, King Agrippa, in order to get from your examination of him something to put in writing. For it 27 seems to me absurd to send a prisoner on, without stating the charges against him."

Then Agrippa said to Paul,   26

"You are at liberty to speak in your own defense."

So Paul stretched out his hand and began his defense.

"I think myself fortunate, King Agrippa," said he, 2 "that it is before you that I am to defend myself today against all the things the Jews charge me with, especially 3 because you are so familiar with all the Jewish customs and questions. I beg you, therefore, to listen to me with patience. The way I lived from my youth up, spending 4 my early life among my own nation and at Jerusalem, is well known to all Jews, for they have known from the first, if they are willing to give evidence, that I was a 5 Pharisee and my life was that of the strictest sect of our religion. Even now it is for my hope in the promise that 6 God made to our forefathers that I stand here on trial, the promise in the hope of seeing which fulfilled our 7 twelve tribes serve God zealously night and day. It is about this hope, your Majesty, that I am accused by some Jews. Why do you all think it incredible that God should 8 raise the dead? I once thought it my duty vigorously to 9 oppose the cause of Jesus of Nazareth. That was what I 10 did at Jerusalem when on the authority of the high priests I put many of God's people in prison. When they 11 were put to death, I cast my vote against them, and many a time in all the synagogues I had them punished, and tried to force them to say impious things. In my extreme rage against them I even pursued them to distant towns. I was once going to Damascus on this business, author- 12 ized and commissioned by the high priests, when on the road at noon, your Majesty, I saw a light from heaven 13 brighter than the sun flash around me and my fellow-travelers. We all fell to the ground, and I heard a voice 14 say to me in Hebrew, 'Saul! Saul! Why do you persecute me? You cannot kick against the goad!' 'Who are you, 15

sir?' said I. The Lord said, 'I am Jesus, whom you are
16 persecuting. But get up and stand on your feet, for I
have appeared to you for the express purpose of appoint-
ing you to serve me and to testify to what you have seen
17 and to the visions you will have of me. I will save you
from your people and from the heathen, to whom I will
18 send you to open their eyes and turn them from darkness
to light and from Satan's control to God, so that they
may have their sins forgiven and have a place among
19 those who are consecrated through faith in me.' Therefore, King Agrippa, I did not disobey that heavenly vi-
20 sion, but first to the people of Damascus and Jerusalem
and then all over Judea, and even to the heathen I
preached that they must repent and turn to God and live
21 as men who have repented should. That is why the Jews
22 seized me in the Temple and tried to kill me. To this day
I have had God's help, and I stand here to testify to high
and low alike, without adding a thing to what Moses
23 and the prophets declared would happen, if the Christ
was to suffer and by being the first to rise from the dead
was to proclaim the light to our people and to the heathen."

24   As he said this in his defense, Festus called out,
"You are raving, Paul! Your great learning is driving
you mad!"
25   "I am not raving, your Excellency Festus," said Paul,
26 "I am telling the sober truth. The king knows about
this, and I can speak to him with freedom. I do not believe that he missed any of this, for it did not happen in a
27 corner! King Agrippa, do you believe the prophets? I
know that you do!"
28   "You are in a hurry to persuade me and make a Christian of me!" Agrippa said to Paul.
29   "In a hurry or not," said Paul, "I would to God that
not only you, but all who hear me today, might be what
I am—except for these chains!"
30   Then the king rose, with the governor and Bernice and
31 those who had sat with them, and after leaving the room,
in talking the matter over together, they said,

[473]

"This man has not done anything to deserve death or imprisonment."

"He might have been set at liberty," said Agrippa to 32 Festus, "if he had not appealed to the emperor."

PAUL'S VOYAGE AND SHIPWRECK, 27:1-44

When it was decided that we were to sail for Italy, 27 Paul and some other prisoners were turned over to an officer of the Imperial regiment, named Julius. We went 2 on board an Adramyttian ship bound for the ports of Asia, and put to sea. We had a Macedonian from Thessalonica, named Aristarchus, with us. The next day we put 3 in at Sidon, and Julius kindly allowed Paul to go and see his friends and be taken care of. Putting to sea from 4 there, we sailed under the lee of Cyprus, as the wind was against us, and after traversing the Cilician and Pam- 5 phylian waters, we reached Myra in Lycia. There the 6 officer found an Alexandrian ship bound for Italy, and put us on board her. For a number of days we made slow 7 progress and had some difficulty in arriving off Cnidus. Then as the wind kept us from going on, we sailed under the lee of Crete, off Cape Salmone, and with difficulty 8 coasted along it and reached a place called Fair Havens, near the town of Lasea.

As a great deal of time had now passed, and naviga- 9 tion had become dangerous, for the autumn fast was already over, Paul began to warn them.

"Gentlemen," he said, "I see that this voyage is likely 10 to end in disaster and heavy loss, not only to ship and cargo but to our own lives also."

But the officer was more influenced by the pilot and the 11 captain than by what Paul had to say, and as the harbor 12 was not fit to winter in, the majority favored putting to sea again, in the hope of being able to reach and winter in Phoenix, a harbor in Crete facing west-south-west and west-north-west. When a moderate south wind sprang 13 up, thinking their object was within reach, they weighed anchor, and ran close along the coast of Crete. But very 14 soon a violent wind which they call a Northeaster rushed

15 down from it. The ship was caught by it and could not face the wind, so we gave way and let her run before it.
16 As we passed under the lee of a small island called Cauda, we managed with great difficulty to secure the ship's
17 boat. After hoisting it on board, they used ropes to brace the ship, and as they were afraid of being cast on the Syrtis banks, they lowered the sail, and let the ship drift.
18 The next day, as the storm continued to be violent, they
19 began to throw the cargo overboard, and on the next, they threw the ship's tackle overboard with their own
20 hands. For a number of days neither the sun nor the stars were visible, and the storm continued to rage, until at
21 last we gave up all hope of being saved. Then, when they had gone a long time without food, Paul got up among them, and said,

"Gentlemen, you ought to have listened to me and not to have sailed from Crete and incurred this disaster and
22 loss. Even now, I beg you to keep up your courage, for there will be no loss of life among you, but only of the
23 ship. For last night an angel of the God I belong to and serve stood before me, and said, 'Do not be afraid, Paul!
24 You must stand before the emperor, and see! God has given you the lives of all the people who are on the ship
25 with you.' So keep up your courage, gentlemen! For I
26 have faith in God that it will be just as I was told. But we are to be stranded on some island."
27 It was the fourteenth night of the storm, and we were drifting through the Adriatic when about midnight the
28 sailors began to suspect that there was land ahead. On taking soundings, they found a depth of twenty fathoms, and a little later, taking soundings again, they found a
29 depth of fifteen. Then as they were afraid we might go on the rocks, they dropped four anchors from the stern and
30 waited anxiously for daylight. The sailors wanted to escape from the ship, and actually lowered the boat into the sea, pretending that they were going to run out
31 anchors from the bow, but Paul said to the officers and the soldiers,

"You cannot be saved unless these men stay on board."

[475]

Then the soldiers cut the ropes that held the boat and 32 let it drift away. Until daybreak Paul kept urging them 33 all to take something to eat.

"For fourteen days," he said, "you have been constantly on the watch, without taking anything to eat. I beg you to eat something; it is necessary for your safe- 34 ty. For not one of you will lose even a hair of his head."

With these words he took some bread and after thank- 35 ing God for it before them all, he broke it in pieces and began to eat it. This raised the spirits of all of them, and 36 they took something to eat. There were about seventy- 37 six of us on board. When they had had enough to eat, 38 they threw the wheat into the sea, in order to lighten the ship. When daylight came they could not recognize the 39 coast, but they saw a bay with a beach and determined to run the ship ashore there if possible. So they cast off the 40 anchors and left them in the sea, at the same time they undid the lashings of the steering oars, and hoisting the foresail to the wind, they made for the beach. But they 41 struck a shoal and ran the ship aground. The bow struck and could not be moved, while the stern began to break up under the strain. The soldiers proposed to kill the 42 prisoners, for fear some of them might swim ashore and escape, but the officer wanted to save Paul, and so he pre- 43 vented them from doing this, and ordered all who could swim to jump overboard first and get to land, and the rest 44 to follow on planks or other pieces of wreckage. So they all got safely to land.

THE GOSPEL ESTABLISHED IN ROME, 28:16-31

When we reached Rome, Paul was given permission to 28 live by himself, with a soldier to guard him.

Three days later, he invited the leading Jews to come 17 to see him, and when they came he said to them,

"Brothers, I have done nothing against our people, or the customs of our forefathers, yet I was turned over to the Romans as a prisoner at Jerusalem. They examined 18 me and were ready to let me go, as I was innocent of any crime that deserved death. But the Jews objected, and I 19

was obliged to appeal to the emperor—not that I had any
20 charge to make against my own nation. That is why I
asked to see you and speak with you, for it is on account
of Israel's hope that I have to wear this chain."

21 "We have had no letters about you from Judea," they
answered, "and none of the brothers who have come here
22 has reported or said anything against you. But we want
to hear you state your views, for as far as this sect is concerned, we understand that everywhere it is denounced."

23 So they fixed a day, and came in even larger numbers to
the place where he was staying, and from morning till
night he explained to them the Kingdom of God and gave
his testimony, trying to convince them about Jesus from
24 the Law of Moses and the Prophets. Some of them were
convinced by what he said, but others would not believe.

25 As they could not agree among themselves, they started
to leave, when Paul added one last word.

"The holy Spirit put it finely," he said, "when it said
to your forefathers through the prophet Isaiah,
26 " 'Go to this nation and say to them,
"You will listen, and listen, and never understand,
And you will look, and look, and never see!
27 For this nation's mind has grown dull,
And they hear faintly with their ears,
And they have shut their eyes,
So as never to see with their eyes,
And hear with their ears,
And understand with their minds, and turn back,
And let me cure them!" '

28 "Understand then that this message of God's salvation
has been sent to the heathen. They will listen to it!"

30 So he stayed for two full years in rented lodgings of his
own, and welcomed everybody who came to see him,
31 preaching the Kingdom of God to them and teaching
about the Lord Jesus Christ openly and unhindered.

THE LETTER TO THE EPHESIANS
· · ·

The publication of Luke-Acts recalled attention to the figure of Paul and to the service he had rendered the cause of Greek Christianity. One or two letters of his were still preserved and occasionally read in Asia, and they may have inspired some Asian reader of the Acts to search for others among the cities mentioned in Acts as visited by Paul. In this way the first collection of Paul's letters came to be made, and from this time on almost every Christian writer we know of was familiar with them.

But those letters were all of them closely related to some immediate pressing situation or problem of their time, and when they were collected a generation later, these were out of date. The collected letters must therefore be introduced by a general letter, addressed to all believers, which should draw attention to their permanent values for Greek religion, and introduce Paul the writer of letters to churches accustomed to think of him as Paul the missionary.

To the man who had collected the letters of Paul and read all nine of them for the first time, they must have been almost overwhelming in their effect. He was himself a Christian, of course, but how meager his own religious life must have appeared beside that of the extraordinary religious genius whose letters now lay before him! No wonder they came to him almost with the force of a revelation. No wonder he bursts into a rhapsody over them and reviews their great ideas with a tumultu-

*ous eagerness that almost baffles the interpreter. The
churches must be made to see the treasures these long-
forgotten letters contain for them. Especially in an age
when Christians of the second generation are losing sight
of the great values of their religion, how important to use
this new-found literature to awaken them to the incom-
parable worth of Christianity! And in an age when the
sects were beginning to honeycomb the church, it was important to bring out the unity of the church, as the body
of Christ.*

*When we remember that almost every line of Ephe-
sians shows indebtedness to one or another of the nine
letters of Paul, we can perhaps understand why its author put it forth under Paul's name instead of his own.
For his purpose was to bring the churches again into
touch with the mind of Paul and with the tremendous
religious dynamic of his personality, so providentially
preserved in these vigorous and profound personal letters
which had lain so long neglected in the chests of the
Pauline churches.*

· · ·

THE ENCYCLICAL SALUTATION, 1:1, 2

1 Paul, by God's will an apostle of Christ Jesus, to God's
2 people who are steadfast in Christ Jesus; God our Father
and the Lord Jesus Christ bless you and give you peace.

THE BLESSINGS OF THE CHRISTIAN SALVATION, 1:3–14

1   Blessed be the God and Father of our Lord Jesus
Christ, who through Christ has blessed us with every
4 spiritual blessing in the heavenly realm. Through him
he chose us out before the creation of the world, to be
5 consecrated and above reproach in his sight in love. He
foreordained us to become his sons through Jesus Christ,
6 in fulfilment of his generous purpose, so that we might

[479]

praise the splendid blessing which he has given us
through his beloved Son. It is through union with him 7
and through his blood that we have been delivered and
our offenses forgiven, in the abundance of his mercy 8
which he has lavished upon us. He has given us perfect 9
insight into his secret purpose and understanding of it,
in following out the design he planned to carry out in
Christ, and in arranging, when the time should have 10
fully come, that everything in heaven and on earth
should be unified in Christ—the Christ through whom 11
it is our lot to have been predestined by the design of him
who in everything carries out the purpose of his will,
to win praise for his glory, by having been the first to 12
believe in Christ. You also have heard the message of 13
the truth, the good news of your salvation, and believed
in him, and through union with him you have been
marked with the seal of the holy Spirit that was promised, which is the advance instalment of our inheritance, 14
so that we may get full possession of it, and praise his
glory for it.

THE GENTILES ENABLED TO SHARE IT THROUGH CHRIST, 2:11–22

So remember that you were once physically heathen, 2
and called uncircumcised by those who called themselves circumcised, though only physically, by human
hands. At that time you had no connection with Christ, 12
you were aliens to the commonwealth of Israel, and
strangers to the agreements about God's promise; with
no hope and no God in all the world. But now through 13
your union with Christ Jesus you who were once far away
have through the blood of Christ been brought near. For 14
he is himself our peace. He has united the two divisions,
and broken down the barrier that kept us apart, and 15
through his human nature put an end to the feud between
us, and abolished the Law with its rules and regulations,
in order to make peace and create out of the two parties
one new man by uniting them with himself, and to kill 16
the feud between them with his cross and in one body

17 reconcile them both to God with it. He came with the
good news of peace for you who were far away and for
18 those who were near; for it is through him that we both
19 with one Spirit are now able to approach the Father. So
you are no longer foreigners or strangers, but you are
fellow-citizens of God's people and members of his
20 family. You are built upon the apostles and prophets as
your foundation, and Christ Jesus himself is the corner-
21 stone. Through him every part of the building is closely
united and grows into a temple sacred through its rela-
22 tion to the Lord, and you are yourselves built up into a
dwelling for God through the Spirit.

THE INCOMPARABLE LOVE OF CHRIST, 3:14-21

3 For this reason I kneel before the Father from whom
15 every family in heaven or on earth takes its name, and
16 beg him out of his wealth of glory to strengthen you
mightily through his Spirit in your inner nature and
17 through your faith to let Christ in his love make his
home in your hearts. Your roots must be deep and your
18 foundations strong, so that you and all God's people may
19 be strong enough to grasp what breadth, length, height,
and depth mean, and to understand Christ's love, so far
beyond our understanding, so that you may be filled with
20 the very fulness of God. To him who by the exertion of
his power within us can do unutterably more than all we
21 ask or imagine, be glory through the church and through
Christ Jesus through all generations forever and ever.
Amen.

GOD'S ARMOR, 6:10-17

6 Henceforth you must grow strong through union with
11 the Lord and through his mighty strength. You must put
on God's armor, so as to be able to stand up against the
12 devil's stratagems. For we have to struggle, not with
enemies of flesh and blood, but with the hierarchies, the
authorities, the master-spirits of this dark world, the
13 spirit-forces of evil on high. So you must take God's
armor, so that when the evil day comes you will be able

to make a stand, and when it is all over to hold your
ground. Stand your ground, then, with the belt of truth 14
around your waist, and put on uprightness as your coat
of mail, and on your feet put the readiness the good 15
news of peace brings. Besides all these, take faith for 16
your shield, for with it you will be able to put out all the
flaming missiles of the evil one, and take salvation for 17
your helmet, and for your sword the Spirit, which is
the voice of God.

THE REVELATION OF JOHN

. . .

*The early Christians lived on a volcano. They prac-
ticed a religion not recognized by the Roman state, and
the government might at any time proceed against them.
Nero had attacked them savagely in Rome in August of
A.D. 64, but in general the empire had paid little attention to their progress. But with the adoption under
Domitian of emperor worship as a pledge of loyalty to
the empire, the church and the state came into sharp collision.*

*Emperor worship had sprung up spontaneously in the
east, as an expression of gratitude to the emperor for the
benefits his rule insured. The empire had brought peace
to a troubled world, and the provincials of Asia and
Egypt could see no better way to acknowledge the new
security and order they enjoyed than by setting up altars
and building temples to the emperor himself. The early
emperors were indifferent to this worship, or positively
discouraged it. But under Domitian it became a part of
Roman policy to accept it and even to demand it, as a
solemn admission of the emperor's sway. To decline to
burn the incense, make the obeisance, and say "Caesar is
a god" would be to deny the authority of Rome.*

*It was a strong temptation to meet this requirement
with compromise, and to comply with the state's demand
—with mental reservations, of course. To prevent such
compromise on the part of the Christian brotherhood in
Asia, the Revelation was written. Addressing the lead-*

*ing churches of that province, John, a prophet of Ephesus,
calls upon them to make no compromise with the situation, but to triumph over it. They must be victorious.
This is the burden of the general letter to the seven
churches, and the special messages to each of them with
which the book begins. In this use of a collection of letters to seven churches as the portal to the Apocalypse we
may see the first reflection of the recent collecting of
Paul's letters to seven churches, which seems to have
been done between the publication of Luke-Acts and the
writing of the Revelation.*

*But the Revelation is for the most part apocalyptic,
not epistolary. In three great visions, full of the grotesque symbolism of the old Jewish apocalyptic earlier
employed in Zechariah, Ezekiel, and Daniel, the prophet portrays the certainty of the ultimate triumph of the
Kingdom of God. No matter what disasters—earthquakes, famines, invasions, wars—they may see about
them, the Kingdom of God is moving irresistibly forward and must finally prevail. The writer has cast his
message in a great super-opera, with arias, antiphonies,
and choruses, having as its tremendous orchestration not
only harps and trumpets but the great noises of nature—
thunders, earthquakes, and mighty waters. Rome itself,
the mightiest empire the world had seen, will fall, for
above the Emperor, the Autocrator, stands the Omnipo-
tent, the Pantocrator.*

*While the grotesque imagery of the apocalyptic in-
vited the minds of the Christian brotherhood, it concealed from Roman authority the meaning of the prophet's message, which in one of the darkest hours in Christian history brought comfort and courage to the harassed*

[484]

*little churches of Asia. It is the prophet's indomitable
faith in God and in the triumph of his cause that is the
glory of the Revelation, but is too often lost sight of
amid the bewildering apocalyptic splendors through
which he views it.*

• • •

THE PROPHET'S CALL, 1:9-20

1   I, John, your brother and companion in the distress,
the kingdom, and the endurance that Jesus brings, found
myself on the island called Patmos, for uttering God's
10 message and testifying to Jesus. On the Lord's day I fell
into a trance, and I heard a loud voice like a trumpet be-
11 hind me say,
  "Write what you see a in roll and send it to the seven
churches—to Ephesus, Smyrna, Pergamum, Thyatira,
Sardis, Philadelphia, and Laodicea."
12   I turned to see whose voice it was that was speaking
to me, and when I turned I saw seven gold lampstands,
13 and among the lampstands a being like a man, wearing a
14 long robe, with a gold belt around his breast. His head
and hair were as white as white wool, as white as snow;
15 his eyes blazed like fire; his feet were like bronze, refined
in a furnace, and his voice was like the noise of mighty
16 waters. In his right hand he held seven stars; from his
mouth came a sharp double-edged sword, and his face
17 shone like the sun at noonday. When I saw him, I fell
at his feet like a dead man. But he laid his right hand
upon me, and said,
  "Do not be afraid. I am the first and the last, the liv-
18 ing one. I was dead, yet here I am alive forever and ever.
19 I hold the keys of death and the underworld. So write
what you have seen, what is now and what is to happen
20 hereafter. The secret meaning of the seven stars that
you saw in my right hand, and of the seven gold lampstands is this: The seven stars are the guardian angels of
the seven churches and the seven lampstands are the
seven churches."

[485]

THE VISION OF THE ROLL OF DESTINY, 4:1—5:14

Afterward I had another vision: There was a door **4** standing open in the heavens and the first voice like a trumpet that I had heard speak to me, said

"Come up here, and I will show you what must take place."

Immediately after this I found myself in a trance, and **2** there stood a throne in heaven with a being seated on it. The one who was seated on it looked like jasper and **3** sardius, and around the throne was a halo of the color of an emerald. Around the throne were twenty-four **4** thrones, with twenty-four elders seated on them, clothed in white and with gold crowns on their heads. Out from **5** the throne came flashes of lightning, rumblings, and peals of thunder. In front of the throne seven blazing lamps were burning; they are the seven spirits of God. In front of the throne was what looked like a sea of glass, **6** like crystal. Around the throne, in the middle of each side, were four animals covered with eyes in front and behind. The first animal was like a lion, the second was **7** like an ox, the third had a face like a man's, and the fourth was like an eagle flying. The four animals have **8** each of them six wings, and they are covered with eyes all over and underneath their wings. And day and night they never cease to say,

"Holy, holy, holy is the Lord God, the Almighty, who was and is and is coming."

And whenever the animals offer glory, honor, and **9** thanksgiving to him who is seated on the throne, who lives forever and ever, the twenty-four elders fall down **10** before him who is seated on the throne, and worship him who lives forever and ever, and they throw down their crowns before the throne, and say,

"You are worthy, our Lord and God, to receive glory, **11** honor, and power, for you created all things; by your will they existed and were created."

Then I saw lying in the right hand of him who was **5** seated on the throne a roll with writing on both sides,

2 sealed with seven seals. And I saw a mighty angel announcing in a loud voice,

"Who is fit to open the roll and break its seals?"

3 But no one in heaven or on earth or underneath the
4 earth could open the roll or look into it. Then I cried bitterly because no one could be found fit to open the roll
5 or look into it. But one of the elders said to me,

"Do not cry! See! The lion who is of the tribe of Judah, of the line of David, has been victorious so that he can open the roll and break its seals."

6 Then I saw standing in the center of the throne and of the four animals and of the elders a Lamb which seemed to have been slaughtered. He has seven horns and seven eyes; these are the seven spirits of God, which are sent
7 on errands to all parts of the earth. He came and took the roll from the right hand of him who was seated on
8 the throne. When he took the roll, the four animals and the twenty-four elders fell down before the Lamb, each with a harp and gold bowls full of incense, that is, of the
9 prayers of God's people. Then they sang a new song:

"You deserve to take the roll and open its seals, for you have been slaughtered, and with your blood have bought for God men from every tribe, tongue, people,
10 and nation, and have made them a kingdom of priests for our God, and they are to reign over the earth."

11 Then in my vision I heard the voices of many angels surrounding the throne, the animals, and the elders, numbering myriads of myriads and thousands of thou-
12 sands, saying in a loud voice,

"The Lamb that was slaughtered deserves to receive power, wealth, wisdom, might, honor, glory, and blessing."

13 Then I heard every creature in heaven, on earth, underneath the earth, and on the sea, and all that they contain, say,

"Blessing, honor, glory, and power to him who is seated on the throne and to the Lamb forever and ever!"

14 The four animals said,

[487]

"Amen!"
And the elders fell down and worshiped.

THE TRIUMPH OF THE KINGDOM OF GOD, 11:15–19

Then the seventh angel blew his trumpet, and loud 11
voices were heard in heaven, saying,
"The sovereignty of the world has passed into the
possession of our Lord and his Christ, and he will reign
forever and ever."
Then the twenty-four elders who were seated on their 16
thrones before God fell on their faces and worshiped God,
saying,   17
"We give you thanks, Lord God Almighty, who are
and were, because you have assumed your great power
and begun to reign. The heathen were enraged, but now 18
your anger has come, and the time for the dead to be
judged, and for rewarding your slaves the prophets
and your people high and low who revere your name, and
for destroying the destroyers of the earth!"
Then the temple of God in heaven was thrown open, 19
and the chest containing his agreement was seen inside
the temple, and there were flashes of lightning, rumblings, peals of thunder, an earthquake, and a great storm
of hail.

THE FATE OF ROME, 18:1—19:6

Afterward I saw another angel come down from 18
heaven. He possessed great authority and his splendor 2
lighted up the earth. He cried out with a mighty voice,
"She is fallen! Mighty Babylon is fallen! She has become the haunt of demons, and a dungeon for every foul
spirit and every unclean and loathsome bird, for after 3
drinking the wine of the passion of her immorality all
the heathen have fallen; the kings of the earth have
joined in her idolatry, and the traders of the earth have
grown rich from her excessive luxury!"
Then I heard another voice from heaven say,   4
"Come out of her, my people, so that you may not
share in her sins, and suffer from her plagues. For her 5

sins are piled up to the sky, and God has remembered her
6 crimes. Pay her back in her own coin, and give her
double for what she has done. In the cup she mixed for
7 others, mix her a double draught. The more she has
given herself to pride and luxury the more you must give
her torture and grief. Because she says to herself, 'I sit
on a throne; I am not a widow, I shall never have any
8 sorrow,' her plagues will overtake her in one day, death,
grief, and famine, and she will be burned up with fire;
9 for the Lord God who has judged her is mighty. The
kings of the earth who have joined in her idolatry and
luxury will weep and lament over her when they see the
10 smoke from her burning. They will stand a long way off
for fear of her torture and say, 'Alas! Alas for the great
city, for Babylon the mighty city, for in a single hour
11 your judgment has overtaken you!' The merchants of the
earth will weep and mourn over her, for no one will buy
12 their cargoes any more—cargoes of gold, silver, precious
stones, pearls, fine linen, purple, silk, and scarlet, all
kinds of citron wood, all kinds of objects of ivory and
13 costly wood, bronze, iron, and marble, and cinnamon,
spices, incense, perfume, frankincense, wine, olive oil,
flour, wheat, cattle, sheep, horses, carriages, slaves—and
14 human lives! The fruit of your soul's desire is gone, your
luxury and splendor have perished, and people will never
15 find them again. The dealers in these things, who had
grown rich from their trade with her, for fear of her torture will stand a long way off, weeping and mourning,
16 and say, 'Alas! Alas for the great city that was dressed in
fine linen, purple, and scarlet, and glittered with gold,
17 precious stones, and pearls, for in a single hour this vast
wealth has been destroyed!' All navigators and all who
18 travel by sea, sailors and sea-faring men, stood a long
way off and cried out when they saw the smoke from her
19 burning, 'What city was like the great city?' They threw
dust on their heads and wept and mourned, crying out,
'Alas! Alas for the great city, where all who had ships
on the sea grew rich through her extravagance! For in a
20 single hour she has been destroyed!' Gloat over her,

heaven! and all you people of God, apostles, and prophets, for God has avenged you upon her!"

Then a mighty angel caught up a stone like a great 21 millstone and threw it into the sea, saying,

"With such violence will Babylon the great city be hurled to destruction and never be seen again! The sound 22 of harpists and musicians, flute-players, and trumpeters will never be heard in you again. No craftsman of any kind will ever be found in you again, no sound of the millstone will ever be heard in you again; no light of 23 any lamp will ever shine in you again; no voice of bride or bridegroom will ever be heard in you again. For your merchants were the great men of the earth; by your magic 24 all the heathen have been led astray, and in you was found the blood of prophets, God's people, and all who have been slaughtered on the earth."

After that I heard what sounded like the loud shout of 19 a great multitude in heaven saying,

"Praise the Lord! Salvation, glory, and power belong to our God, for his judgments are sound and upright. For 2 he has passed judgment upon the great idolatress who corrupted the earth with her idolatry, and he has avenged the blood of his slaves upon her!"

Then they said again,   3

"Praise the Lord! For smoke will go up from her forever and ever!"

Then the twenty-four elders and the four animals fell 4 down and worshiped God who was seated upon the throne.

"Amen!" they said, "Praise the Lord!"

And there came a voice from the throne, saying,   5

"Praise our God, all you slaves of his, high and low, who fear him!"

Then I heard what sounded like the shout of a great 6 multitude and the noise of many waters and the sound of mighty thunders, saying,

"Praise the Lord; for the Lord our God, the Almighty now reigns!"

THE NEW JERUSALEM, 21:1–4, 9—22:4

21 Then I saw a new heaven and a new earth, for the first heaven and the first earth had passed away, and there was
2 no longer any sea. And I saw the new Jerusalem, the holy city, come down out of heaven from God, like a bride
3 dressed and ready to meet her husband. I heard a loud voice from the throne say,

"See! God's dwelling is with men, and he will live
4 with them. They will be his people and God himself will be with them, and he will wipe every tear from their eyes. There will be no death any longer, nor any grief or crying or pain. The old order has passed away."

9 Then one of the seven angels who had the seven bowls full of the seven last plagues came and spoke to me.

"Come," he said, "I will show you the bride, the wife of the Lamb."

10 He carried me away in a trance to a great, high mountain, and showed me Jerusalem, the holy city, coming down out of heaven from God, in all the glory of God.
11 It shone with a radiance like that of some very precious
12 stone, like jasper, clear as crystal. It had a great, high wall with twelve gates, and twelve angels at the gates, which had carved upon them the names of the twelve
13 tribes of the children of Israel. There were three gates on the east, three gates on the north, three gates on
14 the south, and three gates on the west. The wall of the city had twelve foundation stones, and on them were the
15 twelve names of the Lamb's twelve apostles. The angel who talked with me had a gold measuring rod, with
16 which to measure the city and its gates and wall. The city was a square, its length the same as its breadth. He measured the city with his rod, and it was 12,000 furlongs. Its length, breadth, and height were the same.
17 He measured the wall and it was about 144 cubits (216 feet), as men measure, for that was the way the angel
18 measured. The material of the wall was jasper, but the
19 city was pure gold, as transparent as glass. The foundation stones of the wall of the city were ornamented with

[491]

all kinds of precious stones. The first foundation stone was jasper, the second sapphire, the third chalcedony, the fourth emerald, the fifth sardonyx, the sixth sardius, 20 the seventh chrysolite, the eighth beryl, the ninth topaz, the tenth chrysoprase, the eleventh jacinth, the twelfth amethyst. The twelve gates were twelve-pearls; each 21 gate made of a single pearl. The principal street of the city was pure gold, as transparent as glass. I saw no tem- 22 ple in it, for the Lord God Almighty and the Lamb are its temple. The city does not need the sun nor the moon 23 to shine in it, for the glory of God lighted it, and the Lamb is its lamp. The heathen will walk by its light. 24 The kings of the earth will bring their splendor to it. Its 25 gates will never be shut by day—for there will be no night there—and they will bring the splendor and the 26 wealth of the heathen into it. Nothing unclean will 27 ever enter it, nor anyone who indulges in abominable practices and falsehoods, but only those who are written in the Lamb's book of life. Then he showed me a river of 22 living water, clear as crystal, which issued from the throne of God and of the Lamb, and ran through the mid- 2 dle of the principal street of the city. On both sides of the river grew the tree of life. It bore twelve kinds of fruit, yielding a different kind each month, and its leaves were a cure for the heathen. There will no longer be any- 3 thing that is accursed. The throne of God and of the Lamb will be in the city, and his slaves will worship him; they will see his face, and his name will be on their 4 foreheads. There will no longer be any night and they will have no need of lamplight or sunlight, for the Lord God will shine on them, and they will reign forever and ever.

THE LETTER TO THE HEBREWS
· · ·

The later years of the first century found the churches generally composed largely of Christians of the second generation who had inherited their faith and too often had little real sense of its peculiar worth. Apathy and indifference were their worst failings, and when the collision with the empire over emperor worship threatened them with persecution, they were in no condition to meet it. They needed to be convinced of the supreme values of the Christian religion and experience, to steady them for the trials of the hour.

It was to do this that the Letter to the Hebrews was written. It was sent by some great unknown to the Christians of Rome, whom it sought to rouse from apathy not only to renewed devotion but to the leadership among the churches. The Roman congregation ought, in view of its age and its apostolic teachers, Paul and Peter, to be teaching the lesser Christian groups, and to this great task the writer of the epistle seeks to stir them.

He establishes the worth of the Christian religion by comparing it point by point with Judaism, and showing how greatly the new faith surpasses the old. In doing this he employs the allegorical method of interpretation, which had long been popular with Greek and Jewish thinkers. He puts his message in the form of a letter in imitation of the Pauline letter type, but it reads more like a great oration, and in sustained rhetorical power it is unsurpassed in the New Testament.

THE FULNESS AND SPLENDOR OF THE NEW REVELATION, 1:1–4

It was little by little and in different ways that God 1
spoke in old times to our forefathers through the prophets, but in these latter days he has spoken to us in a Son, 2
whom he had destined to possess everything, and
through whom he had made the world. He is the reflec- 3
tion of God's glory, and the representation of his being,
and bears up the universe by his mighty word. He has
effected man's purification from sin, and has taken his
seat on high at the right hand of God's Majesty, showing 4
himself to be as much greater than the angels as his title
is superior to theirs.

THE PERIL OF REJECTING IT, 2:1–4

This is why we must give the very closest attention to 2
the message we have heard, to keep from ever losing our
hold upon it. For if the message delivered by angels 2
proved to be authentic, and every violation or neglect
of it led to a corresponding penalty, how can we es- 3
cape if we pay no attention to such a salvation as
this? It was first proclaimed by the Lord himself, and it
was guaranteed to us by those who heard him, while 4
God himself corroborated their testimony with signs,
portents, and various wonders, and by impartations of
the holy Spirit when he saw fit.

CHRIST THE BRINGER OF THE NEW REVELATION, SUPERIOR TO MOSES, THE BRINGER OF THE OLD, 3:1–6

Therefore, my fellow-Christians, who have likewise 3
heard the heavenly invitation, observe how faithful
Jesus, the commissioner and high priest of our religion,
has been to the God who appointed him, just as Moses 2
was, in all the house of God. For Jesus is entitled to as 3
much more honor than Moses as the builder of a house is
than the house he builds. For every house has a builder, 4
and the builder of the universe is God. Now the faithful- 5
ness of Moses in all the house of God was that of a serv-

ant, in faithfully repeating what he was told to say;
6 but Christ's faithfulness was that of a son set over the house of God. And we are that house, if we keep up our courage and our triumphant hope to the very end.

CHRIST OUR GREAT HIGH PRIEST, 7:26–28

7 Such a high priest we needed—godly, blameless, unstained, removed from sinful men and raised above the
27 very heavens; who does not need, as the old high priests did, to offer sacrifices every day, first for his own sins and then for those of the people—for this last he has done
28 once for all, in offering up himself. For the Law appoints to the high priesthood men full of imperfection; but this utterance about the making of the oath, which came long after the Law, appoints a son, fully qualified to be high priest forever.

HIS HEAVENLY MINISTRY, 8:1–7

8 Now the main point in what I am saying is this: We have such a high priest as this, and he has taken his seat
2 in heaven at the right hand of God's Majesty, to officiate as priest in the sanctuary and in that true tent of worship
3 which not man but the Lord himself set up. But every high priest is appointed to offer gifts and sacrifices, and so this high priest also must have some sacrifice to offer.
4 Further, if he were still on earth, he would not be a priest at all, for there are priests enough provided to offer the
5 gifts the Law prescribes—though the service they engage in is only a shadow and imitation of that in heaven. For when Moses was going to make the tent of worship he was warned, "Be sure to make it all just like the pattern
6 you were shown on the mountain." But, as it is, the priestly service to which Christ has been appointed is as much better than the old as the agreement established by him and the promises on which it is based are superior
7 to the former ones. For if that first agreement had been perfect, there would have been no occasion for a second one.

THEY MUST HOLD FAST TO THEIR RELIGION, AND
REMEMBER THEIR HEROIC PAST, 10:19-36

Since then, brothers, we have free access to the sanctu- 10
ary through the blood of Jesus, by the new, living way 20
which he has opened for us, through the curtain, that is,
his physical nature, and since in him we have a great 21
priest set over the house of God, let us draw near to God 22
in sincerity of heart and with perfect faith, with our
hearts cleansed from the sense of sin, and our bodies
washed with clean water. Let us hold unwaveringly to 23
the hope that we profess, for he who has given us his
promise may be trusted. By observing one another, let 24
us arouse ourselves to rival one another's love and good
deeds. Let us not neglect meeting together as some do, 25
but let us encourage one another, all the more as you can
see that the great Day is coming nearer.

For if we choose to go on sinning after we have so 26
fully learned the truth, there is no sacrifice left to be
offered for our sins, but only the dreadful prospect of 27
judgment and that blazing indignation which is to devour God's enemies. Anyone who breaks the Law of 28
Moses is put to death without any show of pity, on the
evidence of only two or three witnesses. How much 29
worse a punishment do you think will anyone deserve
who tramples the Son of God underfoot, and treats as
worthless the blood of the agreement by which he has
been purified, and outrages God's spirit of mercy? For we 30
know who it is that has said,
"Vengeance belongs to me! I will pay back!"
and in another place,
"The Lord will be the judge of his people!"
It is a fearful thing to fall into the hands of the living 31
God!

But you must remember those early days when after 32
you had received the light you had to go through a great
struggle with persecution, sometimes being actually ex- 33
posed as a public spectacle to insults and violence, and
sometimes showing yourselves ready to share the lot of
those in that condition. For you showed sympathy with 34

those who were in prison, and you put up with it cheerfully when your property was taken from you, for you knew that you had in yourselves a greater possession 35 that was lasting. You must not lose your courage, for it 36 will be richly rewarded, but you will need endurance if you are to carry out God's will and receive the blessing he has promised.

FAITH AND ITS HEROES, 11:1—12:2

11 Faith means the assurance of what we hope for; it is 2 our conviction about things that we cannot see. For it was by it that the men of old gained God's approval.

3 It is faith that enables us to see that the universe was created at the command of God, so that the world we see 4 did not simply arise out of matter. Faith made Abel's sacrifice greater in the sight of God than Cain's; through faith he gained God's approval as an upright man, for God himself approved his offering, and through faith 5 even when he was dead he still spoke. Faith caused Enoch to be taken up from the earth without experiencing death; he could not be found, because God had taken him up. For before he was taken up there is evidence 6 that he pleased God, but without faith it is impossible to please him; for whoever would approach God must have faith in his existence and in his willingness to re- 7 ward those who try to find him. Faith led Noah, when he was warned by God of things no one then saw, in obedience to the warning to build an ark in which to save his family, and by such faith he condemned the world, and came to possess that uprightness which faith 8 produces. Faith enabled Abraham to obey when God summoned him to leave his home for a region which he was to have for his own, and to leave home without 9 knowing where he was going. Faith led him to make a temporary home as a stranger in the land he had been promised, and to live there in his tents, with Isaac and 10 Jacob, who shared the promise with him. For he was looking forward to that city with the sure foundations, 11 designed and built by God. Faith made even Sarah her-

self able to have a child, although she was past the time
of life for it, because she thought that he who had made
the promise would keep it. And so from one man, for ₁₂
any prospect of descendants as good as dead, there sprang
a people in number like the stars in the heavens or the
countless sands on the seashore.

All these people lived all their lives in faith, and died ₁₃
without receiving what had been promised; they only
saw it far ahead and welcomed the sight of it, recognizing
that they themselves were only foreigners and strangers
here on earth. For men who recognize that show that ₁₄
they are in search of a country of their own. And if it ₁₅
had been the country from which they had come to
which their thoughts turned back, they would have
found an opportunity to return to it. But, as it is, their ₁₆
aspirations are for a better, a heavenly country! That is
why God is not ashamed to be called their God, for he
has prepared a city to receive them.

Faith enabled Abraham, when he was put to the test, ₁₇
to offer Isaac as a sacrifice. He who had accepted God's
promises was ready to sacrifice his only son, of whom he ₁₈
had been told, "Your posterity is to arise through Isaac!"
For he believed that God was able to raise men even from ₁₉
the dead, and from the dead he did indeed, to speak
figuratively, receive him back. Faith enabled Isaac to ₂₀
bequeath to Jacob and Esau blessings that were still to
be. Faith made Jacob when he was dying give a blessing ₂₁
to each of Joseph's sons, and bow in worship even while
leaning on his staff. Faith inspired Joseph when he was ₂₂
dying to tell of the future migration of the Israelites, and
to give instructions about his own body. Faith led ₂₃
Moses' parents to hide him for three months after his
birth, because they saw that he was a beautiful child and
they would not respect the edict of the king. Faith ₂₄
made Moses, when he was grown up, refuse to be known
as a son of Pharaoh's daughter, for he preferred sharing ₂₅
the hardships of God's people to a short-lived enjoyment
of sin, and thought such contempt as the Christ endured ₂₆
was truer wealth than the treasures of Egypt, for he was

[498]

27 looking forward to the coming reward. Faith made him
leave Egypt, unafraid of the king's anger, for he per-
28 severed as though he saw him who is unseen. Faith made
him institute the Passover and splash the blood upon the
doorposts, to keep the angel that destroyed the firstborn
29 from touching them. Faith enabled them to cross the
Red Sea as though it were dry land, although the Egyptians when they tried to follow them across it were
30 drowned. Faith made the walls of Jericho fall, after they
31 had marched around them each day for seven days. Faith
saved Rahab the prostitute from being destroyed with
those who disobeyed God, because she had given a friend-
ly welcome to the scouts.
32   And why should I go on? For my time would fail me
if I told of Gideon, Barak, Sampson, Jephthah, David,
33 Samuel, and the prophets, who by their faith conquered
kingdoms, attained uprightness, received new promises,
34 shut the mouths of lions, put out furious fires, escaped
death by the sword, found strength in their time of weakness, proved mighty in war, put foreign armies to flight.
35 Women had their dead restored to them by resurrection.
Others endured torture, and refused to accept release,
36 that they might rise again to the better life. Still others
had to endure taunts and blows, and even fetters and
37 prison. They were stoned to death, they were tortured
to death, they were sawed in two, they were killed with
the sword. Clothed in the skins of sheep or goats, they
were driven from place to place, destitute, persecuted,
38 misused—men of whom the world was not worthy,
wandering in deserts, mountains, caves, and holes in the
ground.
39   Yet though they all gained God's approval by their
faith, they none of them received what he had promised,
40 for God had resolved upon something still better for us,
that they might not reach the fulfilment of their hopes
except with us.
12   Therefore, let us too, with such a crowd of witnesses
about us, throw off every impediment and the entangle-
ment of sin, and run with determination the race for

which we are entered, fixing our eyes upon Jesus, our ₂
leader and example in faith, who in place of the happiness
that belonged to him, submitted to a cross, caring nothing for its shame, and has taken his seat at the right hand
of the throne of God.

WARNING AGAINST MORAL FAILURE, 12:14–17

Try to be at peace with everyone, and strive for that ₁₂
consecration without which no one can see the Lord. Be ₁₅
careful that no one fails to gain God's favor, or some
poisonous root may come up to trouble and contaminate
you all—some immoral or godless person like Esau, who ₁₆
sold his very birthright for one single meal. For you ₁₇
know how, when he afterward wished to claim the blessing, he was refused it, although he begged for it with
tears, for he had no opportunity to repent of what he had
done.

FINAL CONTRAST OF THE OLD REVELATION WITH THE NEW, 12:18–29

For it is no tangible blazing fire that you have come ₁₂
up to, no blackness and darkness and storm, no trumpet ₁₉
blast and voice whose words made those who heard them
beg to be told no more, for they could not bear the order, ₂₀
"Even a wild animal, if it touches the mountain, must
be stoned to death," and so awful was the sight that ₂₁
Moses said, "I am aghast and appalled!" But you have ₂₂
come up to Mount Zion, to the city of the living God,
the heavenly Jerusalem, to countless angels, to the ₂₃
solemn gathering of all God's elder sons, enrolled as
citizens in heaven, to a judge who is the God of all, to
the spirits of upright men now at last enjoying the fulfilment of their hopes, to Jesus the negotiator of a new ₂₄
agreement, and to sprinkle blood that speaks more
powerfully than even Abel's. Take care not to refuse to ₂₅
listen to him who is speaking. For if they could not
escape because they would not listen to him who warned
them here on earth, how much less can we, who reject
him who is from heaven! Then his voice shook the earth, ₂₆

but now his promise is, "But once more I will make not
27 only the earth but the very heaven to tremble!" Now the words "But once more" indicate the final removal of all that is shaken, as only created, leaving only what is un-
28 shaken to be permanent. Let us, therefore, be thankful that the kingdom given to us cannot be shaken, and so please God by worshiping him with reverence and awe;
29 for our God is a consuming fire.

GENERAL EXHORTATIONS, 13:1–16

13   Your love for the brotherhood must continue. Do not forget to be hospitable to strangers, for by being so some,
3 without knowing it, have had angels as their guests. Remember those who are in prison as though you were in prison with them, and those who are ill-treated as being
4 yourselves liable to the same trials. Marriage should be respected by everyone, and the marriage relation kept sacred, for vicious and immoral people God will punish.
5 You must not be avaricious; you must be content with what you have, for God himself has said, "I will never
6 let go of you or desert you!" So that we can confidently say,
> "The Lord is my helper; I will not be afraid.
> What can men do to me?"

7   Do not forget your former leaders, the men who brought you God's message. Remember how they ended their lives and imitate their faith.

8   Jesus Christ is the same today that he was yesterday,
9 and he will be so forever. You must not be carried away with strange varieties of teaching. The true way to steadfastness of heart is through God's mercy, not through scruples about food, which have never done
10 their adherents any good. Our altar is one at which those
11 who serve the tent of worship have no right to eat. For the bodies of the animals whose blood is taken into the sanctuary by the high priest are burned outside the
12 camp. And so Jesus too, in order to purify the people by
13 his blood, suffered death outside the city gate. Let us, therefore, go out to him, outside the camp, sharing the

contempt that he endured, for we have no permanent city here on earth, but we are in search of the city that is to 14 come. In his name let us continually offer praise as our 15 sacrifice to God—the utterance of lips that glorify God's name. But do not forget to be helpful and generous, for 16 that is the kind of sacrifice that pleases God.

THE BENEDICTION, 13:20, 21

May God, the giver of peace, who brought back from 13 the dead our Lord Jesus, who through the blood by which he ratified the everlasting agreement has become the great shepherd of the sheep, fit you by every blessing to 21 do his will, and through Jesus Christ carry out in us what will please him. To him be glory forever and ever. Amen.

THE FIRST LETTER OF PETER
· · ·

The collision with emperor worship made the Christians of Domitian's day acutely conscious of persecution. How was it to be met? One might submit to it most heroically and even die for the faith, yet do it with such inward bitterness and resentment as to make the last hard battle not a victory but a defeat.

This was the weakness of the Revelation. With all its magnificent faith, it had borrowed from the old prophets their vindictive hatred of the persecuting state, and gloated over the fate in store for its new Babylon, the Roman Empire. If such counsels were to prevail, the church would become a seditious and revolutionary group within the Roman world, and while it might unsettle the empire, it would lose its own soul.

Hebrews had called upon the Roman church to become the teacher of the churches, and it was Roman Christianity that now spoke to the churches of all Asia Minor on the true Christian attitude in persecution. But a great name was necessary, if the words of the prophet of Ephesus, who had written in the name of Christ himself, were to be gainsaid. And the Roman church had such names in those of the two apostles who had labored there, Paul and Peter. It was the custodian of their tombs and memories, and from the ancient point of view this entitled it to be their spokesman too. The collected letters of Paul were by this time well known, but the name of Peter might still be used by the church which

*had witnessed his end, to enforce so manifest a reasser-
tion of apostolic teaching.*

*It was in this way that I Peter came to be written,
about A.D. 94, by a Roman Christian, in the name of
the apostle, to the churches of Asia Minor. They must
be impressively reminded of the old sound Christian way
of obedience to the state, respect for the emperor, and love
even for one's enemies. And this is why Paul's influence is so marked in I Peter, for his recently published
letters formed the pattern for it.*

. . .

THE SALUTATION, 1:1, 2

Peter, an apostle of Jesus Christ, to those who are 1
scattered as foreigners over Pontus, Galatia, Cappadocia,
Asia, and Bithynia, whom God the Father has chosen 2
and predestined by the consecration of the Spirit to be
obedient to Jesus Christ, and to be sprinkled with his
blood; God bless you and give you perfect peace.

THE PRECIOUSNESS OF THE CHRISTIAN HOPE, 1:3-9

Blessed be the God and Father of our Lord Jesus 1
Christ! In his great mercy he has caused us to be born
anew to a life of hope through Jesus Christ's resurrection
from the dead, and to an imperishable, unsullied, and un- 4
fading inheritance, which is kept safe for you in heaven,
and you by God's power are being protected through 5
faith to receive a salvation that is now ready to be disclosed at the last time. Rejoice over this, although just 6
now perhaps distressed by various trials; they are to 7
show that your faith when tested is found to be more
precious than gold, which though it is perishable is
tested with fire, and they will bring you praise, glory,
and honor when Jesus Christ is revealed. You must love 8
him, though you have not seen him, but since you believe
in him though you do not now see him, rejoice with

9 triumphant, unutterable joy to attain the goal of faith, the salvation of your souls.

THE CHRISTIAN'S DUTIES IN THE WORLD AND IN THE STATE, 2:11–25

2 Dear friends, I beg you, as aliens and exiles here, not to indulge the physical cravings that are at war with the
12 soul. Live upright lives among the heathen, so that even if they charge you with being evil-doers, they may from observing the uprightness of your conduct come to praise God on the Day of Judgment.

13 Submit to all human authority, for the Master's sake;
14 to the emperor, as supreme, and to governors, as sent by him to punish evil-doers, and to encourage those who do
15 right. For it is the will of God that by doing right you should silence the ignorant charges of foolish people.
16 Live like free men, only do not make your freedom an
17 excuse for doing wrong, but be slaves of God. Treat everyone with respect. Love the brotherhood, be reverent to God, respect the emperor.

18 You servants must be submissive to your masters and perfectly respectful to them; not only to those who are kind and considerate, but also to those who are unreason-
19 able. For God approves a man if from a sense of duty he
20 endures suffering unjustly inflicted—for what credit is there in your enduring being beaten for doing wrong? But if you endure suffering for doing what is right, you
21 have God's approval. That is the life to which you have been called, for Christ himself suffered for you, leaving you an example so that you might follow his footsteps.
22 He committed no sin, and deceit was never on his lips.
23 He was abused but he did not retort. He suffered but he did not threaten, but committed his case to him who
24 judges justly. He carried the burden of our sins in his own body on the cross, in order that we might die to sin and live for uprightness. By his wounds you have been
25 healed. For you were astray like sheep, but now you have returned to the shepherd and guardian of your souls.

HIS DUTIES IN THE CHURCH, 4:7-11

But the end of all things is near. Be serious and col- 4
lected, therefore, and pray. Above all keep your love for 8
one another strong, because love covers up a host of sins.
Be ungrudgingly hospitable to one another. Whatever the 9
endowment God has given you, use it in service to one 10
another, like good dispensers of God's varied mercy. If 11
one preaches, let him do it like one who utters the words
of God; if one does some service, let him do it as with
strength which God supplies, so that in everything God
may be glorified through Jesus Christ. To him belong
glory and dominion forever and ever. Amen.

THE ENDURANCE OF PERSECUTION, 4:12—5:11

Dear friends, do not be surprised that a test of fire is 4
being applied to you, as though a strange thing were
happening to you, but be glad that you are in a measure 13
sharing the sufferings of the Christ, so that when his
glory is revealed you may be triumphantly happy. If you 14
are being abused for the sake of Christ, you are blessed,
because the glorious Spirit of God is resting upon you.
For no one of you must suffer as a murderer or thief or 15
criminal or revolutionist, but if a man suffers for being a 16
Christian, he must not be ashamed of it, but must do
honor to God through that name. For the time has come 17
for the judgment to begin with the household of God,
and if it begins with us, what will be the end of those
who refuse God's good news? If it is hard for the upright 18
man to be saved, what will become of the godless and sinful? Therefore, those who suffer by the will of God must 19
intrust their souls to a Creator who is faithful, and continue to do what is right.

I appeal therefore to those who are elders among you; 5
I am their brother-elder and a witness to what the Christ
suffered, and I am to share in the glory that is to be revealed—be shepherds of the flock of God that is among 2
you, not as though it were forced upon you but of your
own free will, and not from base love of gain but freely,

3 and not as tyrannizing over those in your charge but proving models for the flock; and when the chief shep-
4 herd appears, you will receive the glorious wreath that
5 will never fade. You younger men must show deference to the elders. And you must all clothe yourselves in humility toward one another, for God opposes the proud,
6 but shows mercy to the humble. Submit humbly, therefore, to God's mighty hand, so that he may in due time
7 raise you up. Throw all your anxiety upon him, for he
8 cares for you. Be calm and watchful. Your opponent the devil is prowling about like a roaring lion, wanting to
9 devour you. Resist him and be strong in the faith, for you know that your brotherhood all over the world is
10 having the same experience of suffering. And God, the giver of all mercy, who through your union with Christ has called you to his eternal glory, after you have suffered a little while will himself make you perfect, stead-
11 fast, and strong. His be the dominion forever. Amen.

THE LETTER OF JAMES
. . .

The ancient world was full of preachers. They spoke at street corners or in lecture halls, in synagogues or in private houses. The Stoic street-preacher would seek to reach and hold his little crowd with easy, animated talk—apostrophe, dialogue, invective, anecdote—urging them to fortitude and self-control, and kindling their moral sense.

There is so much about preaching in the New Testament that it is not strange that at least one of its books is a sermon. The ancient preacher was less concerned to present a logical discourse on a single theme than he was to help everyone in his little audience to a better life. And so the ancient sermon was varied, almost miscellaneous, in its composition, aiming always to give moral stimulus of some kind to everyone who heard it.

James is such an early sermon—Christian of course, but touched with the vivacity of the Greek preaching. It is animated, interesting, searching, intensely practical, mingling scorn and humor with tenderness and moral passion. And it was so good that it was eventually published, addressed to "the twelve tribes that are scattered over the world," that is, to Christians everywhere, under the name of James, the "slave of God," of whom nothing is known.

There is something very modern about the Letter of James. Its keen interest in democracy, philanthropy, and social justice strikes a responsive chord in our times.

[508]

*The preacher's simplicity and directness, his impatience
with cant and sham, and his satirical skill in exposing
them, his noble advocacy of the rights of labor and his
clear perception of the sterling Christian virtues that
were to win the world justify the place of honor his sermon has in the New Testament.*

. . .

THE VALUE OF TRIAL, 1:12–18

1   Blessed is the man who endures trial, for when he
stands the test, he will be given the crown of life, which
13 God has promised to those who love him. No one should
think when he is tempted that his temptation comes
from God, for God is incapable of being tempted by what
14 is evil, and he does not tempt anyone. When anyone is
tempted, it is by his own desire that he is enticed and al-
15 lured. Then desire conceives and gives birth to sin, and
16 when sin is mature, it brings forth death. Do not be mis-
17 led, my dear brothers. Every good gift and every perfect
present is from heaven, and comes down from the Father
of the heavenly lights, about whom there is no variation
18 of changing shadow. Of his own accord he brought us
into being through the message of truth, so that we
might be a kind of first-fruits among his creatures.

QUICK TO HEAR, SLOW TO SPEAK, 1:19–27

1   You must understand this, my dear brothers. Everyone must be quick to hear, slow to speak, slow to be
20 angry, for men's anger does not produce the uprightness
21 God wishes. So strip yourselves of everything that soils
you, and of every evil growth, and in a humble spirit let
the message that has the power to save your souls be
22 planted in your hearts. Obey the message; do not merely
23 listen to it, and deceive yourselves. For anyone who
merely listens to the message without obeying it is like
a man who looks in a mirror at the face that nature gave
24 him, and then goes off and immediately forgets what he

looked like. But whoever looks at the faultless law that 25 makes me free and keeps looking, so that he does not just listen and forget, but obeys and acts upon it, will be blessed in what he does. If anyone thinks he is religious, 26 and does not bridle his tongue, but deceives himself, his religious observances are of no account. A religious observance that is pure and stainless in the sight of God the Father is this: to look after orphans and widows in their trouble, and keep one's self unstained by the world.

THE DUTY OF IMPARTIALITY, 2:1–13

My brothers, do you try to combine faith in our 2 glorious Lord Jesus Christ with acts of partiality? For if 2 a finely dressed man with a gold ring comes into a meeting, and a poor man in shabby clothes comes in also, and 3 you pay attention to the man in the fine clothes and say to him, "Sit here; this is a good place!" and say to the poor man, "Stand up, or sit on the floor at my feet," have you not wavered and shown that your judgments 4 are guided by base motives? Listen, my dear brothers. 5 Has not God chosen the world's poor to be rich in faith, and to possess the kingdom that he promised to those who love him? But you humiliate the poor. Are not the 6 rich your oppressors? Is it not they who drag you into court? Is it not they who slander the noble name you 7 bear? If you really obey the supreme law where the Scrip- 8 ture says, "You must love your neighbor as you do yourself," you are doing right, but if you show partiality, you 9 are committing a sin, and stand convicted before the Law as law breakers. For anyone who obeys the whole of the 10 Law but makes one single slip is guilty of breaking it all. For he who said, "You must not commit adultery," said 11 also, "You must not commit murder." Now if you abstain from adultery, but commit murder, you are still a violator of the Law. You must talk and act like men 12 who expect to be judged by the law that treats men as free. For the merciless will be mercilessly judged; but 13 mercy will triumph over judgment.

THE PRACTICAL SIDE OF FAITH, 2:14-26

2   My brothers, what is the good of a man's saying he has
faith, if he has no good deeds to show? Can faith save
15 him? If some brother or sister has no clothes and has not
16 food enough for a day, and one of you says to them,
"Goodbye, keep warm and have plenty to eat," without
giving them the necessaries of life, what good does it do?
17 So faith by itself, if it has no good deeds to show, is dead.
18 But someone may say, "You have faith, and I good
deeds." Show me your faith without any good deeds,
19 and I will show you my faith by my good deeds. Do you
believe in one God? Very well! So do the demons, and
20 they shudder. But do you want proof, my senseless
friend, that faith without good deeds amounts to noth-
21 ing? Was not our forefather Abraham made upright for
his good deeds, for offering his son Isaac on the altar?
22 You see that in this case faith and good deeds worked
together; faith found its highest expression in good
23 deeds, and so the Scripture came true that says, "Abraham had faith in God, and it was credited to him as up-
24 rightness, and he was called God's friend." You see a
man is made upright by his good deeds and not simply by
25 having faith. Was not even Rahab the prostitute made
upright for her good deeds, in entertaining the scouts and
26 sending them off by a different road? Just as the body
without the spirit is dead, faith is dead without good
deeds.

THE POWER OF PRAYER, 5:13-20

5   If any one of you is in trouble, he should pray. If any
14 one is in good spirits, he should sing a hymn. If any one
is sick, he should call in the elders of the church and have
them pray over him, and pour oil on him in the name of
15 the Lord, and the prayer offered in faith will save the
sick man; the Lord will restore him to health, and if he
16 has committed sins, he will be forgiven. So confess your
sins to one another and pray for one another, so that you
may be cured. An upright man can do a great deal by
17 prayer when he tries. Elijah was a man like us, and he

prayed earnestly that it might not rain, and for three
years and six months there was no rain in the land. Then 18
he prayed again, and the heavens yielded rain and the
earth produced crops. My brothers, if any one of you is 19
led astray from the truth, and someone brings him back,
you may be sure that whoever brings a sinner back from 20
his misguided way will save the man's soul from death,
and cover up a host of sins.

THE GOSPEL AND LETTERS OF JOHN
· · ·

The New Testament was written in Greek. It may be described as the literary precipitate deposited by the Christian movement when it impinged upon the Greek world. It was among the Greeks that the new religion found its readiest acceptance and its largest public. Could its message be stated in terms immediately intelligible to them?

Its earliest written expressions—the gospels and the letters of Paul—were cast in very Jewish forms, unadapted to its real public, the people among whom its future lay. This made it all the more necessary to transplant the gospel into Greek soil and to translate it into Greek terms, if the synagogue was not to be forever the gateway to the church.

The Gospel of John is a supreme effort to meet this demand. It was written early in the second century, by a Greek Christian of Ephesus. It is really more a dialogue than a gospel, and it seeks to relate Jesus not simply to the Jewish nation as its Messiah, but to the whole world, as its Light and Savior. It is a book of a few great religious ideas— Revelation, Incarnation, Regeneration, Communication of Life—which appear in the Prologue and to which the writer returns again and again. Its great words "Light," "Life," "Love," "Truth," "Freedom," are still the rallying cries of mankind.

The ancients thought of John as the Theologian—the

[513]

Divine—among the evangelists, and he did set Christian thought upon the rails on which it ran for centuries. But he was quite as much the mystic as the theologian, and the New Testament contains no other such classics of devotion as the upper-room discourses. The gospel is the charter of the Christian experience; to have known Christ through inner experience matters more than to have seen him in Galilee: "Blessed be those who believe without having seen me!"

Historically less convincing than Mark, ethically less exalted than Matthew, the Gospel of John strikes beyond either of them to the very heart of Christianity, as above all an inner spiritual life, of sonship to God and friendship with Christ.

In the Gospel of John the church appears sharply defined against the world, the synagogue, and the sects. And it was against one of these sects, the Docetists, that the First Epistle of John was directed. They were people who believed Christ too divine to suffer agony and death and thought he must only have seemed to do so. They also claimed special enlightenment, closer fellowship with God, clearer knowledge of truth, and freedom from sin. Their spiritual pretensions and fantastic views made them an unwholesome influence among the Asian churches.

Against them and their claims of superiority John urges the fellowship of love. It is the perfect bond between true Christian hearts. Love is of God and God is love. It is his love that has kindled love in us. In this great emphasis upon the place of love in religion the Johannine writings reach their climax.

THE GOSPEL ACCORDING TO JOHN

THE PROLOGUE, 1:1–18

1 In the beginning the Word existed. The Word was with God, and the Word was divine.

2/3 It was he that was with God in the beginning. Everything came into existence through him, and apart from

4 him nothing came to be. It was by him that life came into existence, and that life was the light of mankind.

5 The light is still shining in the darkness, for the darkness has never put it out.

6 There appeared a man by the name of John, with a

7 message from God. He came to give testimony, to testify to the light, so that everyone might come to believe in it

8 through him. He was not the light; he came to testify to the light.

9 The real light, which sheds light upon everyone, was

10 just coming into the world. He came into the world, and though the world came into existence through him, the

11 world did not recognize him. He came to his home, and

12 his own family did not welcome him. But to all who did receive him and believe in him he gave the right to be-

13 come children of God, owing their birth not to nature nor to any human or physical impulse, but to God.

14 So the Word became flesh and blood and lived for a while among us, abounding in blessing and truth, and we saw the honor God had given him, such honor as an

15 only son receives from his father. (John testified to him and cried out—for it was he who said it—"He who was to come after me is now ahead of me, for he existed before me!")

16 For from his abundance we have all had a share, and

17 received blessing after blessing. For while the Law was given through Moses, blessing and truth came to us

18 through Jesus Christ. No one has ever seen God; it is the divine Only Son, who leans upon his Father's breast, that has made him known.

[515]

THE NEW BIRTH, 3:1-15

Among the Pharisees there was a man named Nico- 3
demus, a leader among the Jews. This man went to Jesus 2
one night, and said to him,

"Master, we know that you are a teacher who has
come from God, for no one can show the signs that you
do, unless God is with him."

Jesus answered him,   3

"I tell you, no one can see the Kingdom of God unless
he is born over again from above!"

Nicodemus said to him,   4

"How can a man be born when he is old? Can he enter
his mother's womb over again and be born?"

Jesus answered,   5

"I tell you, if a man does not owe his birth to water
and spirit, he cannot get into the Kingdom of God.
Whatever owes its birth to the physical is physical, and 6
whatever owes its birth to the Spirit is spiritual. Do not 7
wonder at my telling you that you must be born over
again from above. The wind blows wherever it chooses, 8
and you hear the sound of it, but you do not know where
it comes from or where it goes. That is the way with
everyone who owes his birth to the Spirit."

Nicodemus said to him,   9

"How can that be?"

Jesus answered,   10

"Are you the teacher of Israel and yet ignorant of this? 11
I tell you, we know what we are talking about and we
have seen the things we testify to, yet you all reject our
testimony. If you will not believe the earthly things that 12
I have told you, how can you believe the heavenly things
I have to tell? Yet no one has gone up into heaven except 13
the Son of Man who came down from heaven. And just 14
as Moses in the desert lifted the serpent up in the air, the
Son of Man must be lifted up, so that everyone who be- 15
lieves in him may have eternal life."

GOD IN HIS LOVE SENT CHRIST TO SAVE THE WORLD, 3:16–21

3   For God loved the world so much that he gave his only Son, so that no one who believes in him should be
17 lost, but that they should all have eternal life. For God did not send his Son into the world to pass judgment upon the world, but that through him the world might
18 be saved. No one who believes in him has to come up for judgment. Anyone who does not believe stands condemned already, for not believing in God's only Son.
19 And the basis of the judgment is this, that the light has come into the world, and yet, because their actions were wicked, men have loved the darkness more than the
20 light. For everyone who does wrong hates the light and will not come to it, for fear his actions will be exposed.
21 But everyone who is living the truth will come to the light, to show that his actions have been performed in dependence upon God.

THE DIVINE REVELATION IN CHRIST, 3:31–36

3   He who comes from above is above all others. A son of earth belongs to earth and speaks of earth. He who
32 comes from heaven is above all others. It is to what he has seen and heard that he gives testimony, and yet no one
33 accepts his testimony. Whoever does accept it has there-
34 by acknowledged that God is true. For he whom God has sent speaks God's words, for God gives him his
35 Spirit without measure. The Father loves his Son, and
36 has put everything in his hands. Whoever believes in the Son possesses eternal life, but whoever disobeys the Son will not experience life, but will remain under the anger of God.

THE LIVING WATER, 4:1–42

4   So when the Lord learned that the Pharisees had been told that he was gaining and baptizing more disciples
2 than John—though it was not Jesus himself who baptized
3 them, but his disciples—he left Judea and went back
4 again to Galilee. Now he had to pass through Samaria.

So he came to a town in Samaria called Sychar, near the 5
field that Jacob gave to his son Joseph, and Jacob's spring 6
was there. So Jesus, tired with his journey, sat down just
as he was by the spring. It was about noon. A woman of 7
Samaria came to draw water. Jesus said to her,
"Give me a drink."
For his disciples had gone into the town to buy some 8
food. So the Samaritan woman said to him, 9
"How is it that a Jew like you asks a Samaritan
woman like me for a drink?" For Jews have nothing to 10
do with Samaritans. Jesus answered,
"If you knew what God has to give, and who it is that
said to you, 'Give me a drink,' you would have asked
him, and he would have given you living water."
She said to him, 11
"You have nothing to draw water with, sir, and the
well is deep. Where can you get your living water?
Are you a greater man than our forefather Jacob, who 12
gave us this well, and drank from it himself, with his
sons and his flocks?"
Jesus answered, 13
"Anyone who drinks this water will be thirsty again, 14
but anyone who drinks the water that I will give him
will never be thirsty, but the water that I will give him
will become a spring of water within him, bubbling up
for eternal life."
The woman said to him, 15
"Give me this water, sir, so that I may never be
thirsty, nor have to come all this way to draw water."
He said to her, 16
"Go and call your husband and come back here."
The woman answered, 17
"I have no husband."
Jesus said to her,
"You are right when you say you have no husband, 18
for you have had five husbands and the man you are now
living with is not your husband. What you say is true."
The woman said to him, 19
"I see that you are a prophet, sir. Our forefathers wor- 20

shiped God on this mountain, and yet you Jews say that the place where people must worship God is at Jerusalem."

21 Jesus said to her,
"Believe me, the time is coming when you will worship the Father neither on this mountain nor at Jeru-
22 salem. You worship something you know nothing about; we know what we worship, for salvation comes
23 from the Jews. But a time is coming—it is already here! —when the true worshipers will worship the Father in spirit and sincerity, for the Father wants such worship-
24 ers. God is spirit, and his worshipers must worship him in spirit and in sincerity."

25 The woman said to him,
"I know that the Messiah is coming—he who is called the Christ. When he comes, he will tell us everything!"

26 Jesus said to her,
"I who am talking to you am he!"

27 Just then his disciples came back, and they were surprised to find him talking with a woman, yet no one of them asked him what he wanted or why he was talking
28 with her. So the woman left her pitcher and went back to the town, and said to the people,

29 "Come, here is a man who has told me everything I ever did! Do you suppose he is the Christ?"

30 The people went out of the town to see him.

31 Meanwhile the disciples urged him, saying,
"Master, eat something."

32 But he said to them,
"I have food to eat of which you do not know."

33 So the disciples said to one another,
"Do you suppose that someone has brought him something to eat?"

34 Jesus said to them,
"My food is doing the will of him who has sent me,
35 and finishing his work. Are you not saying, 'Four months more and the harvest will come'? Look, I tell you! Raise your eyes and see the fields, for they are white
36 for harvesting. The reaper is already being paid and

gathering the harvest for eternal life, so that the sower
may be glad with the reaper. For here the saying holds 37
good, 'One sows, another reaps.' I have sent you to reap 38
a harvest on which you have not worked. Other men
have worked and you have profited by their work.''

Many of the Samaritans in that town came to believe 39
in him because of the testimony the woman gave when
she said, "He has told me everything I ever did!" So 40
when the Samaritans came to Jesus, they asked him to
stay with them, and he did stay there two days. And a 41
great many more believed because of what he said, and 42
they said to the woman,
"It is no longer because of your statement that we believe, for we have heard him ourselves, and we know that
he is really the Savior of the world.''

THE BREAD OF LIFE, 6:32–40

Jesus said to them, 6
"I tell you, Moses did not give you the bread out of
heaven, but my Father gives you the bread out of heaven,
for it is God's bread that comes down out of heaven and 33
gives life to the world.''
Then they said to him, 34
"Give us that bread always, sir!"
Jesus said to them, 35
"I am the bread that gives life. No one who comes to
me will ever be hungry, and no one who believes in me
will ever be thirsty. But as I have told you, although 36
you have seen me, you will not believe. All that my 37
Father gives to me will come to me, and I will never
refuse anyone who comes to me, for I have come down 38
from heaven not to do what I please but what pleases
him who has sent me. And the purpose of him who has 39
sent me is this, that I should lose nothing of all that he
has given me, but should raise them to life on the Last
Day. For it is the purpose of my Father that everyone 40
who sees the Son and believes in him shall have eternal
life, and that I shall raise him to life on the Last Day.''

THE LIVING WATER, AND THE LIGHT OF THE WORLD,
7:37—8:12–18

7 Now on the last day, the great day of the festival, Jesus stood up and cried out,

38 "If anyone is thirsty, let him come to me and drink. If anyone believes in me, streams of living water, as the Scripture says, shall flow forth from his heart."

39 He meant by this the Spirit which those who believed in him were to receive—for the Spirit had not yet come,
40 because Jesus had not yet been glorified. So some of the people, when they heard these words, said,
"This is certainly the Prophet!"

41 Others said,
"This is the Christ!"
But they rejoined,

42 "What! Is the Christ to come from Galilee? Do not the Scriptures say that the Christ is to spring from the descendants of David and to come from the village of Bethlehem where David lived?"

43
44 So the people were divided about him, and some of them wanted to arrest him, yet no one laid hands on him.

45 The attendants went back to the high priests and Pharisees, and they said to the attendants,
"Why have you not brought him?"

46 The attendants answered,
"No man ever talked as he does!"

47 The Pharisees answered,

48 "Have you been imposed upon too? Have any of the
49 authorities or of the Pharisees believed in him? But these common people who do not know the Law are doomed!"

50 One of them, Nicodemus, who had previously gone to Jesus, said to them,

51 "Does our Law condemn the accused without first hearing what he has to say, and finding out what he has done?"

52 They answered,
"Are you from Galilee too? Study and you will find that no prophet is to appear from Galilee."

8 Then Jesus spoke to them again and said,

[521]

"I am the light of the world. Whoever follows me will not have to walk in darkness but will have the light of life."

The Pharisees said to him, 13

"You are testifying to yourself. Your testimony is not true."

Jesus answered, 14

"Even if I am testifying to myself, my testimony is true, for I know where I have come from and where I am going; but you do not know where I come from or where I am going. You judge by material standards, but I am 15 judging nobody. But even if I do judge, my decision is 16 just, because I am not by myself, but the Father who sent me is with me. Why, in your own Law it is stated that 17 the testimony of two persons is valid. Here I am testify- 18 ing to myself, and the Father who has sent me testifies to me."

THE GOOD SHEPHERD, 10:1–18, 22–30

"I tell you, any man who does not enter the sheepfold 10 by the door, but climbs over at some other place, is a thief and robber. But the man who enters by the door is 2 the shepherd of the flock. The watchman opens the door 3 to him, and the sheep obey his voice, and he calls to his own sheep and leads them out. When he gets his own 4 flock all out, he goes in front of them, and the sheep follow him, because they know his voice. But they will 5 never follow a stranger but will run away from him, because they do not know the voices of strangers."

This was the figure Jesus used in speaking to them, but 6 they did not understand what he meant by it.

So Jesus said again, 7

"I tell you, I am the door of the sheepfold. All who 8 have come before me are thieves and robbers, but the sheep would not obey them. I am the door. Whoever 9 enters through me will be saved, and will pass in and out and find pasture. A thief comes only to steal and kill and 10 destroy; I have come to let them have life, and to let them have it in abundance. I am the good shepherd. A 11

12 good shepherd will give his life for his sheep. A hired
man who is not a shepherd and does not own the sheep,
when he sees a wolf coming, will leave the sheep and run
away, and the wolf will carry them off and scatter the
13 flock. For he is only a hired man, and does not care about
14 the sheep. I am the good shepherd. I know my sheep
15 and my sheep know me, just as the Father knows me and
I know the Father, and I am giving my life for my sheep.
16 I have other sheep too that do not belong to this fold. I
must lead them too, and they will obey my voice, and
17 they will all become one flock, with one shepherd. This
is why the Father loves me, because I am giving my life,
18 but giving it to take it back again. No one has taken it
from me, but I am giving it of my own accord. I have
power to give it, and I have power to take it back again.
These are the orders I have received from my Father.''
22 That was the time of the Rededication Festival at
23 Jerusalem. It was winter time and Jesus was walking up
and down inside the Temple, in Solomon's Colonnade.
24 So the Jews gathered around him and said to him,
"How much longer are you going to keep us in sus-
pense? If you are really the Christ, tell us so frankly!''
25 Jesus answered,
"I have told you so, and you will not believe it. The
things I have been doing by my Father's authority are
26 my credentials, but you do not believe it because you do
27 not belong to my sheep. My sheep listen to my voice,
28 and I know them and they follow me, and I give them
eternal life, and they shall never be lost, and no one shall
29 tear them out of my hands. What my Father has intrusted to me is of more importance than everything
else, and no one can tear anything out of the Father's
30 hands. The Father and I are one.''

RESURRECTION AND LIFE, 11:17–28

11 When Jesus arrived he found that Lazarus had been
18 buried for four days. Now Bethany is only about two
miles from Jerusalem, and a number of Jews had come out
19 to see Mary and Martha, to condole with them about

their brother. When Martha heard that Jesus was com- 20
ing she went out to meet him, but Mary remained at
home. Martha said to Jesus, 21
"Master, if you had been here, my brother would not
have died! Even now I know that anything you ask God 22
for, he will give you."

Jesus said to her, 23
"Your brother will rise."

Martha said to him, 24
"I know that he will rise at the resurrection, on the
Last Day."

Jesus said to her, 25
"I myself am Resurrection and Life. He who believes
in me will live on, even if he dies, and no one who is 26
alive and believes in me will ever die. Do you believe
that?"

She said to him, 27
"Yes, Master, I do indeed believe that you are the
Christ, the Son of God, who was to come into the
world."

With these words she went and called her sister Mary, 28
whispering to her,
"Here is the Master, asking for you."

THE ANOINTING IN BETHANY, 11:55—12:8

Now the Jewish Passover Festival was approaching 11
and many people went up to Jerusalem from the country,
to purify themselves before the Passover. So they were 56
looking for Jesus there, and asking one another as they
stood in the Temple,
"What do you think? Do you think he will not come
to the festival at all?"

For the high priests and the Pharisees had given orders 57
that anyone who found out where he was should let
them know, so that they might arrest him.

Six days before the Passover Jesus came to Bethany, 12
where Lazarus, whom he had raised from the dead, was
living. They gave a dinner for him there, and Martha 2
waited on them, while Lazarus was at the table with

3 him. And Mary took a pound of choice perfume, very costly, and poured it on Jesus' feet, and then wiped his feet with her hair, and the whole house was filled with
4 the fragrance of the perfume. But Judas Iscariot, one of his disciples, who was going to betray him, said,
5 "Why was this perfume not sold for sixty dollars, and the money given to the poor?"
6 But he did not say this because he cared about the poor, but because he was a thief and when he had charge
7 of the purse he used to take what was put in it. Jesus said,
8 "Let her alone; let her keep it for the day of my funeral, for you always have the poor among you, but you will not always have me."

THE LIGHT OF THE WORLD, 12:20–36, 44–50

12 There were some Greeks among those who had come up to worship at the festival, and they went to Philip,
21 who was from Bethsaida in Galilee, and made this request of him:
"Sir, we want to see Jesus."
22 Philip went and told Andrew, and Andrew and Philip
23 went to Jesus and told him. Jesus answered,
"The time has come for the Son of Man to be glorified.
24 I tell you, unless a grain of wheat falls on the ground and dies, it remains just one grain. But if it dies, it yields a
25 great harvest. Whoever loves his life loses it, and whoever hates his life in this world will preserve it for eternal
26 life. If anyone serves me, he must follow me, and wherever I am found, my servant must be also. If anyone
27 serves me, my Father will show him honor. Now my heart is troubled; what am I to say? Father, save me from this trial! And yet it was for this very purpose that I
28 have come to this trial. Father, honor your own name!"
Then there came a voice from the sky,
"I have honored it, and I will honor it again!"
29 The crowd of bystanders heard it and said it was thunder. Others said,
"It was an angel speaking to him!"

Jesus answered, 30

"It was not for my sake that the voice came, but for 31 yours. The judgment of this world is now in progress. Its evil genius is now to be expelled, and if I am lifted up 32 from the ground, I will draw all men to myself."

He said this to show the kind of death he was going to 33 die. The crowd answered, 34

"We have learned from the Law that the Christ is to remain here forever. So how can you say that the Son of Man must be lifted up? Who is this Son of Man?"

Jesus said to them,

"You will have the light only a little while longer. 35 Go on while you still have the light, so that darkness may not overtake you, for those who go about in the dark do not know where they are going. While you have 36 the light believe in the light, that you may become sons of light."

"Whoever believes in me, believes not in me but in 44 him who has sent me; and whoever sees me, sees him who 45 has sent me. I have come into the world as a light, so that 46 no one who believes in me may have to remain in darkness. If anyone hears my words and disregards them, it is not 47 I that judge him, for I have not come to judge the world but to save the world. Whoever rejects me and refuses to 48 accept my teachings is not without his judge; the very message I have given will be his judge on the Last Day, for I have not spoken on my own account, but the Father 49 who has sent me has himself given me orders what to tell and what to say. And I know his orders mean eternal 50 life. So whatever I say, I say only as the Father has told me."

JESUS WASHES THE DISCIPLES' FEET, 13:1-20, 31-35

Before the Passover Festival began, Jesus knew that **13** the time had come for him to leave this world and go to the Father, but he had loved those who were his own in the world, and he loved them to the last. So at supper— 2 the devil having by this time put the thought of betraying Jesus into the mind of Judas Iscariot, Simon's son—

3 Jesus, fully aware that the Father had put everything into his hands, and that he had come from God and was

4 going back to God, rose from the table, took off his outer

5 clothing, and fastened a towel about his waist. Then he poured water into the basin and began to wash the disciples' feet, wiping them with the towel that was

6 about his waist. So he came to Simon Peter. He said to him,

"Master, are you going to wash my feet?"

7 Jesus answered,

"You cannot understand now what I am doing, but you will learn by and by."

8 Peter said to him,

"I will never let you wash my feet!"

Jesus answered,

"You will have no share with me unless I wash you."

9 Simon Peter said to him,

"Master, wash not only my feet but my hands and my face too!"

10 Jesus said to him,

"Anyone who has bathed only needs to have his feet washed to be altogether clean. And you are already

11 clean—though not all of you." For he knew who was going to betray him; that was why he said, "You are not all of you clean."

12 When he had washed their feet and put on his clothes and taken his place, he said to them again,

13 "Do you understand what I have been doing to you? You call me Teacher and Master, and you are right, for

14 that is what I am. If I then, your Master and Teacher, have washed your feet, you ought to wash one another's

15 feet too. For I have set you an example, in order that you

16 may do what I have done to you. I tell you, no slave is superior to his master, and no messenger is greater than

17 the man who sends him. Now that you have this knowl-

18 edge, you will be blessed if you act upon it. I do not mean all of you; I know whom I have chosen; but let the Scripture be fulfilled:

" 'He who is eating my bread
Has raised his heel against me.'
From now on I will tell you things before they happen, 19
so that when they do happen you may believe that I am
what I say. I assure you, whoever welcomes any mes- 20
senger of mine welcomes me and whoever welcomes me
welcomes him who has sent me."

When he was gone, Jesus said, 31
"Now the Son of Man has been honored, and God has
been honored through him, and God will through himself honor him; he will honor him immediately. My chil- 32
dren, I am to be with you only a little longer. You will 33
look for me, but, as I said to the Jews, where I am going
you cannot follow. I give you a new command: Love 34
one another. Just as I have loved you, you must love one
another. By this they will all know that you are my 35
disciples—by your love for one another."

THE FAREWELL DISCOURSE, 14:1—16:15, 25—17:26

"Your minds must not be troubled; you must believe 14
in God, and believe in me. There are many rooms in my 2
Father's house; if there were not, I would have told you,
for I am going away to make ready a place for you. And 3
if I go and make it ready, I will come back and take you
with me, so that you may be where I am. You know 4
the way to the place where I am going."

Thomas said to him, 5
"Master, we do not know where you are going; how
can we know the way?"

Jesus said to him, 6
"I am Way and Truth and Life. No one can come to
the Father except through me. If you knew me, you 7
would know my Father also. From now on you do know
him and you have seen him."

Philip said to him, 8
"Master, let us see the Father, and it will satisfy us."

Jesus said to him, 9
"Have I been with you so long, and yet you, Philip,
have not recognized me? Whoever has seen me has seen

10 the Father. How can you say, 'Let us see the Father'? Do you not believe that I am in union with the Father and the Father is in union with me? I am not the source of the words that I say to you, but the Father who is united

11 with me is doing these things himself. You must believe that I am in union with the Father and that the Father is in union with me, or else you must believe because of the

12 things themselves. I tell you, whoever believes in me will do such things as I do, and things greater yet, be-

13 cause I am going to the Father. Anything you ask for as followers of mine I will grant, so that the Father may be

14 honored through the Son. I will grant anything you ask me for as my followers.

15 "If you really love me, you will observe my com-

16 mands. And I will ask the Father and he will give you

17 another Helper to be with you always. It is the Spirit of Truth. The world cannot obtain that Spirit, because it does not see it or recognize it; you recognize it because it

18 stays with you and is within you. I am not going to

19 leave you friendless. I am coming back to you. In a little while the world will not see me any more, but you will still see me, because I shall live on, and you will live on

20 too. When that day comes you will know that I am in union with my Father and you are with me and I am

21 with you. It is he who has my commands and observes them that really loves me, and whoever loves me will be loved by my Father, and I will love him and show myself to him."

22 Judas (not Judas Iscariot) said to him,
"Master, how does it happen that you are going to show yourself to us and not to the world?"

23 Jesus answered,
"Anyone who loves me will observe my teaching, and my Father will love him and we will come to him and

24 live with him. No one who does not love me will observe my teaching, and yet the teaching you are listening to is not mine but is that of him who has sent me.

25 "I have told you this while I am still staying with

26 you, but the Helper, the holy Spirit which the Father

will send in my place, will teach you everything and re- mind you of everything that I have told you. I leave you 27 a blessing; I give you my own blessing. I do not give it to you as the world gives. Your minds must not be troubled or afraid. You have heard me say that I am going 28 away and am coming back to you; if you loved me you would be glad that I am going to the Father, for the Father is greater than I. And I have told you of it now 29 before it happens, in order that when it happens you may believe in me. I shall not talk much more with you, for 30 the evil genius of the world is coming. He has nothing in common with me, but he is coming that the world may 31 know that I love the Father and am doing what he has commanded me to do. Come, let us go away.

"I am the true vine, and my Father is the cultivator. 15 Any branch of mine that does not bear fruit he trims 2 away, and he prunes every branch that bears fruit, to make it bear more. You are pruned already because of 3 the teaching that I have given you. You must remain 4 united to me and I will remain united to you. Just as no branch can bear fruit by itself unless it remains united to the vine, you cannot unless you remain united to me. I am the vine, you are the branches. Anyone who re- 5 mains united to me, with me united to him, will be very fruitful, for you cannot do anything apart from me. Anyone who does not remain united to me is thrown 6 away like a branch and withers up, and they gather them and throw them into the fire and burn them. If you re- 7 main united to me and my words remain in your hearts, ask for whatever you please and you shall have it. When 8 you are very fruitful and show yourselves to be disciples of mine, my Father is honored. I have loved you just as 9 the Father has loved me. You must retain my love. If 10 you keep my commands you will retain my love, just as 11 I have observed the Father's commands and retain his love. I have told you all this so that you may have the happiness that I have had, and your happiness may be complete. The command that I give you is to love one an- 12 other just as I have loved you. No one can show greater 13

14 love than by giving up his life for his friends. You are
15 my friends if you do what I command you to do. I do not
call you slaves any longer, for a slave does not know
what his master is doing, but now I call you friends, for
I have made known to you everything that I have learned
16 from my Father. It was not you who chose me, it is I
that have chosen you, and appointed you to go and bear
fruit—fruit that shall be lasting, so that the Father may
grant you whatever you ask him for as my followers.
17   "What I command you to do is to love one another.
18 If the world hates you, remember that it hated me first.
19 If you belonged to the world, the world would love what
was it own. But it is because you do not belong to the
world, but I have selected you from the world, that the
20 world hates you. Remember what I said to you: No
slave is greater than his master. If they have persecuted
me they will persecute you too. If they have observed
21 my teaching, they will observe yours too. But they will
do all this to you on my account, because they do not
22 understand him who sent me. If I had not come and
spoken to them, they would not have been guilty of sin,
23 but as it is, they have no excuse for their sin. Whoever
24 hates me hates my Father also. If I had not done things
before them that no one else ever did they would not be
guilty of sin. But as it is, they have seen both me and my
25 Father, and they have hated us both. But the saying of
their Law, 'They hated me without cause,' must be ful-
26 filled. When the Helper comes whom I will send to you
from the Father—that Spirit of Truth that comes from
27 the Father—he will bear testimony to me, and you must
bear testimony too, because you have been with me from
the first.
16   "I have told you this to keep you from faltering.
2 They will exclude you from their synagogues; why, the
time is coming when anyone who kills you will think he
3 is doing religious service to God. They will do this be-
4 cause they do not know the Father or me. But I have
told you about these things in order that when the time
comes for them to happen, you may remember that I told

you of them. I did not tell you this at first because I was still staying with you. But now I am going away to him ⁵ who sent me, and not one of you asks me where I am going, but your minds are full of sorrow because I have ⁶ told you this. Yet it is only the truth when I tell you ⁷ that it is better for you that I should go away. For if I do not go, the Helper will not come to you, but if I go I will send him to you. When he comes, he will bring ⁸ conviction to the world about sin and uprightness and judgment; about sin, as shown in their not believing in ⁹ me; about uprightness, as shown by my going away to ¹⁰ the Father, where you can no longer see me; and about ¹¹ judgment, as shown by the condemnation of the evil genius of this world. I have much more to tell you, but ¹² you cannot take it in now, but when the Spirit of Truth ¹³ comes, he will guide you into the full truth, for he will not speak for himself but will tell what he hears, and will announce to you the things that are to come. He will ¹⁴ do honor to me, for he will take what is mine and communicate it to you. All that the Father has belongs to ¹⁵ me. That is why I said that he will take what is mine and communicate it to you.

"I have said all this to you in figurative language, but ²⁵ a time is coming when I shall not do so any longer, but will tell you plainly about the Father. When that time ²⁶ comes you will ask as my followers, and I do not promise to intercede with the Father for you, for the Father loves ²⁷ you himself because you love me and believe that I have come from the Father. I did come from the Father and ²⁸ enter the world. Now I am leaving the world again and going back to the Father."

His disciples said, ²⁹

"Why, now you are talking plainly and not speaking figuratively at all. Now we know that you know every- ³⁰ thing and do not need to have anyone ask you questions. This makes us believe that you have really come from God."

Jesus answered, ³¹

"Do you believe that now? Why, a time is coming— ³²

it has already come!—when you will all be scattered to
33 your homes and will leave me alone. And yet I am not
alone, for the Father is with me. I have told you all this,
so that through me you may find peace. In the world
you have trouble; but take courage! I have conquered
the world.''

17   When Jesus had said all this he raised his eyes to
heaven and said,

"Father, the time has come. Do honor to your son,
2 that your son may do honor to you, just as you have done
in giving him power over all mankind, so that he may
3 give eternal life to all whom you have given him. And
eternal life means knowing you as the only true God,
4 and knowing Jesus your messenger as Christ. I have done
honor to you here on earth, by completing the work
5 which you gave me to do. Now, Father, do such honor
to me in your presence as I had done me there before the
world existed.

6   "I have revealed your real self to the men you gave me
from the world. They were yours and you gave them to
7 me, and they have obeyed your message. Now at last
they know that all that you have given me comes from
8 you, for I have given them the truths that you gave me,
and they have accepted them and been convinced that I
9 came from you, and they believe that you sent me. I
have a request to make for them. I make no request for
the world, but only for those whom you have given me,
10 for they are yours—all that is mine is yours and what is
11 yours is mine—and they have done me honor. Now I am
to be no longer in this world, but they are to remain in
the world, while I return to you. Holy Father, keep
them by your power which you gave me, so that they
12 may be one just as we are. As long as I was with them I
kept them by your power which you gave me, and I protected them, and not one of them was lost (except the
one who was destined to be lost), so that what the Scrip-
13 ture says might come true. But now I am coming to you,
and I say this here in this world in order that they may
have the happiness that I feel fully realized in their own

hearts. I have given them your message, and the world 14
has come to hate them, for they do not belong to the
world any more than I belong to the world. I do not ask 15
you to take them away from the world, but to keep them
from evil. They do not belong to the world any more 16
than I belong to the world. Consecrate them by truth. 17
Your message is truth. Just as you sent me to the world, 18
I have sent them to the world. And it is for their sake 19
that I consecrate myself, that they also may be consecrated by truth.

"It is not for them only that I make this request. It is 20
also for those who through their message come to believe
in me. Let them all be one. Just as you, Father, are in 21
union with me and I am with you, let them be in union
with us, so that the world may believe that you sent me.
I have given them the glory that you gave me, so that 22
they may be one just as we are, I in union with them and 23
you with me, so that they may be perfectly unified, and
the world may recognize that you sent me and that you
love them just as you loved me. Father, I wish to have 24
those whom you have given me with me where I am,
to see my glory that you have given me, for you loved
me before the creation of the world. Righteous Father, 25
though the world did not know you, I knew you, and
these men knew that you had sent me. I have made your 26
self known to them and I will do so still, so that the love
which you have had for me may be in their hearts, and I
may be there also."

THE BETRAYAL, 18:1–11

When Jesus had said this, he went out with his dis- 18
ciples to the other side of the Ravine of the Cedars where
there was a garden, and he went into it with his disciples.
Judas who betrayed him also knew the place, for Jesus 2
often met his disciples there. So Judas got out the garri- 3
son and some attendants from the high priests and
Pharisees, and came there with lanterns, torches, and
weapons. Then Jesus, as he knew everything that was 4
going to happen to him, came forward and said to them,

"Who is it you are looking for?"
5 They answered,
"Jesus of Nazareth."
He said to them,
"I am he."
6 Judas who betrayed him was standing among them.
When Jesus said to them, "I am he," they drew back and
7 fell to the ground. Then he asked them again,
"Who is it you are looking for?"
"Jesus of Nazareth."
8 Jesus answered,
"I have told you that I am he, so if you are looking
9 for me, let these men go." This was to fulfil the saying
he had uttered, "I have not lost one of those whom you
have given me."
10 Then Simon Peter, who had a sword with him, drew
it and struck at the high priest's slave and cut off his
11 right ear. The slave's name was Malchus. Then Jesus
said to Peter,
"Put your sword back into the sheath. Shall I not
drink the cup which the Father has offered me?"

JESUS BEFORE THE HIGH PRIEST, 18:19-21

18 Then the high priest questioned Jesus about his dis-
20 ciples and his teaching. Jesus answered,
"I have spoken openly to the world. I have always
taught in synagogues or in the Temple where all the Jews
21 meet together, and I have said nothing in secret. Why do
you question me? Ask those who have heard me what it
was that I said to them. They will know what I have
said."

JESUS BEFORE PILATE, 18:33-38

18 So Pilate went back into the governor's house and
called Jesus and said to him,
"Are you the king of the Jews?"
34 Jesus answered,
"Did you think of that yourself, or has someone else
said it to you about me?"

Pilate answered, 35
"Do you take me for a Jew? Your own people and the
high priests handed you over to me. What offense have
you committed?"
Jesus answered, 36
"My kingdom is not a kingdom of this world. If my
kingdom were a kingdom of this world, my men would
have fought to keep me from being handed over to the
Jews. But as it is, my kingdom has no such origin."
Pilate said to him, 37
"Then you are a king?"
Jesus answered,
"As you say, I am a king. It was for this that I was
born and for this that I came to the world, to give testi-
mony for truth. Everyone who is on the side of truth
listens to my voice."
Pilate said to him, 38
"What is truth!"

THE DEATH OF JESUS, 19:25–30

Near Jesus' cross stood his mother and her sister Mary, 19
the daughter of Clopas, and Mary of Magdala. So Jesus, 26
seeing his mother and the disciple whom he loved stand-
ing near, said to his mother,
"There is your son!"
Then he said to his disciple, 27
"There is your mother!"
And from that time his disciple took her into his
home.
After that, Jesus, knowing that everything was now 28
finished, to fulfil the saying of Scripture, said,
"I am thirsty."
A bowl of sour wine was standing there. So they put 29
a sponge soaked in the wine on a pike and held it to his
lips. When Jesus had taken the wine, he said, 30
"It is finished!"
Then bowing his head he gave up his spirit.

JESUS APPEARS TO MARY, 20:11–18

20 But Mary stood just outside the tomb, weeping. And
12 as she wept she looked down into the tomb, and saw two
angels in white sitting where Jesus' body had been, one
13 at his head and one at his feet. And they said to her,
"Why are you weeping?"
She said to them,
"They have taken my Master away, and I do not know
where they have put him."
14 As she said this she turned around and saw Jesus stand-
15 ing there, but she did not know that it was he. Jesus said
to her,
"Why are you weeping? Who are you looking for?"
She, supposing that he was the gardener, said to him,
"If it was you, sir, that carried him away, tell me
where you have put him, and I will take him away."
16 "Mary!" said Jesus.
She turned and said to him in Hebrew,
"Rabbouni!" which means Master.
17 Jesus said to her,
"You must not cling to me, for I have not yet gone up
to my Father, but go to my brothers and say to them that
I am going up to my Father and your Father, to my God
and your God."
18 Mary of Magdala went and declared to the disciples,
"I have seen the Master!"
and she told them that he had said this to her.

JESUS APPEARS TO THE DISCIPLES, 20:19–31

20 When it was evening on that first day after the Sabbath, and the doors of the house where the disciples met
were locked for fear of the Jews, Jesus came in and stood
among them and said to them,
"Peace be with you!"
20 Then he showed them his hands and his side, and the
21 disciples were full of joy at seeing the Master. Jesus said
to them again,
"Peace be with you! Just as my Father sent me forth
so I now send you."

As he said this he breathed upon them, and said, 22
"Receive the holy Spirit! If you forgive any men's 23
sins, they are forgiven them, and if you fix any men's sins
upon them, they will remain fixed."

But Thomas, one of the Twelve, who was called the 24
Twin, was not with them when Jesus came in. So the rest 25
of the disciples said to him,

"We have seen the Master!"

But he said to them,

"Unless I see the marks of the nails in his hands, and
put my finger into them, and put my hand into his side,
I will never believe it!"

A week after, the disciples were again in the house, 26
and Thomas was with them. Although the doors were
locked, Jesus came in and stood among them, and said,

"Peace be with you!"

Then he said to Thomas, 27

"Put your finger here and look at my hands, and take
your hand and put it in my side, and be no longer unbelieving, but believe!"

Thomas answered him, 28

"My Master and my God!"

Jesus said to him, 29

"Is it because you have seen me that you believe?
Blessed be those who believe without having seen me!"

There were many other signs that Jesus showed before 30
his disciples which are not recorded in this book. But 31
these have been recorded so that you may believe that
Jesus is the Christ, the Son of God, and through believing
you may have life as his followers.

THE FIRST LETTER OF JOHN

GOD IS LIGHT, 1:1-5

It is what existed from the beginning, that we an- 1
nounce; what we have heard, what we have seen with
our own eyes, what we have beheld, and touched with
our hands; it is the very message of life—for life has 2
been revealed, and we have seen it and testify to it and

announce to you that eternal life that was with the
3 Father and has been revealed to us—it is what we have
seen and heard that we announce to you also, so that you
may share our fellowship, for our fellowship is with the
4 Father and with his Son Jesus Christ, and we write this
to you to make your happiness complete.

5   This is the message that we heard from him and announce to you: God is light; there is no darkness in him
at all.

GOD IS LOVE, 3:1–3; 4:7–21

3   Think what love the Father has had for us, in letting
us be called God's children, for that is what we are.
This is why the world does not know what we are—be-
2 cause it has never come to know him. Dear friends, we
are God's children now; it has not yet been disclosed
what we are to be. We know that if he appears, we shall
3 be like him, for we shall see him as he is. And everyone
who possesses this hope in him tries to make himself as
pure as he is.

4   Dear friends, let us love one another, for love comes
from God, and everyone who loves is a child of God and
8 knows God. Whoever does not love does not know God,
9 for God is love. God's love for us has been revealed
in this way—that God has sent his only Son into the
10 world, to let us have life through him. The love consists
not in our having loved God, but in his loving us and
sending his Son as an atoning sacrifice for our sins.

11   Dear friends, if God has loved us so, we ought to love
12 one another. No one has ever seen God; yet if we love
one another, God keeps in union with us and love for
13 him attains perfection in our hearts. This is the way we
know that we keep in union with him and he does with
14 us—because he has given us some of his Spirit. We have
seen and can testify that the Father has sent the Son to
15 be Savior of the world. If anyone acknowledges that
Jesus Christ is the Son of God, God keeps in union with
16 him and he with God. So we know and believe in the
love God has for us.

God is love, and whoever continues to love keeps in union with God, and God with him. Love attains perfection in us, when we have perfect confidence about the Day of Judgment, because here in this world we are living as he lives. There is no fear in love, but perfect love drives out fear. For fear suggests punishment and no one who feels fear has attained perfect love. We love because he loved us first. If anyone says, "I love God," and yet hates his brother, he is a liar; for whoever does not love his brother whom he has seen cannot love God whom he has not seen. This is the command that we get from him, that whoever loves God must love his brother also.

JESUS IS THE CHRIST, 5:1–12

Everyone who believes that Jesus is the Christ is a child of God, and everyone who loves the Father loves those who are his children. This is how we can be sure that we love the children of God: it is by loving God and obeying his commands. For loving God means obeying his commands, and his commands are not burdensome, for every child of God is victorious over the world. Our faith is the victory that has triumphed over the world. For who is there that is victorious over the world except the man who believes that Jesus is the Son of God? It was he, Jesus Christ himself, who came in water and in blood; not in water only, but in water and in blood. The Spirit also testifies to this, for the Spirit is truth. For there are three that testify to it, the Spirit, the water, and the blood, and the three are at one. If we accept the testimony of men, the testimony of God is stronger still; for the value of God's testimony lies in this, that he has testified to his Son. Whoever believes in the Son of God possesses that testimony in his heart. Anyone who will not believe God has made him a liar, for he has refused to believe the testimony that God has borne to his Son. And that testimony is that God has given us eternal life, and that this life is found in his Son. Whoever has the Son has life; whoever has not the Son has not life.

THE LETTERS TO TIMOTHY AND TITUS

· · ·

In the life of the early churches there was clearly more enthusiasm and zeal than organization and system. The thought of the speedy second coming of Christ overshadowed everything. But as time went on and the feeling grew that his expected coming had already been realized in his resurrection and the descent of the Spirit, the need of some regulation of church life came to be felt. Its practical side could no longer be neglected. Church officers must be persons duly qualified. The various groups in the churches must be assigned their several spheres and functions. Efficiency must come through organization.

To secure these ends a Greek follower of Paul, well acquainted with the Acts and the Pauline letters, sometime in the second quarter of the second century wrote the letters to Timothy and Titus. They take the form of letters from Paul to his young lieutenants, telling them how to organize and conduct church work. The ideals they express, however, although in the main sound and timely, are not so much those of a great creative religious personality like Paul as of some lesser but more practical systematizer of his results. They are, in short, the work of a priest, not a prophet.

THE FIRST LETTER TO TIMOTHY

THE TRANSFORMATION OF PAUL, 1:12–17

I thank Christ Jesus our Lord who has given me the 1
strength for it, for thinking me trustworthy and putting
me into his service, though I once used to abuse, perse- 13
cute, and insult him. But he had mercy on me, because
I had acted in ignorance and unbelief, and the blessing 14
of our Lord has been given me in the greatest abundance,
together with faith and love that union with Christ
Jesus brings. It is a trustworthy saying, entitled to the 15
fullest acceptance, that Christ Jesus came into the world
to save sinners. And I am the foremost of them, but God 16
had mercy on me in order that in my case as the foremost,
Christ Jesus might display his perfect patience, as an example to those who would later believe in him and find
eternal life. To the eternal King, immortal and invisible, 17
the one God, be honor and glory forever and ever! Amen.

THE WORTH OF RELIGION AND THE WORK OF THE
MINISTER, 4:6–16

If you point this out to the brothers, you will be a 4
good servant of Christ Jesus, living on the principles of
the faith and the excellent teaching you have had. But 7
let worldly fictions and old wives' tales alone. Train
yourself for the religious life. Physical training is of 8
some service, but religion is of service in every way, for
it carries with it the promise of life here and hereafter.
This is a trustworthy saying, entitled to the fullest ac- 9
ceptance. It is for this that we toil and struggle, for we 10
have fixed our hopes on the living God, the Savior of all
men, especially those who believe.

This is what you must urge and teach. Let no one look 11
down on you because you are young, but set those who 12
believe an example in speech, conduct, love, faith, and

13 purity. Until I come, devote yourself to the public read-
14 ing of Scripture, preaching, and teaching. Do not neglect
the gift you have, that was given you with predictions
of your work, when the elders laid their hands upon you.
15 Cultivate these things, devote yourself to them, so that
everyone will see your progress. Look out for yourself
16 and for your teaching. Persevere in your work, for if you
do you will save both yourself and those who listen to
you.

THE SECOND LETTER TO TIMOTHY

CHRISTIAN COURAGE IN PERSECUTION, 1:3-14

1   I thank God, whom I, like my forefathers, worship
with a clear conscience, when I remember you, as I con-
4 stantly do, in my prayers. When I remember the tears you
5 shed I long night and day to see you again, and have the
perfect happiness of being reminded of your genuine faith,
a faith that was seen first in your grandmother Lois and
6 in your mother Eunice; I am sure it is in you also. For
this reason I would remind you to rekindle the divine
gift that you received when I laid my hands upon you.
7 For the Spirit God has given us is a spirit not of timidity
8 but of power, love, and self-discipline. So you must not
be ashamed to testify to our Lord, nor be ashamed of me
who am in prison for his sake, but join with me in suffer-
9 ing for the good news, through the power of God. He
saved us and called us to a consecrated life, not for anything we had done, but of his own accord and out of the
mercy which he bestowed upon us ages ago through
10 Christ Jesus, which has now been revealed through the
appearance of our Savior Christ Jesus. He has taken away
the power of death and brought life and immortality to
11 light through the good news, of which I have been ap-
12 pointed a herald, apostle and teacher. This is why I am
suffering as I am, but I am not ashamed of it, for I know
whom I have trusted and I am sure that he is able to
13 guard what I have intrusted to him for that Day. As
your example in wholesome instruction, keep before you

[543]

what you learned from me, in the faith and love that
come through union with Christ Jesus. Guard that splen- 14
did trust through the holy Spirit that lives in our hearts.

PAUL'S EPITAPH, 4:6–8

My life is already being poured out, and the time has   4
come for my departure. I have had a part in the great   7
contest, I have run my race, I have preserved the faith.
Now the crown of uprightness awaits me, which the   8
Lord, the upright judge, will award me on that Day, and
not only me but also all who have loved and hoped for
his appearing.

THE LETTER TO TITUS

DUTIES OF THE VARIOUS CHRISTIAN GROUPS, 2:1–14

But you must teach people the things that properly be-   2
long to wholesome teaching. Teach the older men to be   2
temperate, serious, and sensible—men of vigorous faith,
love, and steadfastness. Teach the older women, too, to   3
be reverent in their behavior, and not to gossip or be
slaves of drink, but to be teachers of what is right, so as   4
to train the younger women to be loving wives and mothers, and to be sensible, pure-minded, domestic, kind, and   5
submissive to their husbands, so as not to bring reproach
on God's message. Urge the younger men, too, to be   6
sensible. In every way set them an example of good con-   7
duct yourself. Teach with sincerity and seriousness, and   8
present a wholesome, unobjectionable message, so that
your opponent may be put to shame at finding nothing
bad to say about us. Tell slaves always to obey their   9
masters and try to please them, not to oppose them or   10
steal from them, but to show such perfect good faith as
to do credit to the teaching about God our Savior, by
everything they do.

For God's mercy has appeared and brought salvation   11
to all men, training us to renounce godless ways and
worldly passions, and live serious, upright, and godly   12
lives in this world, while we wait for the fulfilment of   13

our blessed hope in the glorious appearing of our great
14 God and Savior Christ Jesus. He gave himself for us, to
free us from all wickedness and purify for himself a
people of his own, eager to do right.

OBEDIENCE TO THE STATE, 2:15—3:7

2　　This is what you must teach and urge and insist upon
3 with full authority. No one is to look down on you. Remind men to accept and obey the constituted authorities,
2 to be ready for any useful service, to abuse nobody, to be
peaceable and reasonable, showing perfect gentleness to
3 everyone. For we ourselves were once without understanding, disobedient, deluded, enslaved to all kinds of
passions and pleasures. Our minds were full of malice and
4 envy. Men hated us and we hated one another. But
when the goodness and kindness of God our Savior were
5 revealed, he saved us, not for any upright actions we had
performed, but from his own mercy, through the bath of
6 regeneration and renewal by the holy Spirit, which he
has poured out upon us abundantly through Jesus Christ
7 our Savior, so that we might be made upright through
his mercy and become possessors of eternal life in fulfilment of our hope.

INDEX

INDEX

⟦ PRINTED
IN U·S·A ⟧